COSMOS, LIFE, AND L
IN A GREEK
ORTHODOX VILLAGE

Cosmos, Life, and Liturgy in a Greek Orthodox Village

Juliet du Boulay

Denise Harvey (Publisher) · Limni, Evia, Greece

First published in 2009 by Denise Harvey (Publisher)
340 05 Limni, Evia, Greece
www.deniseharveypublisher.gr

Printed and bound in Greece

Cosmos, Life, and Liturgy in a Greek Orthodox Village
is the eighteenth publication in
THE ROMIOSYNI SERIES

ISBN 978-960-7120-25-0 paper bound
ISBN 978-960-7120-26-7 cloth bound

To

Rory

and to the

People of Ambéli

ACKNOWLEDGEMENTS

A book which has taken as long in the making as this one owes so many debts to so many people that it is impossible to mention them all. So I would like to begin by acknowledging the presence of all those not here mentioned who in so many different ways, whether they knew it or not, have by their thoughtfulness and companionship led on my thinking and sustained me over many years.

Of those with a direct relationship with this book, my gratitude goes first to my mother, whose trust in me as her 'invisible asset' she somehow maintained against the odds throughout many unconventional years.

Among scholars, the first person to shape my thoughts about Greece was Dr Philip Sherrard whom I met in 1961 when I went to his home in Katounia for a summer job to look after his children. His wife Anna took me to her heart as her 'third daughter', their children became like younger sisters to me, and Philip himself, later to become my godfather, took a unique role as teacher and friend which was to last until he died in 1995. With his vision of Greece, its rural traditions, and its Orthodox and literary inheritance, and his way of relating fundamental principles of religious thinking to subjects apparently as far apart as the great artistic inheritance of Europe and the ecological catastrophe which is now upon us, Philip's thinking was for me a continual opening of doors. Things I had half thought began to come together, and things not yet thought began to be born. In countless conversations with him I always rediscovered the sensation of returning to base, being brought back to the uncompromising clarity that was so much a part of his own life. He was a touchstone, and my debt to him is incalculable.

It was through Philip's advice to go to the Oxford Institute and study social anthropology that I met Dr John Campbell, who died only recently and whose continuing contribution to Greek anthropological studies will be greatly missed. His personal help to me was very great—when I was a student he was always supportive and, even more important, kind, with an unfailing sense of humour which enabled him to take my life as it was and me as I was—failures and all—in a way which was immensely reassuring. As my supervisor for my doctorate, his friendship and understanding—and that of his wife Sheila who gave me endless hospitality—were unstinting, and his anthropological judgement, and his ability to bring a wry scepticism to bear on anything that merited it, was of enormous value. I thank both him and Sheila wholeheartedly. Also in Oxford, the late Professor Rodney Needham is another person whose kindness followed me through my life. He was my tutor for the Diploma, with an interest in symbolic classification which was to influence me more than at the time I understood. And I never forgot his comment when I was preparing to go to Greece for my first period of field work, and wondering how I would find out anything that was worth finding out. All anxiety fell away at his reply: 'The people themselves will tell you.'

Philip Sherrard, before he died, was able to read and comment on some of the earlier chapters of this book, and when the book was closer to a final draft John Campbell and Bishop Basil of Amphipolis were kind enough to spare time and energy, of which they did not have enough, to read it through and give me their advice. Rodney Needham was also generous enough, even in serious illness, to read closely the final draft and to be of great assistance and encouragement. Graham Whitaker lent his expertise to giving my bibliography a polish otherwise quite foreign to it. Elizabeth Wallace, even though she was recovering from a bad accident at the time, gave her best strength to proof-reading an early draft, and it was important also that she was able to give me her views on the way the book struck her from a lay point of view. I am also very grateful to Fr John Raffan, priest of a parish and visiting priest of the monastery of Chrysopigi, both in Crete. Fr John read a draft at an earlier stage and made some valuable comments on how to rectify the somewhat variable tone of some of the chapters. A conversation with him about fate was critical in orienting the form that particular section then took. His knowledge of Greece, with regard both to village life and the life of the Church, has been of enormous help.

Denise Harvey, the publisher of this book and of the still extant edition of my previous one, read the final draft with meticulous care, pointing out numerous details which I had overlooked or got wrong, and she has been the most careful and knowledgeable editor I could have wished for. She has been endlessly generous, with seemingly unlimited reserves of patience, and along with a host of other things she even undertook to do the index. I am more than grateful to her for her unwavering support and her help. I need hardly say that any errors or misconceptions that remain after my readers' comments are entirely my responsibility.

Several scholars outside my own field also gave me generous help with references relevant to particular chapters, and I acknowledge their help with gratitude in specific footnotes. One who should have special mention is the Father Andrew Louth, who pointed me to several patristic and other sources. Again I bear responsibility for the use I made of their suggestions.

My grateful thanks go also to Mother Mary Williams, who has given her professional photographic knowledge and a great deal of her time to sorting out boxes of photographs unlooked at for thirty years, assessing them for possible reproduction, and scanning the best of them onto a CD. There is no doubt that I could never have tackled this task on my own.

Then there are the villagers. That time of my life was unique, and more and more I give thanks that I was able, for a few years, to know and love these people, share their lives, live in their houses, revel in their vitality, walk in their countryside, receive their kindness, value what they valued, see what they saw. There are too many to cite by name in these pages, but I remember them all, living and dead, one by one, and in so far as this book is a true record of what they taught me, it is they who are the authors. I thank them not only for their infinite kindness to me but also for the way they shared their way of life with me, and enabled this book to be written. In particular, in these last years, Evstatheia Korellis, daughter of the ever-memorable Eleni Albani, *koumbára* to my husband and myself and mother of our godchild Penelope, has been unfailing in her willingness to check details of village life either from her own memory or from those with even longer memories than hers who still live in the village.

In Dunblane I will always remember Glenys Sneddon and her husband Peter for the way in which they cared for us during our early years after we moved here from Aberdeen, when I had serious health problems. The fact that our household survived in as good shape as it did, and that we eventually arrived at the point at which we could undertake the sort of work that was in fact waiting for us, was in large part due to them. Frances Paterson did invaluable work typing out many of my notes into a form that I could easily handle—a work enabled by a grant from Aberdeen University sponsored by Dr Nick Bradford and Dr Chuck Jedrez.

The second period of my fieldwork, from 1970–73, was supported handsomely by a large grant from the then Social Science Research Council. Its results were written up in anthropological journals or edited collections which are referred to in the notes, and I am glad to acknowledge these as the original publishers of material which I have summarized in simpler outline in the course of some of the present chapters.

Finally I come to my husband Rory. With his extraordinary empathy he became able, after only a few brief visits to the village, to recall by name and to know by character the many people he met, and his imaginative sharing of my years in the village has made him a uniquely perceptive adviser. Over these many years we have discussed up and down the issues dealt with in this book, to such an extent that it is now in many cases hard to remember whether he thought of something or whether I did. Particularly with respect to sections of Chapters 4, 11 and 12, and to ancient Greek sources, his liturgical and bibliographical skills have been indispensible, but in fact the whole book owes more to him than I can say, for he has read and commented on draft after draft, and undertaken my commitment to it, as he has undertaken my life, with total generosity. In rejoicing at its finishing and in thanks for his sharing of it, I dedicate this book to him, and with him to the villagers, so many of whom he remembers with me.

Juliet du Boulay
Dunblane, Scotland
November 2009

CONTENTS

LIST OF PLATES

LIST OF DIAGRAMS

INTRODUCTION

THE subject of this book is the imaginative world of an Orthodox Christian village in Greece, and specifically the cosmological, religious and moral imagination associated with the characteristic forms of its life. The pattern of this life, formed for the most part by villagers living directly on the fruits of their own labour in their fields and forests, was the subject of my previous book, *Portrait of a Greek Mountain Village*,[1] and the present book aims to reveal the inner world which corresponds to that outer world.

To become aware of the religious imagination in subsistence villages of this kind in Europe involves engaging with a living reality which is often only seen at a distance, through the prism of debates which remain very much alive in the religious history of the West. With a Greek village this is particularly the case: Greece has remained to many the mother of the western world, whether as the first source of free, rational thought or as the source of the Greek language in which the New Testament was first written. And for this reason western preoccupations with Greece have shaped perceptions of the Greek imagination in at least three distinct ways.

First, in the nineteenth century, European Hellenists saw Greece as the birthplace of reason, the heir to classical antiquity; they formed the notion of a self-governing Greek nation state, destined to rise from the ashes of Ottoman oppression and recreate appropriate institutions of free speech and democracy. These lovers of classical antiquity liked to see the traditions practised in the villages almost as an earthy rationality in contrast to Christianity, admiring, for example, the bleak realism of Greek death practices even though at times they were moved to condemn aspects of them as at best magical and at worst destructive.[2] From the folklore industry generated by this perspective, and from some fine historical and ethno-

[1] Oxford: Clarendon Press, 1974.

[2] e.g. John Cuthbert Lawson, *Modern Greek Folklore and Ancient Greek Religion* (Cambridge: Cambridge University Press, 1910).

graphic studies too,[3] the notion grew up that the Greek villages, at any rate as they existed before the flight to the towns, were a repository of thinly-veiled pre-Christian or non-Christian ways of thought—a proof of their classical pedigree.

This way of looking at the religious imagination is associated with the modern period in the West, with its strong distinction between rational and magical thinking, where what is not explicitly reasoned is by definition illusory. Given impetus by the rationalizing tendencies of Protestantism, and later by proselytizing atheists,[4] this distinction continues to surface in some historical accounts as well, such as in those which continue to portray the peasantry of the European middle ages as 'magical' thinkers who used fragments of older thought forms on which the medieval Church is thought to have had little impact.[5]

With time though, European Hellenism has generated opposing evaluations, which point instead to the Byzantine and Ottoman inheritance of Greece, encapsulated in a term which resounds with subtle connotations of both—*Romiosýne* (*Ρωμιοσύνη*), the historical experience of the *Romaíoi* (*Ρωμαίοι*, sing. *Ρωμιός*), the former people of the Eastern Roman Empire. The associations of this term under the Ottomans—reflecting the way in which these people learned to cope with their subjection using a varied repertoire including secrecy, lies, braggadocio and trickery—have gained a new lease of life in a view that sees Greece as possessing not only the institutions of a modern European nation state, and the professional identities which go with them, but also often a contrary identity. This contrary identity is resistant to Europeanism and is kept secret among one's own familiars, protected by lies, jokes, tricks, irony and plays upon words—a *Romiosýne* like that of Ottoman days which, coexisting uneasily with the European values that dominate public life, is deviously asserted in encounters with others, especially with strangers and with insti-

[3] Margaret Alexiou, *The Ritual Lament in Greek Tradition* (Cambridge: Cambridge University Press, 1974); Loring M. Danforth, *The Death Rituals of Rural Greece* (Princeton: Princeton University Press, 1982).

[4] For a recent example see Richard Dawkins, *The God Delusion* (London: Bantam Press, 2006).

[5] e.g. Keith Thomas, *Religion and the Decline of Magic* (London: Weidenfeld and Nicolson, 1971).

tutions.[6] In the villages this perspective has drawn particular attention to the individualistic and competitive behaviour of men, to such things as their blasphemy and their irreverence towards public organizations, their games with auguries and competitive stealing.[7]

This view of the Greek imagination has affinities with postmodern currents of thought in the West. From the 1930s onward, closer encounters with other cultures have been making the whole notion of magical thinking problematic and have encouraged an increasing openness to symbolic languages. Between the wars, social anthropologists working among the varied cultures of the British Empire had already found themselves at the limit of modernist assumptions, and they began to draw attention to other forms of rationality even in African ideas about witchcraft.[8] As a consequence, which was further stimulated in the last few decades by widespread cross-cultural encounters in cosmopolitan cities, a second way of seeing religion has emerged in reaction to modernism which recognizes a variety of alternative rationalities, and, correspondingly, a variety of alternative ways in which individuals may thread together a self-made identity. The individualism of this postmodern sense of identity is indeed perhaps its chief distinguishing mark. Individualism and competitive choice of lifestyles permeate the market for religious experience which goes under the name of the 'new age', just as they permeate the growing fashion for agnosticism. And the implication that both are a lifestyle choice undermines any sense of belonging to a greater whole.

Both these western perspectives on the Greek religious imagination have drawn attention to a part of the reality; but if the Hellenist view was too narrowly focussed on the Greece of antiquity, so too, in a different fashion, has been the postmodern alertness to the disenchantment with western ways which is a facet of the term *Romiosýne*. Another great part of *Romiosýne* is the Byzantine legacy of the Orthodox Christian faith, whose symbols and thought forms are em-

[6] Michael Herzfeld, *Anthropology through the Looking-glass: Critical Ethnography in the Margins of Europe* (Cambridge: Cambridge University Press, 1987).

[7] Michael Herzfeld, *The Poetics of Manhood: Contest and Identity in a Cretan Mountain Village* (Princeton: Princeton University Press, 1985); 'The Significance of the Insignificant: Blasphemy as Ideology', *Man* (N.S.), 19 (1984), pp. 653–64.

[8] E. E. Evans-Pritchard, *Witchcraft, Oracles and Magic among the Azande* (Oxford: Clarendon Press, 1937).

bedded throughout the culture, and Greeks may resist the ethos of the modern European state not only from individualism or scepticism, but also from an Orthodox vision of society.[9] Studies in Greek literature, especially poetry, by writers such as Zissimos Lorenzatos and Philip Sherrard, set a pattern establishing the influence of Orthodox as well as classical symbolism on the Greek poets.[10] Positive revaluation of the Christian influence on the Byzantine heritage had begun in the 1930s with Steven Runciman's *Byzantine Civilisation*,[11] and it continued with Sherrard's historical and theological treatise *The Greek East and the Latin West*,[12] and with the history of the contemporary Greek nation state which the anthropologist John Campbell and Sherrard later co-authored.[13] Ethnographic studies, too, have increasingly noticed the influence of Orthodoxy on Greek popular culture; and for this they are deeply indebted to the vision of their first exponent, John Campbell, for he not only achieved the classic study of patronage, economics and kinship among the Sarakatsani,[14] but he also perceived a whole range of imaginative elements, such as the sacred ties between shepherds and their sheep, the symbolic structure of relations within the household, the sense of release felt after the Easter service, the nature of the blood, moving as a 'mysterious and intelligent force' binding people together. In this way he was the pathfinder, and provided an incomparable base for those who came

[9] The chief theorist of post-Ottoman *Romiosýne* has also remarked on this recently: see Michael Herzfeld, 'The Ethnographer as Theorist: John Campbell and the Power of Detail', in Mark Mazower (ed.), *Networks of Power in Modern Greece* (London: Hurst, 2008), p. 153. This essay takes a hint from the work of Charles Stewart, who 'has consistently and persuasively argued against the conceptual separation of church doctrine from folk practice in Greece', and suggests that 'Stewart's argument should in turn lead us to look for doctrinal principles…and to ask how far those doctrines might determine the shape of social interaction.'

[10] Philip Sherrard, *The Marble Threshing Floor: Studies in Modern Greek Poetry* (London: Vallentine, Mitchell, 1956); Zissimos Lorenzatos, *The Drama of Quality: Selected Essays* (Limni, Greece: D. Harvey, 2000).

[11] Steven Runciman, *Byzantine Civilisation* (London: E. Arnold, 1933).

[12] Philip Sherrard, *The Greek East and the Latin West: A Study in the Christian Tradition* (London: Oxford University Press, 1959).

[13] John Campbell and Philip Sherrard, *Modern Greece* (London: Benn, 1968).

[14] J. K. Campbell, *Honour, Family and Patronage: A Study of Institutions and Moral Values in a Greek Mountain Community* (Oxford: Clarendon Press, 1964).

after him. More recently aspects of church practice[15] and church ritual,[16] pilgrimage centres[17] and monasteries[18] have been described, and monastic teaching has been extensively documented;[19] and even in the more elusive arenas of city, village and mountain pasture, distinctive Orthodox conceptions, for example of the angelic and diabolic worlds,[20] of time and memory,[21] of women's role and the use of household space,[22] of the sacramental quality of substances like wheat, wine and oil,[23] and of the relation between man and the land[24] and man and the natural world,[25] have been found largely intact and persisting.

[15] Lucy Rushton, 'Religion and Identity in a Rural Greek Community', D.Phil. thesis (University of Sussex, 1982).

[16] Margaret Kenna, 'Icons in Theory and Practice: An Orthodox Christian Example', *History of Religions*, 24 (1985), pp. 345–68; 'Why does Incense smell Religious? Greek Orthodoxy and the Anthropology of Smell', *Journal of Mediterranean Studies*, 15 (2005), pp. 52–70.

[17] Jill Dubisch, *In a Different Place: Pilgrimage, Gender and Politics at a Greek Island Shrine* (Princeton: Princeton University Press, 1995).

[18] A. M. Iossifides, 'Sisters in Christ: Metaphors of Kinship among Greek Nuns', in Peter Loizos and Evthymios Papataxiarchis (eds.), *Contested Identities: Genders and Kinship in Modern Greece* (Princeton: Princeton University Press, 1991), and 'Earthly Lives and Life Everlasting: Secular and Religious Values in two Convents and a Village in Western Greece', Ph.D. thesis (University of London, 1990).

[19] e.g. Kyriakos Markides, *The Mountain of Silence: A Search for Orthodox Spirituality* (New York: Doubleday, 2001), and *Gifts of the Desert: The Forgotten Path of Christian Spirituality* (New York: Doubleday, 2005).

[20] Charles Stewart, *Demons and the Devil: Moral Imagination in Modern Greek Culture* (Princeton: Princeton University Press, 1991).

[21] Laurie Kain Hart, *Time, Religion and Social Experience in Rural Greece* (Lanham: Rowman & Littlefield, 1992); Renée Hirschon, *Heirs of the Greek Catastrophe: The Social Life of Asia Minor Refugees in Piraeus* (Oxford: Clarendon Press, 1989).

[22] Renée Hirschon, 'Essential Objects and the Sacred: Interior and Exterior Space in an Urban Greek Locality', in S. Ardener (ed.), *Women and Space: Ground Rules and Social Maps* (London: Croom Helm, 1981), pp. 72–88, and 'Women, the Aged and Relgious Activity: Oppositions and Complementarity in an Urban Greek Locality', *Journal of Modern Greek Studies* 1 (1983), pp. 113–29.

[23] Hart, *Time, Religion and Social Experience.*

[24] Margaret Kenna, 'Houses, Fields and Graves: Property and Ritual Obligations on a Greek Island', *Ethnology*, 15 (1976), pp. 21–34.

[25] Dimitris Theodossopoulos, 'What Use is the Turtle? Cultural Perceptions of Land, Work, Animals and "Ecologists" in a Greek Farming Community', Ph.D. thesis (University of London, 1997).

These observations reflect a sense that in Greece the religious imagination has been particularly rich and influential because it informs the whole culture and not merely the lives of individuals; and an awareness of this power of the religious influence in shaping civilization generally has reawakened in the West. The so-called 'clash of civilisations',[26] suggested as the new face of the world order after the Cold War and debated as a possible element in the events of 9/11 and after, has caused many people to reappraise the way in which the deep levels of a culture continue at a conscious or unconscious level to carry the thought forms of the faith which created it. This recognition is a return to a view which has always had its adherents: the celebrated religious autobiography of Thomas Merton,[27] for instance, records the influence on him of a childhood spent amid the Christian symbols and structures of an old French town. And more recent ethnographic evidence has confirmed the deep Catholic symbolism still present in the life patterns of many western European communities.[28] In the same way, the transition from the medieval to the early modern period in western Europe has been reappraised, overturning the modernist view and revealing in the thought of the peasantry a deep enculturation of Catholic symbolism which had been overlooked.[29]

These discoveries of long continuities in symbolic elements of Greek, and more generally of European, culture have given fresh relevance to my original preference for centering this book on the whole round of life in a single community, and for exploring the varied symbolism by which the community makes sense of that life. And at the same time the religious grounding found in many of these continuities has endorsed a question which the book increasingly set be-

[26] Samuel Huntington, *The Clash of Civilisations and the Remaking of World Order* (London: Simon and Schuster, 1996), and *The Clash of Civilisations? The Debate* (New York: Foreign Affairs, 1996).

[27] Thomas Merton, *The Seven-Storey Mountain* (New York: Harcourt Brace Jovanovich, 1948).

[28] Sandra Ott, *The Circle of Mountains: A Basque Shepherding Community* (Oxford: Clarendon Press, 1981); Joao de Pina-Cabral, *Sons of Adam, Daughters of Eve: The Peasant Worldview of the Alto Minho* (Oxford: Clarendon Press, 1986).

[29] Eamon Duffy, *The Stripping of the Altars: Traditional Religion in England c. 1400 – c. 1580* (New Haven and London: Yale University Press, 1992).

fore me as it developed—the question, how far Orthodox Christianity has provided a central, coherent set of those symbols. This second issue is native to the way Greeks see themselves, whether Orthodoxy is a past from which they wish to free themselves, or one which they take as a matter of course as their own, or one which they long to make more fully present in aspects which have been lost. But these Orthodox Christian roots cannot be explored without also encountering those pre-Christian ideas which others have noticed previously, or those sceptical ways of combining and playing with all such notions, often prompted by the patterns of individual competition and self-assertion already referred to; and since these other aspects of the culture are part of a living, contradictory whole, I have also tried to clarify how they relate to the Orthodox understanding of things, so as to provide as complete a picture as is possible, in the space available, of the Greek religious imagination as I found it within the varied aspects of one community.

These questions I attempt to answer through evidence from the community described in my *Portrait of a Greek Mountain Village*. My first period of living in Ambeli lasted from autumn 1966 to spring 1968; then in autumn 1970 I returned to the village for just under two more years, until summer 1972, to engage on a follow-up study. This type of community has a particular value for the issues explored here: the imaginative world I recorded over these six years belongs to a time when many Greek villages, like Ambeli, were still vibrant working communities living almost entirely off their own land. Globalizing influences were discernible, but minimal, and the rich interlayering of folk beliefs and practices with ecclesial customs and precepts made it a place of extraordinary interest for studying the local understanding of religion and cosmology.

In this comparison of local with ecclesial understandings, my guide to the Church's thinking has been chiefly the Orthodox liturgy. Orthodoxy is known and experienced by the villagers primarily in the visual and verbal symbolism of their liturgical life, which provides a much richer and more authentic touchstone for their faith than conventional dogmatic summaries can provide, though I refer to these, and to some relevant writings of the eastern Fathers of the Church as well. This liturgy of the Church—a term which I use to include all its offices, not just the Divine Liturgy which is the eucharist itself—is the work of early Christian communities, the authors being in many cases little known, though they clearly used not only the words of Scripture in extraordinary richness and profusion but also the words of authors in the patristic tradition who are felt to speak directly out of their experience of God, and are often described as theologians in this sense. Despite the gap between liturgical Greek and village language, this incomparable treasury is a living part of the experience of the Greek villages (as it is of every part of the Orthodox world), whether it has become known to them through immediate knowledge of the services and explanation by the priests, or whether it has penetrated the culture of the people in such a way as to have become, over hundreds of years, part of the oral tradition. The comparison of village imagery with liturgical imagery has a recent precedent; and the systematic use of the comparison which has been attempted here has proved a revealing method for answering the questions of this book, and it is central to its conclusions.[30]

The circumstances which led me to explore the Orthodox liturgy explain why the reflections which I began to make on my material, at a time when the postmodern phase in western thought was at its height, happen now to coincide with the new questions which have recently arisen about religion in the western world. The first draft of several chapters of the book was written using data from fieldwork only, and the book was well under way when, in 1981, I was

[30] For the recent precedent see Stewart, *Demons and the Devil*, Ch. 7. Such comparison presupposes the long-term stability of the Orthodox liturgy, for which see Robert Taft, *The Byzantine Rite: a Short History* (Collegeville, Minn.: The Liturgical Press, 1992). The chief source of variation in recent centuries has lain in the pattern of routine omissions or of transpositions in the sequence which is customary for practical purposes in particular places and periods. In some offices, shortened Greek versions have been in common use in village parishes, including during the period of the fieldwork described here, and in these cases the quotations chosen for translation have aimed to take this into account, and to mark it in a note. For consistency of style in the English translations, the style of the *Festal Menaion* and *Lenten Triodion* translations, which form the bulk of the material, and annotate Greek usage roughly contemporary with my fieldwork, has been the exemplar. In some particular rites of passage, matching this style has meant going to accessible English translations of Orthodox services in the Russian tradition which have worked from comparison with the Greek texts, but care has been taken to check that the translations correspond to Greek usage in any places where it might differ.

disabled by a complex spinal problem. For some years after this, writing a book was more than I could handle, though detailed working out of various intricate and difficult questions that were beginning to emerge from my material became possible with the help of a hand held tape recorder and a typist, and I produced a number of articles over that period which were published in anthropological journals.

Then in the 1990s, a new light began to be cast on my material by experience of the Orthodox Church. I had been received into the Church in 1968, between my two periods of fieldwork, but in Greece my comprehension of the liturgy in the village churches had been seriously hampered by my ignorance of the high language of the Greek Church, though there was much in the action of the liturgy that made sense to me on a level deeper than words. In this context it is relevant to say that Church Greek was a difficulty also for the villagers who did not understand word for word what was being said and needed the Gospel of the day to be explained to them by the priest; but they nevertheless knew where they were as the liturgy progressed, and responded spontaneously to the layers of meaning they perceived in it at each stage, and were deeply focussed in the course of it.

In the village, therefore, my own grasp of the liturgy was largely through their intuitions, and with much less knowledge, and this continued for some time to be the case. It was not only in Greece that my ignorance of Church language hampered my understanding of the Orthodox texts, but in England also, for in those days Orthodox parishes, when they did not celebrate in Church Greek, celebrated almost exclusively in Church Slavonic. However, when my husband and I became involved with the start of a small Orthodox community in our early years in Scotland we began to celebrate in English, and from those beginnings a new world opened up, revealing the relationships lying between great areas of folk belief on the one hand, and the insights of the Orthodox Church on the other. Some of these relationships I had already sensed: asymmetric patterns of giving without reward had emerged as important during my first period of field work, and during my return visit in the early 1970s the dance pattern had begun to appear as a constant theme, later linking in with the same pattern in the liturgy; but the number and detail of the correspondences between the life of the people and the liturgy of the Church only began to dawn on me in the 1990s, though they have been developing ever since.

The interpretation of my material which has resulted from this experience can be compared with the purely anthropological interpretations, freshly made on my fieldwork alone, which I published in the 1980s through to the early 1990s. These are listed in the bibliography. A few small differences are marked in the notes; but otherwise the interpretation of the village material is substantially the same. Differences arise only from the much broader perspective taken here, which requires additional distinctions to be made about the Christian or other origins of village material, but chiefly imparts to it a heightened sense of the spiritual and symbolic heritage from which it springs.

A deep participation in the life of the Orthodox Church is something which few academics in the West, even those closely involved in observing and studying Greek culture, feel called to engage in; indeed, many would shy away from it, feeling perhaps that it might compromise their academic objectivity. But anyone who observes life by participating in it, as social anthropologists have always done, must feel that such an avoidance is a little paradoxical, and that many connecting links in Greek culture might well be more easily seen with a mind sensitive to the formative ideas of the Greek Orthodox Church. For those who do not themselves, for whatever reason, participate in the life of the Orthodox Church, therefore, I offer here what is at once a view from an insider's experience, and a view from the discipline of social anthropology; and as chance and the circumstances of biography would have it, this combination of experience has become apposite to our sharpened contemporary awareness that broad cultural regions of the world have different ways of seeing things, and can contribute to the question of how far the forms taken by Orthodox cultures are shaped by their religious origins.

For all that Greece is so much seen as the mother of the western world, modern studies of the Greek world are not always well understood in the West. Among other problems, there is a potential among readers from western confessions for misunderstanding the Christian history of Greece, though I believe that, when it is rightly read, there is also a potential for their recapturing their own history within it. It became apparent, for example, as I wrote this book, that in the various streams of tradition that had fed into what the villagers of Ambeli called 'the old mind' (*τὸ παλιὸ μυαλό*), there were differing world views available, running alongside one another and intersecting and clashing at various points. This was a culture with very ancient roots which necessarily included choices other than Christian ones, even if the main frame was by that time drawn from Christianity. The drama of village life lies in the vividness with which people perceive these different traditions of thought, how they choose between them, and how the choices work out for good or for ill; and this is why it is so easy to see a variety of different influences in the villages—the classical past, the Orthodox inheritance, the distrust of public institutions which goes back to the Ottomans, and the competitive juggling with all these ways of seeing which is a part of village repartee.

Christianity has played a complex part in its contact with the villages. Initially the Church began by opposing the rural or 'village' conception of the world ('pagan' originally meant simply 'of the villages'), seeing it as something in which the divine was presented as polymorphous, chaotic and conflicting, in much the same way as the world of nature appears to be in its immediate impact on the senses. From this perspective some western readers may begin with a superficial impression that village Orthodoxy is still battling with residual memories of paganism. There are points where this is true in Greece, as it is everywhere, but judging that a custom is inconsistent with Christianity is not as simple as may first appear, since the Church's judgments are graduated. In general it can be said that there are areas of belief which have become accepted as a folk expression of the living tradition, such as not doing handwork on the eves of saints' days, areas with which the Church co-exists while withholding approval, such as belief in nereids, which the Church rejects in the sense that it redefines nereids as a species of demon, and areas—in particular the use of short incantations known as *yítia* (dialect for *γητειές*) or spells—where popular practices avowedly defy ecclesiastical injunctions. At the extreme lie those practices, perceived by both villagers and Church alike as powered by 'demonic energy', which involve manipulation of forces to harm others, in particular the appeal to witchcraft. Recent scholarly writing on Greece has drawn attention to these liminal aspects of the culture.[31] But for the most part, the formative influence of the Church has concentrated on building an architecture of Christian meanings which could embrace, unify and transform the fragments of old cultures that live on in Greece wherever they are not directly in contradiction with the Christian message; and a representative picture will focus more on this broad phenomenon, as I do here, than on more extreme instances like witchcraft.

Thus, while in many of these areas the Church was contending with varying levels of what it saw as erroneous belief, it was also engaged in a great enterprise of unifying the divine and natural worlds in a new vision of creation, and this accounts for the large areas where village experience of the natural world has integrated easily with liturgical and theological reflection within the Church. This cosmic vision is already described by St Paul in a passage which holds the germ of this enterprise fully formed.[32] The architecture of this vision was especially comprehensive in the Greek East, and in the vision of theologians like Dionysius 'the Areopagite', Maximus the Confessor and Gregory Palamas, but it was not limited to the East and something of it penetrated every corner of life in the mediaeval world both East and West.[33] In the West in late mediaeval and early modern times, this vision was disrupted by deliberate separation of thought about the natural world from thought about the divine world—a separation which has created the fragmented and desacralized western cosmos of the present day. Nevertheless in Greece, partly because of Greece's 400-year occupation by the Turks and its resulting isolation from the cultural changes in Europe, the vision has continued until very recently with undiminished immediacy. From this point of view many western readers may have a sensation that in the cosmos of village Orthodoxy they are coming home to a more ancient Christian understanding.

Even within the Christian framework in the culture, however, there are choices. Greek culture is full of what have been called 'con-

[31] Stewart, *Demons and the Devil.*

[32] Romans 8 : 19–23.

[33] C. S. Lewis, *The Discarded Image: An Introduction to Medieval and Renaissance Literature* (Cambridge: Cambridge University Press, 1964); Duffy, *Stripping of the Altars*; Ronald Hutton, *The Rise and Fall of Merry England: The Ritual Year, 1400–1700* (Oxford: Oxford University Press, 1994).

tested identities',[34] belonging to subcultures within the whole, and while some of these (the subcultures of prostitutes, for example, or of the hashish dens[35]) are seen as outside the Christian framework, other conflicts between subcultures occur also within its positive values. One such conflict is that between the monastic and the married life.[36] Other choices, mentioned in this book, involve the tensions set up, for instance, between the duty of preserving the 'strength' of the house and that of generosity to others, and between the obligation to observe saints' days as days of rest, and the demands of the household and of daughters who need dowries. These oppositions, however, though they create certain ambivalences, are ultimately reconciled within the Christian paradigm.

With all this room for choice and contradiction, therefore, this book does not attempt any firm dogmatic separation of orthodox and heterodox elements. Rather, I try to portray the particularities of the villagers' own images of the sacred while presenting alongside them liturgical material which is universal in Orthodox practice. Of course not every person in such a community embodies this tradition without distortion, and in fact the freedom to make subversive choices is an indispensable part of the process by which each generation of the community learns how to live within the whole communal understanding. However, in the overall direction of such a community and of the symbolism with which it lives it is, I believe, not difficult to recognize the extent to which it is an accurate reflection of Orthodox tradition.

These comments have been for those who have some religious or theological interest in the themes of this book, but there remain issues of interpreting Greek religious thought for readers who come with little previous knowledge or sympathy. First there is the difficulty today that Christianity, because it is associated with the past, may also be associated for them with power structures in which masters ruled servants, men ruled women, and nation or empire ruled all.

[34] Loizos and Papataxiarchis (eds.), *Contested Identities.*

[35] Stathis Gauntlett, 'Between Orientalism and Occidentalism: The Contribution of Asia Minor Refugees to Greek Popular Song and its Reception', in Renée Hirschon (ed.), *Crossing the Aegean: an Appraisal of the 1923 Compulsory Population Exchange between Greece and Turkey* (New York and Oxford: Berghahn Books, 2003).

[36] Iossifides, 'Sisters in Life' and 'Earthly Lives'.

Many people today seem unaware that Christianity from the beginning sought to soften and replace all these structures, saying, in the words of St Paul, that 'There is neither Jew nor Greek, there is neither bond nor free, there is neither male nor female: for ye are all one in Christ Jesus',[37] and the struggle against these structures has continued in Christianity with some success up to the present day. But at each stage of the history of this struggle, many of the forms of the society of that time have been accepted as current realities which could only be transformed slowly, and could not immediately be overthrown without worse consequences. In Greek peasant villages the distinction between these brutal realities and the vision of the faith is sharp, but both perspectives are found alongside each other in their language and symbolism, and a casual reader may be deceived into supposing that the villagers do not see the contradictions. It is important therefore to understand that the dialogue between these opposed viewpoints is crystallized in the village accounts of paradise and the fall, and that this dialogue is an inner presupposition of Greek culture and of the Orthodox faith—one which has shown a capacity to sustain realism along with transcendent vision in a way which simple utopianism would find hard to match.

This is illustrated in the position of women in the villages, which has been governed by circumstances that from a modern western perspective are harsh (although less commonly perceived is the degree to which the position of men is harsh too), and this is explained in village life by the story of Eve. But readers who are unfamiliar with Orthodox thought may not appreciate at first that this story is only one of two poles of thought, only one aspect of a paradox well understood by villagers and expressed in the story, told me by a village woman, of Kassiane, a young girl questioned by the emperor's son who was looking for his match in marriage. 'From one woman came all evil', said the emperor's son, alluding to Eve, to be answered by Kassiane with an allusion to Mary: 'And from one woman came all good'.[38] This story makes clear that Greek villages cannot be under-

[37] Galatians 3 : 28.

[38] The origin of this story is the 10th c. Byzantine chronicler known as Georgius Monachus Continuatus, the bridegroom concerned being Theophilus (Byzantine Emperor AD 829–42). Versions of the story continue to this day to be circulated both by oral transmission and in popular pamphlets published by the Orthodox

stood without taking into account the extraordinary significance of the Orthodox title Mother of God, the *Panaghía* (*Παναγία*) or All-holy One, a title which especially as *Panaghía* is found on the lips of these Greek villagers in every kind of circumstance. To unravel the symbolic implications of these phrases is part of the task of this book, for they are inseparable from the understanding also of the nature of the Orthodox cosmos, and the Orthodox view of life and death.

A final question remains as to why I write in a style which is both particular and general, and how far the findings of this book can in fact be generalized.

Unless otherwise stated or referenced the book relies solely on fieldwork material gathered in the northern part of the island of Evia (Euboea)—with very few exceptions specifically from the village of Ambeli—during the periods mentioned earlier. The time and place of the data are thus highly particular, and I believe that the concreteness of the images provided by this particularity is vital to the invocation of the way of thought. Theoretical generalization is removed from place and moment by abstraction, and so inevitably stands at a certain distance from the people from whom the data were derived. Ethnographic description on its own, on the other hand, is limited to these particularities, and opens itself to being relegated to a moment of history which has no abiding significance. In this book I wanted to write somewhat differently, in such a way as to reveal the enduring linkages in patterns of thought found within an ethnographic cross-section taken from one particular moment. I have found myself seeking to depict a particular Orthodox Christian community in such a way as to reveal, through its particularities, its essential nature, and through this to throw light on the essential nature of similar communities. This nature is defined principally by the people's way of seeing the world and responding to it both in work and in symbol—in liturgy—for both overlap in the vision of the sacred in this kind of community: the work of the liturgy and the liturgy of work are parallel activities.

The attempt to convey both the particular and the prototype simultaneously is helped by comparing village talk with liturgical texts,

Church, for Kassiane (or Casia) became a nun and a celebrated hymnodist. I would like to thank Professor Paul Magdalinos for this reference.

as I have done throughout. But I also made a stylistic decision that I would deal in this introduction with topics otherwise omitted, and would eliminate from the main text the kinds of detail which would tend to localize and parochialize the evidence. Hence I have not mentioned myself as observer, and, because my informants are speaking—and very often see themselves as speaking—less as individuals than as people passing on an ancient tradition, I do not cite them individually, even though their individuality emerges with every utterance. Again, in order to reduce distraction from the integrity of the world view described, I have reduced references to comparative material to a minimum, and have omitted for the most part ethnographic variants in other parts of Greece. Most significantly, I have written in the present tense. The reason for this lies in the widespread and long-lasting nature of the thought patterns described, and in the fact that where these patterns correspond to patterns in the Orthodox liturgy, they remain part of a contemporary world view which is retained at the heart of the Orthodox faith, even while many of the agricultural and cosmological implications of that world view may have been reinterpreted.

A further stylistic problem for some may also be my use of 'man' to refer to humankind. The problem does not arise in Greek or the Latin-based languages: in Greek a man and a woman are both *ánthropos*; in Latin, *homo.* Thus this problem occurs particularly in languages with Teutonic roots. However, the modern alternatives either force English writers into the clumsy s/he, or abstractions such as 'humankind', and my purpose in writing in the way I have—using the particular to stand for the general—is better served by the older usage in which 'man' was acknowledged to have two senses, one without gender and corresponding to the Greek *ánthropos*, and the other corresponding to the Greek *ándras*, a person of the male sex.

The only exceptions I have made in the overall style of writing I have chosen are in the case of the moon landings, whose date is relevant because they were a critical catalyst in exposing the village cosmology, and in the case of local saints where local affections expressed in their veneration are a deep principle of the culture. Because such saints are more likely to be perceived in the West as hagiographic stereotypes rather than as real individuals, I have given concrete historic particulars of some of the holy figures of northern Evia as examples of local saints, ubiquitous in the Orthodox world, to whom the people turn, and whom they regard as peculiarly their own. This apart, though, the emphasis is on the generality and durability of the particular ideas and practices I describe in Ambeli.

To recognize the enduring quality of much that I describe is not, however, to ignore the fact that change has always been a part of village life, and indeed so many changes have happened since I was in Ambeli in the 1960s and 1970s that much of the way of life recounted here can no longer be found. Earlier changes begin with the village itself, which had been built around 1800 by families who escaped there from a lower village which had been devastated by the Turks. Before this some of the big families were said to have come in a boat from the north, perhaps Pelion. These upheavals, however, dramatic though they were, did not necessitate a deep change of values but simply a reinterpretation of ancient themes in the new situation. Similarly, most of the twentieth-century wars and economic shifts which I chronicled in my first book, although affecting farming strategies and bringing prosperity or poverty to the people, did not alter the deeper ideas and values which I describe here; and even when young men and women began emigrating permanently from the village during the 1960s, threatening its demographic viability in the longer term, those who had by then married and settled in the village continued to retain the traditional mentality which made sense of their way of life. Before I left the village in 1972 though, a different kind of change had begun to escalate. This process also I touched on in my former book, yet the significant element was not the advent of change *per se*, but of a kind of change which began to relegate the people's sense of who they were from a centre in themselves and in their own village to a centre in an outside world. This outside world, which was more and more making the villagers' choices for them, was one which defined worth and centrality in completely new terms, and found the villagers wanting—saw them, with a supreme irony, as 'far from God'.

A sign of this change which is relevant to the present book was that the villagers had become sensitive to the devaluing of their traditional cosmology by the literate outside world, and thus they were increasingly likely to be reticent about earlier beliefs and to refer to them as 'lies'. This devaluing, of which significant agents were the young children with the crass literalism of their newly-acquired school knowledge, was already apt to lead, in conversations with older people about the cosmos, to such defensive pronouncements as, 'the world is round like an orange'. The sense of embarrassment, almost of shame, about such topics, with which the older people began to be afflicted around the beginning of the 1970s, made details about the earlier cosmology surprisingly difficult to obtain. However, the moon landings from 1969 to 1972 created such a furore in the cafés among men both young and old, and such a stir in the houses, and there was so general a rejection of the American claims, that the subject became the issue of the time and for a period 'the old mind' became more accessible.

A second sign of the new unease was that the 1970s saw the beginning of the departure from the village of some of the settled married householders. In the autumn of 1971 a road was built, and with it came electricity, transport, machines. The chance to mechanize farming, which had already come to other mountain villages and was making Ambeli feel left out, was now available, and 1973 was the last year in which the use of animals for the threshing—insisted on by the old grandmother of one of the last conservative families as the right way to do things—was carried out. The road also brought the possibility of commuting to salaried work in the plains and of bringing a certain prosperity and a greater ease to village life. Yet in spite of these new possibilities of local work, the flight of working householders steadily gathered pace after I left, and in the course of the last thirty years has virtually eliminated the working basis of village life, leaving only a few ageing couples still gaining their livelihood from the village. Now, however, a fresh impetus is bringing a different sort of life to Ambeli: one or two newcomers from the towns have bought and renovated a village house as a weekend cottage, one new couple has arrived and settled permanently, old people return from their children's homes elsewhere to spend the summer at 'their own fire-side', and the village has an appearance of prosperity with many of the houses being re-roofed and modernized by the children themselves, some of whom are returning to their once-deserted houses to use them as holiday homes.

This study thus took place at the end of a long period of stability in the patterns of thought I describe in this book, and on the verge of a great change—one occurring at that time throughout Greece.[39] It depicts the world shared by the married householders of the village, and still sustained there even as young single people were leaving. Most of the customs and beliefs discussed with these settled couples, as also with some of the young, were current during my residence in the village. Many I witnessed personally, though there are some which were described to me which had already lapsed, and to avoid misrepresentation I have identified these in an Appendix. But after I left, the departure of most of these couples was to make the village unsustainable as a centre of communal work, and thus starved of the people who in each generation could validate and create their communal thought patterns afresh in carrying out that work. Undoubtedly the memories they took with them have influenced their way of dealing with the Greek and foreign cities to which they went, but at the time when they began to go many younger people felt they had to catch up with a world that was leaving them behind, and many older people felt unequal to sustaining the culture I have described in this book, against the onslaught of a world constructed by global media, and with recourse only to cultural tools which they had not yet learned how to handle. How far they or their children have in their subsequent lives been able, using new skills in those tools, to adapt or recreate elements of the culture they grew up in, whether in whole or in part, is a story I have to leave to them or to others; but if this account gives them back any part of it, I will feel that I have not written in vain.

As for the generality of the thought patterns I describe, my avoidance, for the most part, of explicit reference to other evidence from Greek ethnography, which I have felt necessary for readability, creates a risk that superficial particularities will be taken as general where they are not. Thus it must be said that variety is of the essence in this culture: there are minor differences in the customs even between neighbouring villages, and people will firmly identify with their own way of doing things as opposed to the way that others do them—'We take exception to that here.' Differences also multiply with distance.

[39] Roger Just has shown that the urban population of Greece became the majority for the first time in 1971: Just, *A Greek Island Cosmos: Kinship and Community on Meganisi* (Oxford: John Curry, 2000).

For instance, the village of Ambeli is a Greek mountain village with inheritance of land through the male line and a pattern of marriage in which women move to live with their husbands, and this has given rise to a particular configuration of kinship and inheritance practices. However, in many of the Aegean islands the female line becomes more significant, and here these shifting elements will be arranged in a different pattern consistent with their reality.[40] But it is arguable that both societies will reveal, even though with different materials, the same underlying patterns constructed in accordance with the unchanging elements of their belief. Both will be recognizable as taking part in the same Orthodox tradition. Recently, I have tried to give an example of how such analysis can be supported by comparing the symbolism of everyday life in Ambeli with that of the Sarakatsan shepherds of northern Epirus, where in spite of sharp differences in communal imagery, a continuity can be shown with the same source texts of the Orthodox liturgy.[41]

Again, there is the question of differences between rural and urban communities. The Christian tradition first spread within the cities of the Eastern Mediterranean, and the city—whether in Augustine's *City of God* or in the symbolism of 'The City' (Constantinople) in the Greek East—became in some ways the paradigm of a Christian community. Philip Sherrard's description of Constantinople from this perspective is full of insights,[42] and similar resonances have been found among the Asia Minor refugees, described by Renée Hirschon,[43] who were settled in Kokkiniá and other urban areas of Athens and throughout Greece after the exchange of populations between Greece and Turkey in 1923, and had sustained, throughout the emigration, a deep Orthodox tradition. Indeed, Constantinople as the Christian City has exercised a powerful nostalgia in Greek cul-

[40] Just, *Greek Island Cosmos*; Muriel Dimen and Ernestine Friedl (eds.), 'Regional Variation in Modern Greece and Cyprus: Toward a Perspective on the Ethnology of Greece', in *Annals of the New York Academy of Sciences*, 268 (1976), pp. 1–465

[41] Juliet du Boulay, 'Bread and Sheep: A Comparative Study of Sacred Meanings among the Ambeliots and the Sarakatsani', in Mark Mazower (ed.), *Networks of Power in Modern Greece* (London: Hurst, 2008), pp. 209–30.

[42] Philip Sherrard, *Constantinople: Iconography of a Sacred City* (London: Oxford University Press, 1965).

[43] Hirschon, *Heirs of the Greek Catastrophe*.

ture, although it has not always engendered wise politics.[44] It is true that there has been a long-standing tension between the people of the towns and those of the villages, the villagers feeling—for the most part correctly—that urban people patronize and look down on them, and at times countering this, in private, by robust comments and gestures which are not entirely polite. But it is probably fair to say that cities with a strong Orthodox tradition have also been cities which had a deep link with the surrounding countryside, and have had the images of village life deeply impressed in their way of thinking. Even now city people in Greece still refer to their *patrídha* (*πατρίδα*), their family village of origin, and return there on symbolic occasions; and with the growth of secularism, of which cities have become the chief dispensers, village Christianity has become in its turn prototypical. This means that it should be possible to find transpositions of village themes in the culture of the cities where faith remains alive. The monasteries and the intellectual centres have also been key elements in generating and preserving the tradition, and we could probably say also that an essential prerequisite of a deep Orthodox tradition is that it is not peculiar either to urban or to village life, either to the monastics or to the folk, but represents a level at which people in all walks of life and in all occupations understand each other's experience as one. A great tradition seeks always to find what is universal in town and country, monastery and shepherd's hut, seeking to make both aware of one another and of the part both play in the welfare of all. Rural Orthodoxy can offer to the cities the natural world and its symbols, while urban Orthodoxy can offer to the villagers its metaphysical and intellectual tradition.

The question then remains as to how far it is permissible to extrapolate from a book of this sort to the wider world beyond the Greek borders. Certainly those who have travelled in the Balkans will recognize some elements in this book, and this suggests that there may be certain common elements which will be found wherever the Orthodox tradition is found. Some of the aspects discussed may also have links with village life in Russia before the Revolu-

[44] Michael Herzfeld, *Ours Once More: Folklore, Ideology and the Making of Modern Greece* (Austin: University of Texas Press, 1982); Michael Llewellyn Smith, *Ionian Vision: Greece in Asia Minor 1919–1922* (London: Allen Lane, 1973).

tion, if descriptions of nineteenth-century Russia are any guide.[45] Of course increasingly, as one moves further from the kind of village about which I have written, there are going to be more and more details which differ—the agricultural cycle, kinship patterns, staple foods, economic activities—but it is nevertheless likely that the way in which Orthodoxy fits these changing elements together is going to result in recognizable patterns at a deeper level. And it is possible, too, that the potential for comparison could be extended to the Christian world beyond Orthodoxy, for Orthodoxy is descended from the united Christianity of the first thousand years, and in Western Europe continuities with this world of the first thousand years of Christianity can be discerned in rural life till well after the Reformation.[46]

As to the extent to which the picture I have drawn can be extrapolated back in history, again I have to leave this question to those with more historical qualifications than I have. Charles Stewart has pointed to Orthodox images of the heavenly and demonic worlds which have remained constant from the fourth century AD to the present day.[47] Concurrences of village patterns of thought and practice with the Orthodox liturgy, and with some of the writings of the Church Fathers, are also a sign that many of the themes brought out in this book are ancient. Liturgists say the Orthodox liturgy was already by the fifteenth century substantially as it is now.[48] Examples are given in this book of village story and song which have come down from Byzantine times, like the story of Kassiane already quoted. And going even further back, it is not difficult even for an

[45] Vera Shevzov, *Russian Orthodoxy on the Eve of the Revolution* (Oxford: Oxford University Press, 2004). Even at the end of the Soviet period, atheist propaganda and forced changes in farming towards an industrial and collectivized model had not by the 1990s destroyed habitual practices in Russian villages which were associated with Orthodox and other aspects of their past, though in the absence in country areas of a fully revived Church, these changes had, curiously, reinforced a reconstruction of many practices as agrarian rituals or expressions of local loyalties. See Margaret Paxson, *Solovyovo: The Story of Memory in a Russian Village* (Washington D.C.: Woodrow Wilson Center Press, and Bloomington: Indiana University, 2005).

[46] Duffy, *Stripping of the Altars*; Hutton, *Rise and Fall.*

[47] Stewart, *Demons and the Devil.*

[48] Taft, *The Byzantine Rite.*

amateur to notice pre-Christian images in, for example, ideas about death. It is not unlikely that we are dealing here with what has been called the history of '*la longue durée*',[49] but how much of this continuity has been preserved in the contemporary Greek and foreign cities to which villagers have gone, and whether and in what form it can be re-asserted, is a question which remains to be answered.

This point having been made, however, my focus as I wrote the book was not on how far it could be generalized, but on how deeply I could give expression to what I found in the village itself. My life in Ambeli gave me a direct and individual experience of what it is to live in such a community, and the wish to write about this for its own sake. I was the only foreigner in the community—was unmarried at the time—and I depended on the people for everything, not only for information about how they lived and what they believed and valued, but for those things without which any life there would have been impossible—hospitality, love, laughter, comfort and companionship. And nothing can replace for me the living experience of this way of life—the rapidity of the people's voices with their soft Boeotian accent, the high-pitched torrent of invective against some erring child or hapless goat, the scent of pine smoke in the winter and the chill of the water under the plane tree in the summer, spring nights filled with the song of the nightingale and with the crowing of cocks and outbreaks of dogs barking, the September air pungent with dried herbs and rotting figs, the long walks over the mountain paths accompanied by the kaleidoscope of the people's talk, the extraordinary charity of their acceptance of myself as a stranger in their midst, the winter evenings sitting with them in the light of the blazing fires and hearing the deep echoes in the drama of their discussions and reminiscences, their intuitions, their stories, their silences. At such times I would feel, as people in such communities do feel when their confidence is undamaged, that I, with them, was at the centre of the world. I hope that something of this experience can be conveyed to my readers.

[49] Emmanuel Le Roy Ladurie, *Montaillou: Cathars and Catholics in a French Village, 1294–1324* (London: Scholar Press, 1978).

1

THE WORLD

THE primary assertion in the pattern of thought which this book is to explore is that this world is created and upheld by God. God is Almighty, he created the universe and everything material and spiritual in it, and nothing in it can occur without his permission. Thus everything is 'from God'—the beauties of the world, the trees, the beasts, the life of man, the corn in the field, the water in the spring. It is not, however, that good things only are from God, but in a sense evil things also. Wars are 'from God', illnesses are 'thrown' at man by God. Even man's nature, which is quarrelsome and prone to sin, is in the hands of God, and the endless imperfection in human activities is due simply to the fact that 'that's how God has made us'.

If God is responsible for all created things, including the existence within creation of evil, there is nevertheless a differentiation made between his responsibility for good and his responsibility for evil, as evil things are thought of as coming from God only in the sense that he permits them through permitting the operations of the devil. God 'holds' or 'contains' (*ἔχει*) the devil, in accordance with his own purposes, allowing him to torment and confuse mankind so that, given the power of choice, man will reveal which side he is really on: 'Will he listen to the devil or to me?' God is thus superior to the devil and ultimately in control of him; but on that lesser level at which the devil is given power, he operates in total opposition to God, striving continually to undo and to pervert those good things which God, or God through the agency of man, has brought into being. A polarity between good and evil thus operates throughout creation, and this polarity exerts its sway on every level of existence, and particularly within man himself. Always on the shoulders of every human being sits Christ and the devil: Christ on the right hand side, the devil on the left, the one summoning to good, the other tempting to evil. Even in church the devil has everybody on a silver halter, tugging their heads around to assess each newcomer.

And even the sanctuary is not proof against him: 'When the priest closes the Royal Doors,[1] tak! It is to stop the devil getting in. But he gets in all the same.' Wherever God is, there is the devil also, locked in conflict, and the bedevilment of mankind in fact finds its origin in this archetypal battle being continually fought out in the universe: 'If God and the devil were not at this moment fighting each other, men wouldn't be fighting and making wars either.'

In spite of this obvious duality between the two great forces, however, the understanding of God as creator of all and as in control of all prevents a radical dualism from holding creation in an irresolvable tension. For all his ingenuity, the devil is powerless to act without the permission of the Almighty; thus the polarity between them, while real enough on its own level, does not act fundamentally to split creation between two equal and opposite forces of good and evil. The power of God is always, ultimately, superior: good is more potent a force than evil and it is because everything is in the hands of divine providence that the world, for all its potential for harm, is essentially beneficent to the creatures it sustains.

There is in this way a grand design in-written in the universe which gives to every part of it a due place and a due purpose. God has set the sun in the heavens 'to warm the neighbourhood'; he has made the moon at the full so that 'the shepherd and the traveller should have light by night', and the dark nights of the moon 'so that hunted creatures should have rest... so that the fishes should shoal'.[2] Folk tales tell of the cat being created to keep under control the mice which were making holes in the cheesecloth that Christ was using for making his cheeses, or in another story, to stop the mice plaguing the monks as they sat on the floor and ate. The pig came into being to rootle up and burst the buried skins of water with which the enemies of Christ were preparing a false miracle. Again, each animal has its natural grace and function—goats give milk which is good to drink and makes a particularly hard well-keeping cheese, while sheep give milk which, too rich to drink, makes a good soft cheese

[1] The Royal or Holy Doors are the doors in the middle of the iconostasis through which no one but the celebrants pass, and then only at set points during the services.

[2] Bright lights cause the fish to shoal, and fishing boats go out at night with lamps hung from their sterns in order to gather the fish around the boat.

which is stored in brine, and excellent yoghourt—'God has shared things out between them'. The cock, similarly, enabling men to tell the time in the darkest hours of night, has a gift from God: 'Do you notice how he crows? At eleven o'clock, at three? God has given him the ability to communicate with the skies.'

It is a reading of the universe not only as essentially beneficent to man but as formed by an intelligence which sets everything in proportion and guides their various relationships. And it is observation of these relationships within the natural world which is one of the strongest arguments for the existence of God. The gifts bestowed on the cock in his communication with the heavens, for instance, may be cited as evidence, or the gracious ordering of the world which allows man to live in it: 'Of course God exists. If we didn't have water, how would we bake? If we didn't have the sun, how would we see?' This continuous flow of God's gifts to his creation is one of the many factors which continually confirm belief in a creator, for he reveals himself in them.

The universe is good, therefore, whole, and rightly proportioned, and powerful as the devil may be, God holds the winning cards. The story of the creation of the buffalo well portrays the typical way in which God and the devil relate to each other on familiar and even intimate terms, and how, for all his panache, the devil is not capable of any real autonomy. This story runs that the devil one day created the buffalo, which he endowed with great feet and a huge voice so that when it walked and bellowed the mountains would shake, and pregnant women hearing it would be so frightened that they would miscarry. However, when it came to the point the devil could not make the buffalo get to its feet and walk. Unable to remedy this situation he went to Christ, saying: 'Hey, friend! I've done this, and this, but the buffalo won't get up!' So Christ went to the buffalo and spoke to it: 'Rise up, O Hoarse-Voiced, and tread lightly!', whereupon the buffalo got up and walked very delicately, and far from bellowing could only utter low groans.

This beautiful illustration of the asymmetric relation of God and the devil reveals that although the devil is credited with a certain creative power, he is not actually effective unless he calls in the power of God. With the invocation of this power, however, the devil's work is inevitably frustrated. The devil is shown to be a plagiarist, living off the original work of God. But in spite of the relatively feeble creativity of the devil in this story, and the fact that at bottom he is all bombast and no real action, the battle lines between God and the devil have nevertheless been drawn, and the sacred balance of the universe is continually vulnerable to the destructive power of the devil because, in the cause of leaving man free, God allows it to be so. The beneficence of the universe is both original and ultimate, working not only in creation but also, as is shown later, in redemption; but in the middle term the goodness in the universe exists in continual tension with evil, and it is within this dynamic flux of opposing forces that man finds himself.

Man thus lives in a universe which is characterized by contrast, and this necessitates in him the capacity to distinguish between good and evil in all the varying situations of life. The teaching of this discernment is an endemic part of the oral culture, taught from children's earliest years by admonition and prescription, by what is 'done' or 'not done', by what is good and what is bad, by what people will 'laugh at' and what they will approve, and at its base lie a number of symbolic oppositions which act as reference points on, as it were, the spiritual map of the universe.

The axis of 'right' and 'left' has already been mentioned in connection with the positions of Christ and the devil at the side of every man. This symbolism is repeated throughout the society: the right-handed position, emphasized as auspicious, is contrasted with that of the inauspicious left hand, and the movement 'towards the right', also described as 'towards the sun' or 'like the dance', is invoked continually in symbolic actions at every level of the social world and is contrasted with the idea of 'turning back', which indicates a movement against the flow of life, away from God and towards the devil. To these poles of reference must be added those of 'up' and 'down', 'superior' and 'inferior', 'straight' and 'squint', and a 'correct' stance which is opposed to that which is 'upside down' or 'the wrong way round'.

In this scheme the situation of God as 'up' and the devil as 'down' is the natural consequence of the superiority of God over the devil, and is testified to by the way the phrase 'God above' comes without thinking to people's lips. The devil, on the other hand, is thought of as associated with the deepest parts of the earth. Occasionally this is put precisely, that 'the devil lies, bound, in the middle of the earth' or that 'the devil, the thrice-damned, is down below our feet'. More often, however, the statements refer not to the devil, the principle of evil, himself, but to the demons which act as his emissaries and pour over the face of the earth doing his bidding. These, while they are accepted as ranging all over the world, are said to have their home, or 'village', in 'the ravines', in 'the holes in the ravines'—that is to say, deep in the clefts of the earth where the mountain rivers flow and where the land is too steep for habitation and cultivation.

While 'up' and 'down', God and the devil, good and evil, are the basic orientations, there are drawn into these a number of other oppositions, some of which have been already mentioned. A phrase commonly used to indicate a girl who has lost her virtue is that she 'put her foot squint', or 'took a crooked road'—a course of action which contrasts with the 'straight' or 'regular' path taken by the virtuous. A spell against the evil eye describes the person who has cast the evil eye coming by, sitting the wrong way round on her animal, with her headscarf on squint, pig-footed. In the art of effective cursing, those who really know how to do it know that you should turn your skirt back to front and put your shoes on the wrong feet. Again, Christ, who is 'correct', who sits on the right or the 'good' hand side, and 'goes with glory', in whose company a man 'moves forward' or 'makes progress', contrasts with the devil, who, on the left hand, 'turns back, the wrong way round'; malicious women, often referred to as 'evil', are also sometimes referred to as 'upside down'. It is with reference to this value given to regularity that at a wedding, when the bride is being prepared for the ceremony, a particular point is made that the parting of her hair should be exactly in the middle, neither to one side nor to the other: 'She's a bride, she mustn't be lop-sided', is the repeated comment. Indeed, custom specifies that all married women, their hair, plaited and wound round the head, bound tightly to frame the face with an under-kerchief, the *tsibér* (*τσιμπέρι*, dialect *τσιμπέρ'*), and then covered with the looser kerchief or *mandíli* (*μαντήλι*) of the colour appropriate to their status, must have a central parting. At the same time, if it is important for an individual person's appearance to be regular and even, collections of individuals must be uneven, lest they become fatally divided. At ceremonial events care is always taken that significant numbers are uneven, 'they must be uneven, they must not form a pair', as it is often said; that is to say, the numbers—whether of people in a ceremonial procession, or of ovens fired for the preparation of memorial bread, or of candles round the dead—must form a symbolic unity, preventing any division into two equal opposing elements.

Squintness and division also have a close relationship with the word for the devil, *dhiávolos* (*διάβολος* or, as it is rendered in the village, *διάολος*), for this is derived from the word *dhiavállo,* meaning to lead astray, to push off true, to set at variance or to put asunder. Inauspicious reversal from the right to the left, from the true to the false, from good to evil, involves a movement towards the devil, and this diabolical movement is summed up in a word meaning to 'turn back' (*γυρίζει*), a reference pregnant with ill-omen. To 'turn back', leaving the right-handed path towards God and taking instead the left-handed road to the devil, is a movement which invariably reverses the auspicious flow of life and sets in motion a sequence of catastrophe and evil.

It is this universe, on whose various levels the mysteries of great good and great evil are continually played out, that is the world in which man lives, and even death does not abolish this geography. In later chapters it becomes clear that there is 'another world' parallel to this one, an invisible world which is the abode both of the souls of the dead and of the saints and angels, with the region of blessedness being above, and of trial and purification below. This 'other' world, like the abodes of God and the devil, is located both above and below the middle ground of the earth, though somewhat as God and the devil invisibly penetrate this world, the 'other world' also invisibly penetrates it when dwellers in its upper and nether region enter the middle ground at certain permitted times and seasons.

In this way, set between the polarities of heaven and hell, God and the devil, man's proper place is to be 'on the face of the earth', the beneficent world given to him by God, with God above him and the devil below. Man thus lives in a world which is the natural arena of cosmically warring forces; and with Christ perpetually on his right hand side and the devil on his left, ever presented with the 'correct' path by Christ but ever tempted to 'turn back' from it by the devil, he is the microcosm of the entire spiritual universe. Man, set in the middle ground between the heights of the skies and the hollows of the earth, on whom the sun shines and for whom the waters flow, is the centre where all things meet.

The consequence of this cosmology is profound, for it is that actions that are conducted within this scheme, however small, can never ultimately be meaningless. This is a world not of chance and relativity, but of purpose and significance. Thus the choices made between one thing and another—between, for instance, work and leisure, fast and feast, when seeds are sown or medicinal herbs picked—are in this setting not only choices between necessity and pleasure but also between help and harm, between good and evil. It is not that work or leisure, fast or feast, are in themselves categorically good or evil, for that varies with the context; it is that a huge range of human activities is governed not solely by the material situation but also by a world of sacred meanings, and it is these meanings which bestow on the man who lives within their rhythms the knowledge of his place in the universe, and the assurance of his integrity and identity.

The universe then, created in accordance with the will of God and sustained by his superior power, possesses a natural stability, but at the same time the ceaseless work of the devil and his ministers brings it about that this stability is continually threatened, the divine order in it constantly imperilled. The world in which man lives sets before him not only the ideal of harmony and balance but also the actuality of distortion and disequilibrium, and the universe is seen not as a static system but as one in tension between opposing spiritual principles—between order and chaos, good and evil, right and left, the straight and the squint. In this universe, order is innate but evil endemic, and in it, as a result, the perpetual endeavour of man and God is necessary to overcome the powers of evil and to restore it continually to its original equilibrium.

This tripartite universe in which God and the devil meet and strive with each other in the middle ground is not simply a physical description but a symbolic system which likewise finds its embodiment in the structure of the physical world—in the heavens and the earth and the centre of the earth. The orientations of 'up' and 'down', heaven and earth, 'high' and 'low', which are central to this view of things, are consistent with a cosmos in which a steady earth with no motion is circled by the heavenly bodies—a cosmos in which direct experience sets the boundaries of belief: 'They say that the earth turns round and round, but do the seas turn round and round too? I don't believe it!', and, 'They say that the sun stands still, but *I* see it rising and setting.' To this observed universe are then added images of the moon hanging by a golden thread, of the dark patches on the moon being forests, and of the ends of the earth which run into a great wilderness, where, although it is impossible to get there, one would find God. The earth itself is said by some to rest on a river: 'The village is 600 metres above the sea. You can see the sea from here. If you dig down 600 metres you will find water.' And together with ideas of this river is the recurrent idea of a great column or columns supporting the earth—a belief which is embedded also in a Christmas myth referring to a great tree supporting the world.

The sacred geography of this universe is consistent with the symbolic system already outlined. It has been said that the demons live 'in the ravines', 'in the holes in the ravines', sallying forth from time to time on their marauding missions. Below these again, around the roots of the tree supporting the world, hobgoblins known as the *skalikantzoúria* (*σκαλικαντζούρια*, dialect for *καλικάντζαροι*, s. *-ος*) hack assiduously at the trunk so as to 'bring the earth crashing down'. At Christmas time, however, they are allowed 'leave' for twelve days to come up and make mayhem on the earth, and this they do with a will. When they return down to the underworld at the end of this period, however, they find the tree healed and the work of the previous year undone. The world tree is saved by the infant Christ. Finally, further down still and in the nethermost darkness, the true home of the devil, 'thrice-damned', is in the centre of the earth.

In this way there exists a general understanding according to which evil and danger increase as the depths increase; nevertheless, even in these depths the devil is understood to be 'bound' (by God), and the world tree, firmly rooted, is cyclically saved from destruction by the birth of Christ. The evil is real but not uncontained; danger threatens but is continually resolved into new life.

By contrast, in the regions of the air above the earth the picture is reversed, but it is also more absolute, for the holiness of these realms is not challenged by evil as the evil under the earth is challenged by God. These regions of the sky are pictured as composed of 'levels' or 'layers' like a house with many floors, while a further layer separates this world from the outer limits of the known universe inhabited by the sun, moon and stars—a region of inviolable purity for it is the dwelling-place of God himself. Here the sun is untouchable because it 'burns', the moon because it is 'light', and above them even God himself does not live. 'Does he live above *that*?' the rhetorical question may be asked, with a gesture towards the sun—an implication confirmed by the appalled comment on the activities of the astronauts,[3] constantly recurring, 'Are they going to go up there above God?' Beyond this level of the heavenly bodies is the end of the universe, described simply as 'a great void'. The word used here, *cháos* (*χάος*), is the ancestor of our own word 'chaos', but though it is sometimes used, as is our word, to indicate disorder, in all contexts concerning the cosmos it is used to indicate something very different—a great emptiness, a nothingness, an unbelievable infinity, void even of God.

The divinely inhabited cosmos then, running from below the earth to the earth, and from earth to heaven, is constructed in levels or layers up to the point where the outer limits of the universe, studded with the sun, moon and stars, sit like a giant lid on the empyrean—apparently a version of the cosmology of Ptolemy (second century AD). The construction and placing of these layers is clearly a question of some speculation, but one thing is certain and that is that in this version they are not cited as metaphors but as material barriers dividing one dimension of reality from another. Said by some to consist of 'earth' or 'land', they are in any event solid and impenetrable, for their existence forms a definitive rebuttal of any claim that man may journey to the moon and beyond: 'Where will they [the men] get through?' These regions of the sky, protected from man's interference, are unapproachable and inexpressibly holy, areas for God alone. Already, before the moon landings, it was being said that God had withdrawn from man because man was penetrating his sanctuaries and hunting him in his private lairs. But it was man's penetration of the further regions of the sky in the space

[3] It was the third moon landing on 31 January 1971 which occasioned the comments referred to in this chapter.

1. Villager ploughing: 'Man, set in the middle ground between the heights of the skies and the hollows of the earth, on whom the sun shines and for whom the waters flow, is the centre where all things meet' (pp. 29–30). But the stony, recalcitrant nature of the ground, lamented in Chapter 2, is also much in evidence.

2. Woman in traditional dress: 'Custom specifies that all married women, their hair, plaited and wound round the head, bound tightly to frame the face with an under-kerchief, the *tsibér*, and then covered with the looser kerchief or *mandíli*...must have a central parting' (p. 28).

exploration of the early 1970s that was seen as the ultimate act of vandalism. Of the moon landings themselves it was asserted on many occasions, 'God won't allow it', and once, prophetically: 'God won't allow it. And if men do get there, the whole world is done for.' The violation, that is to say, of this holiest of holies would inevitably alter the balance of forces throughout the entire universe and bring about catastrophe. And even after general acceptance of the moon landings had become fashionable or unavoidable it was nevertheless still impossible for many people to relate to it, as in the avowal, with a charming smile: 'With my lips I say it, but I don't believe.' It is indeed apparent that with such a violation a deep shift must occur, dividing knowledge of the spiritual world from that of the physical world, and rendering metaphorical or meaningless those physical correspondences to spiritual realities which are rooted in the everyday experience of ordinary people. Tolerance of contradiction between the physical and spiritual cosmos, in hopes of their ultimate reconciliation, is something only learned slowly, and it is as a protest against this breaking apart of the sacred cosmos by the impiety of man, in deed or in thought, that in this context the following apparently self-contradictory remark makes perfect sense: 'It's not true. And if it is true one ought not to believe it.'

Creation is thus seen as a hierarchical ordering of levels, or worlds, although these levels, while distinct, are not totally separate. The power of God is evident in the underworld; God and the devil leave their natural abodes to inhabit the earth; saints and demons leave their places of refuge to visit the world of men; the dead travel, at their appointed times, to their appointed places, above or below. There is thus a means of communication which runs from the heights of the skies to the depths of the earth, from God to the devil, and this takes various symbolic forms. In the imagery of the afterlife for instance, there occur 'ladders' reaching, side by side, to heaven and to hell, and wells as a means of communication between the upper world and the underworld feature at the feast of the Ascension when, covering their heads with a cloth, people gaze into a well and watch, in the water below, the procession of souls. Similarly, there is a hint, in a poem to the Prophet Elias (Elijah) quoted later, that mountain tops are regarded as openings to the heavenly world. This prophet customarily has his churches on the tops of hills and mountains, so the invocation of Elias is the invocation of one who, as the inhabitant of the mountain peaks, lives at the point where earth meets heaven. All these images—ladders to heaven and hell, wells through which people can see the dead return to their abodes, and mountain tops of the Prophet Elias as the means of ascent to God—indicate the existence of a vertical axis by means of which there is communication between one level and another: but this axis is brought out most clearly in the symbolism of death.

At a death, it is the invariable custom to lay out the body on the floor or, as it is put, 'on the earth' (*καταγῆς*), for traditionally floors are of smoothed and hardened earth. In addition to this it is most strictly observed that once the body has been laid out, nothing whatever must be allowed to pass or to be passed over it.[4] The first custom ensures that there is no impediment between the body and the earth on which it rests, and the second ensures that the same is true of the body and the air above, so in this way the dead person is placed at the centre of an axis passing through earth to heaven. This symbolism is reinforced by an implication held in the custom at a death which requires that the door of the house is, until the body is taken for burial, always left open. This is represented as an action which 'does not shut Charos in', that is to say, does not shut death into the house, but in allowing death out, allows also free passage to the departing soul.

This idea of the separation between the upper, the middle and the lower worlds being mediated by transverse axes penetrating all three is, then, prevalent and diverse, and a final illustration of it occurs in the story of the *skalikantzoúria* already quoted. For this adds—to the images of ladders, wells, mountain tops, and the axis between earth and heaven at a death—the explicit notion of a great tree at the world's foundations and thus of a communication between the underworld and the middle plane of the earth.

The idea of vertical axes allowing communication between the various levels of creation thus appears as a vital image in this way of thought, but these axes are the means purely of spiritual communi-

[4] The observances here referred to are related to beliefs concerning the avoidance of the return of the departed soul as a vampire. This is discussed further in Ch. 8.

cation between the worlds, and they involve a journey only to be made by the living in prayer or by the soul at death. Even at death the journey of the soul is perilous, needing to be hedged about by rigorous safeguards both for the living and the dead; but the involvement of anyone in such a journey during life—such as in the case of the astronauts—is unthinkable, and, if thought, is fraught with appalling danger not only for those who make the journey but for the whole world. It is the earth, lying at the centre of creation and poised between heaven and hell, which provides the fullness of the knowledge of God and is the sum of the concern of man.

The hierarchical construction of the universe then, like the relationship between good and evil already discussed, does not embody an irresolvable duality. Even in the most diabolical regions in the centre of the earth, the devil is restrained by the superior power which binds and imprisons him, and further, although the devil cannot penetrate into the heavenly regions, the roots of the world tree draw sustenance from the dark waters of the underworld, and the voice of the newborn Christ summons the demons into the world to waste their time while the roots heal. The place of the devil is limited, whereas the place of God in the freedom of the heavens is his alone.

Thus far, the cosmos that has been described has a recognizable early Christian origin, sharing a Jewish and Hellenistic language about demons, and rooted in the central Christian and Jewish concern with the problem of good and evil, even if some elements of Greek science, in particular the Ptolemaic universe, have also made their appearance. But from this point on, village conceptions of the sun and moon become the main focus of this chapter, and these conceptions have more parallels in ancient science than in anything specific to Christianity, just as early Christian thought assimilated and adapted to its vision many cosmic conceptions of the day. In the village, these ideas are mixed also with other fragments of ancient material which are further discussed in the notes.

In the heavens God has placed the sun and the moon, whose physical light is an image of his nature as light, and whose physical influence over all things visible on earth is a partial reflection of God's nature as lord of all the cosmos. The untouchable and sacred nature of the sun and the moon has been mentioned already, but in addition to this dominant characteristic they also have complex symbolic identities based on ideas about how birth and death, growth and decay, come about. Thought of as 'brother and sister', they possess a 'mother' to whom the sun returns every night and who lives 'far away'. Close observation adds detail to this relationship. The moon is said to 'follow' the sun, that is to say that the full moon rises, broadly speaking, where the sun rises, while the new moon appears in the evening sky above the sunset. The moon is also, however, 'opposite' for the same reason—the full moon rises as the sun is setting; and to this is added the observation that the moon is high in the winter when the sun is low, and low in the summer when the sun is high. That is to say that in the winter, when the sun is rising in the south-east and setting in the south-west, the full moon rises in the north-east and sets in the north-west, while in summer this pattern is reversed. The sun and the moon, classified as masculine and feminine, are, like men and women, complementary opposites.

The sun, however, is defined not just in relation to the moon but to the earth as a whole, and over all the visible creation the sun is 'lord', 'superior', and 'on the right hand side'—attributes which it possesses because it burns, is untouchable, and governs all things. This characteristic is fundamental and holds good whatever the context, even when it appears to contradict the sun's observed motion—'The sun is right-handed, and that's an end to it.' In a similar way, no matter what its current position in the sky, the sun is identified with the east, so that the phrases 'facing the sun' (*πρὸς τὸν ἥλιο*) and 'facing the east' (*πρὸς τὴν ἀνατολή*) are synonymous.

The sun is thus categorically lord, superior, on the right hand side, and associated with the east—the sacrally significant quarter—and it is consistent with this that the sun is particularly significant at birth and death. The symbolism of the sun after a birth is to do with inauguration into life. Traditionally, a birth occurs at home with the local healer and midwife assisting the mother as she walks about and clutches onto supports when the pains get too great. However, at the final moment of birth the midwife takes her hands away from under the child so as to allow it to emerge directly onto the earth—a meeting with the earth of which the same word is used as at death when the body must be laid out 'on the earth'. For the rest of the day of the birth and the whole of the one following, both mother and child must remain unwashed, and during this intermediary period when the child is suspended between the world before birth and the world after it, the three Fates gather around the cradle laying down its future.[5] Very early in the morning of the third day, before dawn, this period is brought to an end by the arrival of the midwife, who washes both mother and child from the blood of childbirth, and dresses them in clean clothes. Following this she washes the dirty clothes and cloths; and when all is purified she goes to the threshold of the front door and calls to the mother to bring her child to the doorway. It is stipulated that the mother must not come on her own—and the emphasis on the role of the midwife makes it clear that this is in fact a second birth, a transition from the liminal post-birth world of the Fates and of the pollution of blood into the fullness of day. On the threshold the midwife instructs the mother to spit three times 'towards the sun' (or 'towards the east'), and three times into her own bosom. Spitting three times is a symbolic rejection of evil which occurs in many occasions when there is danger of the 'evil eye',[6] and it is also found in the baptismal rite of the Orthodox Church symbolizing the casting out of the devil. A woman who is within forty days of having given birth—termed a *lechóna* (*λεχώνα*)—is thought to be particularly vulnerable to malignant forces which threaten both her and her child, and cause mischief, through her, to others, and while for the whole of the period she is a focus for these powers, for the initial three days both she and her child are in particular danger. Thus this ritual which purifies the mother and child as they are led by the midwife from the world of birth and the dominion of the Fates into the society of the village and the light of day, establishes the sun as the beneficent but awesome power which will not tolerate pollution and which is present at the gateway of life.

[5] This imagery is from ancient Greek thought about fate, and village reflections on this are discussed in Ch. 11.

[6] The evil eye is an expression which encapsulates the idea that envy, whether conscious or unrecognized, can do harm to what is envied. The possibility of unconscious envy when something is admired must be recognized and neutralized through disavowing it: 'Let not the evil eye fall on you!', or by a good wish, or by an onomatopoeic rendering of the gesture of spitting—'*phtoú sou*'—which spits out the devil, i.e. any ill will.

As at birth, so at death also the sun is important. It is said that if a person in the throes of death is unable to die, he should be turned 'towards the sun' to permit the advent of death—and the tale is told of this idea being invoked when a small boy, accidentally shot by his brother in a childish game, lay in agony, mortally wounded. So that 'he shouldn't suffer any longer' he was turned to face the sun, and on this being done he immediately 'gave up his soul'. In the actual context of death the word used for dying is never the normal word for 'to die' (*πεθαίνω*), but always to 'un-soul' (*ξεψυχάω*); thus in this context, the sun, synonymous with the east, is turned to at death and symbolizes also the means by which the liberated soul can journey to the other world.

The relationship of the sun to the crisis of death does not, however, end with the moment of death, for after death the dead person must be laid out 'facing the sun', that is to say with his feet, and thus notionally his face, pointing towards the east; the placing of the coffin at the burial service and indeed the orientation of the church itself is the same, 'facing the east'; and finally the grave must be dug and the person buried, again, 'facing the sun'.

The sun, then, is associated with the transition of both life and death; it is invoked as a newly-delivered mother is called to the threshold and crosses the boundary between two worlds, and also as the struggling soul, turned to the east, finds its passage from the body suddenly eased. The power of the sun is thus seen not only as that which presides over the life of growing things on this earth but as the embodiment of a principle which enables change to take place from one category to another, from one level to another, from one world to another. Sought out at birth and at death, it appears to be the principle which is associated with the fundamental categories of human existence and the movement between them; and this same perception, according to which the sun is associated with events of permanence and finality, occurs again in the building of a house.

When the building is begun, holy water is sprinkled inside the foundations, starting from the eastern side—the side described as the side 'facing the sun'—and moving round anti-clockwise 'like the dance'. After this a cock is slaughtered in the same place and the body taken round in a similar movement so that the blood drizzles into the foundations.[7] Again, on the eastern side are buried a bunch of flowers and a silver coin, while a bottle of holy water is built into all four corners. The house is a prized inheritance, built once only in a series of generations, and, made to shelter and nourish a putatively unending line of descendants, it is a symbol of permanence, and it is the sun which is the auspicious power which is associated with its inauguration.

In spite, however, of these majestic attributes, there is a sense in which the sun is influenced by the tension in the rest of the cosmos, for although it is 'lord' and presides over the great cycles of life and death, it has nevertheless a moment of weakness, both in the day and the year. This moment of weakness is related to a perception of the moments of change in the daily cycle of light and darkness—a perception which is acute in people whose lives depend on the seasons and whose activities are ruled not by the clock but by the sun. The day begins at first light, the 'etching' (*χάραμα*, from the verb *χαράζω*, to etch or outline) where the silhouettes of trees or hills are first seen outlined against the paling sky. At sunrise, the sun's power is already well developed, for at this moment it is said to 'burst', (*σκάζει*) a term which when related to natural objects tends to denote power and promise and joy, and parallels the opening of buds in spring. This moves into the time when the sun is full and warm and lifted well clear of the horizon, at about 9 or 10 o'clock, which is known as 'the fullness' (*γιόμα*). 'Midday' at twelve o'clock is followed by 'after the fullness' or afternoon, after which the sun declining perceptibly towards the west is said to 'lean' (*γέρνει*), then, as it sets, to 'reign' in glory (*βασιλεύει*), and finally to 'finish'. Dusk, or twilight, is evoked in a word (*σουρουπώνω*) related to a stem (*σούρα, σουρώνω*) which includes ideas of shrivelling up or wasting away .

The idea of 'leaning' can carry some of the inauspicious connotations of being squint or off-true that were noted earlier, and in spite of the glory of the setting sun there is a clear pattern of growth and decay in the movement from bursting to fullness into leaning

[7] The cock is then cooked in a celebratory meal for those present. Nevertheless, there may be muted overtones of sacrifice in this action, even though a term meaning simply 'slaughter' (*σφάζω*) is used. The placing of the blood may thus reflect ancient practice, but sacrificial associations in Greek village life are rare in my experience and this is not discussed further in this book.

and finishing. Thus the sun has an aspect according to which it is vulnerable, subject to change, and this is echoed in the belief that midday and midnight are susceptible to invasion by the evil hour. The evil hour is a supernatural presence which may be summarized here as a spiritual force of evil which 'passes by', coming and going in a second, afflicting anyone who is vulnerable at that moment with sudden harm. The moments at which this evil may befall anyone are infinite, and largely unknown, but midday and midnight are especially dangerous. It is those burning noontides in summer when the sun's heat is at its greatest that occasion the greatest danger, and the times when the hens cluck sleepily and stir around are moments when the evil hour passes by. In the country everything is hushed by the heat and not a sound is heard—and at these moments the prudent person takes care not to raise his voice or make a sudden noise until the danger is past. Midnight is said by some to be the more dangerous of the two periods, especially the hour leading up to midnight, and this danger is intensified at a death, when people always take care, as they leave a wake, to return to their own houses either well before or well after 12 o'clock.

Danger invests these times, but it is a danger which seems to be related less to an absolute quality of evil in the time than to a fundamental uncertainty, when the balance of forces alters as day turns towards night or night towards day. It is said of these times that at them the 'skies open'—an occurrence graphically illustrated by a swift movement of the hands extraordinarily expressive of the act of opening and swallowing up. This quality of receptivity is also expressed in a phrase often used of the occurrence of spiritual good or harm, involving the idea of finding or 'meeting' one's time,[8] that is to say, coming on a moment at which the time is ripe, or receptive. It is at this time that evil impulses can penetrate the world of men, but at this time also, because 'the skies are open', prayers are most easily received into the heavenly world. At this moment either a prayer or a curse, a good wish or a bad one, can in an instant find its destination, and although this receptivity in the cosmos occurs when it will, it is at midnight at which it is most customary. The characteristic of the midnight period then, and by analogy that of the mid-

[8] See pp. 324 for discussion of this phrase.

day also, is not that it is actively harmful, but that it is vulnerable—a moment of equipoise between darkness and light, good and evil, and so a moment at which the barriers between the spiritual and the material worlds are particularly thin.

In this way the sun, overwhelmingly a kingly and auspicious influence, nevertheless, as it approaches the zenith and 'leans' towards the evening, and as it approaches the nadir and moves towards the dawn, enters a phase in which change and uncertainty render it vulnerable to evil. And as in the day the evil hour marks this moment, so in the year one of the solstices is marked by the demonic apparitions of the *skalikantzoúria*.

Their story has already been briefly mentioned in the context of the world tree, and at Christmas time it features as a very real part of the Christmas mythology—a dimension of the sacred time of this season of which people are strongly aware. The story is told in graphic detail of how the *skalikantzoúria*, throwing down their axes at the approach of Christmas, erupt into the world of men and cause all sorts of harm, ranging from malicious pranks like piddling on the pig that has been killed for Christmas (although they keep away from the sausages on account of the pepper in them) to mobbing and crazing the mortal unfortunate enough to fall into their hands. For the Twelve Days of Christmas they keep up a reign of uninhibited misrule, until on the appointed day, known as the day of the Cross, when the first service for the Theophany (the Baptism of Christ) is held, the priest comes round to all the houses with the cross and holy water, and 'turns them out'. At the approach of the priest they are said to be cast into great disorder, rushing hither and thither, calling out to each other:

> Here comes the priest with the cross
> And the priest's wife with the hot water![9]
> Grab hold of your cucumber-thing and my cucumber-thing
> So that we can go back to our hole.

For all the ribaldry of these tales, however, a startling degree of evil is thought to be abroad at this time. The days are known as 'upside down'; death during this period is considered unlucky, it being

[9] It is the job of the priest's wife, in the absence of a server, to bring to the sanctuary the hot water (ζέον), which is added to the wine used in communion.

said that anyone who dies during the Twelve Days of Christmas goes to hell; similarly, birth on Christmas Day itself is inauspicious, such a birth representing, it is said, the Antichrist.[10] And the *skalikantzoúria* themselves, always to some extent malign, vary from mischievous hobgoblins to messengers of evil carrying out terrifying acts of demoniac power. Especially present by water, they figure in a folk tale in which they gain ascendancy over a girl by learning her name, subsequently hurling her about in a mill stream until, half-crazed, she escapes and returns home to die. Stories are told of people struck immobile or bedevilled in some way by hoards of *skalikantzoúria*, to be saved by the power of the cross or the Lord's Prayer; one dramatic description tells of a shepherd, returning home from his sheep one day in winter, beset by a host of *skalikantzoúria* coming upon him in a roaring wind. They grabbed him, pushing him towards a deep quarry with water at the bottom, and the more he struggled with them, grabbing at plants and tree stumps, the more they pushed him towards the pit. He called out for help but the *skalikantzoúria* stuffed his mouth with wind and his voice barely carried. Eventually, however, people heard him and, rushing to his aid, they found him at the bottom of the quarry in the water; and with their arrival, on the instant, the wind dropped.

It seems at first sight strange that the eve of the birth of Christ should be attended by such a reign of terror, even though the terror is limited since God is said to 'contain' the *skalikantzoúria*, as he 'contains' the rest of creation. Nevertheless, the analogy of the evil hour investing the moments of change at midday and midnight, and the *skalikantzoúria* investing the moment of change at the winter solstice, is suggestive. The risk attending the de-stabilizing of the sun at the two points of its twenty-four hour cycle is echoed in the risk at the winter solstice when the sun is at its weakest—a dangerous moment echoed in the parallel story of the vulnerability of the infant Christ. With the turning point at the winter solstice, however, the danger is greater than at the similar points either at midday or at midnight, for

[10] A birth on this day would involve sexual relations not only during Great Lent, but around the especially sacred time of the Annunciation on 25 March. Continence in sexual relations is understood as an intrinsic part of the control of the appetites which underpins the dietary fast from animal products during sacred periods.

while the recurrent danger of the daily cycle is the momentary encounter with the evil hour, the danger brought about by the weakest moment in the yearly cycle results in a disequilibrium so great that, the world tree nearly severed, the earth staggers on its axis.

Moments of transition thus seem to be also moments of danger, and just as the moments of midnight and midwinter appear to contain similarities, so also does midsummer appear to have correspondences with the moment of peril at midday when the sun halts in the heavens before declining towards evening. The Nativity of John the Baptist is celebrated just after the summer solstice on 24 June, and on this day fires are lit outside and girls and old women jump over them, 'for good fortune'. It seems likely that the earthly fire is on its own level a symbolic representation of the sun, now just beginning to weaken, and though it is not clear why men and boys are excluded from this ritual, the avoidance of the possibility of menstruation and childbearing in the women permitted to leap over the fires indicates an emphasis on their purity reminiscent of the cleansing of the mother and child as they greet the sun on the third day after the birth. Certainly, this time which marks the moment of change just after the zenith of the year has an analogy with the perception of danger at the zenith of the day, and the lighting of fires at midsummer in order to evoke 'good fortune' seems to indicate a concern with the maintenance of equilibrium as the sun passes its high point and starts to drop away towards winter.

If the sun has times of weakness, and if these are especially perilous precisely because they involve its unimaginable strength momentarily being threatened, it is also the case that this very strength, unbounded, is in itself a source of danger. Thus a balance must be maintained between the two possible extremities of too much heat and too little, and man can affect this equilibrium, on which the success of the harvest depends. Sometimes it is obvious how this happens—for example villagers are very aware that in the great heat of summer the pine forests become so flammable that a single spark can wreak havoc over great swathes of country, and the vigilance to prevent this, together with the knowledge of how to halt or redirect such firestorms when they occur—by a 'contrary fire' lit at an exact moment in the path of the oncoming flames—are essential skills in the Greek mountains. But more generally the villager has a sense that human influence on the elements is pervasive, subtle, complex, and not easily traced, and that wishes as well as actions are both implicated, so that vigilance must also be directed to enacting the right wishes at the right symbolic moment. On 1 May a red rug is hung out of an eastern window from dawn to sunset, while at the same time no damp or white washing should be put out to dry. The reason for both actions is the same: it is 'so that the wheat should ripen for bread', and the connecting association is the red rug, an image of the sun in the east, now growing stronger. At the same time, during the rest of the year, on Sundays and saints' days, as well as on the fast days of Wednesdays and Fridays, no washing of clothes must be done and no baking, as this involves firing the ovens, and the reason for this is to do with the sun's power of destruction.

The washing of clothes, always done outside, is accomplished by several gallons of water being heated in a big copper cauldron on a tripod over a fire, near which is placed the washing trough and several tins of cold water. Boiling, or near-boiling, water is then scooped from the cauldron into the trough and diluted with cold, and the clothes rubbed and washed with home-made soap, after which they are rinsed at the spring and hung out on washing lines, bushes, fences or verandas to dry. It is washing done in this way which is the subject of the prohibition, for it is permissible to set some water to heat in the sun and with it to do small amounts of washing, or to do a little washing in cold water at the spring. Thus although the prohibition is enforced universally by the statement 'people don't do the household wash' on sacred days, it is not the washing *per se* but the heating of large quantities of water which lies at the heart of the prohibition, and this is confirmed by the belief that it is particularly important to avoid the water 'bubbling' or boiling, and this, once again, is 'so that the wheat should not be burned up'.

Returning to the similarities between the 1 May practice with the periodic prohibition on the household wash, while both practices evince a concern with the growing crops, the former emphasizes the importance of the sun's heat while the second emphasizes the danger of overheating. A balance in the activities of man has an unseen but beneficial influence on the balance between fire and water, sun and rain, and once again it is the sun, both creator and destroyer, influential over life and death, which is understood to be the focus.

Both in the yearly cycle then, and in the generations of man, the sun influences the fundamental categories of visible existence—the beginning of life and the ending of it, and the bread which sustains it. However, there is a further life-giving principle in the cosmos, and that is the sun's sister, the moon, ruling over an area which, though related, is very different. Not designated explicitly as 'left' or 'inferior', the moon is in fact the sun's complementary opposite as is woman to man, for in relation to the moon as to all things the sun is, as already mentioned, 'superior', 'lord', and 'on the right hand side'. In this way, much as the sun dominates the days of people committed to an unmechanized agricultural life, so the moon rules the nights, for these nights are lit, except for the dim glow from lamp-lit windows, only by moonlight and starlight; and the moon as it waxes and wanes, its position in the sky, its relation to the sun, its companionable presence 'following one to the spring and back again', is a continuing and indispensable part of people's consciousness. The presence of this changing light in the sky is a beautiful and living phenomenon, and a miraculous dispensation to man and beast, especially to those who have to survive in the wild.

To these perceptions of the moon, however, another has to be added, and this is the belief that 'the moon is a cow'. This belief has a literal element. The moon, so often seen to have two horns, is a cow which can, by 'words', that is to say by sorcery, be brought down to earth where it can be milked and the milk used for magical potions, especially those for love. It is not a good thing to bring the moon down to earth; but it can be done, and one of the signs that someone has done this is when it is big and red and low on the horizon. When it wishes to go back again into the sky it is said to bellow, and although it needs 'words' to bring it down it can go back of its own free will. This idea that 'the moon is a cow' is clearly a poetic rather than a rational image, but it is far from nonsensical, and rests on perceptions derived from the living experience of the moon as night follows night, and from direct knowledge of its influence on the seasonal life of growing things.

It is the nature of the moon as variable, constantly changing throughout the month, which dominates this understanding of the moon as a cow, and this variability is expressed in the idea of the moon as 'giving birth' and being associated with a powerful symbolic cycle. In the period of the waxing moon, 'when the moon is becoming full' (*τῆς γιόμουσης*, dialect for *γέμισης*), the first days when the moon is still 'like a sickle' are days when the times are still fragile. But when it begins to get round 'like a loaf', that is to say four or five days after the new moon, the auspicious part of the cycle takes hold, and these are the days in which to inaugurate any important piece of work. A process of matchmaking, for instance, a journey to achieve important business, or the work of planting and sowing, have all to be started during these days, although they may be continued after the full moon without danger. The grafting of plants has to be carried out only over the days of the full moon itself, and the celebration of weddings also.

The period after the full moon, or, as it is said, the days of the 'disappearing moon' (*στὴ χάση*), is the time when the moon 'begins to twist' or 'turn' (*παίρνει νὰ στρίψει*) or to 'go back' (*παίρνει πίσω*), and as in the reference to the 'leaning' of the sun, these are all terms which in many other contexts denote a reversal of the proper order of things, the beginning of an inauspicious era involving connotations mentioned earlier of squintness, being off-true, unbalanced. Thus the 'turning back' of the moon indicates the first signs of weakening, the leaning of this great influence away from its perfect balance, and the beginning of the reign of the baleful forces which gather increasing strength throughout the last two quarters until the final phase when the nights are wholly dark, which is known as the time of the 'lost moon' (*χασοφεγγαριά*).

These days of the waning moon, in general thought of as inauspicious, have nevertheless their value, for they are appropriate for the collection of certain medicinal plants in those cases in which the weakening of the moon is associated with the weakening of the illness. The brooding of eggs under a hen, a process which takes twenty-two days, is also something not to be done 'over one month' or 'over one moon': the turning of the old moon into the new is conceived as being essential to this new life. However, notwithstanding these customs, the period as a whole is conceived as increasingly inauspicious, and there is one moment in the cycle of the moon when this influence becomes not merely inauspicious but actively diabolical. This is the moment when the moon actually 'turns round', for any sorcery carried out at precisely this moment is infallibly effective, and if at this instant someone drops water into a glass, 'Frrrr! it is thrown around in confusion' before their eyes. Sorcery is 'demonic activity', and the ascendancy of sorcerers at that time, in contravention to the normal doctrine of the unqualified power of God, is a statement about the ever-present threat of chaos which is the natural concomitant of birth and change. There is a potential for evil in this particular phase of the moon, and explanation of this lies in an understanding of the moon entirely different from that to which the modern world has become accustomed.

The traditional cosmology of the phases of the moon became explicit in the face of the moon landings in the late 1960s and early 1970s. As mentioned earlier, this constituted a fundamental challenge to traditional beliefs, and the veracity of the American claims to have landed on the moon was the subject of furious debate, and occasioned impassioned resistance. This stemmed to some extent from a scepticism about the motives of those in power, and a simple denial of the idea took the form of arguments relating to the power of American propaganda and the ease with which photographs could be faked. However, there was a deeper reason for disbelief. One has already been mentioned—the impermeability of the layers separating the various dimensions of the upper world—but a further one lay in the problem: 'When the moon is not in the sky in the daytime, where are the men?', and, 'Where are they, also, when the moon is lost?' (i.e. on the nights when there is no moon in the sky). This question was unanswerable, and the inference was a revelation—during these times there is no moon there to be stood upon by anyone. And in illustration, the progress of the 'turning round' of the moon, in diagrams drawn with a poker in the ashes of a hearth, runs as follows: little by little the full moon grows smaller and smaller, until finally it diminishes to a minute speck—illustrated by a tiny tick, a 'little line' (*γραμμίτσα*)—too small to be seen, but there all the same. Then, at a precise moment which comes and goes in a flash, the tiny curl of the old moon 'turns round' (*γυρίζει*) in an instant and becomes the minute crescent of the new. It is in keeping with this understanding that it is at this moment that the demonic forces briefly gain ascendancy, for it is this moment, when this catastrophic reversal is taking place, in this briefest flash of time when the old cycle is vanquished and the new not yet begun, that creation is in chaos, the dark forces momentarily victorious, and everything reduced to a primordial state of flux before the everlasting stability of the regenerative cycle once again informs the natural order.

The moon literally disappears from the sky, then, when it is not visible in the daytime—an idea also expressed by the phrase that the moon 'goes to its mother'—and it physically grows and diminishes throughout its monthly cycle. The moon is thus revealed as a living process of birth, generation, and renewal, constantly dying away into its final phase, constantly renewing itself through its own spontaneous life principle. It has already been mentioned that the moon 'gives birth', an image whose obvious femininity is reinforced in the idea that a fertile mind is thought of as 'feminine', because it 'gives birth' to ideas, or breeds. Thus an intelligible meaning is given to the belief with which this discussion began—that 'the moon is a cow'—for this image, life-bearing and milk-giving, is one which expresses potently the experience of a primordial feminine power, the archetype of motherhood, a regenerative principle so intense that every month it gives birth to itself.

So while the sun has to do with the ultimate categories of visible existence, the initiation of life and the ending of it, the moon governs the cycles of the temporal world and the waxing and waning of the life force. Primarily to do with matter, the elements which are most closely related to the traditional observances connected with the moon are earth and water, the dark womb of creation, the 'clay' of man's existence, the seed bed and the plant graft; the sphere of influence governed by the moon is that concerned with the recurrent themes of health, sickness, and regeneration in the physical world—the perpetual, minute but all-important processes of germination, growth, decay and re-birth, with darkness, fertility, and breeding. In this way the moon is so imbued with femininity and so connected with the processes of earthly fruition, that its description as a cow is far from being the product of ignorance or superstition; rather it is a powerful poetic and symbolic representation of the moon as the nurturing influence which presides over the flux of generation in the natural world.

Both the sun and the moon, in this scheme of things, are understood as profound influences on the rhythms of life in the created

3. Full moon at sunset: 'The moon as it waxes and wanes, its companionable presence "following one to the spring and back again," is a continuing and indispensable part of people's consciousness' (p. 45). At night, apart from moon and stars, there is no light in the village, 'except for the dim glow of lamplit windows' where these are visible.

4. Goats on a crag: '[It is] among the rocks and the ravines of the mountains that the demons are encountered' (p. 54). And 'It is those burning noontides in summer when the sun's heat is greatest that occasion the greatest danger' (p. 40).

world. The sun is lord, superior, on the right hand side, and associated with themes of transcendence and with the east—the sacrally significant quarter; the moon, the feminine counterpart, influences the monthly cycles of material existence and the ebb and flow of the life force in the veins of the world. Both are givers of life, but both hold in their overwhelmingly beneficent cycles inauspicious phases or moments, which allow for destruction as well as creation. Thus while the 'turning back' of the moon inaugurates a prolonged inauspicious phase culminating in a fleeting moment of extreme danger, the sun, even while it is categorically 'on the right', has not only points in its daily cycle which are attended by danger, but also a period during its yearly cycle when it grows so weak that creation as a whole is endangered and the earth threatened with collapse. These periodic invasions by evil occur in both these cosmic forces at similar moments in their cycles. In the cycles of both there appears the auspicious quality of 'fullness', attributed to the sun when it is high and warm and still in the east, and to days when the moon 'becomes full', and it is when this fullness begins to diminish, when the sun shifts into the western hemisphere or the moon begins to wane, that an inauspicious aspect appears in both of them. Again, the critical points of midnight and midwinter in the cycles of the sun find an echo in the dark nights of the moon, for at these moments both are in transition, as it were without substance, with only potentiality, and, neither of the old order nor of the new, can allow demonic forces momentary real power in the world.

Accordingly, while the sun is undoubtedly superior and the moon is its complementary opposite, this opposition consists not in any contrast between them of good and evil but in varying themes to do with the cycles of life and death. Both, being life forces, have the potential for destruction as well as creation, and both suffer, in their own modes of being, the cycles of decay and death that afflict all creation. The sun is thus associated with long cycles of growth, and with ideas of masculinity, authority, superiority, right-handedness, finality, stability and permanence. The moon, paired as the feminine counterpart of the sun and automatically placed in the subordinate and complementary position, is associated with short cycles of growth, and with ideas of relativity, transience, mutability, and process. Thus while the sun is connected with birth and death as categoric changes, and is related to the liminal world where spirit and flesh have their most momentous encounters, the moon relates to those processual aspects of birth and death which are part of the unending regenerative cycles of the natural order and which, although constantly in motion, nevertheless assure within the material world the fundamental continuity of life.

The cosmos which has been described here is founded on the idea of a basic opposition between God and the devil which unfolds in the universe, creating a series of patterns and correspondences throughout the natural world and in the activities of man. Founded on central Christian concerns about the role of good and evil in the cosmos, it makes use in addition of ancient ideas about the powers that govern growth and decay, where the sun and moon are seen as life forces at the centre of a cosmic web of influence over things that are born and die. The importance of a balance between fire and water for life in the cosmos, and the power of the waxing and waning moon over the tides, and thus over the growth cycles of animals and all living things, are found also as contemporary topics in the *Hexaemeron*, the cosmic account of St Basil the Great (*c.* AD 330–79, Bishop of Caesarea in Asia Minor),[11] testifying to the willingness of Christian authors to make use of the scientific observations of their time in working out their own cosmic ideas. In addition though, village thinking dramatizes these ideas in a symbolic language (red rugs, not heating water in cauldrons for washing), and the implications of this are considered more deeply in Chapter 3. In this way the village cosmos integrates patterns of thinking which are both theological on the one hand and partially paralleled by ancient

[11] Basil the Great, *Hexaemeron*, tr. Blomfield Jackson, in *Nicene and post-Nicene Fathers of the Christian Church*, vol. 8 (Grand Rapids, Mich.: Eerdmans, 1983), Homily 3.5, 6.10–11. The idea that water becomes restless between the disappearance of the old moon and the appearance of the new is also accepted by St Basil (Homily 6.11), and the idea that sorcery can bring the moon down to earth is known to him, though he robustly rejects it (ibid.). He also rejects the idea that the waning moon 'consumes itself in all its body', preferring, on the grounds of the shadowed circle visible beyond the crescent of the new moon on a clear night, to say that it wanes 'in the measure that it deposits or absorbs the light which surrounds it' (Homily 6.3).

scientific observation on the other, and it does this at four levels.

The first invokes the absolute qualities of God and the devil, and sets the conditions for states of being in the universe. These qualities are reflected in the natural world in oppositions between good and evil, straight and squint, order and chaos, which are images of the divine and demoniac. Nevertheless, although polar opposites, they are rescued from irresolvable tension by the inherent superiority of God over the devil, by which God is able to contain the power of evil and ultimately to get the better of the devil and convert evil to good.

Secondly, there are also within the universe principles of differentiation which, though fundamentally good, may also take damaged and chaotic forms. These are complementary differences such as characterize the dance of male and female, sun and moon. Femininity and the moon, for instance, are associated with fertile processes contained within the more stable and constant ordering of masculinity and the sun, and neither is associated with absolute evil nor (in an inauspicious sense) absolute left-handedness, unless powers of degeneration and failure temporarily gain the upper hand.

Thirdly, the oppositions of right and left and up and down exist as a particular placing on a continuum which varies with the context. Paired with the 'superior' and 'right-handed' sun, the moon is by inference 'on the left'. But in relation to the world of men the moon is predominantly auspicious and always 'above' and 'untouchable' in God's sacred sphere. In the same way, although women are usually classified as 'subordinate to' or 'lower than' men who are by nature 'superior', men and women together are, as members of the human race, set in a position of authority above the rest of the animal world. In addition, the notion that women are subordinate to men itself varies with the context: as the next chapter shows, this perception is part of the fallen condition of the world, and it can be transcended, and is typically transcended, in the maturing of a marriage.[12]

All these pairs also relate, finally, to a fourth type of opposition which is once again absolute, and which involves movement—going forward and turning back, coming to the full and weakening. 'Forward movement' is movement towards the right, which again is the

[12] See pp. 330–7.

same as movement towards life, towards God. 'Turning back' involves reversing this auspicious flow and redirecting it towards the left, the devil, and death. This capacity for movement is essential in a cosmos where the divisions between the worlds are so firm and the tensions between good and evil so fundamental, for although to move carries always the danger of the fatal reversal, there is also always the possibility of movement forwards and upwards towards the absolute good which is the lode stone of the universe.

Thus throughout the material world a play of complementary oppositions is engendered by the fundamental split in the cosmos between the ultimate good and ultimate evil. Within the created world, however, these oppositions are associated with relative rather than absolute good and evil, strength and weakness—and this relativity not only enables movement between them, but also makes possible the hope of transcending them entirely. Even within these polarities there is in the universe an innate bias towards the auspicious pole, and it is the necessity to realize this innate propensity, to resolve the oppositions and to achieve, even if only in moments, the victory of the divine impulses inherent in the world, which provides in the culture its fundamental dynamic and the motive force for all the activity of man.

In the middle plane, meanwhile, where good and evil are thus locked in a fragile balance which the activity of man can tip for weal or woe, two great elements make up the foreground of the world—earth and water; and these are the subject of the next chapters.

2
EARTH

THE first chapter described a hierarchical universe in which cosmic forces, polarized from the heights to the depths, permeate the material world and give a particular value to every aspect of creation. Here the focus shifts from this total universe to the middle world between the two extremes—the battle zone of God and the devil, in which are embodied all the various oppositions generated by this basic structure. Part of this world is inhabited, controlled, owned, and cultivated, and within this cultivated region the ownership of land, accumulation of property, and so on, exist as central concerns of social life. A picture of the categories used to organize this cultivated zone is given elsewhere;[1] this chapter by contrast concentrates on some of the symbolic categories perceived as operating within the natural world itself, of which the cultivated region forms only a part.

On the earth in which he lives, man himself is the head of an order in which he, as the 'superior intelligent creature', is set over both the animals and the natural world, in the position of mediator between them and their Creator. The capacity for intelligent relationship with the world, involving as it does intelligent relationship with the source of all intelligence—the Logos, the Word—is thus a belief which asserts the relatively greater closeness of man, compared with the animals and the plant world, to God. This world, as the previous chapter has indicated, is by no means thought to lack its own direct relationship with God, but man nevertheless feels himself to be a critical link, and assumes a God-given dominance over the natural world he regards as being there for him to use. Able in certain cases to tame and control animals, the villagers can say of them 'the [domesticated] animals have us [man] as their God'; and although this dominance is gained for the most part simply through the exercise of superior wit and power, subsistence living in an unmechanized culture requires a high degree of cooperation with the

[1] du Boulay, *Portrait*, especially pp. 27–38, 242–52, 265–73.

forces of nature, and a deeper understanding enshrined in stories of the saints, and in some folk tales (of which an example is given below), teaches that true authority over the natural world is in fact gained through the practice of holiness.

The villagers' relationship with the world in which they live is thought of not in the abstract as 'nature', but in terms of the living experience of rock and precipice, field and forest, valley, mountain, and stream, of creatures wild and tame, and of the 'earth' which serves and 'nourishes' both man and beast. And it is this living and particular experience of the natural world which enables it to be seen not as a homogeneous entity but as a series of arenas where sacred and diabolical meet and interact.

In the greatest of these arenas, inhabited places, infused with the presence of heavenly powers, are set over against the wild and demonic places of the wilderness. It is the wilds in which the nereids are seen, and among the rocks and the ravines of the mountains that the demons are encountered, whereas in the village the company of men are both a help in case of accident, and a spiritual defence against the power of demonic attack. 'A gathering of people leaves no room for possession by devils', it is said, meaning that someone among a group of people 'will have gunpowder' (which 'bursts' the demonic power), 'someone will know the "Our Father"...'. On this level, therefore, the village, representing the world of men, is opposed to the wild places, the world of the demons, and there is an essential relationship between the village and the powers of the sacred world, and the wilderness and the power of evil. In the wild, also, there are places of contagion where 'the demon passes by', which infect anyone who comes in touch with them, and an 'evil herb' grows in the wild which can create—or, if properly used, alleviate—a range of demonic sicknesses. It is because of this affinity between the wilderness and the devil that the spells by which certain afflictions are cured have a recurrent theme: the eviction of the sickness 'to the wild branches', 'to the wild places', 'to the wild birds', 'to the wild mountains', to the places 'where the cock never crows', and, in those instances which concern the permanent disposal of a substance contaminated by evil, to somewhere 'beyond the threshing floors'.

The crowing of cocks, therefore, and the presence of threshing floors—such familiar presages of a Greek village—herald for the traveller or those imperilled in the wastes the kindly company of men and the presiding protection of the Church and its sacred presences. However, at the same time as the association is made between the village and benevolent forces, and the wilds and danger, there is another strand of thinking which accepts that the demons are present everywhere and, ironically enough, especially present where there are congregations of people who can be provoked into fighting and quarrelling. And the converse is also true, that just as corruption can be associated with society so can innocence be associated with life in the wild, in illustration of which a folk tale is told of a certain shepherd boy. This boy living a pure and solitary life in the mountains was granted the gift of communion with his animals, as a result of which they were docile and easy to manage, and came to his call. However, coming one day into the village and—a further irony—into church, the boy saw with his uncorrupted vision that everyone present had a saddle (of sins) on their back, while the priest had two. In the course of the liturgy darkness descended and an orgy took place in which he found himself involved, and coming to himself later he found that he had unwittingly had sexual intercourse with his mother. Devastated, he fled back to his mountain fastness, only to find his gift for communion with the natural world lost, his animals wild and uncontrollable, and his peace destroyed.

In this story it is the village and the human company within it that is beset by sin and sexuality, and the virgin life in the mountains which puts man in touch with the reality of nature and of God—a theme which reappears in the making of saints, which on the whole is thought to take place only through the agency of the wilderness. Nevertheless, in these apparently contradictory understandings of the relation between the village and the wild there is a single central idea, for critical to the village is that it is the place of society, though this can manifest itself either in help or in harm, and critical to the wild is that it is a place of spiritual forces in their elemental form, though this also has two aspects, either as threatening harm or as calling forth holiness. The village holds both turbulent humanity and human and divine consolation; the wild, holding loneliness, beauty and danger, is able to confer purity as man's best shield against evil, for it is here that the demons make their home, and where man may typically be overtaken by injury and receive no help, or be beset by legions of devils whirling their tempestuous journey across the face of the earth.

It is in respect of the vast and dangerous solitudes that a certain range of cosmological ideas is especially detailed, since in them man, lacking the advantage of dominance conferred upon him by the socialized areas, meets face to face the ambiguous spiritual presences which inform his world. A primary division which occurs within the elements of this natural world is between 'earth' (*γῆ*) and 'water' (*νερό*), a term which is taken here to include the sea as well, elements which reflect in their different ways the structure of good and evil which is present in the universe, and which represent sources either of life or of danger according to the particular context in which they are encountered.

This capacity of the earth to be either wild or socialized—to provide sanctuary either for the demons or for man—is a fundamental attribute, and in fact the way the earth is experienced by those who live by it is in terms of a constant antinomy according to which it is both friendly and hostile, nourishing and destructive, giving sanctuary and demanding sacrifice. The earth, that is to say, provides a permanent image both of paradise and of exile, and this experience finds continual echoes in the story of the Fall of Man.

This story is one which every one in the village knows, and as told by the villagers the apple, though often referred to as an apple, can also be termed, variously, a fig, a seed, or a tree. Adam and Eve, it is said, were in those days covered with feathers (or, alternatively, hair), but when they ate the forbidden fruit 'so as to become greater than God', their feathers fell off, they became naked and hid, and were thus discovered by God who was walking in the garden and calling for them: 'Adhám . . . Adhám . . . '. Paradise is represented primarily as life without work: 'You wanted to eat, and tak!—there was a loaded table in front of you!' and, 'Whatever you wanted, you had . . . roast chicken . . . whatever you wanted'; and the curse of God is represented in the words: 'You, Éva, with pain and with torments shall you bear children, and you, Adhám, with blood and with sweat shall you till the fields.' The snake at that moment lost the legs with which it had previously walked upright, and lived thereafter on its belly, in enmity with mankind.

Two additions to this basic story, however, are illuminating. The first runs that at that time 'all the stones were bread, and there was abundant water'; but Eve, too lazy to find something to wipe her child with (or, as one version has it, too covetous of the silk scarf which she had for the purpose), took some bread, wiped the child with it, and threw the bread away. 'Is that what you're like? Take that!' God is reputed to have said, and turned her out of paradise.

Every Sunday in the celebration of the eucharist the people see the bread which they have baked with their own hands transformed into 'the Holy Mysteries', and it is universally said that 'bread must not be trodden upon', because of its true nature as the body of Christ. Thus the statement that the stones in paradise were bread is not merely a statement that in paradise endless food was available to man without work: it is a statement that the created order was fundamentally sacred, and that the paradisaical condition of man was a consequence of his recognition of this. Eve, however, in defecting from this understanding and in wiping her child with bread and *throwing the bread away*—thus treating the world purely as a material object to be exploited for her own ends—reversed the sacramental order of reality and found the bread of the world turned to stone for her sake.

The second addition to this story runs that Adam and Eve received a command from God that they should have three children, but Eve remonstrated: 'What, only sleep with my husband three times?'—an expression of the widespread understanding of the sin of Adam and Eve as being fundamentally to do with sexual intercourse. God's answer to this was equivocal: 'Have as many children as you like, only half will be mine and half yours', meaning that half would live and half would die. Thus in this rendering, sin and death entered the world together.

The story of the fall and its variants thus reveal a state of paradise in which man once lived in equilibrium with a beneficent world, a world whose very stones were 'bread', on the condition that he subdued his own will—for sex, for power—and related with reverence to the presence of God in all created things. But the sacrilege of Eve—the wish to be greater than God, the desire for unlimited sex, the unleashing of egotistical self-indulgence—brought this situation to an end and inaugurated in its place an age of pain and suffering as bread turned to stone, streams dried up, children became subject to death, snakes and men became hereditary and mortal enemies, and the world's original integrity became subject to sin and Satan.

It is in the context of the hardship of agricultural life that the story of the fall is uppermost in people's minds. 'Are things otherwise now?' they will say at the end of the story, referring to the 'anguish' (*ἀγωνία*), 'tribulation' (*βάσανο*), or 'tyranny'(*τυραννία*), of dragging a living out of reluctant ground, or indicating the continual exhausting work of maintaining the homestead. Men, as they struggle with the plough, and women as they labour with children and with the household, are the direct descendants of Adam and Eve, still suffering under the curse of God for that original sin. The story and the lived experience thus feed into one another, particularly on the level at which it is the hardship of village life which is predominant, for on this level the people see their lives as involving endless and unremitting work, and nature as, at the least, grudging, and at the most, hostile. In many ways the individual sees himself as working not with the forces of nature but against them, fighting the earth to force it to yield a scant living, risking both physical and spiritual danger every time he ventures into the wilds. Nevertheless, this embattled attitude to the natural world is only a part of man's relationship with the earth, as it is only a part of the story of the fall, for because this story begins with the estrangement of man from his original inheritance in the Garden of Eden, there exists in this understanding of the world not only an encounter with sin and death, but also an encounter with an image of paradise.

'Paradise' is a word often enough heard on the lips of the community, and the primary image it conjures up is that of a garden. 'It is paradise' is the comment often attached to a description of a place with fruit trees and cool breezes and running water, a place of ease, beauty and refreshment. It is because of this image, also, that the visitor is invariably encouraged to come to the village, not in the spring when all agree that the season is at its most exciting and lovely with bursting buds and the greening of the trees, but in the autumn, when the great period of work is over and when the fruit, the free gift of a suddenly generous earth, is offered simply for the picking. 'Come and see us in September,' they say, 'then, whatever you want, you'll find—figs, apples, pears, grapes...'. Vines, of course, require a good deal of care, but a laden fruit tree, to which in most cases very little attention has been paid throughout the year, is not only a particularly clear image of the fecundity of the earth, it is, so to speak, an icon of nature in her unfallen state. It is as if the labourer, as he fills his house with strings of apples, or waits for a hare to come and eat the wind-falls below a wild pear tree, is released from his destiny to be nourished by the earth only if he toils and struggles, and suddenly receives, in uncalculated abundance, a harvest for which he has not lifted a finger.

While, however, the idea of 'paradise' incorporates in this essential sense the vision of a world which yields up its fruits without work, it is used also in contexts referring to the household to invoke the image of abundance, even though this abundance has in fact been gained by the sweat of man's brow. There is a proverb, 'One person alone does not create paradise', which indicates that paradise on this earth is indeed realizable, and defines it as the fruit of marriage. For marriage results not only in a well-provided household with its own cheese, meat and eggs, milk, cereals, bread, fruit, vegetables, wheat, wine, and oil, but in the priceless gift of children through which a healing continuity is assured. In this understanding too is caught up the idea of the garden of paradise, for it invokes a world in which toil and sweat are left behind, the fruit of man's labour safely gathered into the house, and in which the house, and the man and woman within it, have once again been linked with that archetypal garden from which their ancestors fell. It is this image which is being called upon in an old man's delighted comment on the fecundity of his house: 'Look! When the woman is here the house is a garden!' It is this image also which inspires the comment of an old woman, sitting by the ashy debris of the fire, the whitewashed plaster shedding flakes on the floor and the hens pecking in the mud outside, to say of her daughter-in-law: 'We brought her here to live with us in paradise.'

Paradise is in this way the experience of abundance which the people encounter with as much reality as the world of exile in which for the greater part of their lives they struggle. For in its rare moments of unsolicited fruitfulness, the earth provides a clear image of the world before the fall, while in the cornucopia of the household, overflowing with the garnered produce of the year's toil, a different dimension of salvation is offered—the redemption of the world and the regaining of paradise with, as it were, the consequences of the fall put behind. Thus it is at either end of the cycle of work that the fruitfulness of the earth links man once again with his origins in the fundamental beneficence of creation, while the intervening periods of hardship and relentless toil confront him with an earth whose equilibrium is still disrupted by the evil consequences of man's original sin.

The dimensions, then, of wild and socialized earth, which have already been discussed, accord precisely with the story of Adam and Eve which the people clearly feel to be the charter for their agricultural life. Wild places are seen as holding a natural innocence which links them with the world before the fall, and as providing an environment which helps to keep people untainted, without sin, and in touch with the mysterious lore of the natural world. But they also hold characteristics and potentialities receptive to the devil and inimical to man, and these can be overcome only in one of two ways—by great purity, or by work and endurance. Socialized places, on the other hand, lie at the other end of the scale, fraught with the sinfulness of the men who inhabit them, and yet providing to each man his house, his spot of the sanctuary which the earth provides for those who labour for her crops.

In this way, while it is ascetic purity that transforms the wilderness into a place where saints are made, it is in work that the alchemy lies that makes spots of 'paradise' in the social world. The recurring feature in the redemption of the social world from the possession of the devil, and in the maintenance of the social order, is the toil of man.

Work is closely linked with land. The village where a person is born, the *patrídha* or 'place of his fathers', is a reality embedded in the thinking of rural people, and consists in a deep sense of identity with a portion of the land which is part of a person's consciousness of himself. This love of the land, however, is a love which is connected in Greece less with a person's attachment to the substance of the physical earth of his village, as with the place to which he has traditionally been attached by inheritance and the history of his family. Thus while the villagers emphatically state that 'no one would sell his grandfathers' fields', it becomes clear that this is only partly due to a sense of attachment to the piece of land itself, and is more an identification with the value of the labour with which the land and the grandfathers had been linked.

On this level therefore it is 'land', in the form of fields or forest—the pieces of ground associated with the life and the labour of the family—rather than the notion of the 'earth' as an elemental force, which appears to exercise the primary pull over the loyalty of a villager. And on this level the relationship of the individual with his land appears to be one which is practical rather than mystical, active rather than contemplative, exploitative rather than reverential. Nevertheless, the fact that the same word (*γῆ*) is used for both 'land' and 'earth' indicates that no essential split is made between the two concepts, and even on the practical level discussed above, the permanence of the land—its primary material advantage—is seen also as a spiritual quality reflecting this immortality to which man aspires: 'The earth is immortal; does the earth ever die?' And this perception, which provides a continual undercurrent to village life, surfaces at times on highly symbolic occasions of which the traditional good wishes at a marriage provide a clear example:

> May you both live a thousand years!
> As the mountains shine, so may man and wife shine,
> As the mountains grow white, so may man and wife grow white,
> With children and great grandchildren...

The earth therefore, even in so far as it is involved in the hard facts of subsistence living, is by no means experienced only on a dimension of simple materialism; as we have seen, there is a charter for seeing the earth both as man's enemy and, in the story of Adam and Eve, as man's original and ultimate home.

Work too, like the earth to which it is related, has two aspects. Its primary aspect relates it to the curse and presents it as perpetual and unwelcome evidence of that time when the world was set against mankind as a result of sin. Thus as the man comes home tired and filthy, or as misfortune strikes his fields or his household, as he swears at his animals, his children, at Christ, the cross, the faith and the Mother of God, he experiences work as anguish, and he rebels against the constant exhaustion inflicted by the tyranny of his association with the natural world. The secondary aspect, however, is otherwise, for in the green of healthy crops, or in the fruits of toil at the completed yearly cycle of harvest, the earth reveals a different aspect, and the work which results in this revelation is seen not so much as brute slavery as a necessary cooperation with forces greater than him, which acts to reveal the divine order immanent in the world. Man's work becomes the means by which the split between man and God, man and the earth, the village and the wilderness, is overcome, and work is thus transformed from being a purely economic activity into one that has also a direct relationship with the sacred world.

The extent to which this revelation is seen in terms of the regaining of paradise is implicit in much of what has been said already, but it is particularly apparent in the harvest of the wheat. The harvesting of the many crops is spread over a period of several weeks and the whole period is noticeable for a growing sense of completion and fulfilment, even while it involves long hours of exhausting work at the hottest time of the year. It is a time at which the struggle of man with the earth reaches a peak of exertion but one at which also the ripening ears of wheat, the swelling maize, and the hardening pulses, herald the end of the battle and unveil an order of creation which cooperates with man rather than opposing him. The climax is reached in the harvesting of the wheat for the year's bread, and in the threshing of the wheat the whole village is involved in the great celebration of harvest home. The previous evening the threshing floors will have been damped with water and sprinkled with chaff to make a hard surface, and the next day a number of families gather with their mules or horses so that several animals together may trample the brittle stalks while a man or boy runs behind them with a whip keeping them going, and other family members rest in the shade. Five times during the threshing—which takes all day—several people go through the mixed up stalks and grain with long-handled wooden forks and shovels turning over and bringing to the top anything untrampled. At first the workers move forward in rows, but the last time they move forward in a long line from the inside out, one person following the other, 'fork first, shovel after', coiling from the centre until they have covered every last piece of ground. At the end of the day everyone sweeps together the trampled chaff and loose grain into a great mound, ready for the winnowing next day, which they then mark diagonally with a rope in the imprint of a cross. The day finishes with dancing in the houses after the evening meal.

The new day is marked as one of celebration from the moment at dawn when the housewife rises to make bowlfuls of *loukoumádhes* (*λουκουμάδες*) or batter-puffs, and throughout the day this refreshment—a festive food traditionally served only on name days and feast days—together with a sprinkling of honey and little glasses of *rakí*, is served to all present as well as to any passer by who can be haled in, and at noon a meal is served on the threshing floor by the housewife whose harvest it is. While the evening meal is traditionally a cockerel, which are fat at this season, the mid-day food is always green beans stewed with tomatoes and oil, but it is brought out in ceremony from the house in due order, the harvest bread coming first. This bread is made in the same way as bread for a wedding or for the New Year, in a large round copper dish which has been smeared with olive oil, and after baking is anointed with honey and sprinkled with sesame seeds. The decoration of these breads, however, varies with the occasion, and the harvest bread before baking is imprinted all over with crosses made with a fork. Thus the cooked food from the house, led by the festival bread with its decoration of crosses, emerges, to meet the gift of the sheaves of wheat brought in from the wild, and this meeting between wild and socialized takes place on the threshing floor which, as has been said, marks the boundary between the two worlds. This is one of the great moments of reconciliation when through the medium of toil the natural world has produced her bounties for man, and the reconciliation of the wilderness with the socialized world, for however brief a moment, returns the world to its unfallen state and reintegrates the garden of nature with its archetype in the garden of paradise. It is because of this that the day is one of such high celebration, and because of this that the words, 'We are threshing tomorrow!' in fact mean, 'Come and celebrate with us!'

The great meeting of man and nature thus occurs at the harvest of the wheat when the natural world bears fruit, paradise is restored, and man can lay aside his toil briefly and take his rest. But this symbolism is not complete without a further element, and this lies in the synchronicity of the time cycles relating to the agricultural year and the Mother of God. The title *Theotókos*, 'the One who gives birth to God',[2] which has most commonly been rendered in English as Mother of God, is in the Greek primarily an adjective, as in the phrase 'God-bearing and ever-virgin Mary'(*Θεοτόκος καὶ ἀειπάρθενος Μαρία*). This title dates from the third century and was confirmed at the Ecumenical Councils of Ephesus (AD 431) and Chalcedon (AD 451), as a safeguard for the notion that in Christ, God was truly born in the flesh. The cycle of the feasts of the Mother of God has its basis in the *Protevangelion* of James, a second century compilation of Christian traditions about her life, and these feasts occur at significant points of the agricultural year.

The year begins in September, when the fields have lost the parched brittleness of summer and the work of clearing and burning off begins, to be followed, after the autumn rains have soaked the earth, by the two ploughings for the wheat. September and October are months when the sun is clear and warm and the air brilliant, when bright grass springs again in the fields, cyclamen bloom in the forests, and the earth is re-born after the summer drought, and it is in explicit analogy with this renewing of the earth that the liturgical year, beginning on 1 September, has as its first major festival, on 8 September, the Birth of the Mother of God. Following this the next great feast is the Entry of the Mother of God into the Temple on 21 November when she is brought as a child for her dedication. Thus when the earth is renewed and young again after the summer, the Mother of God is also in her infancy. And at the end of the agricultural year a similar correspondence is seen, for on 15 August, with the earth falling to rest at the end of the high summer, is celebrated the great festival of the Falling Asleep of the Mother of God (*Κοίμησις τῆς Θεοτόκου*).

There is thus a correspondence between the earth and the Mother of God which is represented on the one hand by the cycle of the seasons from the sowing of the seed in the autumn to the gathering in of the harvest of the grain in July and August, and on the other hand by the cycle of the Mother of God which, running from 8 September to 15 August, causes her presence to pervade, and, as it were, embrace, the entire liturgical year. This however is not the only correspondence, for, as will be remembered, the celebration of

[2] From *tíkto* (*τίκτω*), to bear, or give birth to.

5. The threshing: 'A time when the struggle of man with the earth reaches a peak of exertion… A number of families gather with their mules or horses so that several animals together may trample the brittle stalks' (p. 62).

6. A fork used at the threshing: 'Five times during the threshing—which takes all day—several people go through the mixed up stalks and grain with long-handled wooden forks and shovels turning over and bringing to the top anything untrampled' (p. 62). While grain and chaff fall straight through the tines, any long stalks tend to be caught where they converge.

the Nativity—when Christ is a baby and the Mother of God at her most vulnerable after giving birth—parallels the weak point of the solar cycle and the time of danger for the world. It has been mentioned that a woman within forty days of giving birth—a *lechóna*—is, together with her child, highly vulnerable to evil spirits, and that the mother is not only liable herself to harm but also capable of bringing unintentional disturbance to others. As a result of this belief, it is customary for such women to avoid visiting other people's houses for fear of household objects breaking unexpectedly, and to observe various rules defining things she may or may not touch. In addition to these, stringent measures are taken to protect both mother and child from the spirits of evil, particularly during the hours of darkness, and it is not until the end of the forty days that both may go to the church for the blessing that brings about their purification from the pollution of childbirth and freedom from its attendant dangers. Only after this period, also, can the child be baptized, and it is because of this that mothers wait 'in anguish' to baptize their infants and only thereafter are able to 'relax a little'.

The parallelism of this understanding of human birth with the Church's portrayal of the Mother of God at the Nativity is striking. It is true, of course, that in the case of the birth of Christ the theme of blood pollution is explicitly denied: 'A great and marvellous wonder has come to pass this day. A Virgin bears a child, and her womb suffers no corruption',[3] because 'Where God so wills, the order of nature is overcome'.[4] Nevertheless, the frailty of the infant Christ is also emphasized: 'A manger and swaddling clothes and a cave are the marks of Thy lowliness',[5] and in February the feast of *Ypapandí* (*Ὑπαπαντή*) commemorates the Meeting of the Lord with the aged Symeon in the Temple when his mother comes to be purified 'according to the law'.[6] The Mother of God 'ever virgin' and giving birth 'in fashion past nature'[7] is nevertheless subject also to 'the law' relating to the customary understandings of the dangers of childbirth. She is the Mother of God

[3] *The Festal Menaion,* tr. by Mother Mary and Archimandrite Kallistos Ware (London: Faber, 1969), Matins of the Nativity of Christ, p. 264.

[4] Ibid., p. 267.

[5] *Festal Menaion,* Compline, Forefeast of the Nativity of Christ, p. 206.

[6] Luke 2 : 22.

[7] *Festal Menaion,* Matins of the Nativity of Christ, p. 281.

but she is also a woman, and is seen as encompassing both dimensions.

There is thus an exact symmetry in the fact that at the time when the earth is in danger from the powers of evil and destruction in the universe, the Mother of God and her new-born child are at the period of their greatest vulnerability. And indeed, the understanding of the Mother of God as *lechóna* is explicitly asserted by the villagers in explanation of the particular peril of the twelve days from Christmas to Theophany. During this period people must cense the house when they come in at night-time and must not go out again till morning, the reason being that 'for these days the Mother of God is a *lechóna*, therefore the customs are as for a *lechóna*'. In this sense, therefore, it may be said that, at the Nativity, the Mother of God as *lechóna,* holding in her arms the vulnerable infant Christ, is symbolically paralleled on the cosmic level by the world weakened and undermined as it waits for the strengthening of the infant sun. And this identification of synchronous moments of turning both in the rhythms of the cosmos and in the cycle of Christian salvation, is illustrated and confirmed by the Christmas demons. The cosmic dimension of these demons is clear in that the focus of their efforts is to destroy the tree that supports the world; their relation to the Christian Gospel is clear in that it is the birth of Christ that instigates their abandonment of this work, and the sanctifying power of the Theophany that banishes them back to the underworld to find their work undone. The *skalikantzoúria*, comic and grotesque as they may be, have in fact become articulations in the folk imagination of the cosmic dimension of the Nativity.

It is, nevertheless, at the harvest, with the united symbolism of Christ and the ripened wheat, that the correspondence between the earth and the Mother of God is at its most profound. The understanding of bread as the body of Christ has already been mentioned, and this understanding gains particular power from the fact that it is the flour from wheat grown on the peoples' own land, and baked with the housewife's own hands, that is used in the liturgy. The great round loaves of the people's daily bread, wrapped in cloths and perched on the beams for the week's eating, although they differ in the manner of their preparation, are not in their material substance different from those loaves which, closely kneaded and stamped with a special seal, are consecrated in the liturgy as the body of Christ. In this way, the ears of wheat gathered in at the harvest, which will become the bread both of the household and of the eucharist, is, of all the foods eaten, the one which most completely links the natural world with the divine.

It is this sacred understanding of the wheat which gives the key to the inner meaning of the harvest, for wheat is not only the staff of life but the body of Christ, and the harvest of the wheat is the living proof also of the reintegration of the world with its original purpose. The stones of the earth have become wheat; the produce of the earth, redeemed from the power of the devil, has become the body of Christ; the earth itself which gives birth to the wheat is linked with the all-holy and compassionate figure of the Mother of God who gives birth to Christ; man and the earth, society and the wild, are no longer divided. And it is because of this that the harvest bread is decorated all over with crosses, and the cooked meal—an act of family communion normally only held within the house—is moved ceremonially out into that area of the village which marks the boundary where the two worlds meet—the circle of the threshing floor.

The symbolism of the wheat is further elaborated in two additional contexts: the memorial services for the dead, and the feasts commemorating the saints, both of which use wheat as food for the dead. The wheat for the saints' days is boiled and left plain, while that for the dead has walnuts, almonds, browned flour, raisins, sugar, parsley and pomegranate seeds mixed in, but the significant difference in this context is that while the wheat for the saint has first to be bruised so that it bursts during the cooking, it is important that that for the dead should remain whole. The difference is critical, for while the unburst grain, closed in on itself and as yet unfruitful, is appropriate for grief, the bursting of the bruised grain calls to remembrance the germination of seed and the bursting of the buds in spring and signifies 'joy'.

It is plain from these three ways in which wheat is understood that it is being seen in three different aspects, as an image of life, death, and resurrection: the ripened wheat of the new harvest representing the eternally renewed gift of life to man, with Christ himself the principle of the resurrection which takes place within it every year; the seed corn of the dead, unburst and in its 'mourning' state, representing the body which must be buried before it can rise again into life; and the burst corn, signifying the joy of the saints, representing the lives which, having born fruit, are now with Christ in paradise. Thus the gift which the earth gives to man—the wheat or bread of his material and spiritual existence—reflects on its own level the gift given to man by the Mother of God in the birth of Christ. It is in response to this understanding that the work of harvesting this wheat, although undertaken in great heat and requiring a pitch of dedication and effort, transcends the normal division between the sanctuary of the house and the 'tribulation' of work in the fields and forest, and losing its punitive aspect, becomes openly an act of evident joy. And it is the Mother of God, whose cycle encompasses and transcends the agricultural pattern of the year, who keeps all under her protecting veil.

It is, then, no accident that the feasts of the Mother of God are placed as they are, for deep in the liturgy of the Church lies this cosmic understanding of her role. This role as the fruitful mother who nurtures the one who is both God and man, linking the fallen world once again with paradise, is expressed in the great Akáthistos Hymn to the *Theotókos*, which celebrates her nature in a series of images taken to a significant extent from the natural world:

> Hail, vine whence springs a never-withering branch,
> Orchard of pure fruit,
> For thou tendest the husbandman who loves mankind,
> For thou hast borne the gardener who cultivates our life,
> Earth yielding a rich harvest of compassion,
> Table laden with mercy in abundance,
> For through thee the fields of Eden flower again...[8]

The link of the Mother of God with the created earth as a whole lies in the action of God being 'made flesh' (*σὰρξ ἐγένετο*),[9] for this flesh which makes Christ man is the common inheritance not only of man but of all creatures; and the relationship goes further, for the flesh which Christ 'shares in' derives from the 'vile clay' or dust of the earth from which we are made.[10] Thus when God was made flesh it is not only man and the substance of living things that became asasociated with this action but the fabric of the entire material cre-

[8] *The Lenten Triodion,* tr. by Mother Mary and Archimandrite Kallistos Ware (London: Faber, 1978), The Akathistos Hymn, pp. 423–37. *Akáthistos Hýmnos* (Ἀκάθιστος Ὕμνος) means the 'Unsitting Hymn', during which everyone stands.

[9] John 1 : 14; cf. *Festal Menaion,* Matins of the Nativity of Christ, p. 268.

[10] *Festal Menaion*, Matins of the Nativity of Christ, p. 271.

tion, and it is because of this intimate link between God and the world that creation can be said to be renewed through the Mother of God and the world can be depicted as caught up in rejoicing: 'When she gave birth in fashion past nature . . . the whole creation sings.'[11] 'God has appeared in the flesh, . . . [and] has made the whole creation shine with joy.'[12] 'Hail, womb of the divine incarnation. Hail, for through thee the creation is made new.'[13] 'For God the All-perfect is born a babe of her . . . therefore let all creation sing and dance for joy, for Christ has come to restore it and to save our souls.'[14]

Thus the Mother of God, whose harvest is compassion, and the earth, whose harvest is the bread of physical and spiritual life in both house and church, are linked in a single overarching understanding in which the curse is overcome and the 'the fields of Eden flower again'. It is of course critical that while the earth is ploughed and sown for the harvest of the wheat, the Mother of God is the 'field untilled' from whom 'has grown the divine Ear of corn . . . Living table that hast held the Bread of Life'[15], and her 'fruitful womb' is made 'as a fertile field for all who long to reap the harvest of salvation . . . '.[16] It is the visible, physical earth and bread on the one hand, it is the invisible, heavenly earth and bread on the other; and while the visible is an image, it is only an image, necessarily imperfect, of the invisible. Yet the parallels in this Orthodox symbolism are clear; and although the earth is so often revealed in its negative aspect as hostile to man and as subject to the curse, it is at harvest time revealed to some extent in its true nature as an image of the Mother of God, re-established in its sacred dimension as a paradise, whose gardener is God.

It has been argued above that the people's predominant experience of the earth is mediated through the story of the fall from paradise, and that it is in the working through of this story and the regaining, however momentarily, of the unfallen world, which gives to purely practical living its life-giving symbolic dimension. There

[11] Ibid. p. 281.
[12] Ibid. Vespers of The Nativity of Christ, pp. 253–4.
[13] *Lenten Triodion*, Akathistos Hymn, p. 423.
[14] *Festal Menaion*, Lity, Vigil of the Nativity of Christ, pp. 265–6.
[15] *Lenten Triodion*, Akathistos Hymn, p. 428.
[16] Ibid. p. 424.

is, however, a further dimension in which the earth is experienced.

This dimension is expressed in customs and ceremonies relating to birth and particularly to death, and according to this perspective the earth is a power holding ineluctable sway over all creatures, giving life and taking it again. In relation to this power man cannot be other than acted upon rather than acting, and towards it he stands in a relationship neither of confrontation nor yet of cooperation, but of simple awe and obedience.

The necessity at birth of the child 'falling onto the ground' has already been described, making an offering of the new life to the earth that gave it and accepting the mother as merely the vehicle for the birth. In this context the earth, as the first recipient of the living child, is acknowledged as the real giver of life, and no intermediary must interpose between the earth and the child. So here the midwife is as it were discounted, and symbolically comes into her own only on the third day when at dawn she summons the mother and child to the threshold to greet the sun. The period of transition for mother and child is, however, not over yet, for this only ends when after forty days both come to be received into the church. At this point there follows a ceremony of which two versions exist,[17] the older and more interesting version citing a practice which once again involves laying the child on the ground.[18] This is the 'churching' of the infant—

[17] In contemporary practice in the village (which continues by and large today), the mother and child, once again on the threshold, though this time of the door of the church, have the prayers of purification and blessing read over them by the priest, who then takes the child into the church. If the child is a boy, the priest, in an action known as 'dancing' the child, carries him up the nave and through the south door of the iconostasis into the sanctuary, round the back of the altar, and then out again through the north door, then gives him to his mother. If the child is a girl this action is replaced by the priest carrying her into the church up to the icon of the Mother of God which is in the iconostasis immediately to the left of the Royal Doors, one which always depicts her as holding the Christ child in her arms. After this the child is given to the mother who is now free to enter the church and light a candle before going home.

[18] Ioannes M. Phoundoulis, *Ἀπαντήσεις εἰς λειτουργικὲς ἀπορίες* [*Answers to liturgical questions*] (Thessaloniki: Πουρνάρος, 1982), vol. 4, pp. 234–5. 'We find a somewhat different order in other manuscripts and in Symeon of Thessaloniki [† 1429]. Here, apart from the usual statement that the service of the forty days is the prelude to the service of holy baptism, and Symeon in particular speaks of it

which is normally carried out before baptism, or may be incorporated into the service of baptism itself—where the priest takes the infant, brings it into the church and presents it at the altar, and then lays it on the ground in front of the Holy or Royal Doors, the gates of the sanctuary, from whence it is picked up by a parent or godparent who before doing so must make three prostrations.[19]

In the context of the present discussion the outstanding idea in this version of the forty days ritual is that just as at physical birth the baby is offered to the earth in acknowledgement that it is the earth which gives life, so on the baby's first visit to the church, it is once again laid on the ground. There is, however, a significant difference,

being carried out even for an infant already baptized, we see how in the middle of the rite of baptism itself, exactly between the last pre-baptismal prayer, "O Master, Lord our God, call…", and the beginning of the service of baptism proper—that is to say the baptismal Divine Liturgy—is inserted the churching of the infant catechumen. [At this point Phoundoulis quotes from Symeon of Thessaloniki, *Dialogue in Christ*, in Migne, *Patrologiae cursus completus*, Series Graeca, vol. 155, Ch. 62, as follows]:

> "And the priest, taking the infant, churches it, singing the *tropárion* 'Hail, Mother of God and Virgin full of grace'. And he chants this thrice. And he places the child before the Holy Doors, and the one who receives it makes three prostrations and lifts up the child." And Symeon says further: "And thus taking the catechumen by the hand as finding one who was lost, he brings him into the temple…showing that he brings him to his lost Lord. And expressing his joy…he sings, 'Hail, Mother of God and Virgin full of grace…', and goes in. And imitating Symeon [the Biblical Symeon who received the infant Christ in the Temple], the chief priest brings the baptisand before the altar, showing how Symeon did the same. And he makes him prostrate three times before God… And the chief priest summons the one who receives him and tells him to prostrate three times to the altar…Then if the one who is to be baptized is an infant, the one who receives him bends down and lifts him from where he lies before the Holy Doors."

After this quotation, Phoundoulis comments: 'This I have seen done even today according to the ancient tradition by some priests.'

This reference was given to me by Fr Raphael Pavouris, to whom I am very grateful.

[19] Phoundoulis cites here 'the one who receives' the baby, leaving open the question of who it is who picks up the child. Presumably, however, the person who receives the baby at this point is, in the case of the forty-day ritual, the mother, and in the case of baptism, the godparent.

for while at the birth the baby is born onto the floor of the house, at the churching the baby is laid on the ground in front of the Royal Doors. Here the dedication is not to the earth but to God the true Giver of Life, and it is from God that the mother receives again the gift of her child. Once again the role of the natural world is not denied by liturgical custom, but brought to a new level: the 'churching' of mother and child culminates in the dedication of the child not to the earth, but to the power that made the earth.

One further custom at birth is relevant to the theme of the earth, and this is the burial of the placenta somewhere in the ground under the earthen floor of the house. Burial outside the house is not permitted as the dogs might dig the placenta up and eat it, and 'dogs mustn't eat man'. But this difficulty would be disposed of if the placenta were burned, and this also is prohibited. It seems, then, that in this first stage the earth which gives life must be the first to receive that life, and the placenta which nourished the unborn baby, just as the earth will nourish the growing child, must be returned to the earth.

At death similar understandings are played out, and just as the newborn baby must 'fall on the earth' so, as already noted, must the dead person be laid out 'on the earth'. Similarly, just as disposal of the placenta must be by burial, so it is burial which is universally considered to be the only proper way of disposing of the body itself. Man comes from the earth and goes back into it, and this understanding of man as clay is underlined by the custom of smashing an earthenware water jar at the threshold of the house as the body leaves the house for the last time, and of laying on the dead person's mouth, just before the coffin lid is put on and before earth is shovelled over it, a fragment of an earthenware tile.

This earth, then, which gives birth to man and nourishes him throughout his life, is also the earth which, in the end, will take him, in the words of the laments, under her 'black mantle' (*μαύρη τσέργα*), stopping his mouth with clay and his eyes with darkness. The earth is the arbiter of all life and the measure of man—it gives and takes, it nourishes and destroys. The saying, 'The earth is immortal', already quoted, thus evokes an additional association in that not only do all creatures perpetually draw their life from it, but also all creatures without partiality are sooner or later absorbed back into it.

The horror of death depends in Greece very much on the context, and great excesses of grief are not considered appropriate for those who have lived their allotted span and for whom death was to be expected. Yet even in these cases the experience of the tragedy of death is not avoided: tears are shed, and the grim conclusiveness of burial, which is the same for old as for young, is caught up in the constant reiteration in the laments on the entombment in the black earth, where the dead 'don't see' and are subject to decay and dissolution. The earth both gives and takes life, inspiring both love and terror, and in many of the laments this image of the black earth as the devourer of humanity is as strong an image of death as that of Charos, the traditional figure of death.

Once again, then, there occurs the pattern of oppositions already becoming familiar, for just as the world of nature is divided into tame and wild, inhabited by God or the demons, so the earth is seen as both nourishing and destroying, both the womb and the grave. Once again, however, this split is not final, but is transcended by a symbolism which overcomes opposition and moves it into a unity. In the case of the world of nature the split is healed, momentarily or yearly, in the recurrent experience in the house of the generosity of the earth and the redemptive season of the harvest; in the case of the dual aspect of the earth, the split between life-giver and life-destroyer is healed by a teaching which relates the destructive role of the earth to the purgation of sins in an action that takes place on the far side of the grave.

This theme is discussed in a later chapter and it is important at this point only to indicate the link made between the dissolution of the flesh and the dissolution of sins, and the consequence of this link in the insistence on burial. According to this way of thinking the soul is not free finally to leave the earth until the dissolution of the body—leaving only the clean yellow bones—which indicates that the sins committed in the body have also dissolved. Thus the action of the earth in devouring life, which at the wake can be resisted with such furious grief, is converted gradually into an action which devours sins, and turns the destruction of the body into the well-being of the soul. The earth, which in the story of the fall is shown, although corrupted, to possess an innate goodness and an order essentially beneficent to man, is in its elemental nature shown to be, although pitiless, the devourer only of what is fleshly and gross. In this way, as the earth is the means by which the seed harvested in the summer is sown and metaphorically dies in the autumn and is renewed again every spring, so the earth is the means by which the human soul, harvested at death, passes through the process of dissolution and the forgiveness of sins and gains its passage to its place in the other world.

The capacity of the earth to receive corruption into itself is, then, a crucial element, just as is its capacity to give life and form to all things: 'The earth,' it is said, 'receives everything' however defiled or defiling, but also 'the earth nourishes everything', the lentils, the grass, the creatures—including man—that live off them. Thus the earth is the matrix from which all fleshly creatures and all physical existence come, and it is the vessel to which all must return; but the exchange is not equal, for while it takes death and pollution it gives life and food. Even in its terrifying aspect the earth is in the end a life-giver, purging all things through the processes of decay, and renewing the world by its capacity for regeneration. The 'undying' earth gives and takes all things, receiving dead bodies with the same impartiality with which it receives the seed-corn, embracing both corruption and purity, both death and life, and in its endless receptivity resolving its inherent dichotomies through the regeneration of the seed corn in the yearly harvests, and through the purification of the soul beyond the grave.

The picture of the earth gained in the preceding pages is one which echoes the basic pattern of opposition and transcendence which occurs within the universe. The opposition of wild and tame is part of the pattern, but this opposition is resolved through the physical toil of man and his eucharistic offering by which the earth once again becomes the garden of paradise. The ambivalence of the earth in its elemental aspect as womb and grave is also part of the pattern, but this ambivalence is overcome by the fundamental attribute of the earth as receptive and purificatory, by which it converts physical decay into spiritual growth, and allows the soul, released from the dross of mortality, to travel finally to its eternal home.

At the liturgical level too, a similar logic of transcendence is worked out, but again by reference to the unifying figure of the Mother of God, that 'earth yielding a rich harvest of compassion', and it is relevant in the context of death that as the richly compassionate figure who bore Christ she also becomes the great intercessor for the world. A tale told in the village of the Mother of God makes this point with some force.[20] This tale runs that the Mother of God with four hundred horses and four hundred angels went to ask the Archangels Michael and Gabriel if she could visit the souls in hell. 'By no means!' was the answer. 'But I want to!' 'No!' Twice she was refused, but the third time she was answered: 'Let it be as you wish.' So she travelled to hell where she saw the souls in torment—people roasting on beds of fire because they had lain in bed when the church bells were ringing, women hanging by their breasts for aborting children, a man hanging by his tongue because he had blasphemed. She asked for him to be unloosed so that he could say 'Lord have mercy', so they unloosed him and three times he said 'Lord have mercy' before they tied him up again. Then, rent with compassion, she asked: 'Can't they be released for a period after Easter?' And after two refusals her wish was granted, so that for forty days after every Easter the souls of the dead are freed to come, rejoicing, to the upper world.[21]

The action of the Mother of God as intercessor before Christ is many times stressed in the liturgical offices. But, as the folk tale above indicates, it is not just for the living but for the dead that the Mother of God is the great compassionate figure. Among many examples in the offices for the dead are these prayers: 'We have thee as both rampart and haven, an intercessor well-pleasing to God whom thou hast borne;'[22] and recalling, and transfiguring, the role of the earth in purifying the bones of the dead: 'We have been returned to the earth, after having transgressed the divine commandment of God. But through thee, O Virgin, we have been raised up from earth to heaven, shaking off the corruption of death.' Further, in an

[20] This tradition can be identified as an orally transmitted version of the Apocalypse of the Theotokos, dateable to the 9th–11th c.: see Constantine von Tischendorf, *Apocalypses apocryphae Mosis, Esdrae, Pauli, Johannis, item Mariae dormitio: additis evangeliorum et actuum apocryphorum supplementis. Maximam partem nunc primum edidit.* (Leipzig: H. Mendelssohn, 1866). In the villages of the 1960s it may also have circulated as a tract among those who could read. For this reference I am very grateful to Dr Jane Baun.

[21] The figure of 50 days (to the Saturday of Souls before Pentecost) and 57 days (to All Saints) may also be quoted by the villagers. However, those who quote 40 days are supported by the fact that memorial services can begin again after Ascension.

[22] *Memorial for the Departed*, tr. Liturgical Translations Committee, Diocese of Sourozh, Russian Orthodox Church in Britain and Ireland (Oxford: St Stephen's Press, 2002), p. 10.

even stronger reference to the part played by the Mother of God in her son's destruction of death: 'He who of old formed from a rib our first mother, Eve, through thy most pure womb puts on flesh, through which, pure Lady, he has destroyed the power of death.'[23]

In this way, the action of the earth in purifying the sinful flesh at death echoes on its own level the action of the Mother of God as the great intercessor for the living and the dead—just as in the harvest the earth which bears the wheat which nourishes man, reflects the figure of the Mother of God who bears Christ, the bread of life, for the salvation of the world.

It is apparent from all that has been said that village attitudes to the earth are at one level systematically ambivalent; yet this ambivalence is not irreconcilable, and a key to its reconciliation lies in understanding why the story of the fall has such resonance. One reason, perhaps the chief one, is that in the way it is told, the story carries the implication that it is not a story about the past, and in fact the rhetorical question 'Are things otherwise now?' refers it unequivocally to present experience. It is because of the 'anguish' and 'tyranny' of the struggle to win food from the ground that men are said to be particularly fluent in their curses as they plough; but even as the heavenly figures are blasphemed for the refractoriness of both soil and animal, the pervasive understanding of the story of the fall provides an alternative pole of reference in which both men and women see themselves as Adams and Eves still replicating the sin which distorted their world in the first place. 'How are Christ and the Mother of God to blame?' they will say in a quieter moment, and this opens the way for an awareness of impurity and self-will in the blasphemer, and the recognition at some level that he is treating the earth as an object to be exploited, failing to see the gaining of the bread, which the earth gives him, as a sacrament, and failing in the ascetic purity which the wild places demand of him. And it follows from this that the perception of the earth as essentially hostile and refractory is—however irresistible as at times it may be—a secondary and ulti-

[23] *Burial of the Dead: Office for a Lay Person,* tr. Liturgical Translations Committee, Diocese of Sourozh, Russian Orthodox Church in Britain and Ireland (Oxford: St Stephen's Press, 2004), pp. 43, 51.

mately false one, projected through man's fallen consciousness. Hence the moments when the earth is perceived as paradise—moments which are also referred to present experience—are given the primary value of ultimate truth, and the delight with which these experiences are greeted partakes in this sense of a return home. Further, just as the idea of the fall, with its concomitant image of a blessed state from which man has fallen, affects the understanding of the struggle to win bread from the earth, so it affects the experience of death. For here burial in the black earth, which is the repayment of the debt of sins by returning to the earth the sinful flesh, is also the means by which the flesh dissolved in the earth over time promises the forgiveness of those sins and the hope that the soul will find paradise.

The story of the fall, spread through the Greek world chiefly by Christianity, can thus be seen to have altered the context for ambivalent attitudes to the earth in such a way that the conflicting perceptions involved can be reconciled. And this reconciliation is a part of the wider Christian resolution of the story, whereby Christ becomes the new Adam, defeating death, and the Mother of God becomes the new Eve, the 'mother of all living'.[24] It is through liturgical reflection on this movement from the fall to the incarnation of Christ that village experiences of the earth, as cursed but also as life-giving, as devourer of the body but also as cleanser of the body's sins, come in the Christian story to be seen as counterposed images of the parts played by Eve and the Mother of God. In the patterns of symbolism discussed here the focus of the villagers is chiefly on the story of the fall as it interprets their concrete relationship with the earth, while liturgical reflection focuses on the correspondences at a higher level, with Eve and Mother of God as contrary prototypes of this relationship. Nevertheless, there remains an evident harmony between the great and the little traditions in the way the contradictions of fallen human experience of the earth are resolved, and the earth is ultimately affirmed as a fragile paradise spoilt by man's fall, and as the long-suffering cleanser of sins until redeemed by man's obedience.

[24] Genesis 3 : 20.

3
WATER

WATER is a subject of continual interest in the villages, invariably treated with appreciation and discrimination and, where it is thought to be especially good, with a certain amount of awe. People will talk of a spring on a mountainside so cold and clear and so health-giving that it inspires a hunger which even 'three great loaves of bread' cannot satisfy. A spring such as this will be renowned for miles around, and many a shepherd or traveller will organize his day so as to bring him to it at midday when he stops to eat and rest.

Springs may well up from the ground or be caught in cisterns, perhaps emerging from the roots of an ancient plane tree, to be enclosed by a stone retaining wall and gush out through taps or stone channels. In many villages these springs have never been known to dry up, and it is commonplace for the quality of the water to be quoted by the people as a particular recommendation for their village and responsible for the healthy life they feel themselves to have. 'Our water is nourishing—it makes one fat' is a statement frequently heard, together with wonder that the water as it comes out of the hillside in high summer is so cold that it frosts the glass, a characteristic expressed in the question sometimes asked of those on their way to the spring: 'Are you going for cold?'

Water, then, is not an ordinary commodity but a life-giving element, and it can be rated so highly as to be used as justification for a family's rejection of an offer of marriage from a man in another village, on the grounds that the water there is 'warm' or indifferent. Whatever the other motives for such a refusal might be, the fact that it should find expression in such terms indicates the strength of the symbolism of water, and in the face of the continual toil necessitated by the carrying of water from the spring, the response to a question about the value of piped water to the houses is telling: 'It's no trouble to go to the spring, and the water would lose its nature that way.' This basic response to a basic element in its natural form indicates the importance in this instance—as in many others—of an unadulterated relationship with the natural world. Water has a 'nature' or 'essence' which is lost to man if too many processes are interposed. Water from a tap is a convenience, but drunk from a hillside or carried from the spring to the table it is a miracle.

Water even within the precincts of the village is seen in this way as an element with its own natural power, but outside the village its power increases and can be not only life-giving but disturbing and dangerous. Water is thus an ambivalent element and this ambivalence is precisely revealed in the apparitions of the nereids or water spirits who, astonishingly beautiful but possessing capacities for great evil, are said to be 'sometimes good, sometimes bad'.

Nereids are commonly found by water, bathing, and they also roam the hillsides in troupes, far from human habitation, headed by a little boy beating a drum. They are said not to kill, but to afflict people with sickness, which can be permanent, or with pains in the arms and legs, and the most dangerous of all these apparitions is a crippled boy who is sometimes seen limping along at the tail of the procession. Dancing in the wilderness, nereids make their own music and the dizzying sound of the flutes, very high, 'dirri-lirri, dirri-lirri', and the panic beat of the drum, 'bi-bi-bám, bi-bi-bám', can be heard in the throbbing noon, far away. However, only people in the wild hillsides actually encounter them face-to-face. They do not on the whole trouble mortals unless addressed or interfered with in any way, and the tale is told, for instance, of a shepherd resting by the roadside waiting for his sheep to catch up with him, who at the approach of a troupe of nereids pretended to be asleep, although, through half-closed eyes, he watched them coming on, 'immensely beautiful' and accompanied by the little boy with the drum. Passing by, they noticed him and he heard one of them say, 'Look at that man who's fallen by the road-side and sleeps', but they did him no harm.

Yet on another occasion the course of events was different. A young girl sent one day to herd the oxen was accosted as she neared a ravine by a nereid masquerading as a fellow-villager. This apparition danced around in front of her, barring her way so that in the end she made the mistake of speaking to it, upon which she fell into its power and, falling sick, remained crippled thereafter. And a twist to this story reveals a further characteristic of the nereids, for the girl's mother had just died, and in the confusion following her death, since 'men don't think of these things', no one had seen to getting her to change her clothes before she went out. The moment of death is thought to drench with blood all those present at the time, and the clothes thus affected need to be removed and washed on the premises before they can be worn again. It was thus the nereid's response to blood pollution which generated this fateful encounter. Intentional harm by nereids, then, seems to be a response which people, to some extent at least, bring on themselves, either by some unconsidered act of interference, or by speaking to them, or by encountering them while in a state of pollution. Again, water in the wild is dangerous to a woman polluted by the blood of childbirth, and the fact that women within forty days of giving birth are not permitted to 'cross over water' is clearly based on an awareness of the possible response of water in the wild to impurity.

Nereids, therefore, are conceived as taking vengeance on those who interfere with them and as resenting impurity, and as at such times actively tempting mortals into their power. With nereids, as with all demons, it is dangerous to speak, and more dangerous still to reveal one's name. But nereids do not, like other species of demon who 'attack one head-on', involve men in an irresistible assault. They are, while unequivocally demonic, nevertheless seen as somewhat ambiguous forces, very beautiful and not altogether malign, thought to be able to 'harm' but not to kill, and having a beneficent aspect which can be harnessed on one specific occasion—if a man, coming across a bathing nereid, stabs her headscarf through with a black-handled knife, he can keep her in his power and compel her to do magical tasks for him. Nereids are associated with help and harm, with beauty, purity, and danger, and this characterization in fact epitomizes the general symbolism of water itself which reveals an essential ambivalence, and makes of it a living force which demands man's active cooperation if it is not to tip from creation to destruction.

The ambiguous nature of water is systematized to some extent by a continuum running from the socialized to the wild, which coincides with the changing nature of water as life-giving and as life-threatening. But this dual essence is part and parcel of a single reality, and the coexistence in it of contrary qualities is seen very clearly in the watermill, set among turbulent waters in the ravines

7. The harvest bread: ‘The new day is marked as one of celebration… the festival bread with its decoration of crosses emerges to meet the gift of the sheaves of wheat brought in from the wild’ (p. 63).

8. A ravine: 'The nereids or water spirits who, astonishingly beautiful but possessing capacities for great evil, are said to be "sometimes good, sometimes bad"' (p. 79). This is summer—in winter, melting snow or rain may cause water to rise in the ravines, 'tearing through in tawny crests and making a sound like the sea' (p. 106).

where the demons have their home, but whose great stones mill the grain for bread and whose walls enclose a vibrant social life as people waiting for their flour gather and eat flat cakes of fried dough, and talk for hours and sometimes for nights on end.

There is a clear physical danger in the force of the mill-race and the power of the great grinding stones, and thus the very technology of the mill is mythologized as an invention of the devil who made the stationary grinding stone like a head of garlic, that is, with curved grooving. This stone lies beneath the upper mill stone into which the grain is fed, and into the hole in the middle the devil stuck his phallus to make it turn round. However, spiritual evil as well as material danger invests the mill-race, and so profound is this association that during the Twelve Days of Christmas it is necessary to avoid altogether the mill and its environs for fear of the *skalikantzoúria* infesting the place at that time. Warnings such as this are not to be taken lightly, and the tale is told of one miller who, careless of the prohibition, was thrown into a deep pool in the river by a crowd of *skalikantzoúria* appearing in the form of priests, after which, terrified, he sold up.

If the mill in some way epitomizes the character of water as both life-giving and peculiarly dangerous, a contrivance called a *dhrystélla* (δρυστέλλα) or *nerotriví* (νεροτριβή), which also runs off the mill lade, epitomizes and elaborates these varied themes of water still more precisely. The *dhrystélla* is a round hole in the earth, maybe two metres deep and the same in diameter, lined with planks, into which the mill-lade plunges, and its function is to pound and work certain materials. Ordinary washing is never done in the *dhrystélla*, but a girl before her marriage will wash her hand-made trousseau there, and the heavy rugs known as *velédzes* (βελέντζες) are softened and felted in the waters. These *velédzes* are made from thick loosely spun woollen yarn which is woven into a solid base from which emerge numerous free ends, and to become the strong soft furry rugs they are designed to be, these *velédzes* need to be put in the *dhrystélla* and left for three days to be worked in the movement of the water. There is always, however, an element of doubt as to the outcome, for occasionally the *velédza*, instead of coming out thick and felted, is torn into holes, matted, lumped, and ruined, and for this reason the most elaborate precautions are taken before the *velédza* is committed to the water.

Firstly, the wool for all the rugs to be treated must not come from anything that has been killed, but must be sheared either from an animal which has died naturally, or from a live one. No one who has killed, even by accident, a cat or a dog, can have anything to do with making one of these rugs, for 'it doesn't do' for the *dhrystélla* to receive anything from hands that are 'polluted'; the rug itself, before it is put into the *dhrystélla*, must have a silver coin sewn into one corner, and is then 'crossed'—that is to say it has each opposite corner drawn into the middle and sewn together—after which it is censed and sprinkled with holy water. Finally, the wool for the *velédza* must not have been sheared, spun, nor woven, by a woman in a state of impurity, and any woman approaching the *dhrystélla* must be 'pure', that is to say she must not be menstruating, nor must she have had sexual intercourse for eight days previously. The reason for all these precautions is simple: 'The *dhrystélla* wants a thing to be pure.' It is in keeping with this that the *dhrystélla* is not seen as an impersonal piece of technology but as a feminine power, referred to on occasions in tones of awe, and given the feminine name Morphoula—the Beautiful One.

The power or presence seen to inhabit the *dhrystélla* has thus very similar characteristics to that of the nereids. The mill-stream by means of which it works is thought to be inhabited by satanic forces; the *dhrystélla* itself is sometimes benevolent sometimes destructive; while the name Morphoula recalls the great beauty of the nereids. Finally, as with the nereids, the pollution of death or of blood must be avoided if the anger of the *dhrystélla* is not to be aroused.

It is interesting that a hand that has killed a cat or a dog should be thought of in this context as polluted, for in fact nobody in this kind of rural life, man or woman, can avoid killing things, if only mice, chickens and rabbits. Sheep and goats, lambs, kids and pigs—even the wild song-birds of the forest—are all accepted as being food for man and proper objects of slaughter; killing snakes, hornets and kindred creatures is looked on as a legitimate or necessary part of man's self-defence. But cats and dogs are not dangerous to man, nor yet food for him; more than that, they are a part of his household, each with its own particular function. It is possible, then, that the specifying of this kind of unnecessary killing is a symbolic acknowledgement for the pollution of killing or death as a whole, a pollution which man cannot wholly avoid even while the *dhrystélla* 'likes things to be pure'.

Purity thus is a notable characteristic of water, and it recurs in the understanding of the sea also as 'pure'. This purity manifests itself in much the same way as the purity of the *dhrystélla*—the sea 'gets angry' at impurity—although in this case the effect of this anger is that the sea 'froths up' and throws the impurity back onto land. Thus suicides by drowning, victims of murder, illegitimate children 'thrown away' into the sea, are all returned to the light of day. It is the terrifying realization of this capacity of the sea to reject, and to reveal, sin, which forms a theme in a folk tale in which a woman who is trying to dispose of an illegitimate child thinks of throwing it into the sea, for at this point she is warned of the futility of such an action by her maid who tells her: 'It's no good throwing it into the sea, because the sea will froth up and everyone will say, "Where did this come from?"'

While the sea possesses a purity consonant with water in general, it does appear, however, to be part of a somewhat differentiated mythology, for there are no indications that the sea is capable of being infested with demons, as are rivers and deep pools in the mountains. The sea is inhabited by 'great creatures', and it is accepted that the devil is present, in the deeps as elsewhere, to provoke these creatures to terrify and destroy. There is no sense, though, that the sea provides quite such an equivocal and unpredictable presence as the mountain rivers, and it is perhaps for this reason that some of the various objects thought to be especially potent against evil are a piece of fishing net, a spiral sea shell, and a small stone which, thought to be 'good' if they are taken from the far side of a river, are 'better' from the sea.

The spiritual danger of water is thus particularly evident in the symbolism of the inland rivers; and the fact that, as already noted, the demons have their 'village' in the holes in the ravines, where the rivers flow and where the upper world meets the underworld, probably has a lot to do with this. While it is recognized that the power of evil can be met with anywhere, it is with the cliffs and the ravines, and the water so often found in these ravines, that demonic forces are particularly associated.

There is in this way a paradox in this dual character of water, in that water is on the one hand inhabited by demons and can be an active danger to man, but on the other hand it is beautiful and 'likes' things to be 'pure'. On the one hand it can kill, but on the other it reacts with fury to pollution, especially the pollution of blood and of death. It seems, therefore, that while water rejects the grosser pollutions of mortality it nevertheless can absorb into itself spiritual evil, so that the ambiguity in water is to do not so much with the contrast between good and evil as the contrast between matter and spirit. Water, in itself neither good nor evil, is in its nature spiritual, incorporeal, and because of this it is both hostile to the fleshly pollutions of man and receptive to the aerial demons of the wilderness.

In spite, however, of this distinction between water in its relation to man and water in its relation to the spirits of the wild, there are certain contexts in which these two worlds meet. One such context has already been mentioned as the mill where conversation and companionship take place beside the turbulence of the waters; another is the herding of sheep and goats. The folds for these animals, roughly constructed out of branches cut while still in leaf, lie on the hillsides beyond the village, and both when the animals are dropping their young and when they are sheared, water acquires a symbolic role. Firstly, it is specified that the herdsmen must not have sexual intercourse, nor cut their hair, shave, or wash, during the entire time during which the animals are dropping their young, 'so as not to cut the sequence'. Secondly, at the shearing, the shearers' final act is to wash their hands and shake the water from their hands, full of the fats and greases of the shearing, back over the flock, saying as they do so, 'And next year!' Sexual intercourse is associated with ritual impurity, and the cutting of hair or beard clearly mirrors the cutting or interruption of the flow of life. For the flowing of water in the middle of the sequence to image the 'cutting' of the sequence, however, the focus must be on the movement of water; thus in the lambing or kidding the use of water is ill-omened because with it the good fortune flows away, whereas in the shearing the use of water is beneficent because with it flow back to the flock all the accumulated fats and oils of the fleeces just gathered. Thus the characteristic of water to flow or move things from one place to another can be, like the nereids, either helpful or harmful, cutting the sequence of births, or returning the essence of the wool harvest to the sheep for the next year; and behind the property of water to cut a sequence or to return a benison lies its initial capacity to absorb the essence of an event into itself. Water, auspicious or inauspicious according to the context, is so because it is impartially receptive to spiritual good or spiritual evil.

The ability to receive spiritual essences appears to be the key to the ambiguity with which the water in the wild is perceived, and this characterization creates the precondition not only for its purity and beauty, but also for its violence and capacity to inspire terror. In the wild, reflecting and absorbing the spiritual nature of its surroundings, water is informed with the qualities both of the divine and of the demonic worlds. Because it is pure, it responds to impurity with violence; but at the same time although not in itself demonic, it is receptive to the demonic forces with which these places are infested. Water is thus a mirror of the incorporeal world, and its spirituality, innate but unregenerate in the wilderness, expresses itself succinctly in the nereids' relationship to man which has already been quoted—'sometimes good, sometimes bad'. Water in the wild is not evil, but dangerous.

This receptivity of water to good or evil forces renders it suitable to a series of esoteric uses which occur in the context of spells, divinations, and herbal cures. Doctors, far away and costing money, are only attainable on mule-back over rough mountain paths; and for the priest to be summoned to give a blessing or 'reading', a gift in cash or in kind is customary, both as recompense for his trouble and as an act which allows his prayers to become the villager's. So village lore of the kind enacted in spells is an expression of self-help, 'Why should I go to the priest if I can do it myself?' Villagers' responses to illness and anxiety thus encapsulate personal experience of specific formulae which have relieved their symptoms in past times and have been passed on from person to person or performed by practitioners as acts of charity to those in need. Of these formulae, many are described as 'spells' (sing. *yítio*, dialect for *γητεία*). These often include mention of the holy figures of the Orthodox faith—typically citing that the sufferer is 'baptized and chrismated and given (*ριχμένος*) to God'—and relief is clearly being sought through the help of these figures. But whether or not these holy figures are cited, a spell also often takes the form of a stereotyped narrative about a figure who casts the evil eye, but is told not to do this to the sufferer named but to go elsewhere. This is noticeably different from the pattern of a church prayer, and is thus regarded with suspicion by the clerical hierarchy. Divination, also regarded by the hierarchy in much the same light, is used in an attempt to diagnose illness, or to satisfy, by some form of heightened perception, curiosity or anxiety about the future and about other matters hidden from everyday awareness; while herbal cures, regarded as competition (and sometimes prosecuted as fraudulent) by the medical profession, are prescribed for a whole gamut of afflictions.

Water is a vital element in village methods for the relief of many of these ills. Many of the herbal cures involve infusing or boiling the herbs with water; a spell may be transported by being spoken over some water which is then taken to the sick person and sprinkled over them. The cure for a particular range of demonic afflictions is to crush in water the relevant homeopathic herb and sprinkle the mixture over the sufferer while perhaps also giving him some to drink, this water being so dangerous that any residue must be thrown away in the wild 'where no one ever treads'. There is a form of diagnosis, *psýchisma* (*ψύχισμα*), carried out with certain words and said over water and hot embers, of which the significant test is whether the embers then float or sink; and there is a way of finding objects that have been lost or stolen which involves saying a spell over a plate of water, into which a child—a boy or a girl—then looks, a cloth over their head, and reports what they see.

Divination recurs also in various other types of ritual that make use of water, two of which fall on the Nativity of the Forerunner (John the Baptist) and are designed to let the girls of the village know their 'fate' in marriage. In one of these rituals, the *klídhonas* (*κλήδονας*), all the unmarried girls put some possession into a bucket of water which is then covered with a red cloth and on the eve of the feast is left out all night under the stars. The next morning a boy returns these objects to their owners, reciting, as he picks out each object, a rhyme which foretells their future in marriage. The second of these rituals occurs either at midday or early in the morning, and on this day the unmarried girls go to a well and, with a red cloth over their heads, look into the well-water with a mirror, hoping to see either the man they are destined to marry, or someone who has died. A similar practice has been cited as connected with the feast of the Ascension, when it is said that the dead are to be seen in well-water as they troop back to their places in the underworld.[1] And again, this link between water and the invisible world is repeated in the belief that water whirls round in a glass, revealing a fleeting vulnerability to demons, as the old moon reaches the end of its cycle and is, momentarily, neither old nor new.[2]

In all of these cases, miscellaneous as they may appear to be, there is a constant thread, and this is the idea that water is capable of taking on neutrally the properties of those things with which it comes in contact, so that it absorbs without prejudice both good and evil and reflects them again in diagnosis, healing, blessing, prophecy, illness or demonic possession. Once again it appears an influence equally for healing as for harm, both receptive and reflective, a medium for the occult yet also transparent to the other world, fluid, changing, and without a single character or constant form.

The village sense of what water is in itself is also, as was noted earlier, accompanied by a lively appreciation of the importance of its relation to fire and heat, especially the heat of the sun. Villagers are highly sensitive to the condition of the vegetation which forms their habitat, and to the point it has reached in its annual cycle, and they dramatize their observations in symbolic forms and express them as wishes or prayers, or as actions and abstinences aimed at cooperating with nature. A prohibition was mentioned in Chapter 1 against heating water for washing on sacred days 'so that the wheat should not be burned up'. Water and fire were there seen in a complementary opposition where the triumph of the sun over the rain must be tempered, and this understanding is found again relating to days known as days of the *griés* (γριές), old women, or alternatively *dhrýmes* (δρύμες), a word derived from that for a coppice or thicket and meaning spirits of the wood. The first nine days of March and, according to some, the first three days of August, are characterized as days of these *dhrýmes*, and on their account no work is done in the countryside by the men, and work by the women in the houses is limited by, once again, the prohibition on kindling fire to heat water for washing. The critical idea is that during these seasons of the year the coolness and moisture of the vegetation is threatened by

[1] See p. 34 above. [2] See pp. 46–7 above.

heat and fire, and this is expressed in the reason given for the prohibition which is 'so that the wheat should ripen into bread, so that the vineyards and all the young green shoots should not come to harm'. Water must be in balance with fire, rain with sun, if drought is not to come to the green growth of the earth.

It is on 1 May, though, that this play of themes of sun and rain finds its most illuminating expression, for on this one day symbols of both opposed principles are acted out. On the one hand the practice, already mentioned, of hanging a red rug from an eastern window and prohibiting damp white washing from being hung outside, indicates the importance attached to the heat of the sun. On the other hand a custom named *Piperiá* (*Πιπεριά*), enacted on the same day, takes the form of a prayer for rain. Here a number of young girls, unmarried but aged about twelve and over, dress up one of their number as the *Piperiá* or sweet pepper bush, so that she is completely covered from head to foot by long grassy stems called *lápatha* (*λάπαθα*) and broad leaved branches from some such tree as the plane. These girls, with the *Piperiá*, then go round to every house, singing a little ditty in a monotonous tune evocative of the rain falling:

> Quickly, quickly,
> Quickly to Saint Elias;
> And Saint Elias to the sky
> So that God will send rain
> For the wheat, for the barley,
> For all the grains of God.
> Holes, holes for the wine,
> Channels, channels for the water.
> The farmer with his mattock
> To stop the water running out.

As the girls sing this song one of them drenches the *Piperiá* with water while another digs a little channel, and yet another pours water into it, miming the actions of the farmer cooperating with the rain. Eggs, cheese, bread, dried chickpeas and suchlike are given in return for this blessing, and when they have been round all the houses the girls retire to eat together.

The song of the *Piperiá* gives village words to the kind of thing that is understood when the influences of fire and water are dramatized in symbolic language: when the red rug is hung out of an eastern window and when it is forbidden to hang out damp white washing 'so that the wheat should ripen for bread', or when washing in hot water is avoided on sacred days of the year lest mixing fire with water on such a day should bring a similar consequence on the greenery. The song takes the form of a call to the village to appeal to the Prophet Elias, previously noted as having his churches on mountain tops in reflection of his vision of God on Mount Horeb,[3] so that he will intercede 'for all the grains of God', and its structure is parallel with a similar prayer made every week in the Divine Liturgy during the Litany of Peace: 'For temperate weather, for abundance of the fruits of the earth, and for peaceful seasons, let us pray to the Lord.' The structure in both is of an intercession made directly to a holy figure, and what is prayed for, translated as temperate weather (*εὐκρασία ἀέρων*), means precisely a good mixture or a good balance of the atmosphere, whose consequence is fruitfulness. Thus the symbolic language, which could be ambiguous on its own, is in the song and the mime that accompanies it made into a pattern of words and actions which is continuous with the pattern of prayer offered in church. It is perhaps for this reason that the symbolic language here does not seem to incur the Church's disapproval, and the fact that 'spells' do incur suspicion probably follows from their differences when compared with church prayers, and from the villagers' disinclination to ask for prayers from the priest in times of illness for the reasons described earlier.

Important as it is, though, that the elements of water and heat should find their best balance in the growth cycle, it is the essential character of water itself, its receptivity, which makes of it the great purificatory force that it can become.

In the village, as has been said earlier, are gathered together all the forces of human companionship which serve as protection against the blatant attacks of the demons threatening in the world beyond the threshing floors. The area of the village also represents the divine world which, imaged in the microcosms of the house and

[3] 1 Kings : 19.

the church, provides the space in which the liturgical cycle is lived out, through which the divisive forces of evil in the natural world are reconciled and redeemed. The borders of the village thus provide a demarcation line between the unregenerate spiritual world of the wilderness and the sacred precincts of the world redeemed by Christ, and it is consistent with this that the character of water within these two worlds shifts so markedly. The change of emphasis as the village is entered makes water lose the character of ambiguity and danger which it possesses in the wilderness, to become a redeeming force with a capacity not to punish man's impurity, but to purge it.

The capacity of water to wash away dirt and to bring about cleanliness and beauty on a material level is one which is constantly before the villagers as they carry water which they heat up in the vast sooty cauldrons and use in wooden washing troughs for the huge piles of washing, and as they rinse heavy loads of clothes and beat out rugs at the spring. It is a cleansing capacity, however, which operates as strongly on the spiritual as on the material level, and it is illustrative of its changed character within the context of society that the water which in its elemental form reacts so strongly against the defilement of death, forms within the village one of the constant themes associated with its purification. Thus the first action with a person newly dead is to wash the body with water and then with wine, while the clothes worn by those present when the moment of death occurs must 'pass through water' before they are worn again. Further, the room in which the death occurred is later washed and whitewashed, as also is the room where the wake was held; and after returning from the funeral meal every housewife will empty all the water jars in her house and fill them again from the spring, thus pouring away from the house the contagion of death and, in the drawing of new water, renewing the flow of life among the living.

Illustrative of this changed potentiality in water once it is brought within the social world is the custom associated with New Year's Eve, in the middle of the twelve days of the unstable winter sun which is also the eve of St Basil's day, when every good action of the year must be inaugurated.[4] This custom consists in one person from each house going to the spring, in the dark of night and without speak-

[4] See p. 107.

ing to anyone on the way. The spring, as described earlier, is usually in the form of a spout set in some kind of stone facing to the hillside or cistern, through which the water flows into a bowl or trough and then away through a channel in the ground. At the spring the person chosen drops into the channel a coin and one of each kind of grain sown by the householder, with the words, 'Just as this water flows, so may money, wheat, lentils, beans [and so on], flow into the house.' After this the emissary washes face and hands in the water, fills a water jar, takes from somewhere near the spring a round stone, and returns to the house. On return, he or she dips an olive branch into the water, sprinkles everyone in turn, and taps them on the head with the stone, saying some variant of the words, 'May your head be strong as iron. Many Years and a happy and prosperous New Year!' This is the period, it must be remembered, when the mill-stream in the ravine is thought to be so dangerous that no one dares go near it; but at the same time, within the village water purifies, blesses, and causes to flow into the house increase of money, grain, oil, and all crops necessary for life. Within the village, water is, then, unambiguously beneficent, its flowing action used to receive and wash away dirt and pollution and, at the New Year, to receive and pass on a fortunate flow of resources in the year to come.

A further example of the changed character of water within the village occurs at a birth, when the water, which in the ravine is so dangerous to the newly-delivered mother that she is forbidden to cross over it, is in the village so full of life that it is brought into the house within the first few moments after the birth and is used for what is known as the 'first blessing'. This custom dictates that as soon as the child has been born, someone from the house goes to the priest to get his blessing on some water from the spring. This water is then brought back and sprinkled over the mother, the child, and the house, and what remains is then mingled with gunpowder (which, as noted earlier, 'bursts', thus destroying the forces of evil) and is marked in crosses on the insides of all the windows, shutters, and doors as a protection against those demons which endanger both mother and child within the first forty days of the birth. For three days, as noted earlier, mother and child must lie in the blood of childbirth, but on the third day after the birth they are washed by the midwife, who at the same time washes the clothes also and keeps as a gift the soap with which this washing is done. After being taken to the threshold to greet the sun, the newly-delivered mother may, although she is prohibited from drawing wine, go to the spring for water, and may also do the washing for the household provided that, until the ceremony of 'churching' on the fortieth day, she does this on uneven, and thus auspicious, days after the birth.

In these contexts it is plain that the characteristic receptivity and purity of water persists as strongly in the context of the village as it does in that of the wilderness, but that the way these principles work has changed. Instead of receiving the dangerous forces of the natural world into itself while rejecting the impurity of man, as it does in the wild, water in the village, although still capable of accepting harmful forces into itself, does so in order to purify. In the case of death, for instance, water not only cleanses of pollution the body, the house where the death occurred, and those who were in the house at the moment of death, but also, with the emptying of the water jars after the funeral meal, washes death from the entire village. Water in the social world, still a great elemental force, has become altogether benign, accepting and purging the impurity of the act of living and the pollution of death and leaving renewal in its place.

Thus in the context of the social world the ambivalent nature of water begins to be resolved. In the wild, water both quenches thirst and is full of demons, is both life-bringing and death-dealing. With the lambing, water is seen as having the power to cut off good fortune, with the shearing as having the power to return it. But within the village this potentiality for beneficence is consolidated. Used at New Year as a recipient of money and grain and a bringer of increase, it becomes after a birth the agent of spiritual purification, not merely beneficent but capable of bestowing a blessing. In the context of church and village, water becomes a powerful spiritual force for good, and this capacity is further consolidated in the 'holy water' (*ἁγιασμός*) which, once hallowed, is kept in the house and used for the healing of both spiritual and physical disorders.

There are various occasions on which water is blessed so that it becomes holy water but the greatest of these is at the Theophany (*Θεοφάνια*), the feast of the baptism of Christ, on 6 January. On the day before the Theophany, the day of the Cross, the Divine Liturgy is celebrated and immediately afterwards the service of the First

Great Blessing of the Waters, after which the priest takes the holy water to every house in the village where, using a bunch of basil to disperse it in droplets, he sprinkles all the rooms in each house to evict the *skalikantzoúria*. The following day at the Second Great Blessing of the Waters, commonly referred to as the Feast of Lights, which again takes place immediately after the Liturgy, both church and people are sprinkled at the end of the service, and then each householder takes some holy water home in a bottle and with it he sprinkles his vineyards, fields, and animals, and so on, keeping the remainder for when it is needed during the rest of the year. The holy water kept from this service is also given as a substitute to any who have been forbidden by a confessor to take communion. A similar blessing of water, known as the Lesser Blessing, is also done on specific occasions—at certain festivals or the visit of the relics of a saint to the village—and it can also be blessed in cases of special need, such as when there is sickness among the flocks. Water blessed in this way for specific misfortunes can be kept and used at other times, but its use is restricted for the purpose for which it has been blessed.

Holy water has in this way a special place in the armoury of the house against the invasion of evil, and on the icon shelf of every house there will be a little bottle kept, whose contents may be increased at any time by adding water from the spring. It has special properties of blessing, purification and healing; it may be rubbed on the diaphragm or sprinkled on the forehead in case of sickness or headache; and is in fact used in almost any time of crisis or illness for which another remedy is not known. If a mouse—a creature thought of as unclean—has got into a water jar, swilling the jar out three times with holy water will cleanse it. And holy water protects in a more permanent sense the founding of a house when, as mentioned earlier, it is sprinkled into the foundations and a bottle of it built into each corner of the walls. Holy water is at the far extreme of contrast with the perilous waters of the wild.

It is at baptism, however, that the spiritual polarities of water and its abilities for harm or healing are most clearly revealed. The blessing of the water in the font is inaugurated by an exorcism: three times the priest dips his fingers in the water and makes the sign of the cross, breathing on it (as a sign of the Holy Spirit) and saying,

'Let all adverse powers be crushed beneath the sign of the image of Thy cross.' Then follows the prayer of blessing:

We pray thee O God that every aerial and obscure phantom may withdraw itself from us; and that no demon of darkness may conceal himself in this water; and that no evil spirit which instills darkening of intentions and rebelliousness of thought may descend into it with him who is about to be baptized. But do Thou, O Master of all, show this water to be the water of redemption, the water of sanctification, the purification of flesh and spirit, the loosing of bonds, the remission of sins, the illumination of the soul, the laver of regeneration, the renewal of the Spirit, the gift of adoption to sonship, the garment of incorruption, the fountain of life.[5]

Once again, the symbolism of the Church, far from denying the folk tradition, takes on the folk understanding of the contradictory characteristics of water but brings it to a higher level. Water is still the element of potentiality, a force for harm or for healing depending on the spiritual influences it receives, but there has been a change. Village lore sees water at one extreme as the haunt of demons who threaten illness and danger, and, at the other, as a pure source of refreshment for the weary traveller. The Church sees water at one extreme as a haunt of the demon capable of 'darkening... intentions', and, at the other, as 'the water of redemption', of 'the renewal of the Spirit'. The world of the flesh is not denied but the drama of demonic attack and the prevention of harm is played out less in the body of man than in his spirit, less in the arena of illness and health than of temptation and forgiveness. Here water has transcended its nature as a pure element flowing from springs and into wells, to become integrated with its symbolic archetype as 'the fountain of [immortal] life'.

To summarize so far: there is a contrast between water in the context of the village and water in the wilderness, according to which the water of the village receives into itself the auspicious presences of the place and becomes an agent for purifying and healing, while water in the wilderness, similarly responsive to context, receives into itself the untamed forces inhabiting the wilds and responds to im-

[5] *Service Book of the Holy Orthodox Catholic Apostolic Church,* tr. Isabel F. Hapgood (Englewood, N.J.: Antiochian Orthodox Christian Archdiocese of New York and all North America, 1975), p. 278.

purity and trespass with such violence as to create illness rather than cure it. Although water includes such a wide range of qualities, a single characteristic underlies both, and this is its incorporeality and its transparency to whatever spiritual powers are encountered, and while this in the wilderness renders it transparent to the powers of the demons which dwell there, in the liturgical context it transforms it into holy water and the water of baptism.

Thus it is in society and liturgy that the ambiguity which lies in water in the wild is unequivocally resolved, and this movement from ambiguity to unquestioned good has its roots once again in the fundamental orientation of the world towards God. Even the wilderness is, like the water which is to be found in it, not so much evil as dangerous, and when set against the grossness of human sins it is seen as 'pure' and untouched. Home as it may be to the forces of spiritual evil which inhabit its wastes, and lacking as it may be in the redeeming presence of the liturgical life which takes place largely in places of habitation, the wilderness is a clean, hard environment, the testing ground of the saints and crucible of the human spirit. Even in the wilderness—perhaps especially in the wilderness—water, though dangerous and untamed, retains an essential relation to the holy in its purity, its beauty, and its miraculous and life-giving nature, while in the social world it becomes unambiguously a force for healing.

This pattern of understanding, though complex and fragmentary, thus possesses its own inner clarity and consistency, which in baptism is brought fully into the Orthodox world. However, baptism is itself underpinned by the Theophany, one of the most important festivals in the Orthodox calendar, and in this feast the various aspects of water, dispersed throughout the culture, are brought together in a single scheme. At this feast the Orthodox Church celebrates, as the Theophany or 'Revelation of God' to the world, the baptism of Christ by St John the Forerunner in the waters of the Jordan, and the descent of the Holy Spirit—a revelation seen not simply as a visible declaration to the people that Christ is the son of God but as a decisive confrontation with the powers of darkness by which the whole world is changed. Thus the *tropárion* (*τροπάριον*), or hymn, for the feast of the Eve of the Theophany gives to Christ the words: 'I am in haste to slay the enemy hidden in the waters, the prince of darkness',[6] and the icons of the Theophany depict Christ standing in the water of the Jordan, while blue streams play about his body and black demons lurking in the depths make to flee away. The descent of Christ into the waters is his descent into a medium imbued with possibilities, an element innately pure and purifying, yet one permeated also by the ever-present spirits of evil in the world. It is an archetypal encounter with the realm of the possible which permits free choice, and so gives room for evil—an encounter in which Christ, foreshadowing his final defeat of death in the harrowing of hell, conquers the demons of the deeps, sanctifies the waters of the world, and, reconciling water with its innate holiness, makes it unequivocally an element of spiritual renewal:

> Today the bitter water, as once with Moses and the people of Israel, is changed to sweetness by the coming of the Lord. Today we have been released from our ancient lamentation, and as the new Israel we have found salvation.[7]

As already mentioned, the feast of the Theophany consists of two Blessings of the Waters: the First Great Blessing carried out on the eve of the Theophany, and the Second Great Blessing on the day of the Theophany itself. For the First Blessing the water that is to be blessed is brought into the church in a large bowl, and similarly on the day of the Theophany itself, except in coastal villages where the second blessing is performed for preference beside—and in—the sea. The central moment on each of these occasions is when the priest plunges a cross three times into the bowl in front of him (or three times throws the cross into the sea, whence after its third immersion it is rescued by hordes of small boys who dive in for the purpose), invoking as he does so the descent of Christ into the Jordan. Here, although the villagers may not understand the word-by-word meaning of the many texts which are read by the priest, their knowledge of the ambivalent nature of water from their daily life harmonizes with the knowledge presented to them by the Church, and they need no books or reading to understand the context of the baptism of Christ, nor to know that at the moment when the cross is plunged into the water, the demons flee and the waters are sanctified. They know, too, that the two services of the Blessing of the

[6] *Festal Menaion*, p. 327.

[7] Ibid. pp. 354–5.

9. Filling a pitcher: 'Water in the social world, still a great elemental force, has become altogether benign' (p. 92).

10. The Baptism of Christ: 'Christ, foreshadowing his final defeat of death in the harrowing of hell, conquers the demons of the deeps, [and] sanctifies the waters of the world' (p. 96). (Icon by Theophanes, 16th c., Monastery of Savronikita, Mount Athos.)

Waters involve a symbolic union of the tame and the wild, the bowl of spring water in the church unified with the waters of the Jordan, and in these services the people see all the waters of the world being brought, renewed once again, into the liturgical cycle.

In the feast of the Theophany therefore, the themes in the apparently rather heterogeneous multitude of folk practices and beliefs concerning water are restated, but this time as part of a consistent theology. The water which in folk tradition is pervaded with the demonic presences, is in the Theophany represented by the Jordan in whose depths the demons lurk; the spirit of water which in folk tradition is capable of being not only 'bad' but 'good' is in the Theophany purged of the demons and sanctified by Christ; the water which in folk tradition is a vehicle for transporting spells and cures to people, and sicknesses away from them, carries in the Theophany a blessing on the people and purification to all the houses; the water which in the prophetic and divinatory practices of the folk tradition is a mirror of the spiritual world, becomes in the Theophany the medium which foretells Christ's descent into hell and his final confrontation with the powers of evil, and makes of baptism a 'type' or prefiguring of his death and resurrection. Finally, village concerns with the relation of the cosmic forces of sun and water find archetypal expression in the Theophany in the completion of God's sovereignty over the cosmic elements, in particular the sun and light, and the waters and seas:

> Of four elements hast Thou compounded the creation: with four seasons hast Thou crowned the circuit of the year. All the spiritual powers tremble before Thee. The sun sings Thy praises; the moon glorifies Thee; the stars supplicate before Thee; the light obeys Thee; the deeps are afraid at Thy presence; the fountains are Thy servants.[8]

This sovereignty, inaugurated in the first creation of the world but challenged after the fall by evil and sin, is restored as Christ enters the river Jordan, an encounter which is itself the encounter of fire and water:

> The waters saw Thee, O God, the waters saw Thee and were afraid. The Jordan turned back, seeing the fire of the Godhead descending bodily and entering its stream. The Jordan turned back, beholding the Holy

[8] *Festal Menaion*, Prayer at The Great Blessing of the Waters, p. 356.

Spirit coming down in the form of a dove and flying about Thee. The Jordan turned back and the mountains skipped, looking upon God in the flesh; and the clouds gave voice, marvelling at Him who was come, the Light of Light, true God of true God ...[9]

The Blessing of the Waters is thus more than a celebration of the manifestation of God to the world; it is a celebration of the manifestation of God within the world, within the icon of his creation, and in the light of this revelation all creation is transfigured and all contradictions overcome. It is thus a feast which gathers together and gives a completed meaning to all the various themes of water faithfully preserved in the rural tradition, but still to some extent unrelated and incomplete. In the baptism of Christ the water of the wilderness is linked to the water of the Church—the wild and the socialized divinized together; the unpredictable and autonomous demons of the wild are brought under the kingship of Christ; water as a pure element, the perfect mirror of the incorporeal world in both its good and evil aspects, appears in the Theophany in its true prophetic function, not for finding lost objects or foretelling marriages, but foreshadowing the Passion and the final victory of Christ over hell.

It will be remembered that this theme of opposed characteristics or elements meeting—fire with water, or the regenerate with the unregenerate aspects of water—in such a way that they are harmonized or one is resolved into the other, occurred also in the discussion of the earth, where the opposition between the wild and socialized aspects of nature is transcended in the meal on the threshing floor, and the fruits of the earth become divinized in the bread of the eucharist. Thus it appears that while earth and water differ in the range of properties and qualities which are attributed to them, earth being the element of matter and water the element of the spirit, the basic symbolic structure according to which either is understood is virtually identical. So it is, for instance, that the earth receives dead bodies while water rejects them; earth is concerned with the possession and loss of paradise and so with ideas of fertility and food, while water is concerned with the presence or absence in it of the demons, and so with the basic categories of sickness and healing. However, an

[9] *Festal Menaion*, p. 355.

essentially similar structure is revealed both in the nature of the oppositions which operate within the two, and in the nature of the transcending categories which act ultimately to resolve and unify them. Hence both earth and water are ambivalent elements according to whether they are inhabited by God or by the devil; and both are unified into a single transcendent whole at certain high points of the ritual year. In this way, at the risk of oversimplification, these parallel schemes might be summarized as follows:

EARTH
Receptive to Matter

tame	wild
divinely protected	vulnerable to demons
makes house as paradisal garden	makes work anguish, tribulation, tyranny
gives life	eats the dead

Transcended by the harvest, and by the dissolution of sins as well as of flesh at death, both echoing the work of the Mother of God.

WATER
Receptive to Spirit

tame	wild
divinely protected	vulnerable to demons
cleanses and heals impurity	rejects impurity

Transcended by the Blessing of the Waters, and following from this the rite of baptism and the consecration of holy water, echoing the entry of Christ into creation.

In this scheme, then, it is possible to see in operation some of the principles which appeared in the first chapter. There appears again the fundamental split between good and evil which is reflected within the separate elements of earth and water, but there also appears a higher and more efficacious principle by which this split is periodically reconciled and an even more fundamental unity enacted. At these times the quality of the sacred which, in the normal course of daily life, is only one aspect of earth or of water, loses its relativity and is revealed in these transcendent categories as the archetypal reality.

The particular interest of these categories, however, lies not only in the fact that they reveal again the essential leaning of the world towards God; it is also that they lie at the heart of some of the most important sequences of village activity. They do not, that is to say, come about by some accident of the culture; they are worked towards and awaited by the people with a most lively expectation. Thus although the process by which the evil in the world is transcended is not one which is intellectually comprehended or analytically discussed, it is a process which is expected and achieved, quite deliberately, by a steady involvement of both the Church and the people in the symbolic dimensions of their material life. The overcoming of duality and the redemption of the world from evil goes hand in hand with the necessity to obtain bread and warmth and shelter and society; and it is in the recurrent enactment of the complex customs dictated by such beliefs that the people are 'shaped'[10] or educated from the cradle to the grave.

[10] The Greek word for 'educated' is *morphoménos* (*μορφωμένος*), literally 'shaped'.

4
TIME

THE view of the world described in the preceding chapters involves complex perceptions of its causation in which spiritual influences play a critical part. These perceptions, however, in no way exist on their own or as part of an 'other world'; they exist as part of an inescapably sharp and vigilant awareness on the part of the villagers of the basic material realities of daily life. Divine and diabolical presences are often felt to work through natural causes, and it is as a unified set of perceptions that both spiritual and physical principles mould the people's eminently pragmatic response to their need to find food, shelter and security, for themselves and their families. There is no break in their experience of either world: at the same time as they are relating to the world about them they are walking through a sacred drama.

Time, the fourth great dimension of the cosmos being described here, is encountered in the same way, not filtered through the artificial measurement of clock or calendar but experienced as something inwritten in the villagers' direct experience of the natural world. The time of day, as already described, is reckoned from the position of the sun—a reckoning which allows for a generous imprecision as to exactly when things happen, and ties activities to awareness of the light in the sky. In the same way events are remembered not by calendrical numbers but by their seasonal context, such as their relation to the harvest or to the time of the sowing of the broad beans. And just as times are marked by the sun and the season, so also are they marked by their placing in the liturgical cycle: 'I remember it was November because it was just before the Christmas fast', or 'The great heat begins at the feast of St Constantine and after'.

In this way seasonal and liturgical cycles govern village time, and return things year by year to the same point. The resulting sense that time goes in a circle is obviously apt to the solar and sacred patterns; but longer passages of many years can also be seen by villagers as a circling movement, forming, through the life cycle and the cycle of marriage, the generations of village kin.[1] They also provide a means of dating historical events which touch village lives by their relation to births, marriages and deaths among kin or in the wider village family: 'It was in the year that Christina collapsed and died in the great heat at the harvest.'

This village time contrasts with another time, the time that is imposed by forces outside the village, and by foreigners and foreign powers; that is largely an experience of wars or occupation, or of emigration which can be welcome for its novelty but also filled with an aftermath of suffering and exile (*ξενιτειά*). In the earlier part of the twentieth century alone, the civil wars in 1943–45 and 1947–49, fought by guerrilla bands in the mountains, had drawn in villagers as forced food providers and forced recruits in a way they could not escape, and the conflict only ended through forced evacuation. These events arose in turn out of the German occupation and the famine which accompanied it. Villagers were called up to fight in the Albanian campaign against the Italians in 1940, and against the Germans in 1940–41. They had also fought in the Asian Minor campaign from 1920–22, the product of the First World War, and in the Balkan Wars of 1912–14. And in the meantime emigration to America, Europe and Australia steadily increased, bringing with it the songs of a different kind of exile, often profitable in money but saddened for many years by the loss of home. Such for many centuries has been the experience of historical time in this small country with powerful neighbours on the contested frontier between the West and Islam.[2]

Against this unpredictable stream of historical events moving from unknown origins to an unknown destination, village time, expressed in the cycle of the seasons and of the liturgy, provides a vital element of constancy. Compared with the West, Christianity in the Orthodox world has in general been less concerned with mapping time as a linear movement from creation to apocalypse, and less troubled by millennial anxieties.[3] Indeed, the liturgical emphasis

[1] The way these patterns of kinship are created is described chiefly in Ch. 7.

[2] For detail, see du Boulay, *Portrait of a Greek Mountain Village*, Ch. 10.

[3] See Timothy Ware (Metropolitan Kallistos of Diokleia), *The Orthodox Church*, 3rd ed. (London: Penguin, 1997), pp. 261–3; and Sergius Bulgakov, *The Orthodox Church*, tr. L. Kesich (Crestwood, N.Y.: St Vladimir's Seminary Press, 1988) pp. 176–80. Bulgakov notes that after the early period, when Christ's coming was felt to be

may seem to be as much on the cyclic as on the forward moving character of sacred history. There is an onward movement in that paradise is succeeded by the fall, and the fall by redemption in Christ; but there is a return in that Christ raises Adam and Eve from the dead. The return is important, even though the place attained is not the same but a recapitulation of a pattern which has moved on.

To this may be added the sense of a world beyond time expressed by the early composers of the Orthodox liturgy. The doxology which forms the continuous refrain of this liturgy runs, 'Glory to the Father and to the Son and to the Holy Spirit, now and ever and to the ages of ages. Amen.' The words 'now and ever' speak of a present moment which takes part in the eternal reality: 'now' in sacred time is also 'ever', and because of this the 'ages of ages' to which time tends are also 'now', in an understanding in which the purely linear components of time are collapsed.

This suggests that the cyclic pattern of the solar and liturgical year has an archetypal importance for the Orthodox conception of time, and the structure of the year which is the topic of this chapter can be seen as a subtle and complex reflection on time, eternity, and the relation between the natural and spiritual worlds. The architects of the Christian year evidently interpreted in Christian terms what could be accepted as true knowledge of the natural year, and pointed to natural echoes of the spiritual world which occurred in the course of it. At the same time popular elements of pre-Christian calendrical practices persisted, often for reasons connected with the natural year, and their resonances or dissonances also became part of the Christian year. Many of these pre-Christian practices were Jewish in origin (notably the feasts of Passover and Pentecost which were related to the natural cycle), and others Graeco-Roman (such as

imminent, a second response emerged in the form that 'the Church already possesses the plenitude of all it should bring to pass. Then, fundamentally, nothing separates us from the end....' Cf. Ware's comment (p. 263) that 'For members of God's Church, the "Last Times" are already inaugurated, since here and now Christians enjoy the first fruits of God's Kingdom.' A possible factor in this was the guarded attitude of the Eastern Church to the Book of Revelation, which some Councils omitted from the Canon (see Revelation, Book of, in *Oxford Dictionary of the Christian Church* (Oxford: Oxford University Press, 1974)). However, Bulgakov also refers to apocalyptic tendencies among the Russian sect known as the Old Believers.

winter solstice festivities of which the Saturnalia are an example, or those related to the opening of the new wine). But villagers do not typically concern themselves with the origins of their practices, and experience the year simply as an expression of the whole range of their life, which acquires its own contextual meaning. This poses a problem for singling out 'survivals' of pre-Christian calendrical practices, because by now they take their meaning from their present context rather than from their origin.[4] Thus it is the natural and the spiritual worlds as the village now experiences them that give meaning to the year, and it is by understanding the way in which the natural and spiritual worlds interlock with one another in the present that the village sense of time becomes accessible. In this village understanding it is the unified experience of both dimensions of time that gives to village life its stability and endurance in the face of its manifest uncertainties and vulnerabilities, for to know your place in these time cycles is to know your place in the universe.

The unity between the sacred and the natural worlds in these seasonal experiences is made possible by the fact that their liturgical and agricultural components have a similar structure. The time of nature is a composite of many cycles of differing lengths and timings, all however reflecting a single movement, from sowing to fruition,

[4] A local example is the pre-Lent Carnival referred to later in this chapter (pp. 116–17). By the 1970s the work of folklorists had percolated into the syllabus of the state schools, and children were being taught that the origin of the Carnival was one of the wine festivals of the ancient god Dionysus. (For the Greek state's need to emphasize its ancient Hellenist credentials to western allies after the War of Independence see Charles Stewart, 'Dreaming of Buried Icons in the Kingdom of Greece', in Mark Mazower (ed.), *Networks of Power* (pp. 95, 104–5). Village accounts of the Carnival did not, however, refer to Dionysus or to wine but located the festivities firmly in the three weeks of preparation for Great Lent, and treated it as a harmless release of satire and animal spirits shortly to be renounced by abstinence. The phallic symbols which were part of the Carnival provided colour for either interpretation, but the village did not debate the issue and took no account of the folkloric alternative. Hellenist concerns were then reinforced in the 1990s with the failure of the magnesite mines which had been the principal local employer, after which the local rural administration identified tourist development as a priority for local employment and began to issue tourist guides which advertised the Carnival as 'a resurgence of the god Dionysus in the Greek psyche'. At the same time, the guide hedged its bets by concluding that the festival enables local people to enter Great Lent with 'a lightening of the soul'.

which follows the yearly cycle of the sun. Liturgical time is similarly many-layered, creating a complex harmony of several cycles of differing lengths, which tell again and again variants of the same story, using the materials provided by the natural world. The simplest way to begin to appreciate the richness and complexity of these resonances is to tell the story of the year in its most concrete form, describing the tasks which have to be accomplished so as to cooperate with the natural cycle, and sketching in briefly their sacred associations. After this it becomes easier to expand on how the sacred story is given temporal form, and how it relates to the village experience of nature.

As described in the introduction, there are many kinds of Greek village which have a basis of subsistence living, and even in very similar villages the timing of the farming tasks will vary with the location; and variation in the local saints celebrated will affect the timing of some of the major festivals. The description which follows is of one kind of mountain village in which subsistence agriculture and some large-scale herding of sheep and goats is backed up by barter, by cash-cropping pines for resin, and by tilling gardens and vineyards. Nearly every household has a plough animal or two, all will have hens and a few household sheep and goats to provide milk, cheeses, meat, skins, wool and goat-yarn, and most will have a pig which is killed at Christmas of which every bit is used to provide meat, leather, and soap.

The ecclesiastical year, beginning, as already mentioned, on 1 September when the sun's heat has usually relented and the first rains have refreshed the earth, has as its first major feast the Nativity of the Mother of God on 8 September, and this month is the time when men and women together work in the fields to clear them and burn them off. In the freshened climate herbs are redolent, and at the time 'of the Cross' (the feast of the Exaltation of the Cross on 14 September) when the cross is laid for veneration in a bed of basil and everyone brings a handful of basil to the church to be blessed, the whole village is filled with the scent. Ploughing begins once the fields are cleared and the earth has been well soaked with rain. All crops need the fields to be ploughed twice, once for the initial breaking of the ground and the second at the sowing; but for wheat and maize, both sown later, one extra preparatory ploughing is necessary. Thus after the breaking of the ground, everyone is occupied with the sowing, first of all of the barley, oats, hay, lentils, vetch, broad beans, garlic, and then with the sowing of the wheat. This is a time of united effort interspersed, for some families, by the olive and the honey harvest, and, for the entire village, by a few pungent, sun-lit, holiday days in the second half of October—the 'little summer of St Dimitri'—when the grapes are cut and brought in from the vineyards by all members of the family, and trodden—by men and boys only—on the wooden deck slotted into the open end of a tall up-ended barrel set briefly in every courtyard. This is the time for 'Dimitri's flowers', chrysanthemums, which flower around St Dimitri's day (26 October), and Dimitri's 'little summer' comes with translucent days, lengthening shadows and long distances, and a last flush of harvesting as mushrooms—parasol mushrooms and saffron milk caps—are gathered, wild pears collected, and apples and bunches of grapes selected and strung from the beams for eating through the autumn.

When a large acreage of wheat is sown and the slow oxen used as plough animals, this sowing is lengthy, and in cases when bad weather has delayed the sowing, work can begin very early and continue well into the dark, so that the working day can start at four in the morning and continue until eleven at night by the light of split-off pieces of heavily resinated wood which burn with a bright smoky flare—a rare overturning of obedience to the hours of the sun. The main sowing of the wheat is carried into November, and the Archangel Michael, celebrated on 8 November and seen on his icons with drawn sword, is a formidable figure associated with the darkening November days with the leaves being stripped from the trees and the smoke gusting in ashy draughts down the chimneys; but this is a month named after the preeminent agricultural task—'The Sower' (*Σποριάς*). And the Entry of the Mother of God into the Temple on 21 November, soon after the Christmas fast has begun, is also in the village given the character of the time as the 'Mother of God Half-Way-Through-The-Sowing' (*Παναγία Μισοσπειρίτσα*). The task of the sowing of the wheat then continues into the time known as 'Andrew's' (St Andrew, whose day is 30 November, but who has given his name to the following month of December[5]), and can go on up to Christmas—and even beyond, if the weather has not been fit.

[5] Villagers make equations between names of saints or farming tasks and months but often, as here, with an evident approximation, and in practice other time markers will become salient before the end of the month concerned; so with December and the advent of Christmas, when the days are known as *toú Christoú* (*τοῦ Χριστοῦ*), the time of Christ.

The autumn is thus a time of consistent preparation in the fields after the harvest of the preceding season has been completed and the seeds for the coming one gathered in. Spare days are used, by the men, to repair their houses and steadings, collect firewood from the forest, or take the last of their resin down to the market town, while the women in a quiet hour might go to the fields with their sewing or spinning to watch the household animals graze untethered, or sit at the last of their weaving in the store-rooms downstairs before the cold of winter closes, until the following May, the open door which is their main source of light.

Deep winter begins around the twelve days from Christmas to Theophany, the time 'of Christ' and the time 'of John', between which St Basil, always first of the great hierarchs of the Eastern Church, holds pride of place on the first day of the New Year, and on this day everyone goes round their fields and animals to wish them good fortune for the coming year. This action is known as *vasilévo* (*βασιλεύω*), which in its normal definition means to reign, but which here also carries an allusion to St Basil (*Βασίλειος*, meaning kingly) and literally means 'to Basil' every creature and every important practice. The cold persists through January and into 'Crippled February' and 'Burn-the-Palings'—a quizzical reference to the fact that in March, the woodpile exhausted, people may be reduced to burning their fence posts in order to keep warm—and these days bring as it were a dormant period which keeps, sometimes for long durations, the men in the cafés and the women in their houses. The day is short and the evenings long, with the sun setting at about five and day breaking just after seven, so people are free to visit each others' houses for a few hours in the evening and everyone gets their fill of sleep—though the old with their aching joints do not sleep well, someone needs to get up at three every morning to stop the animals banging about in the stable downstairs by replenishing the hay in their mangers, and women with daughters needing dowries regularly rise at four o'clock to spin. During these months snow can isolate the village, or more frequently rain, which causes the river to rise in the ravine, tearing through in tawny crests and making a sound like the sea. Animals cannot be taken through the flood and the only way to cross over for the people themselves is by a narrow bridge made from felled pines joined end to end, edged by a flimsy wooden rail. Life during much of these periods is, for all but the shepherds, confined on the whole to the village, and within-doors. In the fug of the cafés the men's talk is ceaseless and emphatic as more wood is piled into the stove and minute cups of coffee or tiny glasses of *rakí* sparingly ordered. Within the houses the women keep a different kind of company, and conversation is accompanied by the quiet movements of spinning, mending, knitting, or embroidery, while highlights from lamp or flame pick out the features of the company, and shadows pool in the corners. In the early dark the firelight is the main source of illumination, and the fireplace, whitewashed two or three times a week, reflects the flames and makes the room glow red-gold. Although the flocks in the folds on the hillsides can give birth earlier, the few sheep and goats who live in the stables on the ground floor of the houses drop their young in February, and these first fruits are often brought into the living rooms to frolic by the fireside, their presence explained to any newcomer with the delighted comment, 'We have offspring!', and their well-being in the face of admiration protected by the classic response: 'May the evil eye not fall upon them!' 'The Meeting' (that is, the presentation of the infant Christ in the Temple on 2 February) falls at this time, marking the end of the forty-day period of the recovery of the Mother of God from her giving birth.

During this period some work outside still persists, for even in bad weather water has to be fetched from the spring by women trudging over muddy paths and under lashing rain, animals must be fed, and bread, in these conditions sometimes taking a whole day to rise, must be baked. Washing sometimes piles up for weeks until a break in the weather provides an opportunity for it to be done in the troughs outside and hung up on any available surface to dry. And there is the wood stack to be replenished, as well as great piles of evergreen branches to be cut from the forest undergrowth as fodder for the household animals, and hay to be carried from the barns to the stables.

The Lenten fast begins around this isolated time or a few weeks later, depending on the date of Easter, bringing unmistakable reference points with the steady passing of the six weeks to Palm Sunday, and whenever the weather eases, further preparatory tasks in the fields await, and further sowing. Even in January a start should be made on the pruning of the vines, and there are the first ploughings for the maize and the chickpeas to be done, while February brings the first hoeing of the vineyards and broad beans and the sowing of the chickpeas and lettuces, and there are the gardens to be prepared. There are trips also to be made to the market town for random needs, the fruit trees to be pruned and, later in the month, onions and spring onions to be sown. March ideally sees the end of the first hoeing of the broad beans and the vineyards, as well as the second ploughing for the maize, thus freeing, in April, the women to hand-weed those crops, such as wheat and lentils, which cannot be hoed, and to plant the green beans. Then on the day of the Annunciation (25 March, soon after the spring equinox) the men 'cross (*σταυρώνουν*) the pines', that is to say initiate the tapping season by making a crosswise cut in the bark with an axe.[6] Holy Week and Easter follow at some point in April or a little either side of it—'Easter flowers' refers to lilac which blooms around the time of the Resurrection—and after the lambs and kids are weaned or slaughtered at Easter, the women, in addition to their normal tasks, need also to milk the household animals twice a day and make yoghourt and cheese and pick up the eggs from the hens which are laying well by this time. St George's day on 23 April is regarded as the gateway of summer as is Dimitri's of winter: the sowing of the maize occurs between mid-April and mid-May, and when the weather warms up in early May it is followed by the planting of the rest of the garden crops.

All the time the sun has been strengthening steadily towards the great heat or 'the burning', which proverbially, as already noted, sets in 'at the feast of St Constantine and after' (21 May), and the crops have been coming on fast. In April the lettuces, spring onions and garlic are ready, and from then on everything is a glut, for the great amount of produce is matched only by the speed at which it ripens, so that by mid-June the lettuces have bolted and the broad beans have progressed from being good for eating fresh to having hardened so much that they can be used only for animal feed or for lengthy stewing.

This period through May and into early or late June is the Pente-

[6] This action involves exposing a small amount of fresh wood to allow the resin to flow, and at the bottom of this making a cut 'in the form of a cross' which will guide the slowly flowing resin into the tin that is fixed to the tree below the cut to catch it. The action needed is essentially the same as that which would result in actually making a cross in the bark, although it in fact is incised in such a way as to result in a 'V'.

costal period which again, like Great Lent, carries clear markers of the passage of time: mid-Pentecost on the twenty-fifth day (on which certain kinds of work are avoided to protect against inroads from mice), the forty days to Ascension with its return of the souls to the underworld, and the fifty days to the feast of Pentecost itself. In the spring months as leaves unfurl and wild flowers bloom, and before the haze of summer descends, the sun shines with a clarity which opens long vistas over the hillsides, and the steady increase in the heat is echoed in a sense of fecundity and a steadily increasing tempo of work. In May the vineyards need to be hoed for the second time and the vines pruned of their excess leaves and shoots, the chickpeas need weeding, and the broad beans become ready for the second hoeing, while towards the end of the month the gardens begin to need watering twice a week, there is the maize to be hoed, the oats and vetch to be cut green for animal fodder, and the hay to be cut and carried. There is a wonderful plenty after Easter, with milk and fresh cheese, yoghurt, eggs and occasionally meat; and with spring onions, lettuces, radishes and broad beans, followed by tomatoes, cucumbers, peppers, courgettes, and melons, while the summer evenings are scented from every chimney with the aroma of fresh green beans stewed with oil and tomato.

Then a week after Pentecost, the day of All Saints brings in the fast of the apostles Peter and Paul, whose subsequent feast is on 29 June. Mulberries and cherries ripen from mid-June, and, from the end of June on, the summer garden produce comes into season. This month sees also the end of any tasks left unfinished from May, as well as the completion of the harvesting of the vetch and those oats which have been left for seed, and of the main crops such as lentils, barley, and broad beans which are by now hard and dry. The tasks of June finish with the earthing up of the growing maize stalks against the summer wind, so that all is in order for the moment when the whole village, as one, 'enters in to the [wheat] harvest' in early July—a month known simply as 'The Harvester' (*Θεριστής*).

The solstice, quickly followed by the feast of the birth of John the Baptist, known at this time as St John the Oregano-Gatherer (*Ἅϊ-Γιάννη Ριγανάς*) is now past. From the spring time onwards the increasing pressure of work has been led by the lengthening day, and as the working day outside begins and ends with the sun, so now in the summer the first task falls in the early dawn at four in the morning when the animals must be fetched from grazing, while the last task is the return from the fields and the shutting up of the hens when dusk falls around nine. Tiny children are cared for by the grandmothers at home, or taken to the fields and placed in cradles made with a blanket wound round two ropes slung from the branches, while older children come and help. All the weeks of the harvest are a time of incessant and pressing activity in increasing heat under cloudless skies; however it is during the wheat harvest that this sense of urgency reaches a peak, when almost the entire population from sunrise to sunset is in the fields—the women, bent double and with aching backs, reaping, the men, with hands which became puffy from the strain, binding the sheaves with tough withies and loading them onto the animals for stacking round the threshing floors. During this time the village virtually empties, the only movement within it being the trees stirring in the summer wind, some hens scratching or a dog or a cat wandering, an old person going for water, a child playing, and the men returning at intervals to the spring to water the animals. But for all the intense work this time is not without its festival, and at about the mid-point of the harvest on 20 July the inhabitants of the three neighbouring villages with contiguous boundaries gather together beside a mountain-top church for a two-day celebration of the feast of the Prophet Elias.

Life, however, returns dramatically to the village at the threshing of the wheat, for the circular threshing floors lie around on its very edge, and 'The Thresher' (*Ἁλωνάρης*) is the village equivalent for August, which also ushers in the feast of the *Panaghía* on the 15th. The threshing is done by combinations of families pooling their work animals to tread the wheat as, roped together, they are driven round and round a central pole, treading the grain free of the ear and the stalks into chaff. It is a period which, unlike the threshing of the other crops, is marked by a great sense of occasion and is for the owner of each threshing floor the culmination of the agricultural year, the high point which combines a sense of community with the reassurance of the continuity of life, and which is expressed in an explosion of joy which has been described already. The cycle of the wheat, from seed corn to seed corn, is completed with the winnowing, and this is done by each family separately, whose members walk up and down, two or three at a time, with long-handled wooden spades, throwing the mixed chaff and grain into the air, so that while the grain falls in a heavy golden pile at their feet, the lighter chaff blows away to settle in a tawny mound down-wind. Finally the wheat is collected into sacks, the ground scoured clean of every last grain with brushes of thorny shrubs, and these scourings are sieved and picked clean of any tiny clods of earth and little stones.

With the gathering in of the wheat the tempo of work falls off, for although the numerous tasks maintaining everyday life still go on, and although there are the chickpeas and the maize still to be harvested and a host of minor tasks with the subsidiary crops to be completed, the work now consists less of harvesting than of storing. The feast of the Transfiguration (8 August), and the days round the middle of August which are the time 'of the *Panaghía*' (the Falling Asleep of the Mother of God on 15 August) come when, with life assured for the coming year, there is a sense of peace and fulfilment. At this time, with the tasks in fields and threshing floors completed, there is time for the women to sit in the shade of their verandas, preparing tomato concentrate, boiling figs with herbs, and making *trachanás* (*τραχανᾶς*)—a kind of dried porridge made by boiling together coarse ground wheat and milk, letting it cool and set, and then spreading it on cloths to dry in the sun ready for crumbling up and storing. There are the pulses for the winter stews to be rubbed from their pods, which are by now dry and brittle, walnuts to be gathered and to have their soft green husks removed, herbs for flavourings and herbal teas from the mountains to be rubbed and stored, maize to be prized from the cob—all peaceful occupations carried out in company. Sometimes looms are brought out into the yards and weaving carried on in the mellowing sunlight of the end of summer.

In this type of economy, then, within the overarching cycle of the year, each subsidiary cycle of animal and vegetable growth and fruition dictates the pattern of work, and because each cycle varies in length and timing for each crop, the combination of all these cycles is a practical work of art. Thus (with the exception of emergency measures when the sowing of the wheat is held up by bad weather) the work of the year is dictated by the passage of the sun, the length of the working day by the length of time the sun is in the sky, the day's work by the placing of each living thing in its cycle of life: everything depends on the synchronous ordering of man's activity with the processes of life in the natural world.

11. The snow recedes: 'February brings the first hoeing of the vineyards' (pp. 108–9).

12. *Midzíthres* hung by the house to mature: 'There is a wonderful plenty after Easter, with milk and fresh cheese' (p. 110)... "Your own bread—not one of those miserable town loaves; and wine from the barrel in the store-room, a *midzíthra*, some *féta*, eggs... ". Such a house truly represents the divine plenitude of which it is an icon' (p. 192).

At the same time, while it is clear that those engaging in subsistence living cannot afford to be anything other than relentlessly practical in the way they organize their daily activities, the sacred world is echoed in these activities at every point. So the holy presences of the liturgical cycle like St George and St Andrew cast their penumbra on the natural seasons in which their festivals fall, and it comes about that the season itself is referred to predominantly not by calendar dates but by the activity associated with it or by the sacred presence presiding over it. So 'The Harvester', 'The Thresher', 'the vine harvest', 'the olive picking', are points of time that need no further elaboration, in the same way as the 'great fast', 'the fast of the apostles', the days 'of Christ', 'of John', 'of the *Panaghía*', 'of the Cross', specify known reference points in a common understanding. And it is as a natural consequence of this mutual assimilation of sacred presences, natural conditions, and seasonal activities, that, as indicated above, the beginning of the flowing of the resin is marked by the feast of the Annunciation, the onset of the great summer heat with the day of Saints Constantine and Eleni, and the last burst of fine weather before the winter closes in with St Dimitri.

Thus far the focus has been on the sense made by the cycles of subsistence tasks in forming the pattern of the year, and the liturgical accompaniment has been described only as a pervasive set of associations whose own meanings are as yet inexplicit, though the holy figures are in some way felt to preside over the times and seasons. It is now possible to look more closely at the logic of the sacred year which, interweaving with the turning and returning of the life cycles within the seasons, engenders its own complex and distinctive movement, and in the process speaks of the relationship between time and eternity. Like the natural year, the sacred year contains subtle overlapping rhythms and is reckoned not only in terms of the wheel of the full year running from autumn to autumn, but in terms also of a series of cycles nesting within one another and replicating each other on a greater or lesser scale. Each of these cycles has a different dynamic and incorporates a different rhythm, but each one relates to the others so as to build up in the end a unified and ordered pathway to the mystery of the sacred world.

Easter, celebrating the Resurrection, is the high point of the liturgical year, occupying a unique position as 'the feast of feasts' and forming the centre-piece of a cycle of its own. Easter falls not according to a set calendar date but according to a recondite assessment of the movement of the heavenly bodies of which the first full moon after the vernal equinox is the significant feature. The sacred periods depending on Easter consequently vary with the date of Easter, these periods being the season of Great Lent preceding Easter and the Pentecostal period which follows it. To both of these periods are tied certain saints' days as well as the great feasts of Palm Sunday, Ascension and Pentecost. Thus within the overarching cycle of the year, through which the individual saints' days run in unending succession, the greatest importance is given to this inner cycle whose meaning gives the form and the dynamic to the whole liturgical year.

Great Lent is a period of six weeks to which is added the seven days of Holy Week that end on Easter Sunday, so that it is on the fiftieth day (counting inclusively) from Forgiveness Sunday—on the evening of which Lent begins—that the Resurrection is celebrated. Following Easter, another period of forty days measures the time between the Resurrection and the Ascension, after which a further ten days completes the period to Pentecost. The balance between the two periods before and after Lent is thus exact, although the effect of this exactitude is to show up the sharply contrasting nature of these times. During the fifty days of Great Lent the divine offices are to do with the fall, the separation of man from grace and his enslavement to sin and death. Because of this the period is marked by fasting, by prostrations during certain prayers, by long penitential services which culminate in the Passion services of Holy Thursday and Holy Friday when people may grieve visibly. During the fifty days between Easter and Pentecost, in contrast, the emphasis is on the victory of Christ over hell and the restoration of man to his divine freedom. During this time therefore, not only prostrations but also memorial services are excluded as inappropriate,[7] and it is a

[7] The Homily of St John Chrysostom, appointed to be read at Easter Matins, contains the assertion, 'Christ is raised from the dead and there is none left in the grave', and the village belief in the release of the souls back to earth for the forty days between Easter and Ascension is the folk response to this, as is their custom during this period to refrain from lighting candles for the dead.

time of feasting and joy inaugurated by the customary greeting of 'Good day' on the village paths being replaced with 'Christ is Risen!' together with the answer, 'He is risen indeed!'[8] In this way, while the fifty days of Lent lead the faithful into the desolate lands of the fall, the fifty days of Pentecost following the Resurrection lead them back into the land of the living and, more than that, into the time which foreshadows the redemption of all things and the defeat of death. Thus the period of penitence and expectation in the time preceding Easter is exactly matched by the period of joy and release in the time after it, and the hundred-day period as a whole, returning year after year, recapitulates in miniature the whole history of humanity from the original loss of grace to the descent of the Holy Spirit.

With the completion of the fifty days of Pentecost the world is returned to its normal equilibrium in which awareness of sin, and joy in the gift of grace, are not contrasted but held together in tension, and it is the recitation by the priest of the three long 'kneeling prayers' at the vespers of the Holy Spirit on the Sunday of Pentecost—known to the people as 'the kneeling church'—which mark this turning point. These are prayers at which—unusually for the Orthodox whose normal posture in church is to stand—everyone including the priest kneels, and they contrast particularly sharply with the practice of the previous fifty days in which any posture of penitence such as kneeling or prostrating is proscribed. With these great prayers in which recognition of human sinfulness is balanced with prayers for the illumination of the living and the dead, the period of the risen Christ ends and the gift of the Holy Spirit becomes the liturgical focus; the people are returned to the world in which illumination must be worked for rather than being symbolically, as it is during the fifty days after Easter, already achieved. The world has become again a place which holds not only joy and festival but also penitence and struggle, and the importance of this transition back into the fallen world and the presence of death is so deeply recognized by the people that they say that when these prayers are being said, anyone in fields or forest who cannot attend should also kneel briefly. It is this kneeling which forms the definitive break from the previous period

[8] Ecclesiastical custom enjoins this greeting for the forty days after Easter, but in practice in the villages of the 1960s this greeting was exchanged chiefly on Easter Sunday, with a few people thinking that the practice should continue for three days.

directly hallowed by the Resurrection, and it re-establishes the normal cycle of the sacred year within which the extremes of the human situation—fall and resurrection—are equally emphasized.

The sequence from Lent to Pentecost is thus paradigmatic for the whole year; and just as there is an overturning of ordinary securities by demonic pranks from Christmas to the time when Christ is revealed at his baptism at the Theophany, so the social order is challenged at the beginning of Great Lent. Lent is inaugurated by a three-week period during which the rules for fasting are partially relaxed before, at the beginning of the last of these weeks, meat is abandoned. During these three weeks, a time known as *apókreas (ἀπόκρεας)*—or the time of 'putting away meat'—the Carnival is celebrated on the Saturday evenings and Sundays, when boys and girls cross-dress or masquerade as old, or mad, or drunk, and visit the houses to be treated with almonds, wine, or sweets, while households will gather together bringing and sharing food, and men and women together will sing and dance, spicing the occasion with the rude songs which are only ever licensed at this time. In many villages these activities cease with the advent of Clean Monday (*Καθαρά Δευτέρα*) when the cupboards are stripped of all but the vegetable products which are the fare of the Great Fast. But there are some villages which on this day act as a magnet for people from all around, and although fasting food only is eaten on this day, they are notorious for other ways in which the norms of society are overturned with men dressing up as women, women as men, and people going round the houses with jokes and songs of amazing obscenity. And it is not only in the houses that ribald poems may be rehearsed but 'At the top of people's voices! Out in the square!' in processions accompanied by the beating of drums and the brandishing of phallic symbols of enormous dimensions. With the end of this day, however, quiet descends and order is restored. Great Lent, the longest fast of the year, culminates in the Resurrection and the Pentecostal period, so here as at the period from Christmas to Theophany—that is to say, at the two greatest festal periods of the Christian year—we see chaos and misrule preceding the re-making of the world.

On these occasions, therefore, the anarchic forces inherent in the world escape from their customary restrictions to be openly acknowledged and released, though the linking of this release to the rhythm of the sacred seasons means that they are in due time re-ordered and controlled. The excesses of the Carnival, particularly, find a notable contrast in the long period of abstinence which is enjoined by Great Lent—an abstinence which does not involve food only, but also sexual relations, for to be 'clean' or 'pure' means abstaining from sex on the eves of holy days and before special activities requiring purity such as visiting the bees or making the liturgical bread, as well as for eight days before communion and, strictly speaking, during the Lenten periods also.

The logic of the Carnival clearly gains force from the natural vigour of a people otherwise answerable to a strict code of sexual control in private, and of decorum in public behaviour. But there is a deeper symbolism at work which is to do with the fundamental truth that in a world where the devil is active it is in the nature of things that the forces of creation are continually threatened by the forces of disintegration: moments of great enlightenment are accompanied by moments of great temptation, revelation is accompanied by spiritual danger. In a world full of conflict and therefore of choices, equilibrium once reached is not a steady state but must continually be striven for and continually regained. Further, the *skalikantzoúria* at Christmas and the public license at the Carnival are comic but vigorous representations of dark forces which in fact threaten death. At Christ's birth the threat to his life by Herod is averted and the world tree healed; but at the end of Great Lent the threat actually matures into Christ's murder. At these premonitory moments, then, the power of evil is focused and crystallized into an image of chaos which is acted out in the social world. But the disintegration at these moments is not only contained by the rhythm of sacred time, it is also the prelude to triumphant reversals, as Christ illumines the world at the Theophany and shatters the powers of death at the Resurrection.

The hundred days of the movable feasts centred on Easter thus form one cycle, the quintessential story of the Christian year. However, there is a second cycle, for circling through the whole year from autumn to autumn, and including the three chief movable feasts as part of their round, is the sequence formed by the Twelve Great Feasts. These celebrate the other principal events involving Christ and the Mother of God which together give the teaching of the liturgy on the central Christian doctrine of the Incarnation, the birth of God in the flesh. The particular importance of the Mother of God in Orthodoxy, and the secret of her close pairing with Christ in these feasts, is the intimate part she plays in bringing about this divine birth[9] and in some feasts the accent is on her part, and in some on Christ's, as laid out below:[10]

	Feasts of the Mother of God	*Feasts of the Lord*
8 Sept	Nativity of the Mother of God	
14 Sept		Exaltation of the Cross
21 Nov	Entry into the Temple	
25 Dec		Nativity of the Lord
6 Jan		Theophany
2 Feb	Meeting of the Lord (Presentation in the Temple)	
25 Mar	Annunciation	
Easter – 7		Palm Sunday
	(EASTER)	
Easter + 40		Ascension
Easter + 50		Pentecost
6 Aug		Transfiguration
15 Aug	Falling Asleep of the Mother of God	

Both these two cycles cover the whole year, though one is nested inside the other and reveals in this patterning a particular relationship. With the feast of the Nativity of the Mother of God on 8 September just before the first of the Feasts of the Lord, and her Falling Asleep on 15 August just after the last of them, the Mother of God has five feasts to Christ's seven, thus being revealed as subordinate to her son. But her cycle is longer than his—she is born before him and dies only after his work is completed.

As discussed in Chapter 2, the Nativity of the Mother of God at the time of the renewal of the earth in the autumn, and her 'falling asleep' when the earth sinks to rest at the end of the great summer heat and the completion of the harvest, suggest that the Church has seen in the

[9] Ware, *Orthodox Church*, pp. 257–61.

[10] *Festal Menaion*, pp. 41–2.

seasonal cycle of the earth an appropriate symbolism for the ritual cycle of the Mother of God, and has perceived it as expressing on its own level something of the inner meaning of her feasts. Thus in spite of the strange and often inimical presences that inhabit the wild, and the sometimes pre-Christian colouring in the popular understanding of them, at every harvest time the whole of the natural world is brought into balance with its original undivided nature, and the Christ-bearing role of the Mother of God is central to this process. But if there is a correspondence between the earth and the Mother of God, there is also a correspondence between the wheat and Christ, between the harvest and the eucharist. Christ stands in the same relation to the wheat as his Mother stands to the earth. Not only the Mother of God but Christ also is imaged in the processes of the natural world.

With the cycle of the sun these correspondences are further underlined. They consist of parallels which have been mentioned already in the discussion of cosmic beliefs in Chapter 1, but which need more elaboration at this point.

It has been argued that the Twelve Days of Christmas symbolize a period of uncertainty and ambiguity which coincides with the wavering times of sunrise and sunset: in both the folk understanding and in the Christian discourse, the end of this period marks the stabilizing of the world into a renewed order, and again this coincides with the definitive lengthening of the day. So it is consistent that the feast at which Christ is revealed to the world is filled with images of the sun and themes of light, and that the Theophany, the 'showing forth of God', is described in terms of light. In the village the day of the Theophany itself is known, familiarly, as 'The Lights' (*Τά Φώτα*), that is to say the 'Feast of Lights'. Similarly, in the liturgy of the Theophany, the manifestation of God is, as we have already seen, repeatedly rendered in images of the sun:

> Today the Sun that never sets has risen and the world is filled with splendour by the light of the Lord... Today Paradise has been opened to men and the Sun of Righteousness shines down upon us... Today we have been delivered from darkness and illuminated with the light of the knowledge of God. Today the blinding mist of the world is dispersed by the Epiphany of our God. Today the whole creation shines with light from on high.[11]

[11] Ibid. p. 354.

Further, not only at the Theophany is the imagery of Christ as the light of the world recurrent, but also at his Nativity, where celestial imagery occurs in the *tropárion*, or hymn, of the feast:

Thy Nativity, O Christ our God, has shone forth upon the world as the light of knowledge, wherein those who served the stars were taught by a star to worship Thee, the Sun of Righteousness, and to know Thee the Dayspring from on high. O Lord, Glory to Thee.[12]

Images of spiritual illumination which refer to the sun as the greatest source of physical light in this world thus resonate throughout liturgical symbolism, and they are constantly restated in the texts of the great feasts.[13]

It is clear of course that the principal theme here is not physical light but spiritual enlightenment—the sun is the Sun of Righteousness, the Sun that never sets. But by now it is clear also that, once the finite, mortal, and unstable nature of physical phenomena is restated, there is felt to be no fundamental discontinuity between natural and spiritual realities; the lesser is an expression of the greater, the Sun of Righteousness finds an image of his glory in the sun of the created world. Both the Nativity and the Theophany hold inner resonances with the cosmic rhythms of nature: in both of these feasts the movements in the natural world are seen as, within their limits, expressing the nature of the sacred season.

Again, while the theme of light is most emphasized at the winter solstice and the Twelve Days of Christmas, it is not limited to these days and in fact reaches its fulfilment at Easter. Easter, whose calculation involves, as has been said, proximity to the first full moon after the vernal equinox, is a festival which again emphasizes light. At the equinoxes the sun and moon are equal partners, the full moon being directly opposite to the sun and shedding its light by night to the

[12] *Festal Menaion*, p. 261.

[13] Further examples of Christ being symbolized as light are: at the feast of the Entry of the Mother of God into the Temple, 'The Father is Light, His Son is Light, and the spirit, the Comforter, is Light: for, shining forth as from one sun, the Trinity divinely illuminates and preserves our souls' (*Festal Menaion,* Matins, Entry of the Most Holy Theotokos, p. 178); at the feast of the Meeting of Our Lord, 'Christ the Sun' (*Festal Menaion,* Matins, p. 419); and it is an image used by Christ of himself, 'I am the light of the world' (John 8 : 12).

greatest extent possible, as the sun does by day. These features of the Jewish Passover, historically tied to the Easter season, make it the time of the greatest illumination both of the day and the night. And again the correspondence of the resurrection of Christ with the coming of spring in the natural world has a symmetry which is explicitly celebrated throughout the whole of the Orthodox world on Holy Friday, when the bier of Christ is decorated all over with wild flowers, and on Easter Sunday, when it is the abundant spring produce which marks the end of the fast and loads the festive tables with food.

In this way the imagery of Christ as the light of the world is presented not only in terms of spiritual illumination but also in the iconic correspondence of his cycle with that of the strengthening sun, just as the imagery of the Mother of God as giver of birth is presented not only by her role in the Incarnation but also by the correspondence of her cycle with that of the awakening and falling asleep of the natural world. Christ, born at the nadir of the year and completing his work on earth with the descent of the Holy Spirit at the approach of the high point of summer, is celebrated in feasts which harmonize with the strengthening light. And this is epitomized in the last feast of the Lord in the year, the Transfiguration, when, the harvest completed and the summer at its height, the moment is celebrated when on Mount Tabor Christ's face 'did shine as the sun and his raiment was white as the light'.[14]

The completed sacred story is thus told in both cycles, but the enfolding of the cycle of Christ, the Light of the World, within the cycle of the Mother of God also provides an image of their relationship with each other, one depicted on countless icons in which the Mother of God holds Christ in her arms. While Christ, both God and man, transcends his mother, he also owes his humanity, and in that sense his earthly life, to her. Though Christ comes down from heaven he is, in being born of a woman and in his birth in the harvest corn which becomes his body, nurtured by the earth also.

A final reflection of this symbolism of the sun and of the related cycle of growth and decay is given after the summer solstice in the figure of John the Baptist, referred to in Orthodoxy as 'the Forerunner', who above all the saints appears to have the most specific

[14] Matthew 17 : 2.

associations with the yearly cycle. The last figure of the Old Testament, St John is in Church tradition regularly associated with the Mother of God, the first figure of the New, and the two of them appear, one on either side of Christ, in the icons above the cross beam of the icon screen that divides the sanctuary from the rest of the church. The sacred destiny of St John, exactly six months older than Christ,[15] was revealed early on when he 'leaped in the womb'[16] at the coming of the Mother of God to her cousin's house, carrying within her the unborn Christ; and the relationship between John the Forerunner and Christ is expressed in the feasts celebrating their conception which fall, respectively, on the autumn and spring equinoxes, exactly nine months before their births. The Nativity of the Forerunner on 24 June, as has already been described, is the day on which fires are lit 'for good fortune' as the sun turns back after the summer solstice. Thus the coming of Christ at the moment of the re-birth of the sun at the darkest time of the year is balanced by the coming of the Baptist just as the sun begins to turn back after the high point of summer.

This counterpoise between Christ and the herald of his coming is a key element in the life of the Forerunner. The Christ whom he foretells, 'the latchet of whose shoes', as he says, he is 'not worthy to unloose',[17] is the one who 'must increase' as John himself 'must decrease';[18] and so, correspondingly, in the Gospel the news of the ascendant Christ coincides exactly with John's own approaching death. It is in the last days of his life that he sends to Christ asking him to confirm that he is indeed 'He who should come', and receives the reply: 'The blind receive their sight and the lame walk, the lepers are cleansed, and the deaf hear, the dead are raised up, and the poor have the Gospel preached to them.'[19] The rise of Christ is inextricably related to the fall of the one who came before him, and this relationship finds a precise image in the association of the birth of the Forerunner with the diminishing sun of the midsummer solstice, while the birth of Christ is associated with the midwinter sun which is about to strengthen.[20]

[15] Luke 1 : 35–6.
[16] Luke 1 : 41.
[17] Luke 3 : 16
[18] John 3 : 30.
[19] Matthew 11 : 2–5.
[20] A. Kyriakidhou-Nestoros, *Οἱ δώδεκα μῆνες: τά λαογραφικά* [*The twelve months: folk traditions*], 2nd ed. (Athens: Μαλλιάρης Παιδεία, 1986), p. 77.

Thus, although the reason given by the people for the custom of jumping over fires on the Nativity of St John is simply that it is 'for good fortune', it seems clear that the underlying association is with the solstice. And this in its turn may provide the interpretation for the association, mentioned earlier, of the Forerunner with the collection of oregano. Oregano is a herb which grows wild on the hillsides and has to be parched brittle by the sun before it is ready to be picked, and it is thus doubly associated with St John, destined for the wilderness and beginning his life just after the height of the midsummer sun. The name 'St John the Oregano-Gatherer' expresses these linkages, and oregano-gathering on the mountains becomes on this day associated with the prophet of the wilderness.

St John is in this way linked with the moment which defines the passing of the summer solstice, and this insight in the great tradition provides the explanation for two practices in the folk tradition which have already been briefly mentioned, both involving unmarried girls finding out their 'luck' or 'fate' in marriage. Firstly there is the *klídhonas*, a form of divination which occurs on the eve of the Nativity of St John, and features a bucket of water and a red cloth which is left out all night under the stars. Secondly, the day of the Nativity of St John is the occasion for a divinatory ritual involving a mirror and a well. It will be remembered that a chief characteristic of water is to convey and mirror the unseen world, and that the red blanket, put out all day on 1 May for the ripening of the wheat, symbolizes the sun. Here, then, the sun of St John and water in its divinatory role come together, and though these divinatory practices have, from the Church's point of view, their questionable aspect, the logic behind them is not far to seek, for St John, who recognized Christ while still in the womb and who in the wilderness prepared people for his coming, is the greatest of all the prophetic figures. These village practices linking the sun with divination thus appear to be related to the liturgical understanding of St John, whose prophetic function is imaged in the brilliant sun of the summer solstice.

The cyclic forms which image and commemorate the Christian story do not end with these great yearly cycles however, for they are continued in microcosm down to the week and the day. The month does not seem to have been absorbed into Orthodox imagery—its natural symbolism has already been discussed in Chapter 1; but the day and the week are different, and each in its own way has parallels in the liturgical year and possesses a cosmic dimension.

The initial conception of the week in the Judaic tradition derives from the six days of the creation of the world, followed by the last, the day of rest, which is the Saturday of the Sabbath. To this the Christian tradition adds the Sunday as the 'first and eighth day',[21] the first of the six days of creation, and the eighth day beyond time on which Christ rose from the dead. From this point, accordingly, the tradition then relates the rest of the week to Holy Week, the week of Christ's passion and death, by marking Wednesday as the day Christ was, as the villagers say, 'taken', and Friday as the day he was crucified. Thus Wednesdays and Fridays are days of repentance, while the Lord's Day (*Κυριακή*, from *κύριος*, lord), as both the first and the eighth day of the week, is throughout the year the day of the resurrection. Every week throughout the year is in this way an image of Holy Week, constantly commemorating in miniature the events of the Passion, and every Sunday is an image both of the beginning of the world, and of the triumph of Christ over death and the inauguration of a new creation.

If the parallels between the week and the year are only brought out by liturgical practice, the parallels between the year and the day are immediately apparent since both are governed by the sun. The progress of the day from dawn to dusk, as measured by the villagers in terms of the passage of the sun, has already been outlined, and from the initial 'etching' of the skyline against the early dawn, through the 'bursting' of the sun, its 'fulness' and its midday point, to its 'leaning', 'withering' and 'finishing', the day is ordered not by a mechanical arrangement of hours and minutes but by a flexible response to the growth and waning of the light which orders all things. In this way the village day is, as it were, based on first principles, related always to the reality of the world of natural phenomena, and since this phenomenal world is related always to the sacred cosmos which lies within and around it, the day also has a liturgical dimension.

The principal characteristic of the liturgical day is that it runs not from sunrise to sunrise, but from sunset to sunset—a perception

[21] Alexander Schmemann, *Introduction to Liturgical Theology*, tr. Asheleigh Moorhouse, 2nd ed. (Crestwood, N.Y.: St Vladimir's Seminary Press, 1975), pp. 60–4.

originating in the creation story in Genesis which defines 'the evening and the morning' as being 'the first day'.[22] The effect of this is to see the world not as moving from light to darkness but from darkness to light, and this makes of the liturgical day an image not only of hope but of salvation, for it brings into the present moment the implication of the eventual progress of the world through darkness and error to the revelation of God. The effect of this image of time is that the twenty-four hours of any holy period are inaugurated not on the morning of the day concerned but on its 'eve', and any ritual custom or prohibition associated with a holy day—and there are many—becomes relevant from the time the church bell rings for vespers at 6 p.m. Since every Sunday is a feast and every Wednesday and Friday is typically a fast day, it is easy to see how this liturgical rhythm becomes grafted on to the rhythm of work and rest, and forms an inseparable part of the village understanding of time.

The emphasis on movement from darkness into light in the timing of the liturgical day picks up themes which have already emerged in discussions of the yearly strengthening and weakening of the sun. For not only does the moment of greatest darkness at the Christmas solstice conceal the birth of the Light, as it does in the natural order, but the moment of greatest light at midsummer, which in the natural world carries only the premonition of winter, in the Orthodox understanding is linked with the birth of the Forerunner who is the herald of the good tidings. Thus in the same way as the transitional moment in the cycle of the sun at Christmas holds the promise of the divine Light, so the liturgical day beginning in the evening represents in microcosm the same theme.

This is exemplified in one of the most reverent moments of vespers. At this evening service with which, canonically, every liturgical day begins, the Evening Hymn is always sung:

> O gladdening light of the holy glory of the immortal, heavenly, holy and blessed Father, Jesus Christ. Now that we have come to the setting of the sun, and have seen the evening light, we praise the Father, Son and Holy Spirit, God. It is meet at all times to hymn thee with reverent voices, O Son of God and giver of life, wherefore the world gives Thee glory.[23]

[22] Genesis 1 : 5.

[23] Author's translation; cf. Hapgood, *Service Book*, p. 8.

This hymn—one of the earliest of the Christian church, its origin unknown even in the fourth century[24]—celebrates the 'gladdening light' of Christ, symbolized at vespers by the lit candle which is carried from the sanctuary into the nave, light brought from heaven to earth.[25] Numerous themes are caught up here, but what stands out in the context of this present discussion is that Christ comes into the world at the approach of darkness. Just as Christ is born at the darkest time of the year, so it is in the setting of the sun when vespers is celebrated and in the gathering dark that there lies the promise of salvation.

Further, this theme of light in the darkness is echoed in the Song of Simeon which the order of vespers places towards the end of the service, following the Evening Hymn. Simeon, a 'just and devout man' who had been told he would not die until he had 'seen the Lord's Christ', recognized Christ when as an infant he was brought to the Temple. Lifting him up in his arms and blessing God, he proclaimed:

> Lord, now lettest Thou Thy servant depart in peace according to Thy word, for mine eyes have seen Thy salvation which Thou has declared before the face of all peoples—a light to lighten the gentiles and the glory of Thy people Israel.[26]

Thus the light of Christ is once again celebrated in the evening, as the shadows gather and as Simeon prepares to die. Not only the darkness of the night but the darkness of death holds the light of the divine life, and it is within this scheme that villagers live when on the 'eves' of Wednesdays, Fridays, Sundays and feasts, the lamp in front of the icons in the house is lit, and when, understanding that this is the 'eve' or preparation of the sacred time, they hear the bell ring for vespers and compose themselves for the holy day already begun.

It has become clear that both the tiny cycle of the day and the whole year's Feasts of the Lord have a congruence with the cycle of the sun, but that this relationship is iconic, not one of equivalence. An icon is not the archetype, but partakes to some degree in the nature of its archetype. Thus although the sun is an image of Christ, Christ is

[24] Taft, *Liturgy of the Hours*, p. 38.
[25] Ibid.
[26] Luke 2 : 28–32.

both the sun and 'the Light that shone before the sun',[27] and while the glory of the Father revealed in Christ is celebrated at 'the setting of the sun', he himself is the 'Light that never sets';[28] the light that is lit at vespers as evening falls in fact honours the 'Lord of the light that knows no evening'.[29] The material world is derivative from the spiritual world through which it comes into being.

This theme of the transcendence of the spiritual world has already become familiar from the first chapter, where God always triumphs over the devil in the end and the universe holds an in-built bias towards the auspicious pole, and it is consistent with this that a persistent asymmetry gives always to the spiritual world a slight but significant predominance. Thus while five of these feasts, from the Nativity to the Ascension, emphasize the inter-relationship of the Light of the World with the strengthening sun, the full seven deny any complete equivalence for they run not from solstice to solstice but from 14 September to 6 August; and Easter, the 'feast of feasts', falls not at the summer solstice but at the vernal equinox. The Sun of Righteousness is imaged—has his icon—in the sun of the natural world, but he is transcendent over it. Yet again in the same way the movement of the day, whose natural rhythm is from work to rest and from the rising of the sun to its 'finishing', is counterposed by a liturgical movement which takes the world from darkness to light, transforming it so as to become an icon of the transfiguration of the world at the end of time.

At the same time the transcendent meanings of the sacred year are found to be immanent in every cycle, from the largest to the smallest, which is nested within it. It has already been mentioned that the year of the Mother of God encompasses the agricultural season from its beginning to its ending, while the Year of the Lord lies within her cycle, from the feast of the Holy Cross on 14 September to the Transfiguration on 6 August. In the same way, within the Year of the Lord lies the loss of innocence at the beginning of the Great Fast to the descent of the Holy Spirit at Pentecost, and overlapping this the drama of the life of Christ from Christmas to Easter, and within both of these the seven days of Holy Week from

[27] *Festal Menaion,* Great Vespers, Transfiguration of Our Lord, p. 475.
[28] Ibid. Matins, Transfiguration of Our Lord, p. 487.
[29] Ibid. Matins, The Meeting of Our Lord, p. 422.

the evening of Palm Sunday to the Resurrection. In yet smaller focus lie the recurring cycles of the week and the day, both representing the movement of the world from its creation to its redemption and restoration. In this way these cycles depicting the fundamental Orthodox account of man in the world—his sacred origins, his relationship with his creator and with creation, and his destiny—tell of the inner drama of the human soul through the multifaceted teachings of the same story continually retold, and are constructed very much like the fractal principle found in the natural world.

The fractal principle is one according to which similar patterns are repeated virtually infinitely on an ever smaller (or larger) scale, so that there are nested sequences of a pattern within a pattern, providing endless possibilities of variation in detail, though always held together in intrinsic harmony by the inspiration within it of a single idea.[30] The same alchemy is at work in the nested cycles of the villagers' year, constantly lifting them out of the perceived world of flux and change and reinstating them in a mode of sacred time where eternal truths become visible, or are 're-presented', within the temporal world.

This shift from the temporal to the eternal is an explicit theme of Orthodox liturgy. The Orthodox re-presentation of sacred events is not to do with a sense of time which involves a 'before' and 'after', or which recalls a past event in the present. It is not to do with the past at all. The significance of the fall, for instance, is not as a historical event but as a mythic event which exists as a present possibility that people are free to relate to and take part in again and again. For this reason the figure of Adam, the universal man, is not a separate individual somewhere in the past; it is 'I', the expression of the consciousness of each person present. Thus the Church sees each person as Adam, praying for a return to the paradise from which all have excluded themselves, as in this liturgical text for the last day before Great Lent:

The Lord my Creator took me as dust from the earth and formed me into a living creature, breathing into me the breath of life and giving me a soul: He honoured me, setting me as ruler upon earth over all things visible, and making me companion of the angels. But Satan the deceiver, using the serpent as

[30] James Gleick, *Chaos: Making a New Science* (London: Heinemann, 1988), Ch. 4 *passim*.

his instrument, enticed me by food; he parted me from the glory of God and gave me over to the earth and to the lowest depths of death. But, Master, in compassion call me back again.[31]

Again, as the fall is not limited to the historical past but is an action of the soul which exists for everyone as a present possibility, so in the same way the liturgical offices of the Church are not commemorations of the past but rituals opening the path to a world that exists now in eternity. And in this way it is not we who call the divine persons of the sacred world into our time but rather they who call us 'back again' into their world beyond time. Thus the liturgy describes itself as celebrating not past memories of the temporal world but present realities of the heavenly one, and this is stated again and again in the Orthodox Eucharist, the Divine Liturgy, where the consecration of the bread and the wine is preceded by numerous references to the origin of the earthly liturgy in the heavenly liturgy described in the vision of Isaiah.[32] The first of these references is the prayer said by the priest before the moment when, carrying the book of the Gospels aloft, he enters the sanctuary from the nave through the Royal or Holy Doors in preparation for the Gospel reading. This prayer is explicit:

O Master, Lord our God, who hast established in heaven orders and hosts of angels and archangels for the service of thy glory: grant that, together with our entrance, there may be an entrance of holy angels, ministering with us [*συλλειτουργούντων*, literally, celebrating the liturgy with us], and with us glorifying thy goodness.

[31] *Lenten Triodion*, Vespers, Sunday of Forgiveness, p. 168. Another example from the same service (p. 169): 'O precious Paradise, unsurpassed in beauty, tabernacle built by God, unending gladness and delight, glory of the righteous, joy of the prophets, and dwelling of the saints, with the sound of thy leaves pray to the Maker of all: may He open unto me the gates which I closed by my transgression, and may He count me worthy to partake of the Tree of Life and of the joy which was mine when I dwelt in thee before.'

[32] Isaiah 6 : 1–8. Allusions to the text of this vision focus on the first three verses in particular: 'In the year that King Uzziah died I saw also the Lord sitting upon a throne, high and lifted up, and his train filled the temple./Above it stood the seraphim: each one had six wings; with twain he covered his face, with twain he covered his feet, and with twain he did fly./And one cried unto another, and said, Holy, Holy, Holy, is the Lord of hosts: the whole earth is full of his glory.'

The liturgy on earth is in this way a reflection of the liturgy in heaven, and cannot take place without it.[33]

In further emphasis that the world of time derives in this way from the world beyond time, the liturgical texts say frequently of any sacred event celebrated that it happens 'today', 'now'. The limitations of the temporal world inevitably involve the Church in rituals which are cyclic and consecutive rather than simultaneous and eternal, but each sacred event celebrated by the Church, because it occurs in the eternal present of the divine world, is felt to be one which occurs also in the present moment of our time. Similarly, the actors in the liturgical drama are not the clergy and the congregation, who are merely participants; the actors are the sacred persons of the eternal world who draw the people of the Church into their own reality. Thus the event celebrated at any particular moment of the liturgical year reflects a timeless divine action in eternity. In the Feasts of the Lord, for example, it is Christ himself who is the celebrant, acting in the present moment according to a particular timeless mode of his being; and through their participation, to the extent that they are able, the human and natural world reflect his action in time. A text from the feast of the Transfiguration is typical:

Today Christ on Mount Tabor has changed the darkened nature of Adam, and filling it with brightness He has made it Godlike./Shining forth with the light of the virtues, let us set foot on the holy mountain that we may

[33] *Divine Liturgy of St John Chrysostom*, tr. Liturgical Translations Committee, Diocese of Sourozh, Russian Orthodox Church in Britain and Ireland (Oxford: St Stephen's Press, 1999), p. 31. After the prayer mentioned comes the singing of the thrice-holy hymn—a reference to the angelic song in Isaiah's vision—which precedes the reading of the Gospel. The second half of the liturgy then begins almost immediately with the singing of the Cherubic Hymn (text in n. 4, p. 141) in which the present congregation is said to represent, or to image (the Greek word means 'to be icons of'), the cherubim—the order of angels which, after the seraphim mentioned by Isaiah, are traditionally regarded as the closest to God in the heavenly liturgy. And at the beginning of the consecration of the bread and wine the Eucharistic Prayer again places the action of the present liturgy in the context of the cherubim and seraphim, singing the thrice-holy hymn (for the text of this fourth reference, see p. 416 below).

gaze upon the divine Transfiguration of the Lord./The sun which makes the earth bright sets once more; but Christ has shone as lightning with glory upon the mountain and has filled the world with light.

Thus the liturgy of the Orthodox Church presents Christ in a particular timeless mode acting in the present moment, now, 'today', and this eternal action is reflected in time both on the human level and on that of the natural world.[34]

This divine action which draws each 'I' into the 'I' of Adam, and which places the liturgy of man and nature in dependence on the heavenly liturgy and sets it in the 'today' of eternity, is rendered in Orthodoxy by the term *anamnesis*, meaning, literally, memory, or recollection. But the memory referred to is not the memory of the past, it is the memory of present realities that the soul has instinctive knowledge of but has 'forgotten': *anamnesis,* in accordance with the term's original Platonic usage, is the soul's unveiling of eternal truths which are present within it but which have become obscured. In the words of an Orthodox theologian: 'During the Liturgy, through its divine power, we are projected to the point where eternity cuts across time, and at this point we become true *contemporaries* with the events which we commemorate.' This comment applies particularly to that part of the liturgy which is actually called

[34] Quotation from *Festal Menaion,* Small Vespers, Feast of the Transfiguration, p. 469. Further examples can be found in any feast, e.g. for the Nativity of Christ: 'Thou hast come forth from a Virgin, neither angel nor ambassador, but the Lord himself made flesh, and to me who am man Thou hast brought salvation. Therefore I cry unto Thee: Glory to thy power, O Lord./Let creation now cast off all things old, beholding thee the Creator made a child. For through Thy birth Thou dost shape all things afresh, making them new once more and leading them back again to their first beauty.' (*Festal Menaion*, p. 212.)

And the Easter Canon begins: 'It is the day of Resurrection, let us be radiant, O ye peoples; Pascha, the Lord's Pascha; for Christ our God hath brought us from death to life, and from earth to Heaven as we sing the triumphal hymn./Let us purify our senses and we shall behold Christ, radiant with the unapproachable light of the Resurrection, and we shall clearly hear Him say: Rejoice! as we sing the triumphal hymn./For meet it is that the Heavens should rejoice, and that the earth should be glad, and that the whole world, both visible and invisible, should keep the feast; for Christ, our everlasting joy, hath arisen.' (*The Pentecostarion*, tr. Holy Transfiguration Monastery (Boston: Holy Transfiguration Monastery, 1990), Easter Matins, p. 28.)

(in both Greek and English church usage) 'The Anamnesis', which leads into the consecration of the bread and wine, though it is true also of the liturgy in its entirety. Thus the word *anamnesis* reflects, within the high tradition of Greek Orthodox culture, the whole sense of continual recovery and return which enables worshippers to participate in the timeless world of the Kingdom of God.[35]

In the little tradition of the villages, of course, the intellectual architecture of this way of seeing time is not expressed; rather it is present as an undefined set of assumptions which has brought into being a time world which is accepted without reflection, where the villagers think of days and seasons as belonging, in this present moment, to guardians of the heavenly world—the summer solstice to St John the Oregano-Gatherer, the 'little summer' of October to St Dimitri, the first day of the year to St Basil, first of bishops. The dark days of Christmas and the eating of pork and sausages are the days 'of Christ'. The Risen Christ in the spring-time of Pascha comes when lambs are ready to be weaned (or slaughtered) and the lactating animals milked. August days of the harvested earth and the Falling Asleep of the Mother of God are the paradigmatic time 'of the *Panaghía*', to be contrasted with her other names and modes of being, for example at the Annunciation in the spring when the pine trees are signed with the cross for the start of the resin season, or in the autumn when she is the *Panaghía* Half-Way-Through-the-Sowing. And, as will be elaborated later, the villagers live imaginatively in this view of time in ways which are unmistakable—when they grieve anew over the recently crucified Christ lying before

[35] For a summary of essential liturgical aspects of the term *anamnesis* see Ware, *Orthodox Church,* pp. 281–2, 286–7. The latter passage is the one which cites the quotation given, which is from Paul Evdokimov, *L'Orthodoxie* (Neuchâtel and Paris: Presses de Taizé, 1959) p. 241. *Anamnesis* (stress on 'e' in English, second 'a' in Greek) originally passed into Christian usage in the tradition quoted by St Paul (1 Cor. 11 : 24–5) and St Luke (Luke 22 : 19, 39) of Christ's words at the last supper, where, in immediate association with the eternal present of Christ's words, 'This is my body... This is my blood', there follow the words, 'Do this in remembrance [*anámnesin*] of me' (*εἰς τὴν ἐμὴν ἀνάμνησιν*). This version of the tradition was enshrined in Orthodox liturgy in the words leading up to the consecration of the bread and the wine in the Liturgy of St Basil, and thus has given to this part of the liturgy the term 'The Anamnesis'.

them and refrain from eating because 'Christ died today', or rejoice anew in his resurrection in words which bring his defeat of death into the present moment: 'Christ is risen!'[36]

In the liturgy then, the timeless reality of the sacred world enters into the cycles of time, and, since the liturgy within the Church gives here its inner pattern to the whole of life, there is felt to be a congruence between the sacred and the seasonal year in village experience, and the name of a sacred person is set as a transcendent sign over the appropriate season. And it is also, as this chapter has tried to show, this holy world whose energies are felt to be, albeit inconstantly and incompletely, reflected in the natural phenomena of the fallen material world, so that there are times when the sun, or the fruitful earth, or the wheat harvest, participate to some degree in a corresponding eternal reality and make present their divine archetypes. And just as the cycles of time in the village nest in and overlap with one another, so these sacred presences, together with the events which they initiate, the liturgical times which they bring about, and the natural seasons into which they enter, all re-enact variants of the same story; and through this continual return to the same story with the experience of time that it involves, there occur in the villagers' lives moments, however fleeting, when they are caught up into a dimension which is 'both now and ever'—a world beyond time. It is this unity of perception which brings together the liturgical cycle with the agricultural seasons, and which is expressed in the comment, made in the context of talk on the progression of the festivals to Easter and beyond and the glories of the opening buds of spring: 'The year runs in harmony with the faith.'

[36] pp. 361–2, 365–9, 376-81.

5
WORK AND BREAD

THE patterning of sacred time in the Greek villages has been described, in broad terms, as being governed by the seasonal cycles and the liturgical ordering of the Orthodox Church. It is now time to detail some of the ways in which this broad pattern enters into daily life by being continually replicated in a multitude of diverse forms down to the minutest area of man's activity. These forms are in essence quite simple and consist in a variety of injunctions and prohibitions applied to certain kinds of activity at certain times. However it is because they are simple that they are effective, for they apply to the most fundamental components of daily life—eating, resting, working, sex—and so are able to link the complex demands of subsistence living to a parallel scheme of meanings in the incorporeal world, and add up to a deep and many-faceted teaching about man's relationship to his own kind, to nature and to God. Central to these activities is the growing, harvesting, giving, and receiving of food—prototypically of bread—and this chapter discusses how, through the basic activities of working and eating, these sacred rhythms are brought into the daily lives of the people and made real.

The organization of the labour by which the household is created and maintained is itself ruled by both practical and symbolic considerations. To a significant extent the work on the land is undertaken as a common enterprise, man and wife and, where possible, the children also, working together in the fields and with the flocks, with only the forests kept as the exclusive province of the men. Conversely, the men's work enters the realm of the household in that men take care of building and repairs to the main structures, they cut and carry wood and, when necessary, take the household sheep and goats with them to graze. However, in spite of this overlap, a broad division of labour between men and women can be roughly represented by a single image: the women in the houses, the men on the land. To the women exclusively, except in case of sickness or other emergency, fall the multitudinous tasks of maintaining the household and all within it, so that they become identified with the house itself, their virtue and their diligence being synonymous with both its upkeep and its honour, and this central role is epitomized in the oft-quoted saying: 'Without the housewife the house cannot function.'

Thus it is the women who care for the children, the guests, the old, and, in the numerous memorial rituals, the dead. It is the women who mend, spin, sew and weave, making a huge array of clothes and household furnishings ranging from shepherds' capes, so heavy and thickly felted as to be wind- and water-proof, to blankets and carpets of varying thicknesses patterned in red and black; rugs woven from strips of old clothes; wool coverings for beds and walls in a variety of rich dark colours of matched reds, blues, mauves and browns; bags, sacks, and cushions; tablecloths, napkins, pillowcases, sheets and bedspreads with lace edgings; and local costumes seamed with ornamental but hardwearing stitches, the festival versions ornate with deep hems stiff with silk embroidery and worn with richly-decorated ceremonial aprons. It is the women who carry the water from the spring, clean the houses and regularly whitewash the sooty fireplaces, care for the animals of the household, make cheeses and yoghurt in season, wash the clothes and thump the rugs free of mud at the spring, collect wild greens in the winter and in summer tend the village gardens, they who cook on iron tripods over open fires, and bake the huge round loaves in the mud-and-brick ovens built in every courtyard.

To all these tasks the man—said to be 'a guest in the house'—is a stranger, returning home only for food and refreshment when he has finished with his own labours; but these labours also are essential to the house and underpin all that goes on in it. No less onerous than those of the woman but merely different from them, the man's labours lie outside the house in the public world of politics and economics, of buying and selling, and of responsibility for care of the land and the production of the raw materials for the family livelihood. The men will work all day in the steep forests collecting resin into increasingly heavy tins, they will cut wood and day after day labour with the ploughing, and the heaviest tasks about the house and the land are their business. And as well as upkeep of the house and repair of barns and steadings, good decisions for the farm and steady and responsible negotiation in business for the care of his family fall to the man. In this way, although it might be said that the work of the women is more central to the family in that it concerns the immediacies of the household, that of the men is thought to be harder since it involves ultimate responsibility for the family's basic survival; it is the men's strength on the land which supports the dedication of the women in the houses, while at the same time their efforts are subject to the unpredictable character of natural phenomena—rain, hail, snow, flood, pests, heat and drought—in a way the women's are not. So it is thought that the man is justified in being easily upset and prone to anger since the burdens ultimately fall on him, while the woman, said to 'want everything ready', is fundamentally spoiled for she, finding herself short of any raw material, is depicted, with an inimitable and imperious gesture of head and hand, as simply demanding of the man: 'Where is it?' The balance of power in the household depends on these realities: the man has a right to chide or even to strike his wife if, for instance, the food is not well cooked or not ready on time; but if the basic materials are lacking then she is the one with the right to reproach.

Within this pattern a further division of labour operates, and on similar lines. Practical considerations appear to determine much of the allocation of work on the land so, as indicated above, the men customarily do heavy tasks such as the ploughing, binding and carrying the sheaves at harvest time, or cutting, carrying and splitting wood, and the women those like weeding and reaping that are lighter and considered 'fiddly' (*λεπτὴ δουλειά*). But at times this is infused by a gender symbolism according to which only men, for instance, being 'pure',[1] deal with pure creatures such as bees, and only men handle the plough and sow any seed scattered broadcast, though women may break with a mattock the clods on newly-turned ground and sow seeds such as broad beans and maize which are dropped one by one into the furrows following the plough.

Work on the land is hard, requiring strength, patience, and endurance, and being typically described as 'tyranny' and 'tribulation', and the connection made between the nature of this life on the land

[1] From the involuntary shedding of blood as in women's monthly periods, or after childbirth. Blood (see Ch. 7) is viewed as a life principle.

and the sin of Adam, mentioned earlier, is openly asserted; and when the people say, as they do, when struggling with the plough, 'Look how we struggle to get our bread', or 'We serve under tyranny—that's how God has ordained it', the background to their thought is the fall and its consequences. But if the fall is a living theme in the imaginations of the people, so also is the garden of paradise which was man's original home, and this also figures as an image binding together ideas of the house, of fecundity, and the completion of toil—of a house in fact which is, as already quoted, a garden. Thus the re-establishment of the nourishing bond between nature and man, which is the culmination of the toil and sweat of the preceding year and is revealed in the overflowing corn bins and barns and storerooms stuffed with produce, bears, for all who share this cultural inheritance, implicit images of the unfallen world.

For all the talk of the 'anguish' and 'tyranny' of the work with the fields and forest it is, then, not for nothing that it is the work of the men which is singled out as being, in various renderings, 'blessed', 'blessed by God', or having 'a blessing'—a state of affairs which is at times explicitly contrasted with the lot of women: 'The man has a blessing and goes to the fields, the woman with the spindle is cursed.' The reason given for this is not one which refers directly to the fall; rather it is explained that day by day men see some result for their labours, whereas the women have no sooner completed their tasks than they have to do them all over again. However, the link with the fall, though submerged, is present. Firstly, the periodicity of the various tasks on the land, in contrast to the endless recurrence of the tasks in the houses, is tantamount to a brief lifting of the curse on that work which is conceptually the province of men, and its reinstatement in the paradisal world of God-given completion and fulfilment. Secondly, it is the annual rather than the daily cycle of work which, through each harvest, brings back nature into that relationship with man which existed before the fall. Thus it is again the work of men rather than that of women which more closely expresses the recreation of the original relationship between man and nature which was his in the beginning and which, year by year, through obedience to the discipline of toil and sweat laid upon him by the curse, brings about, briefly, his redemption from it.

If the work of men throughout the year, however, carries with it echoes of redemption, the work of women is caught up, in a different way, in an identical movement, achieved in their case not through following the rhythms of nature but through a complex ritual patterning of activities within the house.

Wednesdays and Fridays have already been noted as days on which the women's tasks of washing and baking are prohibited,[2] but these are not the only prohibitions relating to them. As noted earlier, the ritual day is inaugurated on its 'eve', or 6 p.m. on the preceding day, and on the eves of Wednesdays and Fridays a range of women's work comes under interdiction. Use of scissors and needles is prohibited, as is any work with wool—the loom and the spindle, as is said, being particularly 'heavy' (*βαρύ*) or 'serious'—although these prohibitions are not carried over into the day itself. Men's work does not come under any prohibition at these times, though this situation changes with Sunday, the day of the Resurrection; here a similar prohibition concerning household tasks for women on the eve is followed throughout the next day by a complete avoidance of any work, for both men and women, other than that necessary for the maintenance of the homestead. These prohibitions, although not a part of the formal ecclesiastical canon, have nevertheless been accepted by the Church in rural Greece as legitimate tradition and have been known to be enforced by confessors; thus together with the other ritual prohibitions relating to work, these customs have the nature of a sacred ordinance.

Although men's work on Sundays—and, as will be seen, on other important feast days—is classified alongside that of women as prohibited, it is generally speaking the women's work, as it is the woman's fast, which is the most critical. The woman in fact is not only the material sustainer of the house but its spiritual guardian also, and this is encapsulated in various rhymes relating to the weekday prohibitions: 'Friday [fast for] your husband, Wednesday [fast for] your children/And if you have neither husband nor children, protect your good self'; 'Wednesday and Friday, don't cut your nails/On Sunday don't wash your hair, if you want to make progress'; and in a more baroque rendering: 'Friday your husband, Wednesday your children/Lest your eyes on Sunday drop out into your apron.' It is clear here that it is to the woman in her own right, as well as to the married woman with dependants, that the prohibitions apply; but the woman is typically a per-

[2] See p. 44.

son with others under her care, and the main thrust of the prohibitions reinforces this emphasis. It is a woman's responsibility for others which singles her out as the one who must keep the sacred observances, and it is for this reason that a certain lifting of the restriction on handwork may be allowed to unmarried girls, 'because they haven't got dependents'; or again because they 'aren't married and haven't any children'.

The rule of abstinence from work does not, somewhat naturally, apply throughout the four long fasts, but nor yet is it confined only to the weekly rhythm of Sundays and the eves of Wednesdays and Fridays, for it is also invoked for the numerous festival days which occur as high points of the festal cycles of Christ, the Mother of God, and certain of the saints. Of these, some are classified as 'light' or lesser feast days, others as 'serious' or important. The lesser saints' days are marked on their eves by the usual prohibitions on women's work, although these differ from the Wednesday and Friday prohibitions in that they extend throughout the following day, that is to say on the saint's day itself; however, on the important holy days not only is the women's work in the house prohibited but also the men's work in the fields. Here again, even though this pattern of ritual prohibitions on work embraces, on the great festivals, the work of the men, particular emphasis is laid on the sacral responsibility of the woman, for it is on her purity, spiritual as well as moral, that the safety of the house rests. Thus when on a lesser saint's day a man cuts his hand on an axe, it is his wife, busy all day (in this instance weaving rag rugs) who is immediately held accountable. 'Look, Ioannina has been weaving all day and Ioannis goes and cuts his hand on an axe![3] The man goes out with an axe, he cuts wood or he ploughs a field, but the woman in the house must keep the saint's day.'

While it is only on the great festivals then, and on Sundays, that men must refrain from work, women have to be alert to the implications of their activities throughout all the various cycles of the sacred year, and are thus drawn into a complex ordering of tasks which makes considerable demands on their resourcefulness and self-discipline.

The reasons for the spiritual protection afforded to the household by the women's observance of these customs may at first sight

[3] Women are frequently known by their husband's name, hence Ioannina means the wife of Ioannis, Periklina the wife of Perikles, and so on.

be obscure, and it may seem that this restriction on women's work at sacred times is fundamentally a practical measure as a charter for relaxation in a world where women have such diverse and arduous tasks to perform. But this is to miss the point of a way of life in which the security of the house rests on the habit of painstaking and unremitting work by all its members. Thus the women, used to the constant accompaniment of handwork during any quiet moment and ever conscious of the material needs of the household, in fact find it difficult to sit hand-idle on long winter evenings, and even with the diversion of the evening visiting they sometimes complain of boredom and have difficulty in keeping awake. In such a context, the prohibition on work demands not so much relaxation from feminine tasks as their due ordering—a sense of propriety and a degree of household management revealed in the slightly self-deprecating self-comparison: 'Today, God forgive me, I knew it was a feast day [the eve of that of the Archangels Michael and Gabriel], so I worked hard all day and now I sit [doing nothing].' While some women, that is to say, might be unprepared and, as it were, caught out by the ringing of the bell for vespers, others would have organized their day around the advent of the quiet evening. The effect of the rule is, then, to concentrate the mind during the day so that, even though the force of industrious habit makes this initially difficult and rather dull, the evening is left free from the customary preoccupations.

In addition to this element of order, there is a further meaning built into the prohibition on work, and this relates to household economics and is revealed most clearly in attitudes to violations of the rule. In one case a woman who had had five daughters to marry used to work all through the nights even at prohibited times. However, she did this, she said, with faith, asking for forgiveness, and after the first two daughters had married she never again broke the prohibition. Again, for an amateur to practise spinning for its own sake, rather than for the purposes of furnishing the house or building up a dowry, is thought pardonable. Thus the rules relating to avoidance of work at sacred times embody an instruction not only to be ordered and careful in the running of the household, but also—except in cases of extreme need—to leave on one side all concerns relating to winning a livelihood. Popular practice on the eves of sacred times can be seen as related to a certain detachment from the preoccupations of daily living, and in this way corresponds exactly with a particular moment of preparation in the liturgy. At this moment, just before the consecration of the Holy Gifts of the eucharistic bread and wine, which is the most sacred point in the liturgy, the congregation, who, in the words of the Cherubic Hymn that is being chanted, 'mysteriously represent the cherubim', is exhorted to 'lay aside all earthly care'.[4]

The liturgy itself is the principal feature of any festal day, and, excepting the fast days of Wednesdays and Fridays, and occasional days such as that 'of the Cross' which have their own sacred dynamic, it is the coming of the festal day which prompts the cessation of work on the previous eve: all feasts have the liturgy as their central point and all are prepared for in this way. Thus the laying aside of all earthly care in the liturgy is precisely and concretely reflected in the cessation of economic activities in the home on the previous evening, and it points to the reason for this cessation: preparation for the eucharistic mystery in the liturgy of the feast the next day. In the period of waiting on the evening before, the women implicitly recognize their proximity to the eucharist in their custom at such times of lighting the icon lamp in front of the household icons; and although the cessation of handwork causes them to yawn and gossip, or complain of boredom, the presence of the lamp is a constant reminder of the coming feast.

There is also a further connection with the eucharist, for the cessation of women's work on the eves of holy days is accounted for by an image drawn explicitly from bread: 'They say that Christ and the Mother of God are eating up there as we are eating down here, and that if you use a needle or pointed thing you pierce Christ, and if you work with wool their bread is full of wool.' Here a correspondence is set up which involves the meal in the earthly household and the feast of the holy figures in the sacred world, so that the meal in the home, imaging the feast of the divine persons in heaven, images also the liturgy at which the consecrated bread is broken and distributed. The house, the church, and the heavenly world thus correspond to one another, the lesser, like the cycles of time, nesting in

[4] The Cherubic Hymn runs: 'We who mysteriously represent the Cherubim, and sing the thrice-holy hymn to the life-creating Trinity, let us now lay aside all earthly care, that we may receive the King of all, invisibly attended by the ranks of angels, alleluia, alleluia, alleluia.'

the greater; and it is not fortuitous that the distaff which, together with the loom, is thought to rank as the most ritually charged of the prohibited feminine tasks, is not only the symbol of the feminine role but also the tool in folk tradition characteristically carried by the Mother of God.[5]

Hence there is a potential for disorder in women's work: it has no natural bounds of night or of seasons to give it periodicity, it is never finished, it is connected with the accumulation of dowries which are a perpetual source of concern, and for all these reasons it can easily infringe on the time for the sacred mysteries. Thus it is logical that men's work, as cited above, is said to be 'blessed', while 'the woman with the distaff is cursed'. The symbolic value given in this way to woman's work carries additional resonances of the irresponsibility of Eve, through whom the nature of work in the world outside paradise became as it is. Woman's work, as an expression of woman's nature, carries a potential for disorder and disproportion which needs continual ritual reordering if it is not to 'pierce' Christ, disrupt the peace of the Holy Family, and bring danger to those under her protection. While the man is free to 'go out with an axe or plough a field', because night or the season will bring his work to fulfilment, the married woman, with the irresponsibility of Eve always a present possibility, must subject herself and her work to the discipline not of the seasons nor of the market-place, but of the sacred persons who protect her family and sanctify her home. And that this is a discipline, rather than merely a welcome relief from work for those normally overworked, is underlined in the fact that the cessation of work must be observed not only on the eves of the feasts but also on the eves of every Wednesday and Friday (symbolically days of mourning for Christ's capture and crucifixion).

The fast at these times illuminates the nature of the prohibition on work, for it reveals it to be related to an ascetic purpose, which is to bring people to a deeper state of preparation for the penitential day that lies ahead. In the same way the cessation of work on the eves of feasts must be seen also as a kind of fast, for its purpose is

[5] In the icon of the Annunciation Mary is normally shown holding a spindle, because she is engaged in spinning the yarn for her weaving of the new veil for the Temple. In the hymnological tradition the veil represents Christ's flesh. My thanks go to Bishop Basil of Amphipolis for this observation.

identical, which is to bring people to a deeper state of preparation for the feast that is upon them. Abstaining from feminine work at these times is therefore not a luxury but an ascetic undertaking, and the achievement of this order in feminine work thus carries with it not just a preventive but a redemptive potential in that, reversing the irresponsibility of Eve, it reverses also the action of the fall and recreates the harmonious relationship with the sacred world which was by Eve's action so disastrously interrupted.

This correspondence between the exhortation of the Cherubic Hymn to 'lay aside all earthly care' and the prohibition on women's work also reveals an extra dimension to the nature of the 'blessedness' which is a property of the work of men, for this work, ruled by natural rhythms which bring along periods of rest as well as periods of labour, already participates, as it were, in that dimension in which earthly care is laid aside. Obedience to Sundays and certain saints' days is necessary to integrate this experience fully into sacred life, but by its very nature the work of men involves the first step of periodic release from particular anxieties. Women's work however, entailing endless involvement in repetitive and essential tasks, conducted in many cases by firelight and lamplight as well as by the light of day, lacks this natural balance, and the insistent injunction to them to subordinate these tasks to the sacredness of the time redeems their work from possession by the world and achieves in it the blessedness already attributed to that of the men. In the way in which both men's and women's work is understood, therefore, it is apparent that a direct parallel is being made between liturgy and life—between the centredness enjoined on the faithful at the singing of the Cherubic Hymn, the blessedness ascribed to the work of men, and the necessity for regular periods of withdrawal from worldly concerns in the work of women. And because of this parallelism it becomes possible to read off from the liturgy what in daily living lies behind the various prohibitions on work at these times. In the liturgy the exhortation to 'lay aside all earthly care' comes at the point of deepening concentration when the awaiting congregation, in the words of the singers, 'mysteriously represent the cherubim' who, as it is said later, with the angels and the seraphim, attend upon God in their tens of thousands. The singers, as the voice of the people, then continue: '... that we may receive the King of All, invisibly escorted by ranks of angels.' The purpose of the laying aside of earthly care within the ecclesiastical setting can therefore also be seen as the purpose written into the custom enjoining the laying aside of earthly care during sacred periods in the home, and the receiving of the King of All is central to both. Man must work if he is to live; but this is not the only truth, for in its due time this work must give place to rest and recollection and to the understanding that behind the work of man lies the work of God.

If the patterns of work are in this liturgical way rescued from their customary characterization as tribulation and integrated with the search for the kingdom of heaven, the same is also true of the way in which the chief product of work—food—is shared and eaten; and one of the most important series of customs governing these meanings, underpinning the liturgical year and giving a continual movement to the weeks and years, is the alternating pattern of fast and feast.

This basic patterning of the fast marks out both separate days and extended periods. Wednesdays and Fridays, as the days respectively on which Christ was taken and crucified, are throughout the year, with rare exceptions, kept as fast days, inaugurated, as already noted, by abstinence from handwork and the lighting of the icon lamp on the preceding evening. And there are, in addition, four extended periods of fasting of between two to seven weeks each. Two of these fasts fall in the winter—the Nativity fast which covers the forty days before Christmas, and the Great Fast which covers the fifty days before Easter. The summer fasts consist of the Apostles' fast, which begins the week after Pentecost and ends on the feast of St Peter and St Paul on 29 June, and the Dormition fast, which covers the two weeks preceding the feast of the Falling Asleep of the Mother of God, on 15 August.

In the Orthodox understanding the fast extends to all behaviour, and, as noted earlier, this applies not only to the desire for food. Thus sexual continence is enjoined at times of fasting, for instance the eves of holy days and in particular the eves of Sundays and the main saints' days during lenten periods, and for eight days before communion; and while within Orthodoxy this is related to the search for freedom from the passions and the movement towards a certain independence from the demands of the flesh, it is also directly related to the descent of man into sin through the fall. Thus fast and feast are complex disciplines which involve a whole range of human behaviour and in this way relate and identify the nature of the sacred times with the normal concerns of everyday life.

The fast from food in the Orthodox Church consists in abstinence from all animal products involving vertebrates, that is to say in refraining from eating meat, eggs, fish, cheese, milk, and so on, to which, in the strict monastic fast, is added abstinence from oil and wine as well. In one instance also—before the Great Fast—there is also a preparatory three-week period leading up to the full fast. The first week allows meat on every day including Wednesdays and Fridays; during the second, meat may be eaten although the normal fast days are observed; and during the final week, known as Cheese Week, meat is not allowed but other animal products may be eaten, and again the Wednesday and Friday fasts are relaxed. The first day of the full fast begins on the first Monday following, Clean Monday, when all the abstentions come into force.

When the full Orthodox life is lived in the Greek villages the fasts from animal products are observed in all their severity, kept by all, even by children and even in times of hunger. So punctilious is this observance that a child who, milking the animals on a fast day, through inattention takes a mouthful of milk, will instantly spit it out. But if the fast is incumbent on the faithful, so also is the feast. It would be unthinkable, for instance, for the celebration of the Resurrection to occur without the Easter feast in the early hours of the morning. In the same way the killing of the Christmas pig is an event ordained by God—'much food and few days, that's how God has made them'; and the killing of the pig is an act which straightforwardly identifies the season with the birth of Christ—'it puts one in mind of the victim of a sacrifice', in the words of one person, and is done, in the words of another, 'because Christ was born'.

The feast is, then, an act of reverence as much as is the fast, and this duty is nicely exemplified in the story of a village saint, Philip the Poor, whose day on 14 November in village reckoning immediately precedes the Christmas fast like his namesake the Apostle Philip. This story goes that Philip slaughtered his only plough animal so as to be able to keep the feast on the day of his patron saint, answering his anxious wife with the assertion, 'God will provide.' The next day, when his wife rebuked him, saying, 'What will we do, old man, now that we want to go and plough and we have no plough animal?' he answered her again in the same vein, and when they went down to the stable, there was the cow once again munching at her stall. The comment of one narrator points the moral: 'He had faith, you see.'

Neither eating nor not eating, therefore, carry in themselves moral connotations; the connotations are given to them by the nature of the time to which they are related. To feast during the fast would be a sign of indiscipline if not of greed; to fast during the feast would be a sign of inappropriate concern for worldly wealth and an insufficient trust in God. Particularly during Great Lent, but to a lesser extent during the lesser fasts, fasting symbolizes a recognition of man's fallen state and the taking up again of the ascetic journey back to his origins before the fall—an understanding beautifully phrased in the Saturday of the Dead preceding the Great Fast: 'Lead me back again to thy likeness/refashioning my ancient beauty.'[6] Feasting is the appropriate response to the climax of this journey in the reintegration, however briefly experienced, of the fallen world with that paradisal world which is man's true inheritance—just as in a later chapter the feast of food on the Easter tables is an icon of the feast of joy which is given to the faithful at the Resurrection.[7]

Fasting and feasting are, therefore, different moments on a single continuum: both fasting and feasting are sacred activities, and the contrast between the two is not between profane and sacred, still less between secular and sacred, but between two different modes of the sacred—penitential and celebratory, fallen and redeemed. In both modes, that of penitence and that of joy, the aim is identical and only the focus differs, for the aim is reintegration with the paradise of the unfallen world, while the focus shifts according to whether what is being expressed is man's distance from that paradise or his closeness to it.

The existence, then, of fast and feast involves two dimensions of the use of food—what is eaten and when it is eaten—and the very existence of ordained fasting and feasting indicates a value placed on food which challenges the pre-eminence of personal will and material convenience and sets up a tension between the demands of the physical world and those of the spirit. The placing in the year of

[6] *Lenten Triodion*, Evlogitaria of the Dead, p. 128.

[7] See pp. 380–1.

the fasts elaborates this point and indeed adds a further dimension, once again emphasizing the pre-eminence of the spiritual world, for while two of these fasts fall during the winter and bring about a natural balance whereby for significant periods scarcity in the natural world is echoed by asceticism in the spiritual one, two fall in the summer when food is plentiful. Thus the existence of the summer fasts precludes any easy argument attributing the fast to the working of natural economics, for no one in a subsistence way of life can miss the paradox of fasting at a time when milk is flowing freely, hens are laying, and cheeses are being made every day. At these times there is an evident disjunction between the natural and the spiritual law which recalls the periodic asymmetry between the material and the spiritual worlds already noted. And again the implication is identical—that the spiritual order, although on the whole interweaving harmoniously with the natural order, nevertheless underpins and is superior to it. In the fasts, and particularly in those fasts which occur during periods of abundance, the pre-eminence of the sacred law is asserted over natural appetite and worldly self-interest; while in the feast—typified in the story of Philip the Poor who risks ruin in order to celebrate his saint's day—lies the obverse of the same point. Taken together, the combined message of the injunctions both to fast and to feast is that both the use and the renunciation of material things has a spiritual dimension, and that the aspect of life which is dependent on economic expedience and physical necessity is, no matter how important, subordinate to the divine Word by which men also live.

The work on the land which produces the food, and the eating of the food itself, are, then, activities which are ordered in such a way as to recognize the needs of both body and spirit, integrating temporal actions with symbolic meanings, and releasing these actions into a dimension of experience which involves far more than the simple struggle to survive. The wheat harvest and the symbolism of wheat have already been briefly discussed — the spontaneous outburst of rejoicing in the meal on the threshing floor and the hospitality of *rakí* and honey puffs freely offered to passers-by, together with the use of wheat as flour not only for the bread of the household but also for the bread for the eucharist, and as grain in memorial food for the dead and the saints. Wheat is thus a food which pre-eminently unites the physical and spiritual worlds, material and immaterial brought together in a single substance, and it is because of this that bread, above all other food and in all sorts of different forms, is used to define and to express the meaning of the great variety of ceremonial occasions.

First and most basic of these ceremonies is the family meal, especially the cooked meal eaten in the house, for this involves not only material sustenance but also a communion between all the individual members of the house and between the house and all those elements which have brought it into being—the land which produces the food, the forefathers from whom the land was inherited, and the sacred world on which all depends. No meal begins before everyone is gathered, sitting round on stools at the low tables set in front of the fireplace, where the single copper pot has been on its tripod over the flames, and always a good wish or blessing is given by the householder—'good appetite', 'welcome', or very often 'All-holy Mother of God, come and let us eat together'. Both at the beginning and end of the meal the sign of the cross, made by all present, acknowledges the source of the life that is given them, while on the table is evidence of family toil on family land—usually a stew of vegetables, or beans, chickpeas or lentils, little glasses of wine, perhaps cheese, and, in season, salads of greens gathered from the wild, tomatoes, cucumber and lettuce. But whatever else might vary, always without fail one of the great round loaves is produced, signed briefly with the sign of the cross, and cut generously into wedges or slices which are piled up on the table and eaten by everybody as an accompaniment to the meal.

At the end of the meal when the plates are taken away the larger pieces of bread are collected to be kept for a future meal or given, often as their only food, to cats and dogs. After this, the tablecloth is gathered up from the corners to preserve all the remaining breadcrumbs, and these are given to the hens. Bread is never thrown away—'It comes from the ground, it is given by God, it is our chief food, it becomes the *andídhoro* (ἀντίδωρο).[8] In the universal saying 'one must honour bread'

[8] The *andídhoro* is what remains of the bread from which the eucharistic bread is cut, and is given as blessed bread after the liturgy.

it is understood that it must be eaten, not wasted, and in particular it must not be left on the ground to be trodden underfoot.

Bread then is in the most basic sense the food of man. Very often during the course of work outside it is virtually the only food, eaten in large quantities, accompanied only by a little cheese or some olives, and draughts of water from, if possible, a nearby spring. It will be remembered that the definition of superlative water is that it creates a hunger for 'three great loaves'. Thus to eat bread is to live, to live is to eat bread, and this is enshrined in the phrase 'to eat bread' which is used not only to indicate 'we are eating a meal', but also, in a different sense, of old people. In this context of old people it is a phrase which involves a series of nuances, from 'I have eaten my bread', in the sense of 'I have lived [and am now ready to die if I have to]', to the more frequent meaning of someone who is in a sense living too long: 'He [or she] eats bread [but cannot work].' Thus to live does not just mean to eat bread, it means to work to produce that bread: to eat without working means that a radical balance has gone astray.

If the growing and harvesting of the wheat is a part of this process, so also is the baking—an arduous and recurrent task involving considerable skill if a series of perfect loaves are to be produced regularly in all conditions of temperature and humidity. For its rising, *prozými* (*προζύμι*)—a piece of naturally-leavened dough kept aside from the previous baking—is mixed with the new batch, and large loaves are pummelled and kneaded and set to rise in the separate compartments of a long wooden trough. When the bread has risen for the second time, the beehive-shaped mud oven, that is set in every yard, is fired—using dead brushwood left over from the evergreen branches cut as winter feed for the animals—and on its becoming hot enough, the glowing embers are raked forward to the mouth of the oven with the use of a long pole, and the floor of the oven cleaned of ash with a dampened mop head made of strips of material. Each loaf is quickly scored with the letters I X, the initial letters of *Ἰησοὺς Χριστός* (Jesus Christ), pierced with the knife top and bottom, signed—with a quick motion of the hand—with the cross, and placed with a long-handled paddle on the oven floor, the mouth of which is then banked up with the glowing embers, and closed on the outside with a sheet of tin.

The sign of the cross is used in all sorts of activities, but bread is distinguished by being actually marked with the initials of Christ; and in this and in its 'piercing'—an action specifically avoided on certain sacred times because of its resemblance to the piercing of Christ—there is more than an echo of the Orthodox liturgy.

The bread that is used for the eucharist is stamped with a seal patterned in the form of a thick equilateral cross whose central square, which is called the Lamb, bears the first and last letters of the two words Jesus Christ (ΙΗCΟΥC ΧΡΙCΤΟC[9]) followed by the word 'Conquers' (ΝΙΚΑ). The right and left hand of the Lamb are designated as if the Lamb were Christ, facing the priest—the 'right' hand of Christ thus being on the priest's left:

'right'	IC XC NIKA	'left'

Further squares on either side of the Lamb bear symbols representing, on the Lamb's 'left', the nine orders, one of angels and eight of saints, and, on the Lamb's 'right', the Mother of God (ΜΗΤΗΡ ΘΕΟΥ), indicated here by her first and last letters in Greek, ΜΡ ΘΥ, while above and below the Lamb are squares identical to the Lamb, but designated for the living and the dead respectively.[10]

		Square for the living		
'right'	Square for MP ΘΥ	IC XC NIKA	Square for the saints	'left'
		Square for the dead		

[9] C is an old form of S, which is written as Σ in modern Greek script.

[10] This interpretation is found in the *Ἱερατικόν* [Service Book] (Athens: Ἀποστολικὴ Διακονία τῆς Ἐκκλησίας τῆς Ἑλλάδος, 1998), p. 99, but it is also common practice to treat the square below the Lamb as representing both the dead and the living, and to treat the square above the Lamb as a reserve Lamb, in case the square in the centre is damaged while it is being cut out.

The loaf with this seal, called a *leitourgiá* (*λειτουργιά*), liturgical bread, or *prósphoro* (*πρόσφορο*), bread that is 'offered' to Christ, is, during the rite of preparation (*προσκομιδή*) which takes place before the liturgy, taken by the priest who with a little implement in the shape of a lance cuts out the 'Lamb'—the central square of bread which represents Christ. This he does by making four incisions—on the 'right', the 'left', the upper part and then the lower part of the 'Lamb'—accompanying his actions with quotations from Scripture: with the first incision, 'He was led as a sheep to the slaughter'; with the second, 'And as a blameless lamb before his shearers is dumb, so He opened not his mouth'; with the third, 'In his humiliation justice was denied him'; with the last: 'And who shall declare his generation?' Then with the words, 'For his life was taken up from the earth', he severs the Lamb from the lower crust of the loaf. After removing the Lamb from the *prósphoro*, the priest places it upside down and makes in it a deep cross-wise cut saying, 'The Lamb of God, which takes away the sins of the world, is sacrificed for the life and salvation of the world.'[11] Inverting the Lamb again so that the seal is uppermost, the priest places it on a flat metal dish (the paten) and pierces it in its 'right' hand side, saying, 'One of the soldiers with a spear pierced His side, and forthwith there came out blood and water. And he who saw it bare record and his record is true.' After this, particles are taken out of the other sections of the seal for the Mother of God, the nine orders of saints, and for the living and the dead, and are placed around the Lamb on the paten.

The explanation given by the villagers for the piercing of the household bread, top and bottom, carries no reference to the liturgy, for it is said to be 'so that it shouldn't rise too much'. However, in every other way this household bread, marked with the initials of Christ and pierced top and bottom with a knife, bears a striking resemblance to the bread of the liturgy, marked, similarly, with the initials of Christ and pierced top and bottom with a spear. In this commonplace action by the housewife therefore, it seems possible that there is being commemorated, however briskly and with however practical an explanation for the piercing of the bread, the sacred actions of

[11] Two phrases are sometimes added to this sentence—see *Ἱερατικόν*, p. 95—but these additional phrases are disputed, and some authorities reject them.

the priest in the rite of preparation which precedes the liturgy. At any rate, at the meal at which this bread is eaten, the communion which takes place is one which has already been said to image the divine feast in heaven, and so is on its own level an image of the eucharist itself. In this way the eucharist is revealed as perfected in the liturgy but already present at a lower level and enacted throughout the whole of life. And while this implied correspondence between the bread for the meal and the bread for the eucharist is not explicitly referred to, this correspondence appears to be part of the people's implicit symbolic universe, as witnessed by their commonplace reference to wine as the blood of Christ and bread as his body.

If this symbolic parallel is true of the household bread, still more is it true of the liturgical loaves baked by the women for the liturgy. The maker must not be menstruating when she makes the liturgical bread, though this does not apply in the making of the household bread, and in addition she must be 'pure' in the sense of not having had sexual intercourse for eight days. The piece of dough kept back from a previous baking which acts as 'starter' for the subsequent batch must also be taken from bread made when the maker was pure. In addition, as already described, the bread for the liturgy—like the household bread—arises as part of a communion, a direct relationship, with the land itself. It is the product of the householder's own toil, won from the earth and harvested by his own hand.

The procedure for baking the liturgical bread differs in certain respects from that followed for bread made for the household—the flour is sifted twice (the flour for ordinary bread being sifted only once), passed through a finer sieve than that normally used, baked for a shorter time, and the top imprinted with the large wooden seal as described above. The result is a dense, neat, round loaf, smaller, paler and flatter than the robust household loaves, and it is this liturgical loaf which is given in to the sanctuary[12] before the beginning of the liturgy. The women do not necessarily bring such a loaf to every liturgy, but they will give one on their men's name days or on other days of their own choice, and three or five on the great memorials commemorating family members. So at every celebration of the liturgy several women

[12] The sanctuary of an Orthodox church is the area around the altar, usually separated from the body of the church by the icon screen.

will be seen going to the sanctuary, each one carrying some pieces of incense in a twist of paper, a little bottle of communion wine, a small amount of money, a loaf of liturgical bread wrapped in a blue and white cotton napkin, together with a candle. Pieces from the seal impressed into one or more of these loaves are used for the eucharist itself, the other loaves being blessed in the rite of preparation, and then cut up into small pieces for the *andídhoro,* blessed bread, which is lifted over or touched against the cup of the sacrament after the consecration, indicating that it is related to the sacrament, though at a lower level; and it is then given out to all the congregation at the end of the liturgy. So even if the housewife's offering is not actually used for the eucharist itself this does not diminish the significance of her action, for this lies in the giving of a gift which is then blessed. In their periodic offering of the liturgical loaves the individual households are therefore related directly to the Holy Gifts in the action of the liturgy, and when these loaves are offered as *andídhoro* at the end of the liturgy, these households stand alongside Christ himself as the hosts of a symbolic meal eaten by the community as a whole.

Bread, then, in this scheme of things, possesses a multidimensional symbolic nature, and it is for this reason that it is bread which is the food used, in numerous different forms and under numerous different designations, to mark a great variety of ritual occasions. In addition to the liturgical bread described above, there is a further bread, *ártos* (ἄρτος), which the women make for the church. These are always made in fives, in memory of the five loaves and fishes, and they are given to the church on various occasions—chiefly on occasions such as the patronal festival (of the church or of the household), the feast of the Three Hierarchs, in fulfilment of a vow, or after the sacrament of confession. These are loaves wider than the household loaves but not so deep, baked with sugar and aniseed and much lighter in texture, and they are set out on a table in the nave and blessed by the priest at some point before or during the liturgy and then are distributed, after the *andídhoro*, to the people.

In addition to the breads mentioned above is a special festive bread, *pítta* (πίττα), which is made with a little oil and decorated with modellings of dough and which features with appropriate variations at many occasions. The baptismal *pítta* is decorated with shapes of flowers, vines and growing things; for the dowry celebrations the bridegroom brings a *pítta* which has its dough enriched by an egg and its top brushed with honey and, together with a cross, is decorated with modelled flowers, with a fresh rose or other flower being placed in the centre. The 'bridegroom's *pítta*' at a wedding is similar to that for the dowry, and for the wedding celebrations the mother-in-law also makes a another specially decorated *pítta*, which she scores into four, six or eight pieces, that is given to her new daughter-in-law as she prepares to enter her new home. Again, the harvest meal on the threshing floor is distinguished by the special *pítta* described in Chapter 2, while New Year's day, the feast day of St Basil, is celebrated with the *vasilópitta* (*βασιλόπιττα*) or St Basil's *pítta*.

The *vasilópitta* and the bridegroom's *pítta* are made basically in the same way as the harvest bread, that is to say, with a little oil in the baking dish and the bread after baking being rubbed with honey and sprinkled with sesame seeds; but the *vasilópitta* differs in its decoration, for this is done with modelled dough impressed on the surface of the *pítta* in patterns representing the type of living made by the household. This can vary, up to a point, according to the inclination of the housewife, but in the case of a smallholder owning no flocks but two horses the following example is representative: the top of the *vasilópitta* is crossed overall with two long sausages of dough, then edged all round with a circle (for the threshing floor); in each of the four quarters are worked, in turn, designs of a) a plough, two horses, and a man with a whip, b) and c) designs of a horse on the threshing floor, and d) a mattock. This is finished off with bits of fig and whole walnuts in their shells, and patterned all over with hollow indented circles made with a reed 'for everything good'. In the *pítta* itself is baked a piece of straw, a piece of a vine, and a coin, all of which bring luck to the finder. A *vasilópitta* such as this, baked with wheat flour and oil, including within it money, representations of wine and animal fodder, and decorated with the figures of the landowner, his horses, the mattock, and the plough, and with the symbols for 'everything good'—all held within the circle of the threshing floor and protected by the cross—is said to 'have the smallholding in it', and is an image not only of life, but of a livelihood.

In addition to the various forms of *pítta*, there are made at certain celebrations little festive breads moulded in different shapes, principally for children, called *kossónes* (*κοσσόνες*) which are decorated with walnuts and figs for New Year, and baked with a hard-boiled egg set in the top, white at Christmas, red at Easter. And for children also are baked, on special occasions, little *kouloúria* (*κουλούρια*), circular bread rings, which they particularly enjoy.

Bread, then, celebrates at every meal the completed work of man and God, and in the great festivals it is used to mark the event and distinguish its nature at turning points in the life cycle. And while it features at the great events of joy and celebration, it is no less important at funerals and memorial services at which food for both the living and the dead is a central theme, and huge quantities of flour are used.

For the memorial services for the dead, of which there are five in any one cycle (see Chapter 9), five liturgical loaves are baked, one for the eucharist which together with the four others is sent into the sanctuary. But in addition to this, a great quantity of breads called *psychónia* (*ψυχόνια*), soul loaves, or *kommátia* (*κομμάτια*), pieces, are baked, which are made with a little oil and formed either in one piece in large open copper trays and incised into diamond shapes before baking so that they can, after baking, be easily divided, or else shaped separately into tiny loaves, each one crossed with a fork and sealed with a small seal bearing the central letters of the liturgical seal—IXNK, Jesus Christ Conquers. These breads have various purposes: they are taken to the houses, together with wheat and wine, to announce a forthcoming great memorial; they are distributed at the end of the memorial service and at the memorial meal of the funerals of the married dead; while in cases of the unmarried dead, though *kommátia* are made, trays of *píttes* replace the *kommátia* normally given at the end of the service. At all funerals, any remaining *kommátia*, as well as *píttes* if they are made, are given to all the guests from other villages as they depart. Remembering that in such a society the journeys of these guests are on foot or on mule or horseback, often over mountainous paths and perhaps in the gathering dark, such a gift of bread has considerable meaning. And given that many of these visitors from other villages are in certain respects 'strangers', with all the significance that such a person carries,[13] this gift of bread for sustenance on the journey home is itself a sacramental act.

In the rituals of death, therefore, as in those of life, gifts of bread are a form of communication, a language, for expressing the various

[13] See also Ch. 6.

nuances of any event. For children the language changes, and the 'pieces' are replaced by sweetened *kouloúria*, the little circular breads which, as mentioned above, the children enjoyed in life. For the young unmarried dead the *pítta*, before being cut into squares, is decorated with imprints made with a branch—usually a bracken frond—and the background filled in with impressions made by a matchstick or, more usually, by the teeth of the long implement used for stretching weaving as it lies on the loom. After baking it is sprinkled with a sugar solution which soaks into the crust. It is hard to avoid the impression that the imprinted fronds, among the seed-like impressions made by the matchstick or the teeth of the stretcher, are to do with the idea of the tree of life and its fertility, and that in this bread lies the sweetness of the life that has been cut off, and the fruitfulness that has never been realized. Memorial food brings 'joy' to the dead who on these occasions mysteriously feast alongside the living, and the sweet and patterned bread for the unmarried dead must therefore be seen not only as a statement of what has not been on this earth, but as bringing a special kind of consolation to them in their new dimension of the other world.

Bread, then, never losing its relation with the liturgy and its inner nature as the body of Christ, and predominant also as the staple of physical existence, is the supreme symbol of life. It is the food which not only nourishes the individual and celebrates the life of the household, it also celebrates and defines the great rites of passage and links the whole community together in acts of sharing and of hospitality which find both their origin and their completion in the eucharist. In this way it carries a universal symbolism at the same time as being capable of taking on and expressing the character of a great range of events—mourning or celebratory, fast or feast. Bread is food in the most profound sense, crossing the boundaries between grief and joy, matter and spirit, and being a chief medium of commensality such that a natural invitation to an unexpected guest who finds his hosts eating is: 'Come! We are eating bread!'

Commensality has two fundamental forms—sharing, and hospitality. The basic act of sharing which underpins all community life, the family meal, has already been described, but this is not the only such action, for there is at the other end of the scale a sharing which stretches far beyond the family to involve the entire community. It occurs on rare but significant occasions, its focus being the festival day of any one of the tiny churches which scatter the hillsides around the village, and when it does occur it is an occasion of an extraordinary collaboration.

In many of these churches the celebration of the saint's day is relatively simple and consists of attendance at the liturgy in the morning, often preceded on the previous day by vespers and on some occasions by an all-night vigil attended by the women. But one or two of these churches—for reasons connected with the history of the village, the importance of the saint of the dedication, the situation of the church or the timing of the saint's day—can hold a much greater place in the common life and provide the occasion for what is essentially a giant party in the open air. Present at these gatherings there may be not only the inhabitants of the village whose church it is but the inhabitants also of two or more of the adjacent villages. These churches, more or less remote and very small, may be visited occasionally by people who for some reason of their own wish to light a candle there and perhaps clean them up, but at this annual liturgy they are revivified. The intervening year will have brought the building into a state of some neglect and a few days before the saint's day a group of women set off over the hills with brooms and buckets, brushes and cloths, whitewash, matches and oil, and, having filled their buckets at the nearest spring, will set to work cleaning away the accumulated debris of dead leaves and mouse droppings, sheddings from the rafters, the odd hornets' nest. The work takes about a morning, and by the time they leave the place is renewed, bright with whitewash, swept and garnished, and the icons glow in the light of the little flames burning in the fresh oil of the lamps.

If the dedication of the church is particularly important, and if it occurs in the summer, a group of women may spend the night of the 'eve' of the sacred day sleeping on the floor of the church in preparation. The action really begins the following morning however, when mules and donkeys are laden with a great array of items. Vast cauldrons and a range of cooking implements are secured on the wooden saddles, together with home-woven napkins and tablecloths, with plates, glasses and cutlery, containers of wine and bottles of *rakí*, with bags and sacks of goat yarn stuffed with bread and oil, cheese, olives, meat and pasta. Once all this has been done, and with a great air of festival, the village empties for the countryside.

The liturgy begins early and ends before ten. By no means everyone can cram into the tiny church and the majority will sit around talking in the sunshine outside, on occasions being harangued by the priest for making too much noise. But all will have fasted since awaking, refraining even from a drink of water, and all will gather round at the end for the final blessing and the distribution of blessed bread, and after this everyone combines to set out a great feast. Groups of families gather together to lay out long tablecloths on the grass with piles of bread and plates of cheese and olives. The meat and pasta, provided from church funds and cooked in cauldrons over open fires, is distributed, wine poured from goatskins and water brought from the spring nearby. When everyone has eaten as much as they can, the dancing begins, the steps traditionally set by the different modes and rhythms of the songs sung by the dancers or by music from local players, or sometimes from gypsies who with their fiddles, guitars, and bass clarinets, tour the village festivals. As they dance the dancers may be treated to sips of *rakí* by a man standing in the midst of the dance with a large container offering tiny glasses to the people as they circle around him. The music and dancing at these events, on the harsh baked grass of the parched fields or in the green of forest glades, are fired by enormous energy and by the spontaneous eruption of a joy and optimism too often cramped by the hardships of daily life, so that the words often used to describe the spirit of the festivities are particularly appropriate, for the music and dancing are said on these occasions to 'raise up the universe'.

Quarrels and disagreements may not be absent from these occasions—they may indeed be provoked by them as people get fired by wine or dispute how long a particular group should lead the dance. But for the event to take place at all the general spirit of competition has to be shelved and be replaced by a willingness to cooperate in the celebration of a real common life. And these occasions can act, also, not only to bring together the inhabitants of one village but those, as noted earlier, of two or three, when churches located on the borders between land belonging to different villages bring together great gatherings which can last for two days at a time.

These great occasions of sharing, then, result from a basic understanding of community life and flow back into it, for in them the generous giving of labour and food and the coming together as one body under the protecting presence of the saint, bring about, for however brief a moment, the reintegration of a world fragmented by sin; and, mindful of the sacred universe in which all live, it is perhaps not for nothing that these occasions occur normally outside the village in the 'paradise' of growing things.

In the village, it will be remembered, the press of society combines the security of human company with the bedevilment of human greed and envy; in the wild the world of nature combines the purity of an innocent creation with its vulnerability to demonic attack. These categories of wild and socialized are normally more or less in opposition; but at these open air festivals, as at rare events like the threshing of the wheat, they are united, and the best of both worlds meet and merge in a single act of affirmation. The daily contentions of village life sink into second place as the customary inward orientation of the separate houses is refocused and the separate families join in large groups and take part in the round dance, 'kin group with kin group'. In this moment, when cooperation is asserted over competition and holiday over toil, a kind of reconciliation is achieved not only between people and their neighbours but also between the villagers and the natural world in which the celebration is set.

In the story of the fall, the nature of work, along with the entire predisposition of man's appetites and relationships, is conditioned by his alienation from God, and this, it will be remembered, brings about a situation in which bread becomes stones and winning a livelihood becomes a matter of 'blood and sweat'. Nevertheless, as egotism and rebellion was the cause both of the fall and of the tyrannous nature of work, so, in the patterns of thought described in this chapter, the antithetical action of subjecting that work to sacred times and sacred meanings—festal or penitential—makes of work an act of obedience to the divine law, through which the earth again becomes bread, and bread the life of man and the body of God.

Within this frame of reference work itself can become holy, like the bread which is the end product of this work. And bread is not merely a metaphor, it is, in the Orthodox sense of the term, an icon of this process; it does not 'stand for' this redemption of the curse, it already takes part in it; it does not, in the eucharist, represent or take the place of Christ, it becomes Christ's gift of himself to his people. Bread thus becomes a composite symbol of enormous power: in the work needed to produce it, it is an image of obedience; in the completion of the wheat harvest on the threshing floor it is a symbol of the true harmony between the house and the natural world; in the growing of the wheat and the baking of the bread it is a symbol of the symbiosis of the work of the man in the fields and the woman in the house; in the contrast between the everyday loaf, the decorated *pítta*, and the various breads associated with death, lie the difference between fast and feast, celebration and mourning; in the bread of hospitality and of festival lies the reconciliation between the house and the outside world; and in the bread of the eucharist is the gift of union between God and man.

The critical element, however, in all these relationships, is work—work both of man and God—and it is because of this that bread and work cannot be separated. It is this that accounts fundamentally for the persistent value placed on growing wheat for the house rather than earning cash and buying bread,[14] for in the many-stranded relationship between God, man, and the world, an essential link is short-circuited and then broken if man abandons the land, goes elsewhere to work for money, and with that money buys his bread.

Through the medium of bread then, gained by the sweat of man's brow, the eucharist, the family meal, and the great acts of sharing and giving described above, bring together themes of work and festival, and reveal festival not as the antithesis of work, but as its apotheosis. Work, carried out in obedience to the divine command, has as its fruit the bread of reconciliation and hospitality, and it is in this context that the unavoidable and tyrannous work of subsistence living is redeemed from the customary connotations of the Greek word for work, *dhouleiá* (*δουλειά*) which means, literally, 'slavery', and brought into the realm of *leitourgía* (*λειτουργία*),[15] which means public or communal work or service, hence the communal service of God, the 'liturgy'. In this light the ritual prescriptions and prohibitions with which this chapter has been concerned can be seen as having come into being so as to make of the commonplace and laborious tasks of everyday living a constant series of liturgical acts.

[14] See du Boulay, *Portrait of a Greek Mountain Village*, pp. 36–7.

[15] Only the accent distinguishes *leitourgiá*, the bread made for the consecration, and *leitourgía*, the Divine Liturgy itself.

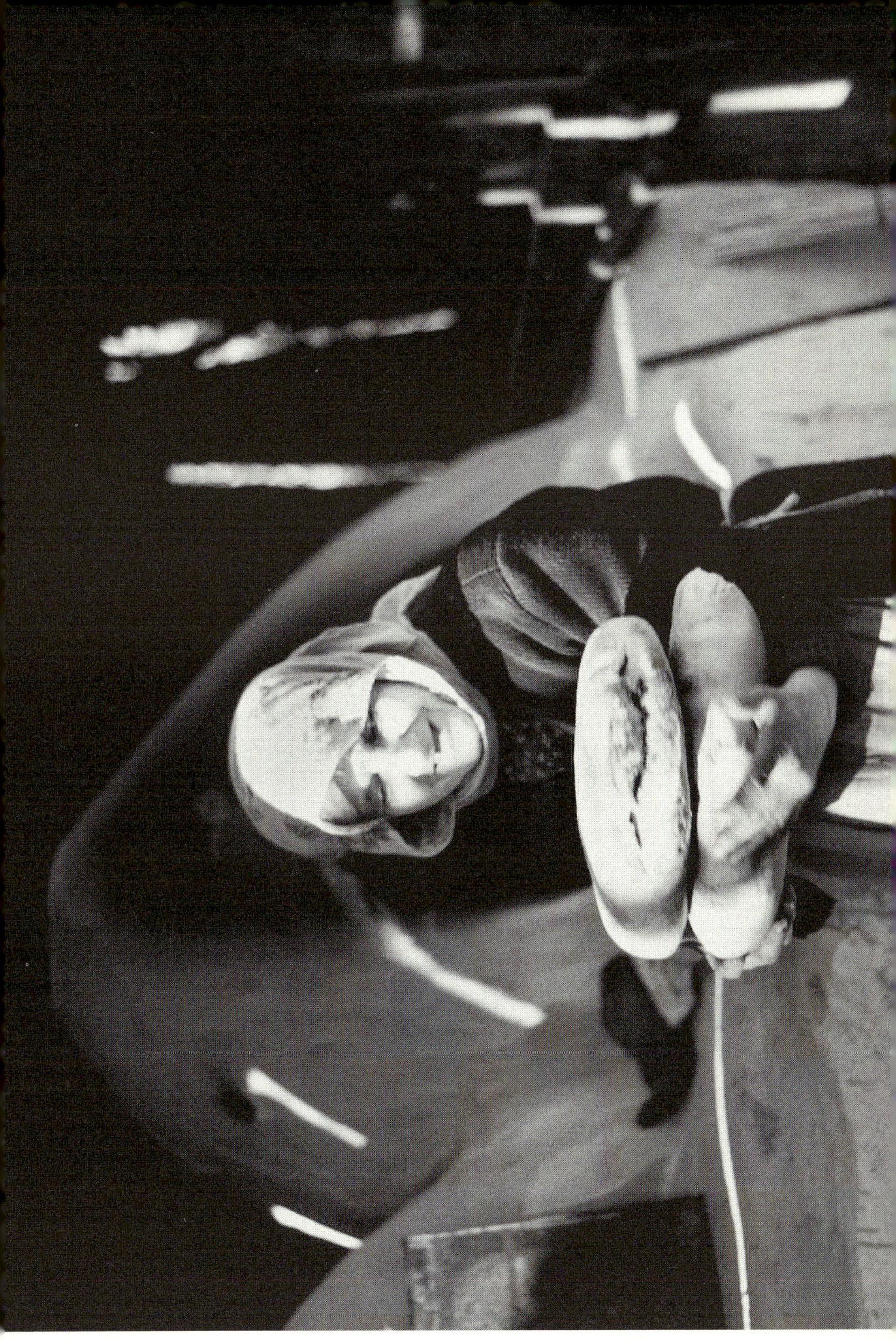

13. The household bread: 'Always without fail one of the great round loaves is produced, signed briefly with the sign of the cross, and cut generously into wedges' (p. 148). Behind is the bread oven, which is set in the yard and has its own roof.

14. Before the feast day of a mountain church: 'These churches, more or less remote and very small, may be visited occasionally… but at this annual liturgy they are revivified' (p. 157).

6
THE HOUSE AND THE STRANGER

IN the ordering of work to allow for quiet recollection before the feast, and in the baking of the bread for the family meal, the last chapter showed that the action of the woman in the house bears strong correspondences with the action of the liturgy in the church. This parallelism between the house and the church is critical to understanding the absolute loyalty to their own household of the members which inhabit it. For it is in the context of each individual house, where practical tasks are inseparable from symbolic meanings, that all that is best and most creative in life is lived out, and it is this assurance of ultimate value which can knit the household so profoundly into a single unit with a single centre. All are involved in the task of creating this house where love, trust and mutual support are to be found, where children are born and thrive—the house of village song and celebration, the 'paradise' of the saying already quoted. Nevertheless, even though the household is an entity to which everyone—great and small—contributes, it is the woman to whom is given the domain of the house, and she who is at the heart of the life-force contained within it. The presence of the woman and the life of the house are indivisible, and this gives rise to axioms such as 'it is the woman who holds the house together', and its converse, also already quoted, 'without the woman the house cannot function'; and it is this that allows it to be said of a dead wife whose widower was then forced to close the family home: 'Katerini took the key in her pocket.'

The woman, however, cannot rise to this stature and dignity without a man, and the creation of the household rests, before all else, on a single institution, that of marriage. Thus it is accepted for all, both men and women, that they will, when the time is ripe, 'marry and have children', and that it is only in marriage that there lies an acceptable environment for sexual relations and any hope for a 'future'. 'God wants you to marry', it is said of women, 'and become a housewife'—a word as filled with dignity in village Greek as it is devalued in English—and that marriage is binding and life-long. This point is sharply made by two stories.

In one of these, a woman, abducted as a girl from her village and forcibly married to her abductor, is said to have been taken by her husband far from her home village to an island, where over the next years she bore him children. But she never forgave him, and when after many years the couple returned to the woman's own village she notified her kin in advance and connived with them to cause her husband to be ambushed and killed. This woman, however, in spite of what might seem to have been the justice of her cause, figures as that worst embodiment of femininity, 'Eve', for having 'kept hatred in her heart'. The second story, in many ways similar, runs that a girl, seduced and made pregnant by a man who then failed to marry her, later dressed up as a man and, waiting for him at a festival at the 'crossing point of the ring dance'—the place where any group waits that wishes to lead the dance—stabbed him to death. At that point she threw off her disguise and told the assembled company of her grievance, on which the man was 'forgotten' and she was applauded by all the people for having 'kept her nerve' (*βάστηξε τὴ καρδιά της*) and redressed the wrong done to her. The different moral drawn in each case makes the identical point with some piquancy, for in both cases it is one which upholds marriage: to the man, however acquired and however undeserving, who is the husband of a woman and the father of her children, the woman must give lifelong loyalty; a false lover, however, deserves death.

It is clear from these stories that marriage is a social fact rather than an individual preference, and indeed marriages are, except in the case of abduction or elopement, 'arranged' by the elder generation between principals who barely know one another and who may have seen each other only at one critical meeting. If the marriage is carried out 'one, one', that is to say engaged one week and married the next, there is little chance of a further close look, and many are the stories of ways in which a plain girl could be passed off as pretty by a clever negotiator, or the plain elder sister substituted at the last moment for the desired younger one, only to be revealed when her veil was removed after the marriage service. Certainly, intense enquiries into the honour and wealth of the prospective spouse's family, and into the character of the prospective bride or groom, all figure exhaustively in the calculation of an acceptable marriage; but, come what may, children must marry, and this combination of inevitability as to its occurrence but uncertainty as to its outcome, brings it about that marriage is characteristically accepted as 'a matter of fate'. It is impossible to foresee how things are going to turn out, and this is not helped by the false promises and the unhelpful attention of gossips that may and usually do abound around a marriage negotiation. But in spite of all, the word once given is final: regardless of second thoughts, the engagement is conclusive—reinforced, if anyone is tempted to backslide, by the fear of infuriated relatives with 'knives and axes'—and the marriage itself indissoluble (in village terms though not in the Orthodox rules of marriage[1]) except by death.

The creation, however, of a marriage which is inwardly as well as outwardly binding, and of a household which is 'paradise', is not achieved overnight, or easily, not least because marriage in this society is a liaison between two groups not two individuals, a great range of in-laws on either side looking to the new bride or groom as 'theirs'. In the early years of the children's marriages, the girls marry out but the sons bring their brides into the parental home where all live together, working together in the house and on the land, and sharing food from a communal dish. When after some years this extended family separates, it is customarily the youngest son who remains, with his bride, to care for his old parents and eventually inherit the house, the stables and outbuildings, the threshing floor and a few extra hectares, along with his 'share' of the family land. Thus within this tradition it is the men who are central to the passing on of the family name, its house and land, its history and its fortunes, and so even though it is only the youngest who eventually inherits the family home, boys in general are thought of by their natal families as 'in the house', with girls being 'destined for a strange hearth'.

Marriage is permitted only between families deemed to be beyond the limits of blood relationship, such families being termed as having 'strange blood' and being 'strangers'. Canon law and popular belief can differ on the exact point at which kin can become strangers, the Church specifying any degree of relationship after second cousins as eligible for inter-marriage, popular belief often pushing

[1] While marriage is conceived as eternal in Orthodoxy (see p. 412), permission to marry again can be given by a bishop as an act of mercy.

this limit further. But wherever this point occurs the effect on the principals is the same, and it is that marriage not only removes the girl definitively from her natal home but also places her among 'strangers'; and that as a result the transition, especially for the bride herself, is extreme. The groom and his family do indeed have to adjust to the individual stranger in their midst, but the bride must adjust to a household of strangers, and, leaving all her former loyalties and accepting that even her own mother was only, as it is said, 'temporary', must take on without reservation the identity of her new family. She must leave her family and adapt to her husband, to her husband's household, to his wider kin. Above all, she must adapt to her husband's mother, for this woman she must now address as 'Mother' and it is this woman who reveals the status of her biological mother as having been, all this time, only temporary.

This adjustment is vital, for while the power given to husbands over their wives makes the acquisition of a 'good' man vital to the happiness of the wife, nevertheless a husband—any husband, even if he is not 'good'—is the means by which she can by pursuing her duty, maintaining her honour, and caring for her children, grow to maturity and realize her destiny as a woman. By contrast, the mother-in-law is less the means of the new wife's fulfilment than her competitor in the same field; and it is in fact at this point where the bride and the mother-in-law meet that the greatest potential tensions arise.

The account which follows does not differentiate between the position of the different daughters-in-law in an extended family, and indeed all are similar to the extent that the long term ambition of each of them is to rule a house of her own; but the wife of the youngest son is in a different position in that it is she who will inherit as mistress the house to which she comes as subordinate. This newcomer thus epitomizes particularly sharply the latent conflict between the generations, but the position of all the new brides in the extended family vis-à-vis their mother-in-law is analogous and holds a dangerous potentiality for schism.

One possible source of conflict lies in the allocation of work. It is for instance normal for the young bride in the joint family to help with the endless and often heavy tasks about the house, but this can become a tyranny if her mother-in-law, as she frequently does, exploits her presence to make her 'run everywhere'. Again, in any tug-of-war between mother- and daughter-in-law, the older woman may use her favoured position with her son to put across her point of view and get her daughter-in-law punished. And there does not need to be wilful exploitation by the mother-in-law for tensions to arise, for they are built into the situation. The daughter-in-law, until she has been fully bonded to her new family and has fully adopted their life and loyalties as her own, is an obvious source through which the private affairs of her new family could leak into the outside world, and thus too much time spent with her natal family is looked upon with disfavour. Again, the bride's identity as a stranger with different ideas as to how things should be done can provide an implied source of criticism and lead to trouble.

There is, however, a particularly fundamental threat which the bride and mother-in-law pose to each other, and this is because the mother-in-law, mistress of her house and mother of her son, has, in the new bride, to receive into her household another woman whose complete fulfilment lies in her eventually becoming mistress of the house herself. The conflict here is inescapable, and the characteristic difficulties which either woman finds with the other are clearly revealed in the proverbial statement, 'mothers-in-law are cross-grained'. Conflict does not arise at first, for the position of the new bride is one of ruthless subordination, and she is at first nervous, 'not speaking' or answering back; but after a year or two, and particularly after the birth of children, she gains in confidence and may start to assert herself in matters of household management which are properly the domain of her mother-in-law. But more than this, it is also in the nature of the situation that the new bride will eventually outlive her parents-in-law, and take over entirely not only the affections of their son, but also possession of their house and their land. And indeed this transfer of power does not necessarily await the death of the old people, for in the normal course of things the old ones become weaker in proportion as the bride, by now a mother of growing children, becomes stronger, and as they become unable to work they are vulnerable in their turn to ill-treatment.

This, then, is the negative side. While the bride enters her new house, a nervous stranger in the hands of strangers, though at the same time hoping for all, she also comes as an ambiguous figure to those by whom she is received. To none of them is she yet proved as loyal, honourable, and industrious, and to her mother-in-law she comes not only as the means by which life can continue, but also as the potential usurper and deposer of the existing power. The problems, then, which either woman encounters with the other are structural, and they are mutual. For if the structural position of the mother-in-law faces her with considerable temptations, an opposing structural position produces the same effect in the bride, who comes to the house temporarily weak but potentially independent, knowing full well the jealousies of her mother-in-law and fearing them in her turn. It is a situation which, for both of them, is filled with hopes and fears, and this is expressed in the comment of a woman asked how she viewed the imminent arrival of her son's wife into her house: 'Yes, why should I go on doing all the work? I'll go on working of course, but… That's how God has made us. The old people age, and a new woman comes.'

The relationship between the incomer and her new family, and particularly between the incomer and her new 'Mother', as she is termed from now on, is thus dangerously full of tensions. At the same time however, the house is the single most secure focus of peace and mutual support in the society, the focus where the sacred values subscribed to by all are most fully enacted. Division within the house is thus a rupture of that complete 'confidence' which should exist within it, a fundamental threat to the entire society. And it is because of this that the marriage rituals, from the ceremony known as 'stuffing the trousseau' (filling the pillows and mattresses with straw and arranging the whole trousseau in an ornamental pile) on the Friday preceding the wedding, to the marriage on the Sunday and its subsequent celebrations, are overwhelmingly geared to meet and to surmount these potential tensions, and to evoke harmony and fruitfulness and that assurance of blessed continuity which is life itself. This inner dynamic is captured in some lines from a lament from the area in which the 'builder of the house of eternity' is besought to make this heavenly dwelling, by analogy with the village house, 'broad for the dance and wide for the promenade, with windows through which the nightingales of spring can come and go', for in this lovely image the idea of the long succession of the generations, the sequence of marriages, the birth of children, and the loving relations ideally lived within the four walls, are beautifully evoked. The particular power of this evocation, though, depends primarily on the image of the dance. This image permeates the wider culture in a great variety of contexts, but so profoundly is it rooted in the idea of marriage that men or women, when they marry, are said to have 'taken their place in the line [of the dance]' (*πῆραν σειρά*).

This image of the dance, used here of marriage but recurring again and again throughout the Greek rural tradition, has as its prototype the great open circle of the ring dance, either single or doubled round in a spiral according to the number of dancers and the area available, though with the ends never joining and always with only one leader.[2] The movement is progressive, forward, and always conceptually 'to the right', the auspicious direction which in the Greek world is anti-clockwise.[3] In this line of dance, people gather in groups of kin, all the dancers being linked by the holding of handkerchiefs, and anyone wanting to enter may do so at any time, joining in individually amongst their kinsmen. But for new groups wanting to lead the dance, to 'take their turn' at the head, there is a set procedure. The group already dancing at the front of the line has pride of place, and among its members different men will take the lead, 'dancing' this person or that person, until all have had their turn—this leader often carrying a table napkin as his kerchief, somewhat larger and stronger than the kerchiefs carried by the rest of the dancers, so as to allow him to cut a dash with leaping and twisting steps. All this time those wanting to lead will be waiting on the edge of the dance, and this point where the dance comes full circle is known as 'the crossing of the dance' (*πού σταυρώνει ὁ χορός*). When 'the dance crosses' those already in the lead are not always as willing to give over as the newcomers wish, claiming yet one more turn, and again one more, but eventually the leading group accepts the newcomers and falls back, and the new party comes in at the head of the dance and takes up where its predecessor left off.

[2] This is the typical dance pattern, though patterns with two facing lines, or solo dances, may also occur, and indeed be prevalent in some places. In terms of steps and music, the round dance in the village described here is associated with the *kalamatianós* (*καλαματιανός*), the *sighanós* (*σιγανός*), and the *syrtós* (*συρτός*).

[3] I recorded only one instance of an auspicious ritual which involved movement in a left-handed direction. This was for un-spelling a particular negative spell.

Marriage, therefore, is entry into a continuing procession in which everyone must take part, and this image which describes the young people 'taking their turn in the line of dance' is one which powerfully evokes both the time of waiting as the dance circles on, passing the newcomers by, as well as the definitive entry into the full movement of the dance once those already in possession have relinquished their place. There is more in it than this though, for at the heart of the advent of new life and energy to the dance of life there lies the implication of the voluntary retirement of the older generations who must in due time—albeit unwillingly—pass on their place to others. The dance in fact, as an image of life, is also an image of the passing of time which, bringing new dancers into first place, holds for the older generations the implication of their own supersession.

It is into this dance, then, that the new couple enter—a dance full of the joy of life and the promise of continuity, but one in which also the old people must give way if the new are to lead—and it is the movement of the dance, with its association of rejoicing, of community and of forward progression, which dominates all the various aspects of the marriage ceremonial. On the Friday before the wedding when the girls come to 'stuff the trousseau', they sew or tie up the larger items so that they will load well onto the animals, after which they then dance around everything as it lies in a heap. Then they fold everything carefully into a high ornamental pile in the middle of the room, and when it is complete they dance around it and shower it with symbols of fertility—rice, wheat, and walnuts. The bride's mother in particular is required to do the same, as also are other relatives of the bride when they come, and the groom and his party when they arrive for lunch. And all day people arrive as they will, friends and relatives, those who have been invited and those who have not, to dance around the trousseau in an action known as 'causing it to become iron', that is to say, bringing it good luck so that the possessors of it will be strong and healthy and fortunate.

On the Sunday of the marriage the dance pattern is even more in evidence. Events are set in motion by the bridegroom and his party who arrive 'right-handed', a term very often accompanied with the description 'like the dance', to collect the bride. This right-handedness involves the participants in leaving their point of departure by a right-handed route and following an anti-clockwise course to their destination; from the point of view of the destination itself, this means that the party arrives from its left hand side and departs to its right. The destination itself—here initially the house and later the church—thus images the 'crossing point' of the dance, where newcomers wait to be taken into the general movement; and the bride, once gathered up by the bridegroom's party at her own home, does indeed enter the dance, for the groom and his male kin take turns in taking her kerchief and leading her in the dance, before they all wend their way, 'right-handed', to the church. During the service the bride and groom are 'crowned'—the part of the rite of union which is carried out by the *koumbáros* (*κουμπάρος*, m.) or *koumbára* (*κουμπάρα*, f.), who thereby becomes spiritual kin to the couple.[4] Circular garlands or fillets joined by a ribbon are held with crossed hands over the heads of the pair, exchanged three times, and finally placed directly on their heads. Immediately after this they are 'danced', or led right-handed, three times round the marriage table by the priest, after which, again 'right-handed', the party return to the bride's house for a meal. The celebrations, in the full traditional wedding, go on all night—the bride being expected to dance all the time—before the party next morning once again departs 'right-handed' for the church. Here there is dancing around the church or in the forecourt, during which everyone 'dances' the bride, and after this the party goes directly to the house of the groom, where again they eat and dance for the rest of the day and the following night, and only the following morning do the festivities end.

At a wedding therefore, the dance, and the right-handed image of the dance, is ubiquitous. The way in which the essential structure of the dance itself articulates the themes of taking and yielding the lead, which has already been described, renders it deeply appropriate to the great transitional ceremony of marriage where new life can only arise out of the death of the old. But the use of the dance at marriage does more than merely state in general terms these realities, for in pervading with its right-handed movement the entire sequence of ceremonies, the dance is also the medium which links together a series of separate rituals which elaborate individually these general themes. Prominent among them are the rituals of

[4] For a detailed description of marriage and the role of spiritual kin, see p. 209 ff.

separation and incorporation which govern the departure of the bride from the house of her birth and her reception into her new home.

Of these rituals of separation, the first occurs on the day of the wedding just before the trousseau is loaded onto the bridegroom's animals. This trousseau, spun and woven by the bride's mother since her daughter's birth and by the bride herself since a girl, consists of bright woollen rugs, blankets, and floor coverings in patterns of red and black, many-coloured wall hangings and bed coverings, cotton sheets, pillowcases and cushion coverings with handmade lace edgings, blue and white napkins, cotton tablecloths with fringed edges, shiny red and black goat-hair bags and sacks, and large coverings for use outside, woven in the arrangement of narrow stripes dictated by locality. This trousseau, piled up on the preceding Friday, is the focus of the last action of the bride as she leaves her natal house after the wedding celebrations there have finished, for just before she leaves her home for her husband's house, she turns her back to the pile and, with her hands behind her and, it is emphasized, *without looking behind her*, pulls it down. In this way the bride enacts her separation from her natal family, her relegation of her former life to the past, and her adoption without reservation of her new loves and loyalties; and this inner meaning is startlingly reinforced when the similarities are realized between the bride's gesture with the trousseau and the gesture with which the dead are said to greet one another in the other world. For there, putting one hand behind them while still keeping their gaze forward, they clasp hands briefly, saying, even in the act of separation, 'Somewhere I've seen you before.' The chief characteristic of this 'other world' is that in its shadowy existence all flesh-and-blood relationships have been broken. Thus the bride, leaving her natal home as a girl for the last time, expresses more clearly than with any words the fact that to her old relationships with her family she is now symbolically dead.

The second action of the bride is very similar, though it occurs in the context of her reception into her new home. At this point she is given, by a small boy standing outside the door, the *pítta* baked by her mother-in-law which was mentioned in the previous chapter—the special decorated loaf baked with a little oil and scored into four, six or eight pieces. This the bride immediately drops on the ground in prediction of the sex of the first child of the marriage—a girl if it falls upside down, a boy if it falls the right way up. Retrieving it from where it has fallen the bride then takes it in both hands, breaks it in pieces over her head, and without looking back throws the pieces behind her, thus giving to any girl who catches a piece her next place in the sequence of marriages. Thus the new bride, who has just 'taken her place in the line of dance', is given the bread of fertility and, casting it behind her, is seen as the leader of the dance who, drawing others after her, goes forward without looking behind to take up her new allegiance.

Such a separation, however, is not easily accomplished either by the bride or by her kin, and this is expressed in ritualized hostility when the groom and his party come on the morning of the wedding to, as it were, carry the bride away. First all those assisting with the preparations, when they see the bridegroom's party approaching, hold the door shut and refuse to let him in—'She's not here, she's gone! She's with the sheep!' And when he has gained entry one of the bridesmaids refuses to part with the pillow for the marriage bed until money has been handed over. These actions, joking but with an undertone of seriousness, express, at the same time as they control, the latent hostility between the two parties; and again the difficulty of parting is enacted by a young male relative of the bride who, as the groom urges her forward with her right hand in his, pulls on her left hand and tries to keep her back. But even in these actions the auspicious movement is always the movement forward. It is by her 'right' or 'good' hand that her departure for the church with her future husband is instigated, and with her left, and by a child, that she is held back; while during the final moments of her departure she must not look back as, however reluctantly, she pulls down her trousseau, the fruit of her girlhood, and leaves the house in which she was born. The momentum of the dance is the one that must prevail, and this momentum is forward into the unknown future, through a kind of death, and into a new life.

If the rupture of the bride from her family is expressed, however, in terms both of the necessity and the pain of that separation, still more emphasized is the necessity and the joy of union into her new family, and this is expressed in a sequence of gifts,[5] including the gift of hospitality, and in rituals designed to defuse potential hostility

[5] This theme is discussed in more detail in Juliet du Boulay, 'The Meaning of Dowry: Changing Values in Rural Greece', *Journal of Modern Greek Studies*, 1 (1983), pp. 243–70.

within the house. As has already been indicated, hospitality is a key theme throughout the wedding celebrations, and the meal at the dowry celebrations precedes further meals at both bride's and groom's houses during the wedding celebrations. But while that at the celebration of the dowry, being on a Friday, is a simple meal of beans and rice, those at the wedding traditionally necessitate 'four mule loads of flour'[6] and a number of beasts slaughtered, for not only do kin come from afar for the celebrations, but every household in the village which holds a kinsman or friend is invited. Further, not only is the giving of food formalized in celebratory meals, but it is also the custom for the bridegroom's party, on the road to the bride's village, to bring along wine in order to treat anyone encountered. That this is an obligation founded in the strictest canons of hospitality is revealed in the story of one particular wedding party who, scornful of a shepherd they met on the way, gave him nothing. His answer was to lay on the bridegroom the curse of impotence, and although later it was discovered that it was he who had done this and he was asked to take the curse back, he refused and the ill was never put right. The story stands as an awful warning against meanness at this critical juncture, and the blighting of the marriage as a consequence of one ungracious act is eloquent testimony to the fundamental necessity, on these occasions, to give to all comers without partiality.

In this traditional patterning of marriage, custom dictates not only generous hospitality, but also the giving of gifts. At the engagement ceremony, 'good' rings of plain gold are exchanged between the bridal pair, but in addition, while the bride gives to the groom certain items of clothing and a tasselled white covering for his horse or mule made with her own hands, she receives from him a ceremonial embroidered apron, a long red silk belt—the *kadém* (*καντέμ*)—a silk headscarf, a pair of shoes, and a full set of traditional jewellery. This last consists of bracelets, a necklace with five rows of dangling coins, a large ornamental buckle, and two worked pins—all of which 'must' be given as permanent gifts and 'must' be freshly plated with gold. These gifts from the bridegroom in fact have been known sometimes to cost so much that they can necessitate the family getting into debt

[6] A heavily laden mule should not carry more than 100 kilos. The loads here would probably have been estimated at less than the absolute maximum.

or mortgaging some fields, and in this way they may far exceed the value of the dowry brought by the bride who, in a society which values honour over money, is said often to be received with 'whatever she has'. In this way, in spite of the customary lamentation over the provision of dowries for girls, girls are in fact given away with as little of the inheritance as possible, while of sons it is said ruefully that 'no one who hasn't had a son knows anything about expense'.

This relative expense of sons compared with daughters contrasts piquantly with the relative emotions connected with either, for while the dowries of daughters are subjects of continual lamentation, the expenses of sons, though they may be a burden, are not subjects of institutionalized grief. A rhyme depicts this nicely: 'I have a boy and I'm full of joy/ because I'll become a mother-in-law./ I have a girl and I'm full of bitterness/ because I'll be spinning day and night.' However, the reason for the joy and the lamentation is less to do with the amount of work involved in either child as with the critical fact that while the girls move on, the boys remain 'in the house'. Because of this, while the dowry consists only of moveable items such as cash, some animals, and pieces of household equipment, and while a boy's inheritance and gifts to his bride are very substantial, boys are nevertheless a net gain to the natal family, girls a net loss. The boy's inheritance and his gifts of jewellery to the bride become part of his own family's history, its own wealth, whereas those things given by the bride's family are, together with the bride herself—her fertility, her purity, her loyalty, her capacity for work—lost to them for good.

In this way the gifts of the bridegroom to the bride, which are non-negotiable, stand in startling contrast to the dowry provided by the bride which is strictly dependent on whether she is rich or poor. But the notable thing about these gifts is that, being overwhelmingly ornamental, they appear to have nothing to do with economic values and everything to do with the conferring of honour, the adorning of the new bride with the regalia of the married state. As will be seen in the next chapter, the principle of the family's survival through time is carried by the male line, but the principle of life in its generative aspect lies in the women. Thus it seems that it is the meaning of the bride in herself, as wife and future mother—more than any material possessions which she may bring with her, important though these may be—which is celebrated in the cultural insistence on these gifts of ceremonial clothes and jewellery, for these gifts, creating and confirming the bride in her new status are, if one may put it like this, a coronation of the new source of life within the house.

One final gift from groom to bride must be mentioned, and this is the kerchief of the kind known as a *tsibér,* that is to say the woman's kerchief which, tied tightly around the hair but with a raised roll in front, causes the light decorated headscarf arranged over it to make an attractive frame round the face. This gift is essential, it is worn for the first time on a girl's wedding day, and significantly it must be red, the colour of blood and thus of life. This scarf will be worn daily by the young bride until she is considered to be no longer newly wed, after which it is restricted to festive occasions for which she will wear it until widowhood.

While the bride and the promise of her fertility is graced by the gifts given to her by her groom, the same themes are expressed in the gifts which she gives on her wedding day to her wedding sponsor and his wife (who are by right relatives or friends of the groom); to her mother-in-law; to her father-in-law; to her husband's best man, and all her husband's brothers and sisters. These acts of giving to her bridegroom's kin and friends are referred to by the term *mandilónei (μαντηλώνει)* meaning 'gives a kerchief to'. The term covers both the giving of headscarves to the women, and, to the men, hand-woven cotton handkerchiefs which may be worn ornamentally, pinned to the jacket, but which may also be used by the recipients both at the meal and to perform the wedding dances. And table napkins, also, as noted above, used in the dance, are the gifts given to those who load the dowry onto the animals for transference to the bride's new home. The kerchiefs thus represent the gift which the bride herself brings to her new kin group, the newcomer giving fresh impetus to the dance of life in her new kindred.

There is a further implication in these gifts which is to do with the movement of women in marriage to the households of the men, and with the customary reference to 'giving' a daughter but 'taking' a bride. Women are the mobile element in a society whose fixed points are the men, and in this context the right-handed processional movement so frequent at a wedding is not only a generally auspicious movement: it represents, quite precisely, the movement of the women themselves throughout the society as they 'dance' (i.e. move in an anti-clockwise procession 'like the dance') from their natal families to the houses of strangers, bringing new life with them. The gift of kerchiefs for the dance from the bride to her groom's kin thus appears as a further elaboration of this central theme, for not only do these kerchiefs enable the dance, they also reflect it, for given unilaterally by the bride to the groom's kin with no return being made, just as is the case with the dowry and the trousseau, they image in themselves the unending forward movement of the dance. The irreversibility of the gifts from the bride to the groom's kin is a reflection of the irreversibility of her movement from her natal family to her new alliances.

With these gifts therefore, an unambiguous statement is being made of the ultimate value of the new bride to her in-laws, in that she brings in her own person the promise of new generations to revive the house. But true as this is, the future relationship of the bride with her mother-in-law remains a specific problem and that also has to be dealt with. It has been said that at the same time as the bride brings new life to the family of her marriage she also longs to take over the household herself, and this fateful implication of her presence, and the response of her mother-in-law to it, is startlingly expressed in two proverbial warnings. One of these is that the first woman to receive the glance of the other during the period between the 'crowning' and the entry of the bride into her new home, will die soon afterwards; the other that the older woman is at risk of early death if, between the bride's 'crowning' and her departure from church, and in her mother-in-law's presence, she utters a spell against her.

The liminal period between the marriage itself and the incorporation of the bride into her new home is thus the period of greatest danger for both women, and it is managed quite simply by the custom prohibiting the parents of the groom from attending not only the wedding ceremony itself but also the subsequent celebrations at the bride's house. In this way they do not set eyes on their new daughter-in-law until she arrives with their son to take up her abode in their house. They first meet her, that is to say, when she has finally left the jurisdiction of her natal family and comes to place herself unequivocally in their charge. Even so, this first meeting between the bride and her mother-in-law is pregnant with danger, and this also is strictly controlled. Initially the old couple remain hidden behind the door while the bride performs two ceremonies, one with the bread already cited, and the other which prescribes that she takes honey and marks the doorway with a cross at the top, bottom and right hand side, saying as she does so: 'As honey is sweet so may the bride be sweet. May we live and may we be sweet together.' The meeting between the women is then negotiated by both having their heads covered by a long silk kerchief and, thus blindfolded, exchanging money. This money should be silver, 'to stop evil from making progress', with the mother-in-law sometimes placing the silver in the bride's mouth in order to prevent the 'ugly words' from which so much harm can flow. Only after this are the blindfolds removed, and only after this does the bride step over the threshold. As she does this, she puts her right foot on a poker and a pomegranate which have been placed there, crushing the pomegranate so that it spills its seeds. With this image of the release of the bride's fertility the rites of passage are almost complete, and as the couple enter they are welcomed into the house by the father-in-law with the words: 'Welcome! May you live in strength and with sons, may you live like the mountains!'; and as he speaks he shakes a sieve of flour over their heads, making them white like the old age of snow on the everlasting hills.

These customs face and voice with extraordinary realism the deep fears attendant on this intimate and critical meeting of strangers, and, in identifying the temptations, they at the same time indicate the way in which these may be surmounted. In marking the door with honey and in accepting the silver in her mouth the bride wishes life and harmony to all in the house, and accepts that it is her responsibility, if she comes under pressure, to maintain that harmony by holding her tongue. In accepting silver in her turn the mother-in-law also accepts that she too must not allow evil 'to progress' from her. And finally in wishing the young couple strength, sons, and old age, the older couple implicitly accept with grace their own eventual departure from the scene, leaving the younger people in possession. Thus it is made clear that discord in the house will only arise if the due ordering of things is subverted—if the bride resents her present subordination and allows herself aspirations to power before it falls due, or if the old people use their authority unjustly at the outset or fail to relinquish it when the time comes. At the moment of the bride's entry into the house the existing hierarchy is restated, while at the same time the assurance is given to her

15. Picnic and dancing at a feast day: Above, 'The meat and pasta...cooked in cauldrons on open fires.' In the background to the left can be seen the first of the waiting picnickers, who gather on either side of a long line of rugs. Below, 'As they dance the dancers may be treated to sips of *rakí* by a man standing in the midst of the dance' (p. 158).

16. Bride-groom and *koumbára*: the bride-groom's *pítta* (p. 154) is in a plastic bag in his right hand. Behind, over the saddle, is the bride's gift of the white saddle cloth, the edges laced in this example, which she has made with her own hands (p. 172). On changes from traditional dress here and in Plate 17 (and elsewhere), see Appendix, note concerning p. 281.

that her legitimate hopes will eventually be fulfilled. Time, only, is necessary to the just resolution of all, and patience and obedience on the part of the bride will bring about her eventual inheritance.

The marriage rituals, then, make clear that marriage, as well as being part of the divine pattern for the continuation of life and the only true fulfilment of men and women, is also a meeting fraught with fateful possibilities of conflict through the advent of a stranger into the household. These rituals however, in a series of symbolic statements, not only state the problem but enact its solution, making clear that while all must play their part in making the transition, the bride can only earn her place in a strange house by a selfless and absolute transfer of loyalty. If she does this, she becomes increasingly over time the person whom the wedding adornments prophesy—the woman without whom 'the house cannot function', who epitomizes the life of the family and the continuity of the generations, in whose care the young and the old, the living and the dead, the past and the future, all repose.

If the entry of the bride into the house of her marriage is the point of danger for the household, in the ordinary commerce of village life it is the meeting of the house with the outside world which is the point of danger for society, for it is here that the enclosed and mutually supportive family group meets the potentially hostile world of strangers. In the case of marriage the tension between the house and the bride is overcome by a total identification of the bride's interests with those of her new family, so that she becomes no longer a stranger, but 'ours'—an identification which becomes complete when she first gives birth, for this child is a child of the house and the inheritor of the family name. In the case of encounters with the outside world, however, a different resolution must be found—one that does not eradicate the conflict between differing interest groups, but which nevertheless finds ways to bridge the divide.

This conflict which is endemic to society needs a brief explanation here, for it may appear to sit strangely with the sacred values with which this book is concerned, and with the deep liturgical centre of family life which was discussed in the previous chapter. In metaphysical terms the explanation for this conflict is related to the familiar theme of the archetypal conflict between good and evil. 'The devil has many feet', as the saying goes, and individuals are not exempt from blame if they follow the path of evil; but the villagers are clear about the primary causation in that, as already quoted, 'If God and the devil were not at this moment fighting each other, men wouldn't be fighting and making wars either.' Thus this metaphysical understanding takes full account of individual responsibility while at the same time acknowledging that social life is lived in a world whose structure involves a degree of evil. In sociological terms, too, the same balance is evident, for it is clear that the conflict so prevalent in village life arises in principle not from individual ill-will —although of course ill-will is involved—but out of a particular combination of social factors which individuals are powerless to alter.

One of these factors, already mentioned, is the categorical nature of the love and loyalty found within the house, for the intense inner creativity within it carries with it the more negative corollary of a profoundly exclusive attitude to those outside. The second factor lies in the significance, in a subsistence society such as this one, of a harsh economic environment where material resources are scarce,[7] the land steep and stony, and the strength of man and animal the only way to gain a living. This combination alone is enough to create competition, but competition over resources is exacerbated by a third factor to do with the system of values in rural Greece, for this is founded on a code of honour which for both men and women links social worth to the extreme demands of public reputation. Claims to honour are in this way drawn into the arena of scarce resources as being amongst the things for which people compete, and reputations become perpetual targets of discussion and gossip, more easily lost than they are gained. The consequence of this situation is that while the 'confidence' that exists within the house is supremely prized, outside the house there lies an environment of competition and quarrelling so characteristic of community relations that people will say of themselves, 'We hate one another here.'

People, of course, must and do bear some responsibility for such hostility, to the extent that they are involved in it, but this having been said, each person is also a victim of circumstances in that the strug-

[7] Juliet du Boulay and Rory Williams, 'Amoral Familism and the Image of Limited Good: A Critique from a European Perspective', *Anthropological Quarterly*, 60 (1987), pp. 12–24.

gle for survival in the context of an exclusive loyalty to the family lays on everyone the necessity to protect their own family even at the expense of the families of others. The survival of one's house, or within a joint household of one's line, is in the end a primary value, and a story told of a village family in times of great hardship provides a vivid illustration. This story concerns a man who, having killed a fellow villager in a blood feud, persuaded his somewhat simple-minded younger brother to take the blame, promising that in return he would look after his brother's wife. The younger brother duly went to prison for four or five years, but the elder brother, finding the burden of an extra mouth to feed too great, turned his sister-in-law out in the middle of winter, forcing her to go around the village, destitute, looking for crumbs of work and charity. This story becomes intelligible when it is recognized as a memory of hard times in a peasant economy remote from a reliable administration of justice. It reflects a situation where the feud is still a duty—here performed by the elder brother on behalf of his family, thus giving him a claim over the younger—and where in scarcity the food goes first to those who can take responsibility, do the work, and continue the line. Hence, while the story is told in illustration of the shocking nature of the elder brother's betrayal of his promise, the village comment which follows the narrative recognizes also the harshness of the limits under which the elder brother laboured and the imperative to which he responded, and it does so in the image of the dance: 'He didn't want to lose his place [in the line of the dance].'

The central pivot of the social and moral world is, then, the family—elementary or extended as the case may be. Even within this nucleus there are, as has been said, potential lines of fracture in the entry of a new daughter-in-law into the house; and the growth of strains between members of too large an extended family living in too small a space is the classic catalyst for the removal of some of the couples from the joint family into their own dwellings. But the norm is for the house to provide a single focus of unity within which the distinction between 'us' and 'not us' does not, or should not, penetrate, and as long as people are still together in the same house the norm is for community of interest within the house to be absolute and for the good of all to be the good of each. Outside the house, however, things are different; but at this point there lies a range of kin which provide as it were a buffer between the exclusive world of the house and the hostile world of strangers. Since each of these kinsmen owes a primary loyalty to his own house, even relations with kinsmen are not proof against conflict of interest and consequent rupture of relations, and indeed some of the most bitter quarrels can occur over inheritance and between siblings. But the norm is for kinsmen who live in different households to 'support one another'. This support grows weaker as kinship weakens, but between first and second cousins—possibly even to third—there is a presumed cooperative relationship of some kind, and the real break occurs not with the different houses but, as has been said earlier, with the limits of blood relationship. At this point 'one blood' has converted into 'strange blood', 'kin' into 'strangers', and it is at this point that social encounters move definitively from being presumed to be in harmony with self-inerest to being presumed to be potentially in opposition.

The harshness of the environment thus has two countervailing properties. On the one hand it lays on each individual house the necessity both to give and receive support—a situation which finds pithy expression in the following comment: 'What can we do [but help one another] since we live in such a harsh place?' On the other hand the 'harshness' of the place, which between kinsmen acts for solidarity, acts, in the local community of 'strangers' beyond the kindred, in reverse. Thus between non-kin, to whom no categorical loyalty is owed and who may be presumed to have fundamentally divergent if not inimical interests, a degree of distrust is normal, and this, where the provocation is great enough, can blow up into ferocious quarrels.

Conflict within the community, either latent or overt, is thus inescapable in those cases where two sets of self-interest collide, and this is a cultural, rather than a psychological, fact, and requires a cultural, rather than an individual, resolution. Thus the complex web of giving and receiving by which this resolution is negotiated is composed not only of individual acts of goodwill but also of culturally determined occasions of hospitality and reconciliation; and it is expressive of the fundamental value given to such reconciliation that the greater the social distance between fellow villagers, the more such giving loses its overtones of direct reciprocity and acquires the nature of a free gift.

The nature of the house as the repository of sacred values and the centre of mutual trust and confidence makes it inevitable that within the house it is sharing rather than giving which is at issue, since all members of the family are one, and in giving to the others they are in a sense giving to themselves. In cases of the cooperation of kinsmen living in separate houses the inter-dependence is less, but nevertheless there is a constant movement of assistance between the parties—for instance, whenever more hands are needed in the fields than the family possesses, or in cases of difficult repairs to the house or barn, or in lending animals for the threshing, in giving assistance during sickness, or in offering a loan of money or a plate of food, or providing company for a journey. These are essentially acts of giving rather than of sharing, but in spite of this the movement of gifts is one which is strictly reciprocal, for although the gifts are freely given, they carry with them the unspoken assumption of an obligation which will be returned at some later date, and the person who is able to return such an obligation but who fails to do so, invites the pitying assessment: 'He (or she) doesn't understand.' These acts of assistance are, then, explicitly understood to be mutual—they are part of the common network of survival, and for survival people do not turn to 'strangers' but to 'their own', for from others they can expect at best ambiguous support coupled with a reliable proclivity to damaging gossip.

It is interesting therefore that when the limits of kinship are reached, together with the onset of institutionalized competition customary between 'strangers', the many occasions of giving begin to change their character and to incorporate ideas not only of an expected return but also of more disinterested values. Reciprocal giving between such people includes, for instance, the midday and evening meals customarily offered to day labourers at events such as the sheep shearing or the hoeing of the vineyards, and at the threshing where it is understood that all (both kin and non-kin) who assist the householder with their own and their animals' labour on one day will be assisted by him in their turn. These are all occasions which arise freely at the will of the giver or the receiver, and the gift is coupled with the assumption of reciprocity. There are, nevertheless, significant occasions in which giving to those outside the kindred is customary, not to say obligatory, and in which the occasion of giving is an act complete in itself. These occasions include, notably, events connected with death—funerals and memorial services—where the entire community receives without obligation the hospitality of the bereaved household. These acts of hospitality, being prescribed throughout the entire community, are necessarily over the course of time received by all the households as well as given by them, though not all in the same proportion. But in the event the giving is unilateral in that it is motivated by the occasion, not by any calculation of return; and at a funeral meal the phrase, 'So-and-so (the name of the dead person is given) invites you to sit down to table', is an invitation premised on the understanding that no return in kind to the dead person can ever be made.

There is a further great occasion of hospitality involving 'strangers' as well as kin, and this is the 'name day'—the saint's day on which any male member of the household named after the saint holds a special celebration. In the morning the woman of the house takes to the church a loaf of liturgical bread and some candles and incense, and the family attend the liturgy at which the saint is celebrated. After the liturgy a few guests—nearly always relatives—will be invited to a loaded table, with a main dish consisting typically of meat cooked in oil and tomato paste and combined with some sort of pasta. After this the house is opened to all comers who pass by to wish the household 'Many years' or 'A good year', and to be treated to tiny glasses of *rakí* or sweet liqueur and a spoonful of sweet preserved fruit, followed by an array of hors d'oeuvres of little bits of fried liver, toasted chickpeas, bread, cheese, walnuts and honey, sweet pastries known as *kourambiédhes* (*κουραμπιέδες*), and, in season, chunks of apple, tomato, or cucumber. Further, not only will visitors be treated with these things at the houses, they will be encouraged to fill their handkerchiefs with handfuls of delicacies before they leave. Particularly important to these occasions are *loukoumádhes* or batter-puffs, characteristic of any celebration and yet another variant, as it were, of bread, for like bread they are made simply of flour, water and yeast. Of these ingredients a batter is made which is then dropped by spoonfuls into hot oil so that each spoonful puffs up immediately into a crisp airy bubble. Anything opening out, unfolding like a flower, or bursting, is full of life, 'good', and signifies 'joy'; so batter-puffs, blown up to golden bubbles known as 'pufflets' or 'little bubbles' (*φουσκάκια*), and eaten with honey—which, being sweet, also indicates joy—are, like the decorated *píttes*, symbols of the feast.

Since the giving and receiving of hospitality is an essential part of all celebrations, name days should properly be honoured by the whole community. Thus it is normal for housewives on the morning of such days to make great basinfuls of batter-puffs against the time when virtually the entire community passes through the doors of every house celebrating the name. As this visiting occurs normally in groups, anyone harbouring resentment is able to remain relatively invisible among his or her companions; but even those on bad terms with the family come by to wish the house good fortune and it is considered an insult if anyone neglects to come. If they are not able to come in the day, they come in the evening after their work is done. Such celebrations therefore, originating in the saint's day and particularized in the names of individual householders and their sons, are occasions of communal reconciliation where at least hospitality is given and received, and the lines of communication—characteristically broken by a quarrel—once again opened up.

These acts of generosity, specified by custom and recurring constantly in the long histories of the various households, are, whether occasioned by a death or by a saint's day, of enormous significance, for they occur not only between relatives but also between those thought of as 'strangers'. They thus provide an opportunity even for those households who are opposed to each other to perceive something other than the obsessive issues of the quarrel, and at the least they speak of a value placed on unity and peace struggling, in spite of all the difficulties, to transcend the customary competitiveness of social life.

In this way all these occasions of giving within village society form a continuum running from the sharing within the house to the communal sharing in the open air festival described in the previous chapter, and to the unilateral giving which characterizes name days, memorials, and other festivals, so encompassing the outer reaches of the community. And so complete is this inclusion that this unilateral giving also includes not only those who are entirely outside the nexus of kinship, but also those who are at any one time quarrelling with the givers and so not on speaking terms with them. Thus, for all the hostility so lamented by the people who participate in it, there is at any moment a healing stream of gift-giving running through the common life, and the response it elicits is similarly uncalculated and generous, for it is one of goodwill and good wishes. As well as the wishes of those visiting a house celebrating its name day, already mentioned, those given any kind of refreshment from the house of the dead will offer forgiveness, 'May God forgive him/her'; a recipient of a gift from an unmarried girl will answer not with thanks but with a benediction—'A good bridegroom', 'May you become a good housewife', 'A rich man!'; acknowledgement of a gift or a good act from a married man or woman will be of the order 'Health to you', or 'May you rejoice in your children'.

In addition to these contexts in which gifts are given and acknowledged, the expression of goodwill is in many cases independent of any kind of gift giving and simply part of the normal currency of village life. In this way—leaving aside those people for whom generalized suspicion has become personal hostility and who are therefore avoiding contact with each other—daily life is interspersed constantly, in casual meetings between both kin and non-kin, with blessings and good wishes. These are so numerous that there is room here to mention only a few: to someone who is ill, 'May it pass'; to a pregnant woman, 'A good birth'; to a woman within forty days of giving birth, 'May the forty days pass well'; to the owner of any harvest just gathered in, 'Here's to next year' or 'A good harvest'; at the beginning of Great Lent, 'A good Lent'; to the owners of new born animals, and on founding a house, 'May they/you put down good roots'; on an engagement, 'With health'; as one sees a person leaving the spring with washing, 'Good fortune in the dirtying'—and so on and on. And in addition to these daily greetings there are also a few occasions in the year when the children, young men, or girls go round all the houses indiscriminately, acting out the appropriate ritual and being 'treated' with food—bread or cheese, eggs or walnuts, and so on. Some of these days give the occasion for a joke—as at the Carnival,[8] and at the ritual of the 'camel' on the Monday after Easter, where a property-camel—constructed with broomsticks, rugs, and a horse's skull—is brought round the houses by the unmarried boys to extract gifts of food at a time when every house can be expected to have an abundance: 'Give something to the camel/ so that he doesn't trample your vines./ Give bread, give cheese,/ give a good slice of lamb.' Finally, laden with spoils, the boys retire to dance in the square and

[8] See pp. 116–17.

share their feast together. Other days are occasions of blessing rather than burlesque, as in the 1 May ritual of the 'sweet-pepper bush',[9] enacted by the unmarried girls who also finish their round of the houses with a feast, and Lazarus Saturday (the day before Palm Sunday)[10] when the children visit the houses to herald Holy Week.

All these wishes, ritualized or casual, being only words, may perhaps be thought not to mean very much, but in fact good wishes are blessings and are, like curses, serious currency within a religious cosmology, capable of being realized if, as has been said, 'the time is propitious'. And it is significant that the characteristic ending of quarrels is through a good wish being offered and received between two people who up to that moment have not been on speaking terms. The normal conduct of a quarrel, after the initial exchanges of insults and possible recourse to law, involves the parties 'not speaking' to each other, that is to say that day in and day out they steadfastly ignore each other's existence. It is therefore consistent that while it is the disruption of the normal interchanges of blessings and counter blessings which, in particular, marks a quarrel, it is their resumption which signals its end.

Finally, in the context of communal life between members of the same community there should be mentioned the incidence of gifts given to the poor or the needy. It is customary, for instance, to offer to a pregnant woman any simple item of food for which she suddenly yearns, 'lest she come to harm'; the local healer may enact her rituals freely for any who come to her door; and small gifts of coffee or ouzo may be given to the local down-and-out, or a part of a loaf or plate of food taken to the family of a schizophrenic by a non-related neighbour. In the latter case these gifts are of necessity strictly limited, since more total involvement with the needy would involve a dangerous weakening of the giver's economic strength; but there is nevertheless a symbolic value here which again, as in the earlier instances of giving between 'strangers', or non-kin, acts to reinforce the values of community and charity so bedevilled under normal circumstances by the daily struggle of individual households to survive.

Gifts are, then, given and received on all levels of society, and at the most general level their meaning is the same: it is to express a free flowing generosity of spirit all too often limited by institutionalized

[9] See p. 88.

[10] See pp. 369–70.

competition and lack of means. The context within which the gift is given, however, alters the resonances accompanying the giving and highlights both the limitations encountered in the society and the freedom to which it aspires. Within the house the gift is, as it were, part of the fundamental act of living, for here uniquely a 'confidence exists' (*ὑπάρχει ἐμπιστοσύνη*) making unquestioned mutual support the lynchpin of family relationships. This solidarity grows less, but is still important, between related families in separate households, where gifts and support of various kinds are given freely, but where there is an unspoken obligation to make a return gift at some time. Finally though, where the distance between giver and receiver reaches its maximum in the lack of blood relationship, the occasions of giving diminish again, although when they do occur it is on occasions of hospitality across the community where the giving is unilateral and without calculation of return.

As was said earlier, it is of course true on these latter occasions that since every house follows the same customs, every house will, as the years come and go, receive as well as give. This equalizing effect of the passing of time, however, is not talked of as a consideration by either host or guest on these occasions, who act quite simply in obedience to the nature of the time. In each individual case the gift is experienced not as an intrinsic part of a network of mutual survival but as an uncalculated act of unilateral hospitality in which any delayed reciprocity is deliberately unstressed. While the impetus for giving between kin is embedded in material necessity, that between unrelated neighbours arises from moments in their family's sacred history and is conditioned by a value derived, as will be seen below, directly from the sacred world, for it is to do with the hosts giving without conditions, and the guests receiving without reserve. In this way, at the same time as there are forces working to unite those who are related by blood and to divide those who are not, other forces are working to link the gifts exchanged between relatives to notions of reciprocity, while those exchanged between the wider community partake much more in the nature of a disinterested and symbolic act.

There is thus a point of tension within the society in which the value of preserving the house and family from hardship and failure runs up against the value of giving freely both to friend and enemy, and this tension is resolved by the fact that although self-preservation enforces a basic and continuing level of competition between non-kin, the obligation still exists for every household, at specific points in its life cycle, to give freely to the entire community. It is a resolution which, given the frequency of these ceremonial events throughout the community, is of incalculable importance in overcoming the fragmentation of society which occurs in daily life; and its success in transcending—if only from moment to moment—this fragmentation is once again graphically revealed in the dance, for here, 'kin group with kin group', the varying elements of the community dance and sing together as one.

This image of the 'stranger' as competitor has centred round non-kin who live in close proximity to one another and who therefore can comprise the greatest threat to each other's interests. Since, however, it is the proximity of unrelated neighbours in an environment of competition which creates the conditions for hostility, it follows that with the increase of distance between the parties the incidents of aggravation grow less. And this is indeed the case with what may be termed 'distant strangers'—non-related people from other villages, districts or countries—in which the competitive basis of relationship is entirely changed.

In the case of 'distant strangers', that is to say, unrelated members of neighbouring communities, once again their classification as friend or competitor depends on the particular focus of common interest. Thus there may be a sudden coalescing of hostile feeling against a common enemy if anything occurs which threatens the community interest—a quarrel over water, charges made for grazing rights, or a fight over the relative merits of the communities at a wedding. But it needs a specific competitive context to trigger such feelings, and, in the normal course of things, members of a neighbouring community will be accepted with a quiet friendship and recognition, with exchange of news and casual help as it is needed, and the competition so common between fellow members of the same community will be left behind.

With the stranger from more distant parts of Greece or from abroad this tendency persists and is reinforced. In many instances—as, for instance, in the case of travelling salesmen or tinkers—these people come about their business and go again, arousing no more than the customary exchange of greetings or of news, and there is a definite understanding that such people, as 'strangers', and therefore by implication not fully acquainted with local custom, are exempt from the normal cut and thrust of intra-village relations and should be allowed a certain leeway for error. And if this is the case for a man following his trade, still more is it so with people who possess little or nothing, such as gypsies or beggars, and these people are, it is said, almost always given something, a bit of bread, a hunk of cheese; while in the case of visitors such as foreign travellers the customary offer is of bed and board coupled with an extraordinary degree of interest and compassion. The stranger here is far from being an object of competition; he—or she—is an honoured guest. Thus the tendency within the village for the weakening of the blood tie to be accompanied by the strengthening of hostility, appears to be reversed when the 'stranger' comes from elsewhere and is thus categorically strange, and this paradox does not escape the people who often comment, 'I don't know why it is. We hate one another here, but we love strangers.'

The 'hatred' of neighbours and the love of strangers seem in this way to accord with the presence or absence of causes of competition, and to reveal at the heart of village life two overwhelming and contradictory impulses—to keep and to give. The impulse to keep has in the main to win out over the impulse to give, since a close regard for self-interest is vital for the preservation of the house, and in this context to be unsuspicious, generous and innocent, all virtues in the spiritual realm, is to be 'simple' or 'lacking' in the social one. In addition, 'one must have' [in order to be able to give]. Yet this contradiction is rendered painful by the very values that have been the subject of the preceding chapters—by the people's experience of the limitless bounty of nature, their awareness of the freedom and purity of the divine world, their recognition of the working of the devil and of the distortions of sin in themselves and in others. This is the tragic position of man in the fallen world, and people do not dodge its implications: 'We are all sinners', 'Are our sins forgivable?', 'Whatever we do, we sin'.

In spite, however, of the apparently inescapable nature of this contradiction between duty to one's own family and duty to one's fellow man, there are times when a more satisfactory resolution is available, and this is hinted at in certain statements about the gift. It is a sin not to give to beggars—'They [also] are in God's care'; and to gypsies—'Wherever you give, it is effective. You see, they [also] are God's creation.' *Piánetai* (*πιάνεται*), or *piánei* (*πιάνει*), translated here as 'being effective', means, literally, to 'take', in the sense in which a graft is said 'to take'. Fast food, the village version of which is fried eggs, as opposed to bean soup, is said 'not to take', i.e. to leave one feeling hungry soon afterwards. Particularly, though, *piánei* in this sense is a word used to denote effectiveness in the spiritual world, so that a candle lit by a menstruating woman, or a memorial service at which there is quarrelling, is said not to 'take', while of any ritually correct activity for the dead, or in honour of a saint, and so on, the word is used to indicate that the material action finds an echo in the unseen world. This term used, then, of gifts given to beggars, together with the reference to beggars being in God's care, places the action unambiguously in the spiritual world. In this instance the split between the two visions of the ideal world—between duty to the family and duty to the neighbour—is resolved, for by giving to God's creatures the family also wins its spiritual salvation. This kind of giving, in fact, comes under the heading of actions carried out 'for the sake of the soul'. This phrase is used, for example, of the act of baptizing a child, or in a report that a renowned local healer, as she neared the end of her life, refused to accept gifts in return, saying that she wished to use her skills freely 'for the sake of the soul'. Again, someone offering good advice may underline its disinterestedness by saying that it is given 'in order to save my soul'. The spiritual value of the gift to beggars is of the same order, for the action enters into the spiritual world where the 'good works', which all agree are necessary for entry into paradise, are received, and in this way, in spite of the customary tensions and conflicts, opportunities do exist in the normal daily life for, as it were, untarnished acts of giving. However, a further and more powerful occasion of unilateral giving does occur, and this is the advent of what might be termed the total stranger, the person utterly outside the normal village economy. This is encapsulated in various folk tales relating to hospitality.

In one such tale, a poor widow, left out of the wedding celebrations to which the whole village had been invited, had put loaves of cow dung to bake in order to deceive her hungry children until the wedding guests had returned home and she could go out to earn a handful of flour. A knock at her door revealed an old man with a staff, whom she invited in and to whom she apologized for not being able to offer any refreshment. All the same, he told her to take the loaves out of the fire for the children, and to go to draw wine, and, obeying, she found the cow-dung loaves changed to aromatic bread, and the rotten barrels, long empty of wine, brimming again so that the house was filled with the fragrance. Again, a poor man with two daughters to marry, who welcomed in a ragged old man, found later that his daughters 'spoke pearls, spat pearls' and gained rich dowries. And not only are families saved through giving, but souls also, as in a tale of a woman who gave away an onion. This woman had never in her life given anything away, and one day was working on her onion patch when she was accosted by a pregnant woman who asked her for an onion. In spite of the custom of giving pregnant women any food they requested lest they 'come to harm', she refused, but was countered by continuing requests: 'Just one onion, surely you can spare one!', till eventually she gave one onion away. When she died, the onion, the only thing she had ever given in her life, came out of her backside and by it she was hauled up to paradise.

As powerful, however, as these stories of hospitality given are those of hospitality refused. In direct contrast with the story of the poor widow is that of the householder, watching over the cooking of a rare and delicious meat stew, who three times deliberately ignores a knock on the door. But on turning back to the stew after the third and final knock, he finds it transformed, disgustingly, into human flesh. In another story, one brother among three gives bread to an old man, who eats, but still the bread isn't consumed. All three have wishes granted: that the crows should become goats, that the spring should flow with oil, and that the mountain should become plain. But years later when the old man returns, beseeching the froth of the milk or a little oil to soothe his sores, and is refused with insults by the two eldest brothers, the goats become crows again, the oil becomes water, and the fertile fields rocky heights. The youngest brother though, who is prepared to give the old man the blood of his only son, in the morning finds his son alive again, the old man gone, and his farm prospering; and his brothers finish up working for him. Finally, a story of a nearby hamlet runs that at a festival a ragged old man appeared, only to be mocked. He was hauled into the dance, and then pestered to sing. Eventually he gave in: 'Will you sing too?' he asked. 'But of course we'll sing.' And the old man sang: 'Ach! to seven, ach! to eight, ach! to nine, and back again!', and departed, since when there have never been more than nine houses in the village. In all these stories the unknown suppliant is, of course, Christ, and a sequel to the final story elaborates the theme by telling how

Christ comes again to the same village, this time as a handsome young man in gorgeous attire. He is duly made much of, but sitting at the table with food in front of him he does not eat, but taking the hem of his sleeve and dipping it into the dish, says: 'Eat, clothes! Eat, clothes!', and vanishes.

In these stories the value placed on hospitality is overwhelming. It is no longer a case of the non-related neighbour within the village being treated with suspicion and hostility, nor of the generalized welcome given to such a person at a death or on a name day, nor is it any longer a case of the general beneficence accorded to visiting tradesmen or beggars: it is a case of the necessity of the stranger being welcomed with the best and dearest possession that the house can provide. This cannot be explained simply by the fact that the stranger is no longer perceived as a threat, for in this case a simple neutrality would meet the case. Nor can it be answered by fear of the consequences if hospitality is refused, for these consequences are the product of cultural perceptions of the sacred, and the basis of these fears still needs to be explained. The answer, then, lies in a positive value to do with the necessity to give.

The particular context in which this hospitality takes place has already been indicated: sheer economics mean that the strength if not the very existence of the house depends on a close regard for self-interest, and that in this context to be over-generous and innocent is to place the family—the central repository of sacred values—in jeopardy. In this type of society, therefore, lies an endemic conflict between two worlds—a sacred world and a fallen world, an inner world and an outer world—the two realities locked in a perpetual struggle.

It is a struggle, however, which can be reconciled at significant moments and one of these moments is the arrival of someone who is what one might call the 'complete' stranger—that is to say, the stranger who, as he passes through the village, is seen to be in 'exile', sojourning in foreign parts, and coming from quite outside the local nexus of competition. Locally, the chances of giving without looking for return, even to the destitute, are limited by what the house 'has', and no house 'has' enough to support any other person or family indefinitely. But this necessary limitation on what the house is able to give, while still ensuring its own survival, is not challenged by this complete stranger who by definition comes from outside, is not in competition, and will not stay. In addition, such a person is also, by definition, lacking food, shelter, and probably company as well. Consequently, the complete stranger is the only person who can represent the outside world in a form that does not challenge the economic basis on which the house rests; while conversely this stranger is virtually the only person to whom the house can give, while not, in some form or another, giving to itself by creating the expectation of a return. This stranger is the supreme reconciler, representing for the house its greatest chance to break out of the ever-constricting limits placed by necessity on the sacred imperative to give, and to free what are thought of as natural well-springs of generosity and hospitality which are normally frustrated and locked up within its doors. The person who combines in his own figure the possibility of reconciliation, celebration, and responding to need—all shown earlier to be catalysts to the giving of gifts in this society—while freeing the gift from even the most tenuous association with self-interest, is a person who calls into being a transfigured household, one which is no longer dedicated by necessity to keeping the stranger out, but which delights in its ability to set on the table, if someone comes, 'Your own bread—not one of those miserable town loaves; and wine from the barrel in the store room, a *midzíthra*, some *féta*,[11] eggs . . .'. Such a house truly represents the divine plenitude of which it is an icon, and is truly the house, hyperbolized in the folk tales, in which cow dung becomes bread, water becomes oil, barrels long empty flow with wine, and within which the sacrifice made returns as a blessing. Conversely, the family which turns its back on the stranger, turning its back on one of the rare chances to give freely and without reserve, in a sense turns its back on the kingdom of heaven, and finds the sources of its prosperity withered at the root. In this sense the stranger, receiving so much and giving, in visible terms, so little, is a person who calls forth in the household an awareness of its essential and sacred nature, and in that sense is an aspect of the divinity. The celebration which surrounds the reception of the stranger becomes the celebration of the divine blessing on the family, and of the family's ability to transmit that blessing freely and without reserve into the outside world.

[11] *Midzíthra* (local pronunciation of *μυζήθρα*) is a cheese which when fresh is eaten as a table cheese, and when matured becomes hard and is grated and sprinkled on food; *féta* (*φέτα*) is a soft cheese that is preserved in brine.

17. The Sunday of the wedding: 'The groom and his male kin take turns in taking [the bride's] kerchief and leading her in the dance, before they all wend their way, 'right-handed', to the church' (p. 169). Behind the dance, the trousseau is being piled up, ready to load on to the animals. On matters of dress, see caption to Plate 16.

18. A stranger from another village: 'In the normal course of things, members of a neighbouring community will be accepted with a quiet friendship and recognition, with exchange of news and casual help as it is needed' (p. 187).

7
THE LIFE IN THE BLOOD

IN the last chapter marriage was described as the necessary condition of a fulfilled life and the accepted goal of every family for every child, whether boy or girl. Marriage is permitted only between non-kin, those classed as 'strangers', and this category is defined in sharp opposition to those sharing blood relationship and thought of as 'one's own'. Thus the universal dilemma inherent in any rule of marriage—how to reconcile the family's desire to keep itself intact with its need to receive new strength from outside—is here given a particular edge, since the 'strangers' between whom, exclusively, marriage is countenanced, are seen as being *a priori* in competition with each other's interests.

The sacred principle involved in this paradox has emerged as the principle of reconciliation and union, between man and woman, the house and the natural world, the known and the stranger. This principle at once binds families together, and then forces them to open themselves again to all that is most foreign to them; and these contradictory impulses are so important that the only solution is to confront them directly and live them out to the full. The same metaphysical principle, and the same paradox, is to be found in the living substance of the blood, and this chapter looks in turn at how blood binds families together, and how it compels them, nevertheless, to embrace in marriage what is strange and new.

In the solidarity of blood kin it is the relationship with children which is closest, and in which lies the strongest tendency to self-perpetuation and unchanging identity. Girls learn not just that they must marry, but that they must 'marry and have children', 'marry and produce a family'—a view well encapsulated in the gnomic comment: 'That is what life is, to marry, to have children and to look after them.' So although people may recognize that an evil fate may render a couple childless, or deprive them of their children once born, they do not differentiate in any serious way between the fact of marriage and the begetting of offspring. It is in children that life resides, and the childless, whether men or women—said to be 'heavy going' or lacking in joy—are said also, with terrible finality, 'not to have a future'.

This future which is embodied in the children involves both a corporate and an individual identity. There is a saying used so frequently as to be a basic axiom of village life: 'That's how we found it and that's how we leave it.' It is a phrase which features as a total explanation of any custom or activity: once it has made its appearance, nothing more need be said. The people who use this phrase are seeing themselves as heirs to a tradition and a way of life of which they are the servants, not the masters, and in which their function is to stand between the earlier generations who have passed life on to them, and the children to whom in turn they will pass it on. They are the bridge between past and future, and what they look to pass on is not simply life itself, but an entire culture by which that life is given a meaning. So not only are houses, land, and animals, faithfully delivered to the next generation, but also practices of agriculture, forestry, and animal husbandry, arts of building, making and mending, knowledge of birth and death, of herbs and cures, of good and evil—an interwoven pattern of practical skills and sacred knowledge transmitted in unbroken continuity. So the 'future' which is embodied in the children is to do with the perpetuation of society itself and of the particular perceptions which shape and inspire it. But it is also to do with the communal life of the kindred, and, importantly, with an individual self-fulfilment, in which an inbuilt reciprocity between children and parents is realized over time, and converts the early care of the old for their young into the later care of the young for the old.

It is the duty of children to give, in return for the care they received in their youth, reciprocal care for their parents in their old age, and this is particularly so in the case of the youngest son. While, as has been said earlier, all sons are thought of as being 'in the house', it is especially the youngest who has this designation, for it is he who remains with the old people to look after their minimal wants until they die, and to inherit once they are gone. The child who gives most will inherit most, and in this way the old people are assured of a roof and food in their failing years. Couples with no children, on the other hand, are quite literally on their own, and there is no answer to their rhetorical question 'Who is going to look after us?', for only those of the household can look after those in the household, and in this sense the following comment is the exact truth: 'Brother: stranger. Sister: stranger. Mother-in-law and mother don't live for ever. Only children will look after you.' And it is perhaps in an echo of these mutually dependent relationships that the generations are charmingly confused in the endearments often used by a mother to her infant, 'my mother' or 'my little mother', and in the way in which older children can in familiar conversations address their parents as 'my child'.

There is, then, a basic reciprocity enacted in the care by the young for the old; and although when times are hard this caring for people who cannot work but who still 'eat bread' may be given with little grace, in the final analysis what is important are the simple decencies of warmth, shelter, cleanliness, and food, and so long as the old receive this from their children—and all do because communal opinion would not tolerate it otherwise—they are said to say, 'As long as they look after me, even though they shout at me...'.

Care for the old people, however, does not end with their death, for as important as their physical care during their old age are the memorial customs carried out for them after they are dead. This duty falls nominally on all the children, but again the main responsibility lies on the youngest son with his wife who care for the old ones and inherit the house and land. Thus the toil of the past generations, the land which nourishes the present, and the memory of, in particular, the recently dead, are all bound together in a series of commemorative acts which are conducted not purely through customary duty, but, as it is said, in understanding and gratitude for what they now possess.

All children are potentially carers for the souls of their parents in this way, but the burden of responsibility varies with the sex and status of the children. Since it is the women who guard the ritual life of the household, it is the women who remember and prepare the memorials, though these are also attended by the men. Thus it is the daughter-in-law who cares for her husband's parents and who with her husband inherits the house when they die, on whom the responsibility falls of being the chief guardian of their souls after their death. These memorial services are described in Chapter 9, but a brief indication should be given here of their importance, for they are believed to have a direct effect on the welfare of the dead in the other world. The memorial food eaten by the living community is thought to be imaged in the other world by the dead person who feasts in parallel with the living. The final memorial, which centres around the exhumation of the bones, is likewise a critical stage in the progress of the soul in the 'other world'. Every candle lit to a person's memory appears before that person bringing a moment of illumination; while for those in hell, up to their necks in pitch, each prayer that is said, each candle that is lit, each memorial service that is held, acts to pull them out, just a little, from their torment. So the care given by their children to the old after their death is a service as real as that given before it, and at death the relationship of practical assistance, far from ending, moves, rather, into another dimension.

This form of memorial is not, however, the only way in which people are brought life by their children, for this occurs also through the passing on of the name. The surname, passed down through the male line, is a factor in the especial value that is put on sons who, as well as being 'in the house', are also the only children to be 'heard'—they are the only ones to carry on the family name. But although, as it is said, 'only sons are heard' in this generic sense, there is an individual commemoration enacted through daughters as well as sons, and this lies in the giving of the Christian name. The name given is customarily the name of a saint, and the pattern of naming typically follows a sequence in which the first son is called after the father's father, the first daughter after the father's mother, the second son after the mother's father, and the second daughter after the mother's mother. After this the choice of names is free. Thus the name comes and goes, appears and disappears, calling back to earth and to memory that generation now passing into old age and death, and the enormous joy with which the individual greets the passing on of his or her name to a grandchild indicates its significance as bestowing on them a kind of extension of earthly existence. '[It is] so that the name should be heard again', someone is bound to say, when discussing any particular naming—or its corollary, '[It is] so that the name should not be lost'. And in the renewal of the name and of the individual in the name lies a value capable of overruling even that placed on care in old age which was referred to earlier. For, in a curious antithetical echo of that sentiment ('as long as they look after me, even though they shout at me...') this runs, 'Never mind if they don't look after me so long as my name is heard again'. Thus through the children and particularly through sons 'the name is heard again', the immortality of the land becomes indivisible from the history of the family, and those who have no children or whose children are dead are said to be consumed by an unquenchable grief for they know that 'their name will be extinguished'.

The name, then, has the power to bring the memory of the dead back to this world, and it in some way participates in their identity. The giving of the name at baptism, one of the critical actions of the ceremony, in this way associates the child with a particular forebear, but it has a further dimension in that it also associates the child with a particular saint. The majority of Christian names are just that—the names of saints—and even those with classical names such as Andromache and Pericles still celebrate their name within the dispensation of the Church on the first Sunday after Pentecost—the Sunday of All Saints. The pronouncing of the name during the service of baptism is the prerogative of the godparent, except, significantly, in one situation, and this is when the name to be given is the same as the godparent's own; for in this case to pronounce the name is said to be to 'give' one's own name 'away', and someone else must be appointed to act as proxy. In some sense then, the name is identified with a person's inner reality, and it is this that lies also behind the belief already cited that to reveal one's name to the demons is to give oneself into their hands: 'It is dangerous to speak to the demons, but it is still more dangerous to say one's name.' The name does not merely confer a social identity, it participates symbolically in a person's most integral self; and it is from this understanding that there can arise a variant of the phrase already quoted ('[it is] so that the name should be heard again') in which 'name' is replaced by 'type' or 'stock' (*σόι*)—'[it is] so that the type [of myself] should not be lost'. Thus for 'the name to be heard again' is for a complex reality to be once again called into being, a reality which does not merely indicate but represents the individual, and it is this that gives additional depth to the common assumption that to have no children is to have no future.

The passionate love of children and the absolute conviction that life without children is only half a life is in this way related both to an intense love of life in this world combined with an intense awareness that this life does not go on for ever. At the same time as causing the individual person to be as it were subsumed into, and sacrificed to, the greater cause of perpetuating life in the future generations, children bring with them also the assurance that in them not only the ageing but also the dead are renewed, so that in them the progenitors rejoice in what they feel to be a kind of reprieve from extinction, a kind of relative immortality.

Thus far then, the blood tie binds the generations together in a single continuing identity. But even here the forces which are to scatter the family are already at work. Even as the parents reach their fulfilment in the birth of their first child, they are by this event being pushed up one level into the first of the ageing generations; the care that was lavished on them they now begin to lavish on the newcomer to the family, and hopes for themselves become hopes for their children. And this is strikingly portrayed in a kinship structure in which the extinction of one level of progenitors is implicit in the birth of every new generation.

Kinship is calculated from a starting point in the individual, who looks back to his or her primary progenitors, or 'roots' as they are called, in the four pairs of great grandparents, and sees himself or herself as the centre of a network of relatives originating from them. With roots at great grandparents, a person's lateral relations extend to second cousins, since all second cousins have one pair of great grandparents in common (Diagram 1).

Diagram 1

A pair of 'roots' descending to two groups who are second cousins to each other

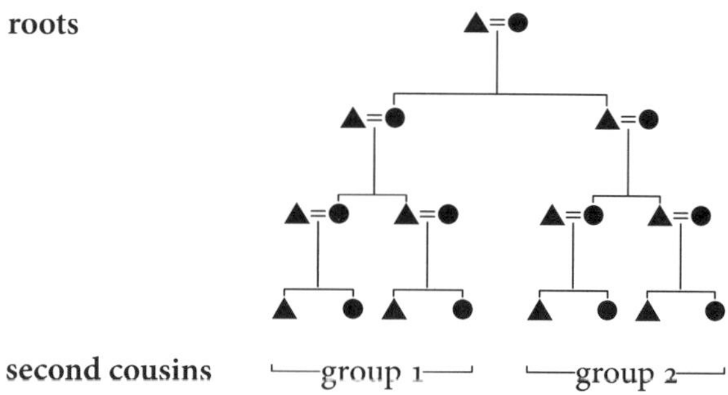

Thus the degree of kinship between any two people is dependent on their relative closeness or distance from a common 'root' or 'roots', and this is made clear in the way in which people typically speak of

kinship. 'I am her niece from her first cousin—my grandmother and her mother were sisters', someone might say, or 'He is my second cousin—his grandfather and my grandmother were siblings.' And reference to this original sibling group carries always with it the implication, spoken or unspoken, of the original progenitors from whom the siblings themselves were born: 'Our parents [grandparents etc.] were siblings and *from the same womb.*'

In this way it is the sibling group, rather than the individual, which is the building block of kinship, for since siblings all share the same parents, all have all four pairs of 'roots' in common and share precisely the same category of kin. But it is only within the sibling group that this absolute identity of kin resides. The 'roots' of parents lie one generation back from the 'roots' of their children; as each new generation is born it forgets its parents' roots and looks to its own roots in the next generation of ancestors, and the whole configuration of aunts and uncles, first and second cousins, changes as a result. It is children in any house on whom attention is concentrated, and their kin therefore who come to feature most significantly in the life of the house; thus while all kinship is derived from common identity in the same roots three or four generations back, the point of reference which defines these roots increasingly comes to lie in the child (Diagram 2).

Diagram 2

'Roots' from the perspective of the child (ego)

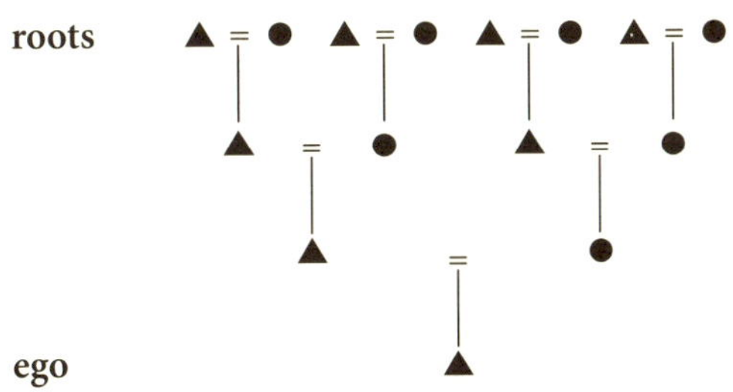

This child-centred perspective is important, for it creates of the village kindred a particularly finite entity, continually hardening off at the edges as it sheds another level of great grandparents into the undifferentiated ancestors of the past, disclaims distant aunts and uncles and cousins, and moves with every generation into a new grouping related centrally to each new child or group of siblings. 'Kinship passes', people will say of a family whose links with themselves have now lapsed, or, 'We have left them [i.e. that stock]'. Nevertheless, although the kindred is finite, the fidelity with which this movement is repeated over the generations perpetuates it in its essential formation, and thus gives it a sort of infinity within the temporal order. Birth is matched with death and death with birth, so that as each new generation comes into being the older one fades into oblivion. It is a pattern which, accepting mutability and change, is based essentially on process and renewal, and one which invokes, as in the marriage rituals, the image of the dance; for the dance of life continues as long as there is a new generation to step onto the dancing floor and to bear for a brief time the image of the family before passing it on. By the birth of children life is quickened and the victory of death relegated yet again. But just as the dancers coming in at the head of the circle cause the preceding party to drop back, so each child or group of siblings entering the dance of life causes one level of progenitors and their descendants, all kin to its parents, to drop out of kinship and out of memory.

Thus there is no cult of the ancestors in this society; on the contrary, the death, memory, and final forgetting of the individual is necessary to the movement of the whole, so that one by one the dead generations vanish, after a time, into oblivion, to leave room for those who come after.

The village construction of kinship, then, has at its heart processes which presuppose an unflinching acceptance of the transitory nature of this life, but at the same time place an absolute value on the defeat of death. Children are the key to this defeat, for not only is the individual revitalized in his or her descendants, but so also is the kindred as a whole, which although constantly changing is also constantly reformed, and in which the endless recurrence of death is overcome by an endless succession of lives. Children represent the ever-completing, ever to be completed, work of the previous generations; they represent eternal life for the kindred. And this centrality of the child to the kin relationships which spread from it is demonstrated in the complete identification of kin relationships that occurs on marriage—aunts and uncles and cousins, nephews and nieces, of both bride and bridegroom henceforth being held in common—while to all these relatives the newcomer is the same: 'bride' (*νύφη*) or 'groom' (*γαμπρός*). To all the members of a person's kindred, that is to say, the newcomer into the family has a single significance—he or she comes as bridegroom or bride to bring new life to the kindred and overcome death by generation. This is the context behind an old man's looking round the room at his niece's engagement and saying, 'Look how many nephews and nieces I've got', and, also, behind the sage confirmation of this statement in the answering comment, 'Thus the kindred increases'. The wedding wish that was quoted earlier—'May you grow white... with children and great grandchildren'—epitomizes this great collective yearning for the knowledge of honourable continuity in old age, while amongst the most terrible curses are those which attempt to undo this life-directed process and set in motion the exact reverse, 'May your feet not recognize the paths they tread, and may the owl hoot from your roof-beams'—for this is an invocation of individual madness, ruin of the house, and the extinction of the line.

The pattern of kinship which has just been described consists of two dominant images both involving the idea of a 'root', and to present these images of 'roots' accurately it is necessary to replace the idea of 'descent' pictured in Diagrams 1 and 2 with the idea of a plant or tree which grows upwards from these roots (see Plate 20 facing p. 209). One image is the perception of the direct lines traced upwards from all the 'roots' through grandparents and parents to any particular child; the other is all the proliferating lines of blood from a particular great grandparent which diversify upwards through the generations to form an ever-widening pattern of branches above. It is significant therefore that two images which reflect this dual perspective are found very commonly in folk art, and found very commonly together. One is the triangular image of a cypress, in which hidden roots produce a condensed upwards-pointing tip of directed growth; the other is the spreading form of a flowering shrub, or flowering plant in a pot, in which hidden roots produce a growth which bifurcates into an increasingly diverse form. There is a strong resemblance between both these images and the way in which kinship is thought of, and indeed the flowering plant has in folklore studies long been taken to be an image of the family, or of the family tree. Thus it seems there is an analogy here between processes in the natural world and those within kinship. The upwards springing cypress images the perspective on kinship which focuses on the way in which each new child forms a spearhead into the future. The flowering plant images a more static perspective which focuses on the common origin of an ever more diffuse category of collateral relatives. The very word 'root' for the original progenitors is in itself suggestive of organic growth, and it seems that in these folk motifs the natural world provides two powerful images of human life—of a child's lines of origin in its roots on the one hand, and of the lines of new births spreading out from a common ancestor on the other.

If the structure of kinship finds apt parallels in images of natural growth, the medium of kinship, blood, is also perceived as an organic substance, for it is blood which both binds together and scatters the members of a family. Even though, strictly speaking, it is only the sibling group which is seen as sharing identical blood, kin in general are defined as being of 'one blood', and this is counterpoised to those who are 'not kin' and therefore 'not blood', 'strange blood', or 'strangers'. So the insistence that marriage must be with those outside the kin group is another way of saying, as people do, that marriage must be with 'strange blood', and the reason for this is phrased also in terms of blood: 'Blood that is like should not be united' (*αἷμα που οὐίζει* [*τεριάζει*] *δὲν πρέπει να ἑνωθεῖ*). Thus marriage at any point within the kindred amounts to incest, for which the exact translation of the Greek term is 'the mixing of [similar] blood' (*αἱμομιξία*). Approved marriages, taking place beyond the kindred, therefore involve primarily the joining of those who are to each other 'not blood' or of 'strange blood', and it is in these terms that any permitted marriage is customarily legitimated: 'They are not blood: they can marry.' The point at which 'same blood' converts to 'strange blood' is open to negotiation, for while the Church permits marriage beyond second cousins, a popular saying prohibits marriage between third cousins also; but wherever it occurs it embodies a concept of blood similarity ceasing abruptly at a particular point.

Blood relationship is thus the foundation of kinship, and the movement of the blood which governs the varying degrees of relationship within the kindred finds expression in the image of the *zinári* (ζινάρι, also ζουνάρι). The primary meaning of *zinári* (pl. *zinária*), dialect from *zóni* (ζώνη) or *zonári* (ζωνάρι)), is the long woven belt worn by men circling round the waist. The metaphorical meaning, however, is what is at issue here, and this metaphorical meaning is invoked in a proverbial expression relating to the length of time the blood continues to reproduce characteristics down the generations: 'The blood lasts for seven *zinária*.' What is a *zinári*? The answer comes with a continuous right-handed circling gesture of the hand imitating the series of turns by which the belt is put on.

Zinári is a complex term which has to be unravelled rather than translated.[1] Siblings are said to belong to the same *zinári*, parents and children to be separated by one *zinári*; and first, second, third cousins and so on, to be, respectively, one, two, three etc. *zinária* from each other. Cousinship may, as a result, be reckoned straightforwardly in *zinária*: 'What are you? Are we kin?' 'We're fifth cousins'. 'Ah! five *zinária*!'... One *zinári*, then, does not mean 'one generation', since any set of siblings are, although on an identical generational level with their cousins, distanced from them by one or more *zinária*. Nor does it mean one (canonical) degree of kinship, for siblings belong to the same *zinári*, even though canonically they are one degree apart. The spiralling *zinári* is not so much a way of counting degrees of kinship as a representation of the process which enables kinship in the first place.

This process which is imaged in the spiralling *zinári* is made clearer in the two following descriptions, one by the village priest and one by a villager. Priests, who have to adjudicate on whether a couple is eligible to marry, are taught a way of reckoning kinship termed 'by affinity' and rendered diagrammatically by a right-handed spiral which widens progressively. Taking the man of the proposed couple

[1] For a full analysis of this image of kinship see Juliet du Boulay, 'The Blood: Symbolic Relationships between Descent, Marriage, Incest Prohibitions and Spiritual Kinship in Greece', *Man* (N.S.), 19 (1984), pp. 533–56.

first, this runs as follows (Diagram 3): 'You start with a [common] root [A], who has a child [B]. This boy marries and has a son [C]: another generation. This boy marries and has a son [D]: another generation. [If the same is true of the woman of the couple] in this way with one cycle you arrive at [a couple who are] third cousins [to each other].'

Diagram 3

Priest's drawing of kinship reckoning 'by affinity'

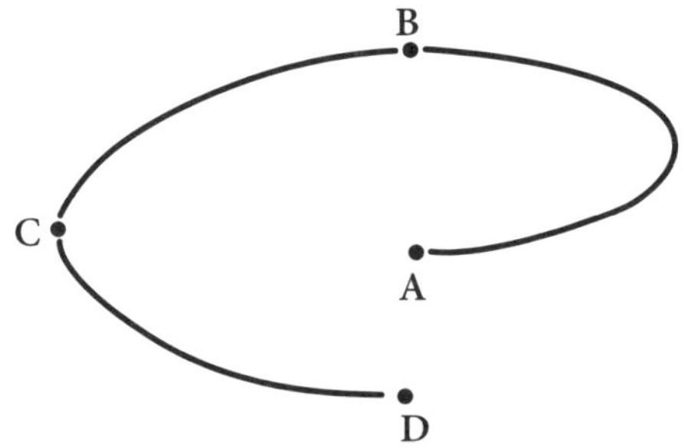

'By affinity' thus reckons the distance of specified individuals from a common root by calculating the number of marriages which intervene between them, and it sees this progressive distancing, up to third cousin (who canonically are 'strangers' to each other), in terms of 'one cycle'. However, a local description of the same process is more illuminating, for it does not merely calculate distance but provides a description of the means by which this distancing occurs: 'You mingle the blood, you get a cross—another stock. You mingle the blood, you get a cross—another stock. One stock is one blood.' (*Σμίγεις τὸ αἷμα, ἔχεις διασταύρωσι—ἄλλο σόι* [twice]. *Ένα σόι ἕνα αἷμα εἶναι.*)

It was mentioned earlier that the sibling group is the building block of kinship since only siblings share precisely the same categories of kin, and the thinking behind this has now become apparent—it is because the 'one blood' or 'one stock' of kinship lies not in the 'root', but in the child or children in whom a new mingling of the blood is, uniquely, created. Here, therefore, we see the exact constituents of the logic which places such an emphasis on the sibling bond: between siblings there are no '*zinária*' for they share identical blood; but successive minglings of the blood, weakening by a specific amount the original stock, produce successive distancing between cousins, and each 'mingling' constitutes a further *zinári*. First cousins, children of siblings, inherit half the original blood, and are therefore separated by one *zinári*. With second cousins the common inheritance is halved again—two *zinária*; and so on. Each successive 'cross' then weakens the blood by one step so that, even within the category of those who are defined as being within the kindred and therefore broadly speaking as of 'one blood', that blood is actually seen to be steadily weakened as from one 'crossing' to another it is diluted down the various lines of descent.

The *zinári* is thus revealed as a way of understanding differentiation between one member of the kindred and another, not in terms of generations, nor of degrees of kinship, but in terms of an integral vision of the transmission and renewal of the blood. And it is an image of considerable power in that it appears to be capable of combining two ideas that were described earlier: the blood lines which flow to a single point (the cypress tree), imaged in the one blood of siblings, and the blood as it disperses across the collateral generations (the flowering plant), imaged in the successive minglings of the blood. More than this however, the *zinári* catches up a third significant element in that in its circling movement it recapitulates an earlier theme, for it takes, like the dance, the form of a spiral, right-handed, irreversible, and continually renewed.

It is becoming clear that the movement of the dance, already seen so persistently in the wedding celebrations, is but one embodiment of an image which appears in other contexts. This image, wherever it is found, is not only overwhelmingly auspicious and life-directed, but also invariably symbolized as 'right-handed' and irreversible. In kinship it takes the form of one 'cycle' of marriages and births from a common root to the outer edges of kinship (the priest's description), as well as the continuing right-handed cyclic movement of the *zinária* which in varying degrees separate kinsmen (the villagers' description). Thus just as in marriage it is the women who are, in themselves, the dance, in kinship the image applies to the blood, passing onwards in a uni-directional flow of marriages to strangers until sufficient generations have passed for it to complete the 'cycle'—to have been diluted enough to allow for marriage to the descendants of the original stock. This is the fundamental meaning of the image of the *zinári*: it is the dance of the blood. And this image has a further elaboration, which involves an additional marriage prescription known as *katameriá* (*καταμεριά*).

This prescription stems in the first place from an uneasiness about marriage between people who are closely related to the bride or groom of an earlier marriage—for example, the brother of a groom may not marry the sister of his brother's bride, unless both couples are married on the same day, so that there is no previous relationship of close affinity preceding either marriage. The way in which this impediment is felt to happen is made clear in the following description of the union of the blood in marriage: 'If you drink water it becomes part of you. So it is with blood.' And the consequences are unequivocal too—the relatives of the pair who have thus married and 'drunk' each other's blood, 'become affines, but like kin'. And there are some unexpected though logical consequences to this belief. In the case of a man, for instance, whose first wife dies childless and whose second wife bears him children, these children are forbidden to marry any children of the first wife's siblings since, in words reminiscent of those quoted above, they are 'like cousins'. The blood of the first wife and her siblings, 'drunk' by the father, remains in him into his second marriage to create a 'blood' relationship between his children by his second wife and his dead wife's nephews and nieces.

If two brothers may not marry two sisters except on the same day, there is a still more stringent interdiction on marriage between the sister of a groom and the brother of his bride, who may never in any circumstances marry, for if they did 'the blood' would 'turn back'. And between two siblings marrying two first cousins, or between first cousins marrying two first cousins, this turning back of the blood is only prevented if marriages are regulated by the principle that they must, like the two brothers marrying two sisters, be *katameriá*, that is to say going one way:[2] in other words, if a man A marries a wo-man

[2] The word *katameriá* as a general term indicates everything of the same type being collected together in one place, and it can be used, for instance, to indicate a grazing arrangement whereby all the sheep are grazed *katameriá*, in one area, so as to leave the sown ground free, or be cited in the telling of fortunes from a drained coffee cup when all the grounds collect in one place. The rule of *katameriá* in marriage described here includes local variations elaborating the basic marriage rules. For a description of other variations of this sort in Greece see Just, *Greek Island Cosmos*, pp. 107–10.

B, more kinsmen of A may marry more kinswomen of B, but no kinsman of B may 'turn back' to take a woman from the kin of A—successive marriages between affines are only countenanced so long as they preserve the original movement of the sexes in marriage.

There is more to it than this, however. It will be remembered that 'only boys are heard' in the sense that only boys inherit the house, work the family land, and carry on the name, while daughters on marriage leave their family of origin and sever their close connection with their own kin, for the house, the mother, and the kin of their husband. And it will be remembered too that the terminology of marriage—to 'give' a daughter in marriage and to 'take' a bride—is a reflection of this reality, since it is the men who provide the axis of stability and continuity 'in the house' while the women are mobile, leaving their homes on marriage to go as 'strangers' to their new kin, bringing their 'strange blood' with them. The proscription on 'return' marriages between unrelated pairs of kinsmen then, while it appears at first sight simply to enforce a reciprocal and consistent movement of either sex in opposite directions—men going one way and women another—is not in fact reciprocal and does not bear equivalently on either sex. Rather, it assumes the men remaining 'in the house' while the women are 'given' to these men in marriage, so that it is on the passage of the women that the uni-directional movement is enforced. What is being preserved by *katameriá* is, then, the integrity of the two groups of wife-givers and wife-takers, which may not be confused lest, once again, 'the blood' should 'turn back'.

'Turning back', or reversing the right-handed, onward, and life-directed movement, is always, as has been said, deeply inauspicious, and those marriages which are not '*katameriá*'—which do not continue in the same direction—partake in this same inauspicious reversal. This is a fatal counter-flow which brings about the same evil consequences as marriage within the kindred, for it causes 'the stock' to become 'polluted' and provides a catalyst for misfortune and death.

Just as close affines can be seen as 'like kin', so the 'return' of the blood is seen here as occurring between people who are not physiologically related but are linked only by the marriage of two of their relatives, and thus between two groups of people who need to be specifically defined as 'strangers' for the initial marriage to take place at all. In spite of this, however, what is thought to 'return' in marriages of this sort between pairs of cousins is the blood. A blood link, then, is assumed, firstly, to occur between any pair who are joined in marriage, and secondly, to extend through a considerable range of relatives, especially on the 'taking' side. It is only if this occurs that the 'blood' can be said to 'turn back' in a marriage which is not *katameriá*, i.e. when the 'taking' side becomes the 'giving' side.

The range of kin at risk in this way is a matter of debate, though it is felt by some that it extends to the limits of the kindreds involved. But whether the limits fall across a broad or a narrow spectrum of kin, the principle is the same, and it is one which posits a theory of the blood which has moved from a physiological to a symbolic understanding, and assumes that blood, passing mysteriously between the two partners to a marriage, also flows through them typically to their relatives on the 'taking' side to whom the new relationships are particularly important; and the rule of *katameriá* is designed to protect people against the return of this mysterious blood link which makes bonds 'like' kinship, just as the normal marriage rule specifying marriage out of the kindred is designed to protect people against the return of the physiological stream of the blood of kinship itself.[3]

Katameriá thus reveals more than the existence of this symbolic blood link on marriage; it reveals a critical principle which relates the movement of the blood to the movement of women, and it builds on and illuminates the general marriage rule that blood should go to strange blood. The basic marriage rule enforces the uni-directional movement of the blood in insisting on the outward movement of marriage to strangers, and prohibiting the return of descendants in marriage—for a specified number of generations—to any line from which they derive. The rule of *katameriá* adds to this a further element of irreversibility, prohibiting men of a kindred from 'taking' women not only from among the descendants but also from among the close affines of a woman whom they have already 'given'. Both rules are thus embodiments of a single principle—that the procession of the blood should be irreversible, avoiding the death-bringing marriages which would return the blood to its source; and both rules operate in the same social context in which

[3] This account of *katameriá* makes some small modifications to the account in du Boulay, 'The Blood'.

19. Two Marias: The old Maria danced like a young girl at the baptism of her grand-daughter, for joy that her 'name should be heard again' (cf. p. 196). The old man is her husband, blind for some years.

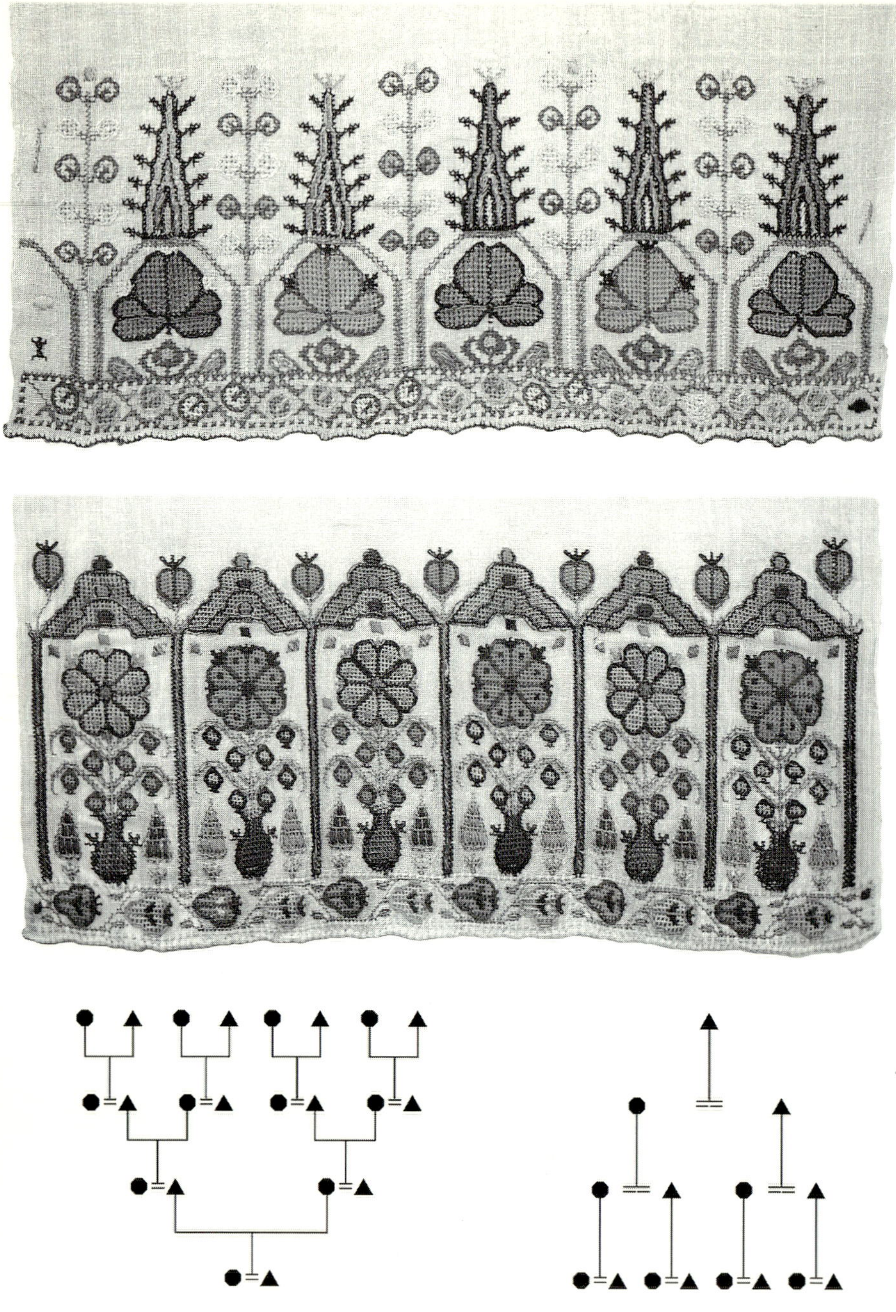

20. Flowering plant and cypress motifs: Two table runners (*tsevrédhes*) compared with the kinship patterns of Diagrams 1 and 2, both diagrams inverted to place the 'roots' at the ground level of the pattern, and the newest births at the top. The lower runner magnifies the flowering plant motif and places small cypress motifs in between; the upper runner places the flowering plant inside a roofed house, and crowns the roof with the cypress motif.

the men remain 'in the house', 'taking' the women who are 'given' to them. Both rules are therefore elaborations of the auspicious onward circling movement of the blood, embodied in the women moving in marriage 'right-handed' through the community, and it is for this reason that the dance and the dance pattern feature so prominently at a wedding, and for this reason that in the ceremonial gifts of the bridegroom to the bride is included the valuable and much prized adornment of the *kadém*, that is to say a *zinári* (belt) made of red silk. In the light of the foregoing discussion of the *zinári* it is clear why this red spiralling *kadém*, a potent symbol of the circling of the blood through the generations, is so vital a part of the bride's regalia as a new wife, for it is the women who, bringing fresh blood to their new families and providing a new and irreversible impulse to the circling process of generation, are the living embodiments of the giving to the stranger which the *zinári* signifies.

Thus far this discussion has concerned blood kinship only; but the same idea of giving recurs in spiritual kinship.

A spiritual kinsman or woman, *koumbáros* (f. -*a*), is one who, together with his or her spouse, is sponsor at a wedding or godparent at a baptism. This relationship created between the sponsor and the couple, or between the godparent and the godchild, is very close, and it is the mainspring of an understanding by which all members of the two respective households are involved collectively in the spiritual relationship of any one of them, saying of the person concerned, 'We have baptized him' or 'We have crowned [married] him'. Indeed a simple acknowledgement of the link can spread a good deal further than the two households concerned, and it is possible, for instance, for the siblings of a baptizing *koumbáros* to address all the uncles and aunts of the child as '*koumbáre*'.

The action of a wedding sponsor is to follow the priest in the action of 'crowning' the couple—an action of the marriage service so important that the word 'to crown' is used interchangeably with the word 'to marry'. These 'crowns' are in the Greek Church two white circlets joined with a ribbon and representing garlands, placed on the heads of bride and groom, each of which at a certain point in the service is taken by the priest who inserts one circlet at right-angles into the other and with them makes the sign of the cross three times over the groom and then three times over the bride. As he does this he repeats three times, for each of them, the words: 'The servant of God, X, is crowned to the servant of God, Y, in the Name of the Father, and of the Son, and of the Holy Spirit. Amen.' The crowns are then passed to the sponsor who, holding them separately with his hands crossed right over left, receives them, and holding the garlands in the air, changes them round above the heads of the couple three times before finally placing them on their heads.

The ceremony of crowning in the Orthodox marriage service has a complex symbolism in which the crown represents, amongst other things, the glory of the giving which each person will make to the other and to their children, thus bringing into being the mutuality of sacrifice on which the marriage is based. It is in demonstration of the differing sacrifices involved that at the beginning of the service the man is taken by the priest to venerate the icon of Christ, and the woman the icon of the Mother of God. The crowning thus symbolizes for the couple their birth into a spiritual mutuality of which the relationship between Christ and the Mother of God is the full expression, and it is through the crowning that the sacramental reality is called forth which will sustain the future. In this way the *koumbáros* is critical both to the marriage and to its outcome, and since children are the intended outcome of the marriage it is natural that he or she should be confirmed and in a sense rewarded by being given the first child of the marriage to baptize—a sequence enshrined in a popular expression, 'If you plant a vine you'll eat grapes.' The planting of the vine of marriage culminates for the *koumbáros* in the fruits of baptism, and a 'proper' or 'full' (*κανονικός*) *koumbáros* is one who has both sown and reaped in this way.

The duties of the godparent at baptism initially involve renunciation of the devil and a confession of faith, but the chief action is the pronouncing of the name and the anointing of the child with olive oil. The moment at which the name is given is awaited with anticipation, for though godparents have a duty to follow customary practice they in fact have the right to give any name they please, and they have been known to defy the wishes of the parents and to commemorate in the naming some dead relative of their own. It is partly to avoid the spectacular row which can ensue if this happens, that the parents themselves are not present at the baptism but wait to be told of the name by the children who rush from church with the news the moment they hear it pronounced. This moment is critical, for whatever name is said it cannot be unsaid, and it is this name which brings the child into relationship with the person commemorated and into the community of saints, establishing him or her as a unique personality in both the social and divine orders. After the naming the child is completely covered with the baptismal oil—the 'oil of gladness'—by the godparent before being immersed in the water three times by the priest, who also, when the child is dressed in its baptismal garments, anoints the child with the holy chrism, a fragrant consecrated oil compounded from olive oil, balsam, and other ingredients, signifying the gift of the Holy Spirit, which is marked with the sign of the cross on the forehead, eyes, ears, nostrils, mouth, breast, hands, and feet.

The triple immersion is 'after the pattern of Christ's death and resurrection'—a parallel made possible by the symbolic power of water, once again a force for both destruction and creation in that it carries the double symbolism of burial and re-birth, of un-forming and re-forming. So the descent into the waters of baptism here images both the child's encounter with the world of chaos and un-becoming and the washing away of the imprint of the fallen world, and the child's emergence from this encounter as a 'new man' formed in the freedom of the world redeemed in Christ. It is this that creates the conditions for the child to be born again, no longer a 'child of the body' but a 'child of the light',[4] and while it is the priest who is the initiator into this mystery, it is the godparent who in carrying out the first anointing prepares the child for this transition and accompanies him through it. Standing at the gateway between the fallen and the unfallen worlds, giving the name and anointing with oil, the godparent is the spiritual guardian and guarantor of the child's safe passage from one to the other, and it is because of this that godparenthood is 'higher than kinship' and the godparent has the freedom to choose the name; and it is also because of this that when the child is returned to its mother she must prostrate before the godparent in order to receive her child back. The godparent thus has an extraordinary significance, so much so that the role of the priest is somewhat taken for granted in popular thinking and it is the godparent who is indicated as the protagonist,

[4] Hapgood, *Service Book*, pp. 274, 275.

for it is this person who, as it is said, 'puts the oil on' and 'makes the child a Christian'.

The action of the godparent and that of the wedding sponsor are thus symbolically parallel. In both cases it is a priest who performs the sacrament, but in both cases the wedding sponsor or godparent performs the vital action with the crowns and the oil, mediating between the two worlds, standing by the participants and guiding them through. Thus the action of the wedding sponsor in planting the 'vine' of marriage in the sacramental reality is both replicated and consummated when he or she as godparent brings the child into the same mystery. And the sequence does not end here, for the godparent, or someone nominated by him, is normally also the sponsor at his godchild's wedding, and again the same preference should be observed on the birth of the first child of that marriage. This obligation to refer to the original *koumbáros*, and to accept a relative of his if he does not wish to or cannot attend himself, is one which must last for his lifetime. Only after his death may the relationship with that particular family end, and be freely taken up elsewhere. In that case however, the sequence is over and even relationships already contracted with the descendents of the original godparent who stood as proxy for him, can be—and often are—permitted to lapse.

Sponsorship at marriage and baptism are thus not one-off actions but are thought to set in motion a chain of relationships which only ceases on the death of the original *koumbáros*—a situation which is encapsulated in the comments, 'That's how God has given it to us—one to baptize another and then to crown him', and, 'That's how God has given it to us: a person puts the oil on and then he crowns him.' Baptism and marriage thus form a continual interweaving of oil and crowns, oil and crowns, a long chain of relationships created between the families in ordained and sacred procession. And it is here that a similar prescription enters in as was noted for relationships created with affines, for in baptism, as in marriage, the stream of relationships must continue the same way, *katameriá*; and return baptisms involve, though in relation to oil rather than to blood, the same catastrophic conclusion—'the oil turns back', bringing death with it.

Katameriá in the case of spiritual kinship proscribes the godchild from 'turning back' and baptizing anyone in the godparent's family, but as in blood kinship there is a certain imprecision in the boundaries accepted by different families, so that *katameriá* can also be thought to involve both the families concerned, in which case neither the baptized person, nor his parents, siblings, children or grandchildren, should 'turn back' and baptize any similar member of the family that holds a godparent of theirs. Wherever the line is drawn however, the consequences of defiance are serious, and it is typical that after the baptism of a baby by the brother of a girl who had been baptized by the baby's grandfather, the reaction should be: 'Niko shouldn't have baptized the child. The oil turned back, and it died.'

Even, therefore, if the range of people affected by *katameriá* is open to negotiation the principle is nevertheless categoric, and just as the on-going open-ended spiral of the blood and of new births is the consequence of *katameriá* in the world of natural kinship, so in the world of spiritual kinship the identical principle enforces an on-going open-ended spiral of spiritual life. And it is in the context of these meanings that a familiar image suddenly leaps to prominence and indicates an unmistakable parallel between the two types of relationship, for when a man dies and is being laid out, the question is asked, 'Has he got godchildren?' If the answer is yes, then the *zinári* around the waist is bound up and fastened; if 'no', it is left loose and dangling. The explanation for this runs that it is 'shame' (*ντροπή*) to go unkempt before one's maker; but in view of the foregoing discussion on the *zinári* it becomes plain that this action has a more precise significance, and that the unloosing of the *zinári* in the case of those who have no godchildren is a statement of that person's failure to do in the spiritual world what it is his duty also to do in the physical world, and that is to act as a vehicle for the continuing flow of life. The man who goes to his grave with an unwound *zinári* is a man who goes to his maker with the symbolic acknowledgement of the dead-end in him of the life-giving spiral of the oil.

There begins to appear, then, a precise correspondence between spiritual and physical kinship. While the kindred is formed by an understanding of blood kinship set in motion by marriage and birth in the body, the godparent relationship is set in motion by the same events—by marriage and re-birth in the spirit. Both call on substances which have a symbolic as well as a material dimension—in the case of physical kinship, blood, and in the case of spiritual kinship, crowns and oil. Both set up a series of relationships which are devolved through the original participants to a series of relatives on either side, with whom relations must continue in one direction, *katameriá*. Both patterns of thinking are thus seen as parallel and complementary dimensions of the same process, with the movement of both oil and blood being guided by the identical ordering principle in the right-handed and auspicious pattern of the dance, so that failing to have godchildren is equivalent on its own level to failing to have children, for both are a negation of life. But if it is bad to block the flow of the oil, it is worse to reverse it, and the spiritual parallel of incest is found in 'returning' the oil, the initiator of spiritual life, to where it originated, just as a type of physical incest is seen in return marriages between certain categories of affine. Again, an identical symbolism is faithfully proclaimed, for in either case the spiral of life is unwound, and the fateful consequences are in either case the same. In both cases these relationships must continue their progression in a direction which is unambiguously forwards and onwards—a direction which is created and maintained through the observance of the correct categories by which the gift of life, once given, is not passed back again; in both cases the penalties for 'turning back' are identical and terrible; and both find a common image in the spiral of the traditional *zinári*, which is an image of the endless recreation of a single pattern according to which the gift of life, freely passed on, is the means of an endless and miraculous regeneration.

There is one final observation to be made on this parallelism between oil and blood, for while the distinction between spiritual and physical, oil and blood, is clear, and while it is categorically stated that spiritual kinship involves 'relationship' but not 'blood', the theme of blood does nevertheless appear in spiritual kinship. This, once again, manifests itself in the form of a prohibition on marriage between a limited category of people connected with a baptism. Chiefly, marriage is forbidden between the godchild and his godparent or his godparent's children, and between a godparent and a parent of his godchild, if both are widowed. But it is also considered inauspicious for co-godchildren to marry, or for any of the siblings of a godparent to marry any of the godchildren, or for any siblings of the godchild to marry the godparent, and those marriages of this sort that are contracted are looked on as inauspicious and as preventing the couple from 'making progress'. The reason for this has a familiar ring.

In general, it is the similarity of the godparent to a physical parent which is invoked in explanation of this proscription on marriages. The godparent is 'like a parent' to the godchild, his children are 'like godparents' or 'like siblings' to him, and the godparent's other godchildren are 'like siblings' also. But this is more than a metaphor, for the physical analogy is understood quite literally: 'It is as if the godmother has suckled the child herself.' And behind these explanations there runs the recurrent theme of a metaphysical understanding of the blood: 'When a person baptizes a child, the child takes one vein (of blood) from him, and however much it takes after the parents, it will take a little after the godparent. After that, all the different godchildren of that person are as if of the same blood, and are not allowed to marry each other.' Once again, a tie *like* blood kinship is created by the oil, just as in marriage a tie *like* blood kinship is created between those brought into relationship by a marriage, and therefore the gift of oil must not be reciprocated by a gift of blood.

The rule of *katameriá*, the principle that gift relationships once instituted should not permit the return of relationships to their source, thus appears to be a local extension of certain basic understandings about kinship, and provides as it were a magnifying glass with which to see the basic principles of relationships through both blood and oil.[5] First, the blood, like the oil, must continue in a forwards movement away from its source, and any 'turning back' is deeply inauspicious. However, with the passing of a certain number of *zinária* the blood is weakened enough to have 'left' the original kindred and become 'strange' so that cousins of a certain degree are considered not to be related. At this point the full cycle is completed and marriage between such cousins no longer represents a turning back but a movement onwards. Second, even with legitimate marriages between 'strangers', the principle of the union, or 'drinking', of the blood on marriage, means that there is an extended area within which marriages which 'take' from a kindred to whom 'we' have already 'given' are considered as involving a 'return' and consequently prohibited. Third, blood and oil are contrasted but analogous sub-

[5] For similar variations in ideas about blood in Greece see n. 2 above; for similar variations in ideas about godparenthood see Just, *A Greek Island Cosmos*, pp. 133–54.

stances which govern relationships through the body and the spirit respectively, and subject them to similar laws. Blood must not 'return' to blood, nor oil to oil. Nor must the blood as the vehicle of the gift of life be given in return for the gift of the oil of baptism. This does not deny the difference between blood and oil, body and spirit; but because the gift of either can make bonds 'like' kin, so in these cases, too, the principle of *katameriá* is applied to questions of marriage between spiritual kin. What we see, in fact, in *katameriá*, is a particularly rigorous working out of the injunction to give to the stranger, revealing it as an organizing principle of quite extraordinary force.

If we return to the two images of kinship developed earlier in this chapter, it is clear that this emphasis on giving (daughters) to strangers is part of the image of the flowering plant, with its continually bifurcating branches, rather than the perspective imaged by the cypress tree with its concentrated focus on the direct line of descent. However, the perpetuation of the line is also a powerful image in this culture, and the question arises as to why the scattering of seed to strangers has been given such vital significance, rather than, as in many societies, the retention of family identity and property in the marriage of cousins with each other. The attempt to answer this involves two questions being asked: what determines that from second cousin or thereabouts kin become strangers, and why insist on marriage to these strangers?

A descendant becomes a stranger by blood at a particular point, canonically after the degree of second cousin but in popular understanding at third, a principle enshrined in the saying 'for three *zinária* people don't marry'. Nevertheless, the discussion of the *zinári* also showed that, without compromising this principle that 'same blood' becomes 'strange blood' at the boundary of the kindred, there is a concurrent stream of thought according to which the blood is understood to be diluted gradually with each *zinári*. Thus, even while acknowledging that in strict terms they are 'not blood' or 'not kin', if two people can at any point in their genealogies identify a similar 'root', they acknowledge 'slight relationship' with each other, saying that they are 'kin, but not close'. And it is because of this ambiguity that there will always be found those who are uneasy at a marriage taking place between two people who are just beyond the edges of canonical relationship—'Is it all right? I don't know…after all we/they are related.' The reason for this unease is unequivocal and reminiscent of former statements about the blood: it is that even after the limits of the kindred have been reached, 'a vein [of blood] continues'. And this 'vein', as is apparent in a universal saying relating to the inheritance of characteristics, continues down to the seventh generation: 'The blood endures for seven *zinária*.' (Diagram 4.)

Diagram 4

The seven *zinária* – degrees of prohibited marriage and of inherited characteristics

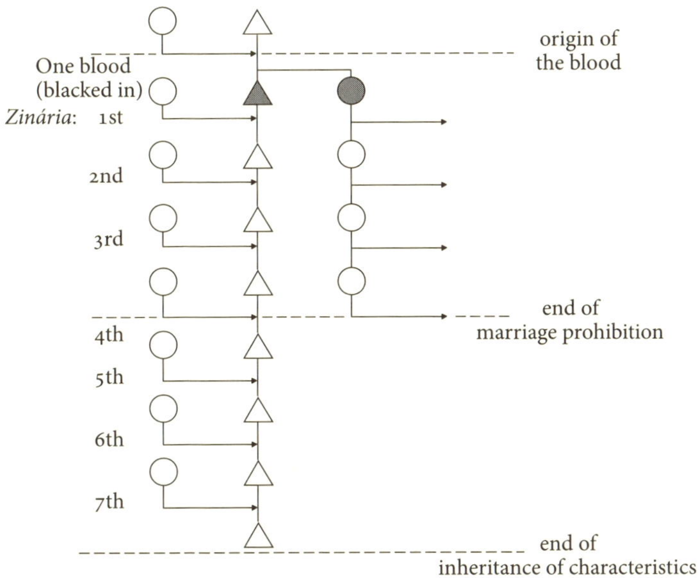

In this statement, therefore, there lies an inclusive and continuing view of kinship which is in direct contrast to the exclusive view in which kin are at a particular point abruptly demarcated from strangers, and this inclusive view adopts the progenitor's perspective, discussed earlier, which sees that all offspring in his or her direct line of descent must to some extent share his or her blood. The exclusive view, however, comes into being through a different perspective—that of the descendants who, four generations away from their common root and at a distance of third cousins from each other, are looking to marry, and feel themselves free to understand significant blood relationship as having lapsed. Thus the unease which commonly accompanies marriages of distant cousins does not stem from the 'slight relationship' still existing between the principals of the marriage, so much as from the blood relationship still existing between them both and the common 'root' of whom they are both 'grandchildren'—a word used impartially for all direct descendants. And that this is the point of reference for any real unease occasioned by such marriages is pointed by the fact that on such occasions the progenitor, if he or she is still alive, is sympathized with for 'having to watch [their] descendants [inter]marry'.

There seems therefore to be a correlation between the perspective of any common root and an unwillingness to see the marriage of 'grandchildren', and between general approval of such marriages and the point at which the common root of such descendants is typically dead. This is supposition only, but it finds confirmation in a belief about the soul after death which runs that for fifty years after death the soul 'waits', or retains in the other world an expectation of some service of love or of memory from those still on this earth. After that the soul waits no longer, for the reason, it is said, that a man might have a memory of 'his great grandfather, but no further back'. And tellingly, this level of great grandfather—the remotest generation of which any individual is expected to have a living memory—coincides with the generational level of second cousins which marks the limits of the kindred. Thus it appears that the time during which an individual's kin are seen as 'one blood' coincides with the longest period during which that individual's 'roots' might reasonably be expected to be alive. The apparently arbitrary moment at which 'same blood' converts to 'strange blood' coincides with the moment at which death is expected to remove one level of progenitors—the great great grandfathers, the roots of third cousins—from that same individual's experience. It seems, then, that the principle at work in the definition of the kindred has to do with the range of forebears of which anyone might normally have first-hand experience, and the time when these forebears can be expected to have died. And it is significant that in spiritual kinship, which follows so closely the patterns of blood kinship, the chain of relationships also ceases on the death of the originator.

Once again it appears that the blood is conceived to possess a symbolic as well as a physical dimension, for if the death of the root is to be critical in freeing blood relationships between that root's descendants, it must be because an element in the blood, potent during the lifetimes of the 'roots' but vitally weakened at their death, is being thought of as if it springs continuously from the living progenitors, and it is this symbolic and life-giving aspect of the blood which is withdrawn when they die. After this point, physiological blood links, deprived of this force, can then act to the seventh *zinári* to transmit characteristics and to provide identity, but not to create that particular vitality in the relationship which it is death to confuse. If this is so, it is this gift of life, springing organically from the living 'roots', which provides that dangerous element in the blood which must not mix with itself, and that, continuing always forwards, must never be allowed to 'turn back', to dam up and frustrate its own impetus; and it would be as a logical consequence of this that the closer limits of the incest prohibition (at second or third cousins rather than the seventh cousins of the seven *zinária*) have evolved. For if the relationships between which marriage is prohibited arise from the continual and mysterious gift to both parties of the life-blood of the progenitors, then the point at which society may deem that the giving has stopped and the relationships it created are at an end, would be the first point at which a whole level of progenitors may be presumed to be dead.

The exact level at which this point is institutionalized is naturally open to some negotiation, depending on the customary age of marriage and involving presumably a tendency to extend the limits of the incest rule on the part of the old people, and to whittle it away on the part of the young; and these different perspectives may well account for the popular belief, where it occurs, that the marriage prohibition should be set at third cousins rather than at second. Nevertheless, whatever the particular equilibrium negotiated at any one time, it is consistent with the symbolism of the blood, and the facts of relationship and marriage already stated, to suppose that the gift of life is transmitted in the blood and continues to be given as long as the origins of that blood are expected to be alive and active; and on the corresponding principle that death, depriving the kindred of one entire level of its progenitors, deprives it also of the possibility of that calamitous return of the life blood which originated from them.

If the death of the oldest level of progenitors is the factor which determines the point at which the child of cousins of 'one blood' is said to become 'strange blood', there remains to be answered the final question—the origin of the insistence on giving daughters to strangers defined in this way, rather than keeping daughters and property within the family.

It has been argued that blood is the vehicle of natural life, which is contrasted with the oil of the spirit; that it is an organic force capable of transcending individuals and binding them into a wider communion (of which one result is that while in western Christendom only the individual has the same blood as himself, in Greece it is the whole group of siblings which is prototypically united in this way); that through marriages grafted onto this paradigmatic form of unity there is a mystical or metaphysical sense in which blood is given continuously to descendants from living generations of progenitors; and that blood must not return and mix with itself but go to the stranger. There is, then, laid out under these four heads a conception in which blood is seen as much more than a merely physical substance enabling a purely material existence; it is the medium of a growth and communion which, although peculiar to the natural world and in this sense contrasted with the spirit, partakes with spiritual kinship in the sacred character of life itself, and thus is subject with spiritual kinship to the same metaphysical laws.

The idea that the gift of blood has a particular vitality capable of creating active relationships so long as its originators are alive and active, and that this living quality in the blood marks it out from the simple genetic resemblances it carries after the originator is dead, is consistent with these principles just listed. But it is also consistent with the image, already mentioned, of those sprung from an individual progenitor as a tree of life—a growth of branches and flowers springing from a central stem, where the sap rising from the 'root' penetrates as a living principle the entire growth which springs from them. The death of these roots puts an end to this flow of sap, though growths already sprung from them continue to pass on their genetic inheritance, and continue to re-establish the identical structure with different relationships as they themselves become roots.

This then appears to be the inner logic of the irreversible and right-handed progression of the blood, and of the way in which it defines the metamorphosis of kin into strangers, and prescribes marriage to none but strangers; and the effect of this logic, together with the rule of *katameriá*, is to create exceptionally wide networks of relationships throughout society. Applied only to the physiological blood links within the kindred, the simple prohibition on the union of the blood would cause each individual to look away from his kindred in seeking a wife, but could result in a sort of endogamy in which separate houses give and take women between themselves. But the symbolic union of the blood which is understood to take place on marriage, together with the consequent adoption of the principle of *katameriá*, enforce as great a degree as possible of giving to the stranger, and ensure the ongoing movement of the blood throughout the whole of the social world.

Marriage, in joining blood to 'strange' blood, is thus the means of a great rapprochement and reconciliation in a society habitually caught, as has been described, in competitiveness and mutual suspicion. The way in which blood is perceived enforces a spreading of marriages, a wide dispersion of the greatest gift any family possesses—its women. And it is remarkable that St Augustine in his analysis of the differing laws of marriage[6] describes the dispersion of this gift with the word which in the Christian tradition has ultimate value: 'love' or (in the older translation) 'charity'. After noting earlier tendencies to endogamy within close kin, Augustine argues that, as the population multiplied, 'There was a just care had of charity, that they to whom concord was most useful might be joined together in divers bonds of kinship and affinity; not that one should in his sole person occupy many relationships, but that every special relationship should be bestowed among many, and so many, by as many, should be joined together in honourable marriage.' Accordingly, the same person should not be father-in-law and father, or father-in-law and uncle,[7] for if these roles were kept separate 'thus were the social amity scattered, and not gathered together all into two or three'. Augustine's fifth century expansion of this principle was followed by the extension in the sixth century of the prohibited degrees of

[6] Augustine of Hippo, *De Civitate Dei* 15.16, from *The City of God*, tr. John Healey (London: Dent, 1945).

[7] Augustine's reference here is to marriage between brother and sister, as e.g. practised by the Egyptian royal house, and to marriage between first cousins.

marriage in European peoples living within the influence of the Christian Church.[8]

Thus to seek a spouse from outside the kindred, or, indeed, to forbid 'return' baptisms within a close category of kin, is one way of obeying the injunction to 'increase and multiply'[9] which, embedded in ecclesiastical teaching, is known to and often quoted by the people, even though they see it in terms of physical procreation only. Relationships, and the gifts which accompany them, must not turn back on themselves but must travel onwards and outwards through society, and this imperative is expressed and enforced through a symbolism of the blood according to which blood is far more than a fluid transmitted once and for all in the act of reproduction; it is the vivifying principle of the body and of the natural community, instinct with a life of its own, pressing onwards on its own purposes of self renewal, and creating in the process a natural union among living kin.

In this context 'right-handed' uni-directional movement carries a precise set of connotations which are to do with the creation of relationships through the act of generosity. The circling open-ended dance pattern, the right-handed processional route at wedding celebrations, the winding on of the *kadém*, the spiral of the blood in the *zinária*, all on their own levels speak of a flow of life moving fearlessly onwards, in which any turning inwards or looking back is death. In the effect of the *zinária* in creating a rigorous rule of marriage to outsiders, the right-handed movement takes on the additional dimension of the giving of hospitality—once again, of hospitality to the stranger. Thus the law of hospitality itself which was discussed in the last chapter, in which gifts flowing freely from the house to the stranger are, by definition, not returned, is revealed as a parallel to marriage and as yet another expression on its own level of the symbolism of the dance. In marriage, however, and in the prohibition of marriage up to and including third cousins which has been described above, this principle of hospitality is seen at perhaps its most fundamental, for here it concerns the free giving not just of food and of shelter but of life itself.

[8] For the crucial role of the 6th c. Church Councils in the development of the western family see Jack Goody, *The Development of the Family and Marriage in Europe* (Cambridge: Cambridge University Press, 1983).

[9] Genesis 1: 28.

8
THE VIOLENCE OF DEATH

THE Greek kindred has been shown to be governed by the principles of death and renewal, and it has been argued that these principles carry with them a certain deep consolation. The living know that a personal immortality awaits them, for a period, in their children, their name, their house and fields, in the memorial services, and in the regenerating power of memory and the continuity of the customs and beliefs which they inherited and passed on. Conversely, because it is not by their lives only, but by their deaths also, that past generations contribute to the continual re-birth of the kindred, and because it is, in a sense, in the very act of forgetting that new generations find new life, there is a type of solace here for all those who long for immortality. In this understanding the individual plays a supporting role, as the bearer and guardian—for a time—of the blood that, renewing itself in him, pours ceaselessly into future generations; and in accepting his role as the servant, through the gift of himself, of a principle far greater than he is, he gains the dignity of serving the cause of life itself.

In these two senses then, the society is permeated with a healing understanding of the interweaving of individual life and death in the renewal of the life of the community as a whole, and it is in part this understanding that gives to the society its immense stability, and to the people within it their capacity for acceptance of the passage of time and the approach of death: 'Up to the age of forty you build your life. After forty you fold your hands, look after your children, have the company of your spouse, and go down hill towards death.'

The uncompromising acceptance of death which is so characteristic of this culture is assisted by the fact that the people are no strangers to it, and from their earliest years they see the older generations one by one succumbing to the onset of infirmity which, it is accepted without fuss, will lead to the stones of the burial ground. Children are allowed freely into rooms where people are sitting with the dead, they see the open coffins of the Orthodox funeral, and with the rest of the congregation they go up to kiss the dead person at the end of the funeral service in the ritual of 'the last farewell'. And the community's physical care for the body does not end with the funeral service, for after the required number of years in the ground the bones are dug up by the relatives to be washed with water and wine, put in the church over Saturday night and Sunday morning, and then set aside in the ossuary. The exhumation is an encounter with the nature of physical existence so sharp that invariably someone is moved to remark involuntarily, 'Look at what we are!' or, 'That's what man is—a handful of little bones', and someone else to reply, 'We are only temporary here'. So the dissolution of the flesh is in its own terms the final reality, and this is faced with a certain robust realism which defies any easy comfort referring to the life of the soul in paradise: 'A fat lot I'll see when I'm under the earth!' and 'No-one's come back to tell us!' It is an acceptance of death firmly based on a repeated confrontation with the limits of physical existence—a continual following through of the cycle of life from the birth of a child onto the earth from which it came, to the return of the body to the earth when that life is finished.

But although the people accept death, because they must, they do not thereby weaken in their love of life. It is this life in which people eat, drink, and feel the light of the sun, in which they dance, laugh, and love, which is celebrated with such passion, this life in which even the simplest things occasion the most profound delight—the planting of chickpeas in the vineyard so that the worker among the vines can 'go eating', a drink of cold water from a mountain spring, a special find of mushrooms in the autumn which are borne back pierced through one after the other on a long withy, the use of the round leaves of the arbutus as spoons to scoop off the froth from buckets of new milk, or the rosy translucent vein of pine wood which smells wonderfully of resin and burns with a brilliant flare. It is this world of precise and personal experiences that represents life, and this world which man, because he cannot bear to leave it, leaves behind to his children who inherit it in his stead and in their turn re-people it and hold the past in their memories.

This view of immortality in which life is recreated again through new generations springs from one perspective, but there are others. Elements in the tradition which speak of the sacredness of the dead, the purgation of the soul, and the journey to paradise, emerge early in the rituals of death, and become increasingly clear as time passes and the response to death develops. Nevertheless, dominating the foreground of daily life, and treated in ordinary contexts as the overwhelming reality, is the extraordinary joy of living, and ever present in the background is the idea of death the destroyer as its ultimate enemy. It is a picture of life as both triumph and tragedy, and of a world so full of richness that in it man longs to defeat the odds, but so constructed that in the last resort this defeat is impossible. So, in the word often used in the context of mortality, this world is a 'deluding world' (*ψευτοντουνιά*), which beguiles us with a sensation of permanence even while it prepares remorselessly to give us over, together with all living things, to the grave. The love of life and the awareness of death are bound together in a powerful irony as dual aspects of a single understanding.

This love of the world, however, is given a further dimension by the symbolic values discussed earlier which are attributed to the cosmos in general—sun and moon, fire and water, village and wilderness. It is matter infused by spirit, not matter alone, which is the indivisible stuff of this world and is ravaged by death, and in the same way as the blood of life is both a material and a spiritual substance, so death, which spills this blood, is not only the physical but also the spiritual enemy. And its great power lies primarily not in the fact that it destroys the body, but that in destroying the body it destroys also the possibility of the union of soul and body which is the precondition for life. Even at its darkest, this way of thought does not deny a future life in some form, but it is easily clouded by the image of a future life in which the soul is fundamentally flawed by the lack of the body. So while there is no doubt of the tragedy of death for the community and for the bereaved, the tragedy is principally for the one who has died, who now lies under the earth's 'black mantle', who 'no longer sees', and who in the half-life of the 'other world' laments his absence from the celebration of the life he once knew.

The blackness of death, then, comes down like a shutter on the light and colour of physical life, and against this picture of contrasts the subtler theology of the life of the spirit after death is at first more elusive, drawn in half-tones, forming a subtext only readable as it were between the lines. The view of death as the final and total enemy, which takes up the foreground during life and is overwhelming at a death, is a view which derives from a particular perspective; this is the perspective of the natural man, strong in the fulness of the body and the passion for living, for flesh and blood, hillside and water, sun and earth. Within this perspective death cannot come otherwise than as a sundering from all that is good, and the life of the soul in the other world cannot appear other than as a thin and etiolated existence, and within this perspective, while on the one hand death is accepted without equivocation and often with some humour as a grim reality which awaits us all, on the other hand it is feared by the dying and is greeted by the bereaved with the most passionate resistance and rebellion.

The degree of communal resistance to a death varies with the circumstances, and although it is great for children, it is greatest of all in the case of a young unmarried man or girl, at the peak of their youth and promise. In these cases the capriciousness and cruelty of death is seen at its most acute as it seizes a person at the very moment that they step into life, robbing them of their inheritance and snatching from them the priceless gift of marriage and children at the very moment at which it has been offered. So it is typical that the death of an exceptionally lovely sixteen-year-old girl should be remembered years afterwards for the pity of such beauty 'being lost'. This is not a generalized pity at beauty being lost to death, but specifically that such beauty should be claimed by the grave before it has been claimed by a man, before it has left its imprint on a new generation. Those who die at the peak of their perfection before they have stepped into the transfiguring cycle of marriage and procreation are those who are lost to posterity, lost to the very cause of life itself, and leave a permanent void in the family of their birth. A married woman, buried in the customary best clothes and with her marriage crown, is witness in her death to her human fulfilment which has thus been ended; but the bridal dress, the crown of flowers, and the sugared almonds which accompany a young girl to the grave image instead the grim fact that her consummation is in the bridal chamber of death.

The focus on death therefore, as the focus on life, is child-centered. For your children to die before you is a grotesque violation, and because of this the terror of a woman at the possible onset of civil war—'It's not for myself, I've eaten my bread. It's for my children, my nephews and nieces…'—is the authentic voice of the culture, as is the comment of some old women at the exhumation of the bones of a young man killed just as he reached maturity: 'It should have been us.' And for the dead also the perspective is child-centered—a mother dying young is thought to have been cheated of the joy of seeing her children growing up, and of an older woman who dies before seeing her grandchildren it is said that she 'ought to have lived to see her sons married'. It is not until the age of seventy and over, the allotted span of human life, that death ceases to be an outrage and becomes accepted—albeit reluctantly—as a necessity. By this time people have 'eaten their bread', they have lived their life and reached the point at which it is inappropriate to insist on making further demands on it, so that the following explanation, on the death of a very old woman, is characteristic: 'For a young person, people wail. You should see what they do for a very young man. But for such an old woman, why weep? She has passed through so many trials and griefs, she has had so many years of life. Why weep that she is gone?' Nevertheless, the point has to be returned to, that whatever the differentiation made in general between different deaths, it is life in this world not the next which is the prime value, and a characteristic prayer is always for a bit more time: 'Give me five days [more], and my son and my grandchildren.' And even the old, living in great poverty and increasing decrepitude, can express the glory of this life in the voice of purest poetry: 'We eat, we drink, we celebrate our joys. Life is sweet, it is hard to surrender one's soul.'

While, then, individual responses to any death vary along a certain continuum, these individual responses take place within a common cultural awareness, and the particular pageantry of rural Greek life is derived in great measure from the heroic nature of a communal life lived with colour and panache in the awareness and defiance of death and its encircling darkness. It is an awareness best expressed in song, and it is encapsulated in the following song from one of the Greek islands which accompanies the dance:

> Dance, dance, take pleasure in your youth
> Since in this world you'll come by it no more.
> Give the dance wings, this earth will eat us!
> This earth will eat us, give the dance wings!

All those with giving hearts who always join the dancing,
Only these take joy in this deluding world.
This same earth we're treading down wants us all to enter in it.
It wants us all to enter in it, this same earth we're treading down.

Dance! dance! Don't spare your shoes
Since they'll rest when you're asleep at night.
Give the dance wings, this earth will eat us!
This earth will eat us, give the dance wings![1]

The dance of life is celebrated in, so to speak, the very jaws of death.

Death then, which will eat us all up, is the ultimate enemy, and death at its most extreme finds dramatic expression in the dark figure of Charos, also referred to as the 'Angel', who at the command of God comes with drawn sword to sunder the soul from the body. In village tradition the Angel of Death is identified with the Archangel Michael, who, like Charos, is always depicted with a drawn sword. With this sword he is said by the Church to defend Christians from the devil at the hour of death;[2] but his identification with Charos is in Greece so deeply rooted that on St Michael's day, 8 November, there is a strict injunction against killing anything for the reason that on that day 'only one [person] slaughters'. Whether it is Charos or the Angel that kills however, the moment of death—the moment when each person's 'oil lamp [in the spiritual world] burns out'—is a matter for God alone. A folk tale relates how the Angel, sent to fetch the soul of a young man, had pity on the weeping wife and children and took the soul of an old man instead. Arriving back before God he was told, 'Is this the soul I told you to fetch?', and was struck a blow from which he became deaf and never again able to hear the wailing of the mourners. Then God sent the Angel down to the bottom of the sea to bring up what he found there, and he brought back a little pebble. 'Now let's open it and see what's inside', said God, and he gave it a tap and split it open, and there inside was a little worm. 'How has it lived all this time inside this stone?' God

[1] *Songs and Dances of the Islands: Local Traditional Ensembles*, 'Pidhichtos', musical supervision by Domna Samiou, Lyra Record Company, no. 2007 (Athens).

[2] The Church's interpretation is based on Jude 9 and Revelation 12 : 7; for details see Michael the Archangel in *The Oxford Dictionary of the Christian Church*.

asked the Angel, but the Angel could not tell. 'Just as I have my intentions for this worm,' said God, 'so I have for people.'

Charos, or the Angel, is thus unambiguously connected with the divine will, serving a purpose far beyond the understanding of man. But the will of God is no consolation to the bereaved, and Charos, deaf to all beseechings, is not seen as a figure of mercy delivering souls from this vale of tears, still less as a mere allegory surviving from a picturesque past to preside over the customs of death. He is the actual embodiment of a terrifying power whom all but the very young have encountered in terms as stark as those of the following lament:[3]

> There I see Charos, he comes advancing over the plains,
> Black he is, black are his clothes, and black too is his horse.
> He takes the young men by the hair, the old men he takes by
>   the hand;
> He takes the little children, and hangs them from his saddle.

To meet death thus is to encounter an extraordinary violence and come face to face with an absolute separation, and it is this which prompts the terrible despair of the mourners, and this, also, which provides the frame of reference within which all the funeral customs are carried out. Given that this initial separation of the soul from the body and the dead from the living has occurred, the changed estate must be established irreversibly, for only in this way can the original act of violence be taken up into the healing processes which safeguard the soul on its journey to the other world. To confirm the separation is now the only course which is not pregnant with disaster, and of all the ideas which guide the transition of the dead person from earthly life to that of the spirit, this separation of categories is by far the most immediate.

The violence of death is seen at its most extreme at the actual moment of death, for this is perceived as an act of slaughter and is portrayed in images of blood. These images of death are said to have originated in the story of a girl whose pieces of dough, saved from

[3] The laments cited in this chapter were, except where otherwise stated, all taken from Ambeli or the surrounding area. In some cases they were recorded privately on the hillside or in houses with people who wished an opportunity to sing in my presence about a recently dead relative, and who did not mind the tape recorder. They were also recorded or written down in discussions about how laments and table songs were sung.

her baking, turned to incense which she burned in honour of God so that the whole place was filled with the scent. Asked by God what gift she would like in return, she requested to be given foreknowledge of death, and although warned that this gift would not bring her peace, she insisted. The answer she received was that if, on entering the room where the sick person lay, she saw Charos sitting on a roof beam, the person would recover, while Charos sitting on the pillow was a precursor of death. One day, entering such a room, she saw Charos with his sword raised ready to cut the sick man's throat, and saw also, as he plunged in his sword, the blood spurting out with such force that the whole room was drenched. Rushing from the room she picked her way homewards, shaking her feet and answering those who questioned her that it seemed to her as if her feet were covered in blood. In this way every death is brought about by Charos who with drawn sword slits his victim's throat, and covers with blood the room and everyone in the house.

The word 'slaughter' (*σφάζω*), which is used for this action of Charos, evokes a particularly violent image and is normally used to describe the killing of an animal—a deed involving the cutting of the throat and the spilling of blood. Thus a typical reference to the moment of a man's death is: 'Charos slaughtered him.' But Charos also has the duty of bringing the soul before God, and this is emphasized in a parallel image also often used: 'Charos took his soul.' This parallel meaning is underpinned by the invariable use of the word 'to un-soul' rather than 'to die', for the action of dying. Once again this image is, like the slaughtering action of Charos, far from being merely figurative, for the soul at death is said to come out of the mouth with the last breath 'like a little child'. So both the shedding of blood and the departure of the soul are bound together in a single idea, and here, locked together in the same moment, are implications of a double symbolism which is crucial to the complex unfolding of the rituals and ceremonies of death, for the soul coming out of the mouth 'like a little child' carries undeniable inferences of re-birth, while the bloody act of slaughter portrays death as violent and conclusive.

The first response of the mourners to the blood pollution of death is to wash the body with water and soap, and then a little wine, and to clothe it in the good costume which the person has set aside for this moment. Everybody present in the house at the moment of death, whether they are members of the family or visitors, must likewise change their clothes, and these clothes must all be left in an outbuilding and on no account be taken into any of the houses of their owners until they have been washed. This washing is done on the third or fifth day after the death, and on that day also the floor of the room in which the death occurred, as well as that in which the body was laid out, is also washed, and the walls whitewashed. The reason for this is the same as in the folk tale: 'It seems as if there is blood everywhere.'

The savagery of the action of Charos thus calls forth an immediate response of purification, and this inaugurates the beginning of a transformation in the dead which becomes explicit with the cutting of the *sávano* (*σάβανο*). This garment is an unsewn length of white material which is approximately one foot wide and measured to be twice the height of the dead person, with a hole cut in the middle so that it fits over the head and stretches the full length of the body both front and back. The *sávano* represents, within village tradition, the stole or *epitrachílion* (*ἐπιτραχήλιον*, dialect *τραχομάντηλο*) which is the indispensable ceremonial garment worn by priests in the performance of any sacred function, and it here represents the priesthood of the laity; and just as the priest wears the stole over the cassock but under the over garment or *phelónion* (*φαιλόνιον*), so the *sávano* on the dead is placed over all the clothes but under the jacket or its equivalent. Thus the *sávano* as the lay equivalent of the stole is a statement of the sacramental function in every man, and this is underpinned by the fact that it is universally accepted as the most important of all the clothes worn, for it is in the *sávano* that the soul appears in the other world.

By the time the church bell tolls as a sign that the community may begin to visit the dead person, the body has been placed on the ground[4] in the position known as 'facing the sun', with the feet, and thus the face, towards the East. Censed from time to time, the body lies on a white sheet which in turn lies on a folded rug, the eyes closed, if necessary with a coin on them, the mouth sometimes shut with a little wax between the teeth which is shaped in a cross over

[4] The necessity for the dead body to be placed 'on the earth' has been noted on pp. 34 and 72.

the lips, the hands crossed right over left on the breast. Sometimes a cloth is laid over the face. A little wheat is scattered over the body, and a number of lights placed around it which, as at all ceremonial events, must create a symbolic unity by being of an auspicious uneven number. Thus an icon lamp is placed on the right of the body; a candle in a glass of 'unsorted', literally 'unclean' (*ἀκάθαρτο*) wheat, that is to say, wheat still mixed with tiny bits of grit and grass seeds from the threshing floor, is placed to the right and left of the body and at the feet; and the *ísou* (*ἴσου*), a unique kind of candle whose name is derived from *ísos* (*ἴσος*) meaning 'equal' or 'equivalent', is placed on the navel. The object of the *ísou*'s equivalence is in fact the dead person, and this is expressed in a complex symbolism.

It is while the body is being washed and dressed that the *ísou* is made, by women who rub wax around a collection of threads which have been cut to the same length as the height of the dead person. It thus forms a long thin flexible candle which is then coiled right-handed (or anti-clockwise) round and round, spiralling outwards from the centre in a flat circular mat, and when this is done the centre of this coil is pulled up and lit, so that in its burning the candle consumes itself, right-handed, in the direction in which it was made. During the night of the wake the *ísou* must be allowed to burn itself down to one third of its original length only before it is extinguished, placed on the window-sill with some incense and a plate of water, 'to make three', and an ordinary candle lit in its place. The second night, now on the floor where the head of the dead person rested, together with the water and the incense, it is lit again and burned down to the last third of its length, and on the third night it is lit again and entirely consumed. The *ísou* has a direct congruence with the *sávano* not only in that both are made to the height of the dead person but also in that both are related to the journey of the dead into the other world. According to the tradition derived from the vision of St Makarios, described in the next chapter,[5] this journey takes a period of forty days to be fully accomplished, during which time the soul is taken by its angel to re-visit the places of its life on earth before being shown the mansions of heaven and hell and finally being brought before God for judgement. Like the *sávano*, the *ísou* also represents the full

[5] p. 269.

measure of the person, body and soul, and just as the *sávano* is the most essential piece of clothing, so the *ísou* is the most essential of all the candles, for it is the *ísou* which gives the soul of the dead person light for the three days during which, with its angel, it journeys over its past life, and it is with the *ísou* that the soul appears before God.

The placing of the *ísou* on the navel powerfully reinforces the right-handed symbolism of the flame as it burns down, for the navel is conceived as the centre of the body and as itself being formed in a spiral. This spiral can at times become unwound, giving rise to pains in the area, and sickness—an ailment known as the 'unwinding'—but it can be cured by twisting it back 'like the dance' in a clockwise direction—not, it is specified, left-handed: 'You don't dance like this (i.e. in an anticlockwise direction); don't do it that way or the person will die!' The *ísou* then, set over the navel and burning in the life-giving right-handed spiral, is plainly an image of life rather than death, and because of this it is not, as might at first appear, a symbol of the extinction of a life. Nor, however, is it the contrary representation of the continuance of the soul into immortality. The precise nature of the life revealed in the *ísou* lies in fact somewhere between the two states, since the three days of the burning of the *ísou* on earth are thought to correspond with the days of the soul's journey over its past life. Thus it becomes apparent that the *ísou*, representing the interim period during which the soul is neither of this world nor of the next, relates the one to the other through the judgement finally passed on the soul's accumulated lifetime of deeds. The burning of the *ísou*, that is to say, represents, from birth to death, a re-play of the life that is just ended; and it is all the gathered deeds both good and bad, recollected by the soul and its angel as the past years and places are revisited, and judged when the soul appears before God, that the flame of the *ísou* symbolizes.

In this way the body passes through a vital transition from the moment of death until the preparations are completed for the visiting of the community. The blood pollution of death is washed away by water and wine, and the purified body then dressed in clean clothes. The dead person is thus recovered from limbo and brought back into society; and the *sávano*, proclaiming the divine image in man and the invisible life of the soul, sets it apart as belonging now to the sacred world. Corn, symbolizing the seed corn of the resurrection,[6] is scattered, the *ísou* placed, the candles lit and the body censed, and with the completion of these preparations the change from pollution to holiness is so extreme that the body is, as it awaits burial, conceived in the same terms as that used for the relics of the saints—'the holy relics' (*τά ἅγια λείψανα*).

There is, then, over these first hours of a death a steady movement away from the dead as a polluting presence defiled with blood, to the dead as a fit object for veneration, placed at the centre of the community. However, the achievement of this state of holiness in the dead is one which is, until burial, essentially unstable, and must be kept in equilibrium by continual watchfulness, and this is one of the considerations behind the unquestioned assumption that 'the dead must have company'. Thus from the moment of death to the last action of the burial, there are people around the body carrying out the numerous little actions of the wake. At intervals the body is censed, using the customary anti-clockwise circular movement of the hand—'right-handed' and 'like the dance'—to spread the incense, with a complete right-handed circle round the body being described before the incense is again set down beside the head. As the candles burn down they are replenished, so that they always add up to an uneven number, three or five. Care is taken that the door of the room in which the body is laid out, as well as the door of the house, is left slightly ajar, so that Charos should not be shut into the house and 'come again' to take another member. But one injunction above all is most urgently heeded, and this is the requirement not to 'step over' (*δρασκελάω*) or 'pass [anything] across' the body, for if the body is crossed over in this way, either by someone stepping across the body or handing anything across it, or by an animal running over it, it is in the last degree inauspicious. Avoidance of the fatal action is not easy, taking into account the fact that throughout the wake the body lies on the floor of a room which is almost invariably small and crammed with people—but it is virtually automatic; and, as chairs, cushions, cups of coffee and so on are needed and passed round, and as people come and go, the injunction is continually reinforced that they should 'take care' and not 'cross over' the body of the dead. The consequence, if they do, is fearful for both the living and the dead, for

[6] See John 12 : 20–4.

to cross over the body of the dead is to make a pathway for the sudden catastrophic reanimation of the original blood pollution and the transformation of the departed soul into a vampire.

This form of the vampire is an image from outside the Christian tradition, derived from the Slav cultures of the Balkans,[7] and typically represents the reanimated dead which returns nightly to its own household, either in its own human form or in that of some animal, to suck the blood of its flocks or its kin, causing terror and confusion and, if allowed to continue, death. The remedies which then have to be practised, while they free the living from further depredations, cause the irremediable destruction of the soul. Thus the phenomenon of the vampire is an image of the wrong management of death in which the transition from pollution into holiness is aborted; the correct negotiation of the critical period after a death represents the auspicious face of death in which the soul is enabled to pass freely into the other world. For the first twenty-four hours between death and burial, therefore, extreme holiness and extreme pollution are held in a delicate balance, and it is only after the burial when the earth has closed over the coffin that this dangerous phase of death comes to an end.

The moment when the body is ready for the visiting to begin is marked by the tolling of the church bell, but news of any death will already have travelled round the village by means of the children who run from house to house telling people what has happened. The advent of death to the village is acknowledged by all, and a kind of tension hangs over everyone until the burial is completed and the confrontation with death absorbed into the united experience of the community. So during this period the customary preoccupations of everyday life are partially obliterated by the force of the drama into which the whole community is thrust; for death confronts the people not only with their own personal experiences of loss, but also with the loss from amongst them of one of themselves, and with, as a result of this, the image of their own death. In the death, therefore,

[7] K. M. Wilson, 'The History of the Word *Vampire*' in Alan Dundes (ed.), *The Vampire: A Casebook* (Madison: University of Wisconsin, 1998); Felix Oinas, 'East European Vampires,' in Dundes (ed.), *The Vampire*, pp. 47–8; Lawson, *Modern Greek Folklore*.

of the least of the villagers is seen the play of forces in their most final form—the processes of life and death and the destiny of the individual soul in the life after death—and each death is an element in each person's experience of his own mortality and of the mystery of the unseen world which encompasses it. It is because this individual experience is set in a pattern of perceptions common to the entire community that there arises the true solidarity of the community in the face of death, and the particular, indescribable, character of the wake.

During the day, after the tolling of the church bell, people come as they can to the house of the dead for a brief visit, returning in the evening or the night to stay for a longer period, sometimes for the entire night. Entering the room, which is often crowded with people sitting around the body on little stools or on the floor, each newcomer greets no one present but goes directly to venerate the dead where they cross themselves, as they do before an icon, and with the words 'May God forgive him/her' they lay a candle and perhaps a bunch of flowers or foliage against the body. Sometimes they might bring a few sugared almonds or walnuts and shake them over the body, or perhaps a little round loaf with a hole in the middle, an apple or some other fruit, which they place in the crooks of the arms—gifts given to rejoice the soul on its arrival in the other world, although they can sometimes be given for other known dead with the words: 'Take this to my mother', 'Take this to my son'. Similarly, when any feel it is time to go, they rise, cross themselves, and leave without a farewell to any of the company except perhaps for a solemn and wordless handshake. From time to time little cups of black coffee will be handed around—a suitable refreshment at a wake because of its blackness and bitterness; tasks are seen to as they arise, and all the time the conversation, varying over a wide range of topics, circles back continually to hover around the flower-strewn, candle-lit, body of the dead.

Although the expression of grief varies with the type of death, there is a tradition that none should go unwept to his grave, and laments may be sung and tears can be shed even at funerals for wastrels and drop-outs. These laments may be sung by anyone present, for all are moved at the spectacle of death, but there is a broad distinction between those closely affected by the event and those more removed from it; while it is for the relatives to give voice to their anguish at the fate of the dead and their rebellion against the tyranny of

Charos, the rest of the community represent a different pole of reality, and one that is to do with accepting the inevitable, maintaining the continuity of life, and giving expression to the mystery into which the dead has entered. It is with these understandings made explicit that the people at the wake act as a kind of chorus as they gaze upon the dead and are stirred to the elegiac comments of their tradition on the vanity of life: 'We are temporary here'; 'This deluding world!'; 'We only briefly have permission to come here'; 'That's where we shall all go'; 'That's how we're made'; 'That's how God has ordained us'. These are comments heard at every wake, and they never lose their freshness.

By contrast, the lament belongs to that foreground of people's thinking, vividly dominant during the initial phase of any death, which is a view of death as total tragedy, against which there is no appeal and for which there is no comfort. It is clear, certainly, that this view is modified even at the moment of death by certain beliefs and customs which speak of the journey of the soul to God, and also by the emotional distance between the various members of the community and the bereaved. Those closely involved in the pain of loss respond with rebellion and despair, those further removed with a philosophical acceptance. Nevertheless, at these times all participate in the same imaginative world, and this world is dominated by images related to the darkness of the earth and to the idea that any life lived by a soul separated from the body can only be a thin and enfeebled reflection of the life lived in the glory of this world. In this 'other world', the soul which leaves the body 'like a little child', or as 'a breath', still exists as an individual presence, but one which now takes the form of 'air', a 'shadow' or shade. Here, relationships bear some resemblances to those of the former life and people recognize each other, but they recognize each other 'strangely', 'not in the form in which they were'; and their greeting of each other is infinitely poignant for, in the gesture described earlier, as they pass each other by they stretch out one hand behind them to grasp the hand of the other, while, still looking forwards and even as they part, they say, 'Somewhere I've seen you before.' So the 'other world' exists not as a creative continuation of this one but as a shadow-play of it, a place seen in terms solely of its negative contrast with the life of the flesh, where people are as they were on earth but bodiless and with only partial memory, a place defined by the absence of physical joys where 'there is no drinking or merry-making', and where 'people don't sit down' and 'don't see'. In so far as one can imagine a bodiless life, a thin echo of this one in a kind of negative image—'that's the sort of thing that goes on there'.

There is a further level, however, to the dimensions of experience during this phase of a death, and this concerns the completeness of the transition from one world to the other. It has been said that Charos in a moment severs the body from the soul, a severance which is—or should be—final. Yet a further series of images exists which also relate to the newly dead, and these reveal that this initial severance is only the beginning of a process which in fact takes much longer to complete. Superimposed, therefore, on the imagery of the bodiless life of the soul, half seeing, half recognizing people, half alive, as well as on the imagery of the soul journeying with its angel, is another view in which the soul is not yet completely free of affection for the body even though this is now subject to dissolution in the grave, and according to this vision the newly-buried dead are portrayed as still associated with their physical life, lamenting their isolation in the blackness of the earth. In spite, then, of the consolation of the sacredness of the dead and the presence of the divine world, slaughter, separation, and isolation in the darkness of the grave remain predominant themes of the phase which immediately succeeds a death, and the urgent and tragic expression which they seek is found in the lament.

The lament, *moirológi* (*μοιρολόγι*), is a genre of folk poetry which expresses loss in any of its forms, and includes subjects such as sickness, exile, and the departure of a daughter from her natal home in marriage.[8] But it is at death that the lament is at its most vivid and uncompromising. Laments are sung exclusively by the women, and they have a role throughout the whole progress of mourning, both at the formal burial and memorial rituals, and during the course of daily life when a woman, seized with the need to express a sorrow suddenly too heavy to be born, will voice her grief in her house or on the hillside. The lament is an art form which combines, as do so many traditional expressions of the people, a highly organized basic structure with individual interpolation, invention, and innovation, and which allows the imagination of the singer to be nourished rather than stifled by the convention within which it operates. Thus

[8] Alexiou, *The Ritual Lament*.

these laments are, for those who sing them, genuine expressions of loss springing from personal pain, but possessing also a greater function, for they allow those who sing them to relate to the depth of their experience through the traditional images of their culture—fate, love, life, beauty, loss, the darkness of the earth, and the power of Charos—and thus to transcend the particularity of their own suffering and take part in the universal nature of separation and death.

The poetry of the lament is formed in a fifteen-syllable iambic line with rhyming couplets, but in the singing of it the most characteristic element is that the lines are broken up into a number of phrases, involving, at the beginning and end of each phrase, a stressed upwards keening note, 'Och!' or 'Ach!', pitched well above the musical line. With some singers the break occurs in the middle of the line, which is then completed by the second half, but some singers break off before the middle, with the new phrase picking up a word or two of the phrase which has already been sung, and again breaking off before the end of the line and repeating the process, thus forming a continuous interweaving movement of the verse. Sometimes a half line will be sung twice, or the whole line repeated. Often a phrase invoking the dead such as, 'Ach, my dear little mother!', 'Ach, my little sister!' is interpolated in the middle of lines in a voice half-singing, half-sobbing, and an invocation of the dead usually concludes every line with an upward inflection which, in those experiencing violent grief, is intensified into something midway between a sung note and a shout, so that the line begins and ends with what is essentially a ritualized cry.

The traditional lament is in this way a form of expression which is common to everybody, since it is a mode of singing easily adapted to phrases of distress, and in addition can be adapted to the phrases of ordinary speech with the upward inflection again on the first and last syllables, as in, 'Ach! How many times she asked us to ease the pain and we couldn't do anything to help her!', or, 'Ach! How she suffered, poor soul, and we could do nothing!' Like the way in which the lines can be broken up or reiterated at the wish of the individual singer, the formation of notes around the melodic essentials is at the discretion of the singer, and while with some people the words are sung with a relentless hammering on the bare elements of the melodic pattern, with others there is a greater play on a number of variations surrounding this basic phrase and the familiar pounding rhythm is less marked. Again, just as the music of the lament can bend, within the limits of its formal structure, to personal inspiration and the need of the moment, so the use of words and images allows for individual adaptation. Names may be linked with diminutives and be replaced by differing invocations: 'My lovely young man!', 'Tree of my house!', 'My cypress tree!', 'My daughter!', 'My water sprite!', and so on. Changes of phrase within the main theme may occur to suit the relevance of a particular occasion, as in the line 'Ach! I beg the Master Mason who builds the house of eternity...', which may be altered, for instance, to 'Ach! I beg the Master Mason who builds my sister's little house, Ach! the house of eternity!'

The identification of the singer with the song is thus a vital element in the creation of the lament. But there is more to it than this. So deeply infused is the performance of the lament with the lament itself that it is very often the practice rather than the content which distinguishes the lament from a song suitable for occasions entirely unconnected with sorrow. This is partly because, since on this level death is perceived straightforwardly as the absence of the life of the body, songs that celebrate life and those that bewail death in both cases do so in images derived from this world, so the difference between the two modes lies to a great extent less in the nature of the imagery than in the manner in which the song is rendered. So the universality of the lament lies in the common stock of folk poetry from which it is drawn, while its particularity lies in the fact that its performance as a lament lies in the hands of the singer, who 'can take it [i.e. the poetry] wherever they want'.

Some of the ways in which the basic structure of a poem may be modified by the singer are given below. In the following poem the same basic theme is used, with slight adaptations, both for a lament for a dead husband, and a song for a sick son.

> Ach! Sing, nightingale, sing your song in all the gardens, ach! my Thanassi!
> Ach! But in our garden don't sing,
> My Thanassi you are dead, and sorrowful,
> Ach! to my Thanassi don't sing, ach! my dear little Thanassi!

and:

> Sing, nightingale, sing in all the gardens
> But in my garden don't sing because I'm sad

Because my son is gravely ill and near death.
All the day long I'm thoughtful, in the evening I'm sad
Because my son is gravely ill and near death,
And in my garden, nightingale, don't sing.
My Fate has thrown sorrows on me...

Here a similar poetic core is adapted to two different modes of singing, one which takes the form of a lament and the other which takes the form of a 'table song' (*τραγούδι τοῦ τραπεζιοῦ*) or song for entertainment, and in these cases it is not the change in the words so much as the altered melody and style of singing, which marks them for what they are. Sung as a table song there is no initial exclamation or final invocation, and rather than being sung in the harsh mode of the lament they are sung in a vibrant melismatic voice; and it is these differences which indicate to the listener immediately whether the song is sung to entertain or as a ritual expression of grief. In the following poem the words of the main text remain unchanged whether rendered as a lament or a song, though if sung as a song, the refrain is added: 'Charos, don't take me away, because you'll never bring me back again!'

The nightingales of spring deceived me one day at dawn,
They deceived me and they said that Charos would not take me.
And I made a house for myself, high and wide
...... [text missing] ..... higher than the others
With seven and eight floors and with forty windows.
And as soon as I had finished it I went up to a high window
And I gazed far abroad towards the East. I see Charos coming
Mounted on a horse, treading the plains.

This wonderful poem illustrates the point made earlier about the awareness of mortality which throws into relief the people's joy in life, for the 'deluding world' of the popular imagination, here expressed with such irony, can become according to the context a fit theme not only for a death but also for a convivial gathering.

The next poem again illustrates the proximity of life and death and again shows that the images which feed folk poetry in general are a natural part of the expression of both. Equally as lament and as table song the poem is rooted in the universal themes of love, house, family, children, springtime, and if considered purely as literature, the focus is on the gentle shaping over the years of generations of successive lives. But if the poem is sung as a lament it is apparent from the first syllable that the whole thing is opened up to reveal the unfathomable perspective of loss.

Rendered as a song the poem runs:

I pray the builder who builds the eternal home,
May it be wide for the dance, broad for companionship,
And on the right hand side may you leave windows
So that the little birds can come in and out, the nightingales of spring.
Gently with the mattock and softly with the spade
So as not to break the glass and shatter the crystal.

As a lament it is thrust into a different world entirely:

Ach! I pray the builder who makes your little house,
Ach! My little sister, ach! the house of eternity.
Ach! May it be wide ach! for the dance, broad for companionship, my little Harikli!
Ach! And on the right hand side may you leave windows, ach! my little sister!
Ach! So that the birds can come in and out, the nightingales of spring, ach! my little Harikli!
Ach! Gently with the mattock and softly with the spade,
Ach! So as not to break the glass and shatter the crystal.

Finally, in perhaps startling illustration of the degree to which this poetic tradition places the song in the hands of the singer, there follows a song which not only may be sung either as a lament or as a table song, but which, if sung as a table song may be presented either as serious romance or as bawdy analogy.

'Militsa, where are you on the cliff, loaded with apples?
I am worried about your apples and fearful of the precipice.'
'If you fear the precipice come by way of the path.'
The path brought me out at a little church;
I see the memorial stones thickly clustered, clustered and making a brave show,
And one memorial on its own, separate from the others.

I didn't notice it and I stepped on it, on the eyes and eyebrows,
I hear the memorial stone boom and groan deeply;
'Who is this who treads on me, on the eyes and eyebrows?
Can it be my dear mother, my beloved sister?'

References are common in folk poetry to girls weeping over their stolen basil or their broken water-pitchers, and in everyday conversation someone firing her fields or being unable to control an animal properly can, if the company is in the mood, be taken up in a barrage of repartee and give rise to shrieks of laughter. Similarly in the poem quoted above, the reference to the apple tree's fruit, the pathway up the mountainside, and the eventual arrival at the lonely little church, can all be taken in the same way. Even more startling an example of such flexibility is the famous image of the 'marble threshing floor' which is found both in the most poignant and exalted references to death—the struggle with Charos on the marble threshing floor—and in a carnival song of great obscenity which refers to the priest threshing on the marble threshing floor and reduces everyone, including the singer, to hysterics.

There is of course a huge variety of songs which resist the change of categories demonstrated here; but the examples which have been given establish the lament as a living expression of the people, a creation of their own moment and their own immediate situation, even while it transcends mere individualism by carrying with it the accumulated wisdom and sorrow of generations. It is able to contain and channel the grief and despair of the recently bereaved, catching these emotions up into a known form, and giving them a voice which is not purely their own.

There is thus a creative interplay between the performer and the tradition, and the context in which the song is sung is all-important—a context which in the laments is to do with the immediate experience of death, or its remembered passion. To establish the contextual nature of the despair expressed in the laments, however, is not to minimize the strength of this despair nor the totality with which it is experienced, and two final examples of laments reveal beyond any doubt the terrible logic of this perspective on death, and the clear-sighted and inexorable realization of the dissolution of beauty under the black earth.

Ach! Oh birds, come down out of the sky and disappear, ach!
  the very stars are groaning,
Ach! And you, my brave young man in all your glory, ach! are
  descending into the gates of Hades.
Ach! Where are you going, my silver coin, to be lost for ever?
  My marble statue, to dissolve into corruption?
Ach! My crystal jar to be broken in pieces?
Ach! Your eyes are dark, your breast is a city, ach! and your naked
  body a flowering garden.

Finally, a lament which follows a typical pattern according to which the bereaved person asks the dead: 'How are you getting on in Hades?':

Ach! 'Why do you want to find out, wife, "How are you,
  my Thanassi?"
Ach! Here there is no dancing, ach! there is no singing,
Ach! The only thing you can do for me is to remember to burn
  incense and light a candle on my grave.'
Ach! 'Who do you have for company, who do you have to talk to,
  my Thanassi?'
Ach! 'I have the heavy stones for company, ach! the black earth
  I have to wife.'
Ach! 'I am preparing a meal for you, my Thanassi, to honour you,
Ach! To celebrate your name day and invite guests along,
Ach! But you, my Thanassi, are not coming to keep us company.'
Ach! 'When I departed, my wife, from the old house,
Ach! I departed for ever, never to return.'
Ach! 'My Thanassi, I have never drunk wine, ouzo for its
  sweetness;
Ach! Now I shall drink both, my Thanassi, to celebrate life.
Ach! I sing you mournful songs, and again songs, Nassio, ach!
  my Thanassi.
Ach! Where did my silver piece go? It is lost!—my marble statue,
  that it should dissolve?
Ach! Where did that beloved slender body go, ach! to melt away
  into the black earth?'

This black dimension of despair is, as has been said, not the only perspective on death, nor in a sense is it the most permanent, but it is overwhelming in the initial period after a death, and dominant for some time after it. The newly-bereaved live imaginatively with their dead, whose eyes see nothing in the darkness, and whose mouths are stopped with earth.

Although laments may be sung for some years after a death, the chief occasion on which they occur is at the wake, and at the wake they are so essential that for them to be sung by non-kin who know a large body of the laments, and are skilled in singing them, is in no way an indication of lack of genuine grief. The lament is the fitting response to a death, whoever sings it, for Charos is the common enemy of both young and old, both for the individual and for the society, and all present are steeped in a similar understanding of what this enemy means. Thus the outcry of the mourners against the brutality of death, whether voiced by the bereaved themselves or by those appointed to do so, is an expression of the voice of the people. Those who join with the bereaved in their lamentations are sharing them in an act which involves the primary meaning of 'compassion'.

There is a further element to this compassion however, and this emerges in the talk about the person who has died, for the conversation about this person is natural and straightforward, but it is radically altered from the previous everyday attitudes. The customary reference to the dead, both at the wake and for a period after it, is to couple the name with the adjective 'forgiven'—as in 'Maria, the forgiven one' (*ἡ Μαρία, ἡ συγχωρημένη*)—and although the life which is now ended is called to mind with clarity and sharpness, the comparisons and judgements which operated in life are, at the wake, entirely absent. So at the wake of an old wastrel, for instance, who began as a thief and ended as a drunkard and a beggar, a man unmarried and 'fallen out' of community life, the talk is truthful, of his inordinate drinking and smoking, of how he went to a doctor but would not take his advice, so that 'his liver rotted away', 'his liver burned up, pneumonia got him'. His boasting is called to mind: 'That's all gone now, the "I'll fix this person" and "I'll fix that person".' Yet the tones of contempt or mockery so often used about him in his lifetime have disappeared, together with the nickname referring to a famous robber by which in life he had been invariably known, and instead it is 'Uncle Stamatis, the forgiven one'. And like a litany, repeating itself at intervals, the comment of extraordinary acceptance and mercy: 'That's how God has made us, to every person his own character.' The entire wake is in its way a rehearsing of the life of the dead person as people recall this and that characteristic, but the competitive relations of daily life are entirely absent, and the forgiveness evoked is no abstraction but a concrete reality expressed by all who come.

It has become apparent that the wake is a deeply communal event in which people of a similar understanding come together in response to an event which affects them all. Nevertheless there is a particularity about the wake, because the catalyst for the general mourning is the loss of a single person and the grief of that person's relatives. As well as being an act of communion between all members of the community, the wake is also the stage where the meeting between the outer world of normality and the inner world of chaos and disruption, the outer world of society and the inner world of bereavement, is played out. And because there are those present who are less, as well as more, involved in grief, the wake is undertaken by the community at large with a kind of healing familiarity and pragmatism. Against the collective seriousness and recollection of the occasion, there is a tapestry of colour given by the various responses as people react individually to the death, and a continuing undertone not only of people doing little tasks as they arise, but also of the natural conversation of members of a single community passing the long night hours together. Somebody melts wax and, with the help of another person, makes candles; someone else yawns and, amid discussion, takes a thread from her dress and places it on the body—a symbolic 'sewing' of the mouth to prevent the corpse yawning and swallowing her up. The universally understood prohibition on allowing anything to cross over the body is continually reiterated. And all the time the conversation waxes and wanes, concerned both with the continuing drama of the dead, and, especially as the night wears on, with devices to keep the company amused and awake.

Because gossip at such a time is always avoided, the talk is forced to remain largely on general topics or personal reminiscences, and as a result the telling of folk tales and ghost stories becomes a feature of the wake, as well as discussion on random topics which get thrown up in the course of talk. A man tells of passing the church one dark night when suddenly a shadow reared up in front of him. Thinking it was a ghost he loosed off his shot-gun, only to find that he had narrowly missed killing his mule. Or someone starts a discussion which focuses on the conception of twins, and this, not unnaturally, ends with the entire room collapsing in gales of laughter.

It is inevitable that from time to time in a gathering of so many people laughter should arise—even at wakes for the young and tragically dead—and it is just as inevitable that there should be, after such outbreaks, a general withdrawal by the company as they renew in themselves a sense of the impropriety of such behaviour. A woman, earlier criticized for the robustness of her comments, is later asked to tell a joke to keep people awake. Her response to this is good-humoured: 'What am I to do? If I don't talk you don't like it; if I do talk you take offence.' Or a man, having put everyone into fits of laughter by his bawdy comments, might, after the company had sobered into a quick remorse for behaviour that 'didn't do' in front of the dead, put consciences to rest by a typical comment: 'He said them himself. Uncle Nicholas won't take umbrage at us.' And later the joker's absence may be lamented: 'If only Ioannis was here to make us laugh.' Laughter, then, occurs at a wake, but common as it is, it exists as separate incidents of light relief occurring against a serious communal engagement with the reality of death, and it is this reality which causes even people only remotely connected with the dead to sit late at the wake, and ensures that a small body of people is always willing to remain to watch through the long hours of the night until the dawn.

As already indicated, the initial phase of death gains its power particularly from that element in the tradition which represents the terrible finality of death as the devourer of both soul and body. It is the principal mourners who are most open to these images and from them in particular that the great outbursts of pain and despair arise, in the laments which state with such terrible clarity the changed situation of the dead and the immeasurable gulf which has now opened up between them and their loved ones. Thus rebellion and despair characterize the responses of these people, and the agonized searching for the dead, the conversations which are held with them, the vivid concern with their fate—all strong elements in the lament—reveal an abyss of grief which threatens real danger to the living by binding them imaginatively to the dead, from which they must be drawn back by those about them. And it is in answer to this that the community, who do not share the personal grief that afflicts the close relatives, are able to voice also a different aspect of the tradition—one that emphasizes the continuance of life for the living and the irreversible change that has come upon the dead, enjoining acceptance, and painting in with the lightest of touches the existence of an overarching divine will.

It is from this standpoint that the comments quoted earlier arise ('That's how God has ordained us', 'We only briefly have permission to come here'), calling to mind the spiritual setting in which the death is to be seen, and opposing the traditional understanding of the will of God to the involvement of the bereaved in their experience of Charos and the finality of physical death. It is from this standpoint, too, that the community take over much of the organization of a wake, telling those who mourn what they should do, carrying out tasks themselves, ordering the proceedings with rough kindness, sometimes forcing the mourners to bestir themselves, to do what needs to be done, to continue with life.

It is because of this that the comfort given to the bereaved is very often of an order which sounds to western ears uncompromisingly harsh. 'What can you do, it was your fate to lose him', 'He's gone now, he won't come back', 'He's gone now, weeping won't bring him back', are words frequently heard being said even to the most bitterly bereaved, or to a young woman greeting her dead mother for the last time before the funeral: 'Don't beat your breast. Keep quiet.' For this attitude, springing, as it must do, from the ability of those less closely involved to be detached, and resulting, as it does, in a reiteration of terrible but irresistible truths, serves a vital purpose in forcing the bereaved back into life, in establishing the distinction between the living and the dead, and initiating the long process during which the separation becomes accepted by the bereaved. Laughter at bawdy jokes may be, as indeed the villagers feel it to be, a scarcely legitimate extension of this function; but it remains true that the voice of the community in its acceptance of the situation of all men, its irrepressible normality, its trust in the providence of God, and its solid representation of the imperative demands of daily life, is a vital force in counteracting the mourners' rebellion against Charos, their despair at separation, and the nihilism which can be engendered in them by too prolonged a contemplation of disintegration within the tomb.

The day which dawns on the wake, roughly twenty-four hours after the death, is the day of the funeral. By this time the body will have been placed in a coffin made during the preceding hours, and the communal action continues in that everything is done by relatives, friends, or neighbours. From the washing and laying out of the body, to the wake, the making of the coffin and the congregation in church, everyone has known, and was known by, the person who has died. The priest is a villager, the gravediggers also. Nothing is given into the hands of professionals but everything is taken care of by the rough hands and familiar faces of those who shared the life of the person who has died, whether for good or ill. By now, some people will have gathered outside the house, waiting for the priest to come to the house and sing the 'Thrice Holy' as it is popularly known[9] over the body. This done, the coffin is 'raised' and carried out, feet first, and as the bearers cross the threshold a pitcher of water is broken with a crash just outside the door. The reason cited for this is that Charos should hear the crash and 'distance himself', but the breaking of the pitcher clearly also images the fact that the body, that vessel of clay, has also been broken and is leaving the house for the last time.

The procession sets out with the priest in the lead followed by a boy carrying aloft a cross on a long pole, two more boys with the *exaptériga* (ἑξαπτέρυγα) or long poles topped with gilt images of the seraphim and each bound round with a napkin or a handkerchief given as a gift to the bearer by the house of the dead, and then by the coffin borne by four men. As they leave the house the church bell begins tolling, and people gather by the pathway, the men with their caps in their hands, to watch it go by and join in behind, so that by the time the coffin has reached the church virtually the whole vil-lage is present. In the church the open coffin is laid on a low cloth-covered table in the centre of the church, with the feet towards the Holy Table, the face of the dead oriented towards the east. The dead person is in this way proclaimed as still being a member of the community, which

[9] *To Trisághio*, or more precisely in church parlance, *Akolouthía tou nekrosímou Trisaghíou* [Ἀκολουθία τοῦ νεκρωσίμου Τρισαγίου].

stand on three sides around the familiar form, leaving open the end facing the altar, and all the candles brought to the dead at the wake are now lit and pressed on to the inner edges of the coffin,[10] while the candles which people buy at the door and then lay on the body are lit in due course, so that throughout the service the coffin dazzles with tiny flames and people from time to time have to step forward to re-arrange the candles and prevent the flower stalks from catching fire. Further candles are given to every member of the congregation by the family of the dead, and these are lit and held in the hand, remaining alight throughout the service.

In the funeral, many of the themes which run through the wake and the preparation for the wake are expressed again, though this time they come into focus as aspects of the Orthodox faith and are explicitly linked with the great themes of the Christian Church.[11] Forgiveness for the dead, the reception of the soul by Christ, and its rest in 'a place of light, a place of refreshment, a place of repose'[12] is the first and last theme of the funeral, and the service represents a great union of the living on behalf of the dead, continually beseeching and at times arguing for his salvation in litanies which return and return again, until towards the end of the service the priest faces the dead person and pronounces the absolution. While verses from Psalm 119[13] express again and again the repentant human search for God, the lighting of candles and the frequent censing—such a dominant feature also of the wake—are seen to be images infused with ideas of purity and forgiveness and are exact embodiments of the popular saying that '[only] incense, a candle and a pure soul' can approach God.

Meanwhile, expressed in the 'Blessings [*Εὐλογητάρια*] of the dead',

[10] The candles are slim beeswax candles which, softer than paraffin candles, warm easily in the hand and can be pressed against a wooden edge where they stand upright. These candles tend to spit and pop with impurities, and they fill the place where they are burning with the scent of honey.

[11] Quotations from the funeral service follow the shortened form of the service in the *Μικρὸν Εὐχολόγιον* [Small Prayer Book], Ἐπιμέλεια Ἐπισκόπου Ταλαντίου Παντελεήμονος (Athens: Βασιλείου Σαλιβέρου, n.d. (1960s)), which was in common use in Greek village parishes at the time of the fieldwork recorded here.

[12] *Burial of the Dead*, Threefold Litany for the Departed and Short Litany for the Departed, pp. 17–18, 71–2, 81–2; cf. Hapgood, *Service Book*, p. 368 ff. (corresponding to *Μικρὸν Εὐχολόγιον*, pp. 225, 238 (=221–3), 244 (=221–3).

[13] Psalm 118 in the Septuagint.

a second theme emerges, which again unites all present, living and dead, in the person of Adam, and recalls the familiar images of paradise and the fall as the charter for this severance of soul and body:

> Of old thou hast created me from nothing
> And honoured me with Thine image divine,
> But when I disobeyed Thy commandment
> Thou hast returned me to the earth whence I was taken.
> Lead me back again to Thy likeness,
> Refashioning my ancient beauty.
>
> I am an image of thine ineffable glory
> Even though I bear the marks of sin;
> Take pity on Thy creature O Master,
> And cleanse me with Thy loving kindness.
> Grant me the fatherland for which I long
> And make me once more a citizen of Paradise.[14]

These affirmations of the divine image in every person thus reinforce the symbolism of the *sávano* and the *ísou*, and the effect of this is to restore, transfigured, the relationship between the living and the dead which has been broken not only by death, but also sometimes by life. While relations in the community at large are characterized in life by competition, both at the wake and still more at the funeral service the living and the dead become one in the common awareness of the common need for mercy and forgiveness, and the common honour of still possessing, however defaced, the divine image.

Finally, a third theme appears towards the end of the funeral service, in the form of a dialogue between verses which are close to the words of the village laments, and the Epistle and Gospel which declare the resurrection. Twice the bleak realism of these words is heard, mourning the world of the fall, once before the two resurrection readings, and once after, these latter verses being sung as the 'last kiss' is given by all to the dead in the open coffin. At this point the priest removes all the candles from the coffin except for three at the head, places an icon depicting the resurrection on the right

[14] Evlogitaria of the Dead: this translation is from *Lenten Triodion*, p. 128; cf. *Burial of the Dead*, pp. 32–3, Hapgood, *Service Book*, p. 379. Verses from *Μικρὸν Εὐχολόγιον*, p. 228.

breast of the body, and, men first, the entire congregation including the children file past to make their last farewell, crossing themselves, kissing the icon, and kissing or bowing towards the face or the hands of the dead person as the quiet singing continues.

In the dozen or more verses which are sung in this mourning tone, the shadow side of Greek consciousness is confronted head-on. Two verses from before the resurrection readings may suffice as examples of the similarities of all these sorrowing church texts with the village laments—similarities which are, however, subtly redirected by the brief prayer at the end of each verse:

> What pleasure of life remains without a share of grief? What glory stands immutable on earth? All things are fainter than a shadow; all things are more deceptive than dreams. In an instant death overtakes them all. But in the light of thy countenance, O Christ, and in the sweetness of thy beauty, give rest to him whom thou hast chosen, for thou lovest mankind.
>
> I remembered the prophet who cried out: 'I am earth and ashes.' And again I looked into the graves and saw the naked bones, and I said: 'Who then is the king, the soldier, the rich man or the pauper, the righteous or the sinner?' But give rest, O Lord to thy servant with the righteous.[15]

In these verses the tragic vision of the laments is endorsed, but it is made to point towards the declaration of a world to come; and this declaration follows in the singing of the Beatitudes, which summarise Christ's teaching about those who will inherit the kingdom of God,[16] and in the reading of the funeral Epistle[17] in which the drama of the resurrection is summed up in the words 'So shall we ever be with the Lord', and again in the reading from the Gospel of St John.[18] In this Gospel Christ's words, 'The hour is coming, and now is, when the dead shall hear the voice of the Son of God, and they that hear shall live', bring instantly to the Orthodox mind the icon of the risen Christ breaking the chains of the captives in Hades and sweeping up Adam and Eve with either hand to join him in the glorious world above.

[15] Verses attributed to John of Damascus, sung before the Epistle, *Burial of the Dead*, pp. 60–1, 62-3; cf. Hapgood, *Service Book*, pp. 385, 386, corresponding to *Μικρὸν Εὐχολόγιον* pp. 229–30, 232.

[16] Matthew 5 : 1–12.

[17] 1 Thessalonians 4 : 13–18.

[18] John 5 : 24–30.

After the last kiss and its accompanying laments, the Epistle's image of Christ with his people gathered round him, together with the Gospel's image of Christ emptying Hades, return in the prayers of the 'Thrice Holy', which close every encounter with the dead, and every memorial service. When the coffin—still uncovered—has been carried to the graveyard and set down at the grave, the 'Thrice Holy' begins with the following verses:

> With the souls of the righteous dead
> Give rest, O Saviour, to the soul of thy servant,
> Preserving him to the life of blessedness
> Which is with thee who lovest man.
>
> In the place of thy rest, O Lord,
> Where all thy saints repose,
> Give rest to the soul of thy servant,
> For thou alone lovest man.
>
> Glory to the Father and to the Son and to the Holy Spirit,
> Thou art God who didst descend into Hades
> And break the bonds of the captives,
> Give rest also to the soul of thy servant.[19]

In this way, the grief and despair of the lament is re-stated at the funeral in uncompromising terms, but is met always by the image of the risen Christ searching out his people and gathering them in from the land of the dead.

The open coffin is now lowered with care into the stony ground. The family of the dead will often place a bottle of wine on the body for the washing of the bones at the exhumation; little gifts may be put into the grave—ouzo in a tiny bottle if the dead person liked it, more apples or walnuts; and if the grave used is one in which there has already been a burial and from which the bones have been exhumed, several people will throw small coins into the grave as payment to the previous tenant so that he will not evict the new occupier. The final acts are initiated by the priest. The lamp burning before the icon of the *Panaghía*, extinguished at the end of the funeral and its wick removed, has been

[19] Cf. *Burial of the Dead*, pp. 2–3, Hapgood p. 368, corresponding to *Μικρὸν Εὐχολόγιον*, p. 221.

carried to the graveside, and the priest now pours its contents of oil and water over the dead, places a piece of tile over the mouth, and with a spade takes some earth which someone then sprinkles with water and throws into the coffin. After this, the coffin lid, bearing the two initial letters of the person who has died, and the four letters I X N K for Jesus Christ Conquers, already noted as the inscription on the seal of the bread of the eucharist,[20] closes the coffin. Everyone then throws a stone or a clod of earth onto the coffin, and no one leaves until the grave has been filled and a rough cross stuck in the ground at the head of the grave and fixed with stone, and perhaps some flowers in a jam jar put at its base. The last act, as people leave, is for them to be offered by the family of the dead some plain boiled wheat which all accept with the words, once again, 'May God forgive him'.

Back at the house of the dead, the bereaved family, together with all those who were in the house at the moment at which the dead was carried from the house, again gather in the room where the person died for the priest to come and sing once more the office of the 'Thrice-Holy'. On a table in this room there is a plate of hot food, the same that will be served at the meal, 'which should be steaming' so that the aroma with the rising steam may nourish the dead, a glass of wine, some smoking incense, a plate with three 'pieces' of bread,[21] and a plate of wheat with a candle stuck in it—wheat which, for the first time since the death and in an image of the purification of the soul by now well under way, is cleaned of any little bits of debris and washed. After the Thrice-Holy, the ceremonies of burial end with the funeral meal.

The meal, consisting of stewed beans and rice with some bread and a glass of wine, is given in the name of the dead person who, as mentioned already, is said to have 'invited' everyone 'to sit down to table'. So the first action of the dead person in, as it were, their new estate, is to provide hospitality, without discrimination, to the whole village, and in this action the sacred nature of hospitality becomes touchingly evident. For here not only is the house open to all who come, but the act of giving is answered by an act of forgiving, to the extent that the phrase normally employed for proposing attendance at such a meal, 'Let us go and eat', is replaced in this context by the words 'Let us go and forgive' (*πᾶμε νὰ συγχωρέσουμε*). This meal is

[20] See p. 150.

[21] See p. 155.

attended first by the men of the village and afterwards by the women, everyone going in installments and cramming into the small room as best they can. At the beginning, crossing themselves before they begin to eat, the guests replace the customary grace, 'Come, Mother of God, let us eat', with the prayer for the dead, 'May God forgive him', and they do the same again after they have finished. They eat, unusually, with a certain rapidity and a minimum of conversation, and their farewell greeting as they leave the house is 'May you have life!' The closing act of the drama is for everyone as they go back to their houses to pass by the spring to wash their hands, return home to throw out every drop of water in the house, and return again with their empty water jars to fill them up freshly at the spring.

The death, then, of any individual, is an event which in this society cannot be private: for all its schisms and fragmentation, the social world forms an organic whole in which the infection of death threatens every household and one man's death diminishes the whole community, and the answer to this diminishing is an intuitive and immediate impulse towards reconciliation. This finds expression on the most practical level in the fact that a particular catalyst for the ending of quarrels is 'at a death', when women who have not previously been speaking together encounter each other as they lay out a body. It has been noted that quarrels in the village are often of great length and extreme intensity, and that people who are quarrelling will pass each other on the paths and wait together at the spring without acknowledging each other's existence. It is therefore not the fact of meeting which is the cause of the ending of the quarrel, but the fact of meeting at times of prescribed hospitality and particularly in the presence of death. Similarly, no matter how bad the relations between any villagers before the death of one of them, it is exceptional for anyone deliberately to avoid going to the wake or burial, or to refuse to accept the memorial food, or to fail to say the brief prayer for the salvation of that particular soul. No matter what the customary relations are between villagers who find themselves in each others' company as they attend the wake, there is a general and perceptible relaxation of tensions as people meet on the ground of their shared understanding of the nature of existence, rather than on the ground of their competing temporal situations. The community's response to death is forgiveness, and at the wake it is not just the dead who need, and who receive, forgiveness, but the living also.

In this way the ferocity attributed to Charos at the moment of death, itself a reflection of the death given by humans to animals, is the catalyst for an opposing impulse of reconciliation and sanctification: the body polluted by blood becomes a 'holy relic'; the sinner becomes 'the forgiven one'; the 'unsorted' or impure wheat which contains the candle of the wake becomes the clean wheat, picked over, washed, and censed, in which is set the candle of the Thrice-Holy; the despair of the mourners is contained by the necessities of hospitality and instructed by the community in a difficult consolation; and the community itself, sobered by the realities of this 'deluding world', is moved towards a communal singleness of purpose which is in normal times only intermittently achieved. The final end of all these ceremonies, seen in the next chapter, is the freeing of the body from the bonds of the flesh and of the soul from sins, while at the same time working through the worst of the grief and rebellion in the mourners to something of a vision of a further reality beyond this world. Thus in this initial phase up to the burial, the cleansing of the body and the purification of the soul are two aspects of a single process—the pollution of the act of Charos echoes the pollution of life, and both are washed away by water, wine, incense, prayers, hospitality, and forgiveness.

One final aspect remains to be defined, and this is the way in which these Christian images co-exist with the negative images of death outlined earlier in the chapter. It is here that the prohibition, already mentioned, on stepping over or passing anything across the body, needs further interpretation.

Firstly, if a body lies on the floor in the middle of the community, and if there is a prohibition against crossing over it, a space is preserved above the dead into which no one and nothing must enter. The earth, on which the body is traditionally laid, is linked to the heavens by the flight of the soul, and the newly-dead, now transformed into the 'holy relics', provides the central point at which the two worlds meet. A statement is thus being made here about the free passage of the soul from this world to the next, and this is illustrated by the icon of the Falling Asleep of the Mother of God—whose feast on 15 August is one of the great feasts of the Orthodox year—which provides the archetype of the death of the faithful after Christ's resurrection, for while it shows the disciples gathered around the body, only the person of Christ occupies the space above. Further, in this icon the person of Christ is shown receiving the soul of his mother in an image which calls to mind precisely the village vision of the act of 'un-souling'[22]—that is to say it depicts the soul which has left the body in the form of a little child, though with the addition in the icon that the soul is now held on the arm of Christ. In receiving her, the resurrected Christ embodies to her, and to all the faithful souls of the Church whom she represents, the rebirth of soul and body announced in the Gospel of the funeral service.

There is, however, a second consequence of having a space into which nothing earthly must enter, and this is that earthly things are forced to go round instead—a movement around the body which must, like all other auspicious processional movements, be 'like the dance', any left-handed movement being emphatically repudiated: 'The devil comes from there.' So the prohibition on passing anything across the body has the direct result of creating a continual reassertion of the auspicious right-handed movement as people, cushions, chairs, babies, cups of coffee, and all the paraphernalia of the wake, process in an unending dance of life around the dead person in the centre. The world—to use an exact translation of the Greek word for 'people', 'community' (*κόσμος*)—revolves around the dead, at whose centre, on the navel, the right-handed spiral of the *ísou* burns.

This principle of the auspicious flow of life around the body is also echoed in the practice of the lament. Alexiou[23] describes a formal rendering of the Greek lament as consisting of antiphonal singing between two groups seated on either side of the body, with the changeover being initiated by the receiving group whose chief mourner stretches out her left hand to 'take' the lament from the right hand of the mourner opposite. However, if passing anything over the body is precluded, then this clasping of hands must take place in the space west of the head or east of the feet. Further, the insistence on the right-handed movement involved in the 'taking' of the lament with the left hand implies that the two chief mourners

[22] For 'un-souling' see p. 38. [23] *The Ritual Lament*, p. 40.

must sit, respectively, on the south side of the body at the head, and on the north side at the feet (Diagram 5).

Diagram 5

Implied movement of the lament between the two sides of mourners

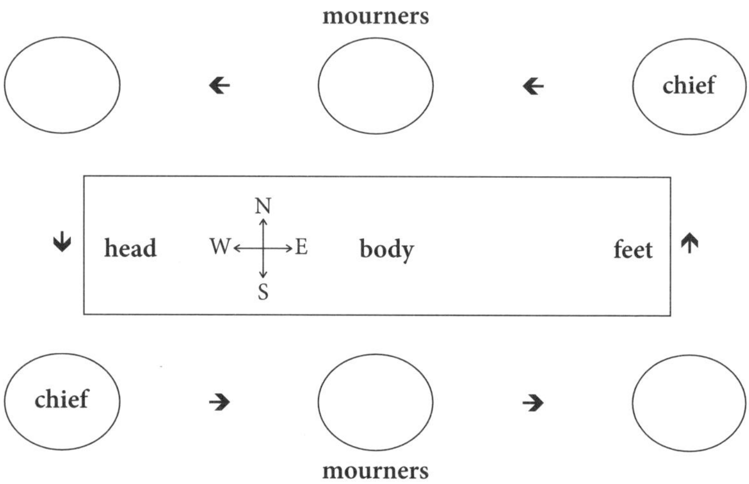

Thus the lament, taken from the left and given to the right, and, similarly, received by one person and then given to another, is, although sung antiphonally by two groups, symbolically passed on and on in a continuous right-handed circle. In this way the lament itself is drawn into the movement of the dance which protects both the dead and the living, and asserts in them both the continuity of life.

Once again, therefore, the cyclic pattern of the dance appears, this time as a dance around the body, and this is added to the washing with water and wine, the *sávano*, the *ísou*, the placing of the body on the ground facing east, the right-handed censing movements, and the folding of the hands right over left, to form the image of a good death. As we have seen from its symbolic associations, this image is a Christian one, and harmonizes with the accompanying symbolism of forgiveness to create a coherent shape for the period between death and burial.

It is perhaps surprising, then, that intermingled with these

Christian images are those quite different images, first, of the soul as being consigned to the underworld as an ineffective shadow, and, second, of the body as at risk of being turned, through no fault of its own, into a blood-seeking vampire terrorizing its kin. And the fate of the vampire itself is even worse, for the only remedial actions which can be taken involve, possibly, formal exorcism by a bishop, or, most commonly, pouring boiling oil and vinegar into the hole which is said to have opened up in the grave as a result of the presence of the vampire, and in both cases village thinking holds that the remedies are for the protection of the living only, the soul having already 'become a demon' and been lost. After such an event, no memorial services are held, no candles lit in the name of the dead, and no exhumation carried out, for these ceremonies are now to no purpose.

These perceptions, so much at odds with the resolution involving the movement of the soul to God and the accompanying pattern of forgiveness and repentance, have survived with extraordinary force, and this raises the question why such negative ideas should have remained so influential, even though the Church has generally repudiated these particular perceptions and sought to free its people from them.

The image of the soul as a shadow confined under the 'black earth' where all is defined in negatives of the life now lost, and where even memory is incomplete, derives both from the Jewish *Sheol*, the 'land of forgetfulness' of Psalm 88,[24] and from related ideas of the Homeric underworld in the Hellenic past, where the contrast between life and death is defined principally in terms of the opposition between blood and not-blood. Here the soul, which leaves the body for the 'other world' at the moment when the last of the blood of this world pours symbolically out into the house, is depicted in images which are the reverse of blood—a 'shadow', a 'breath', 'air'. And it is consistent with these contrasts that the new habitation of this bloodless soul is equally insubstantial, a place of continual drifting motion, of perpetual non-encounter in a world lacking all definition, and a principal feature of the dead body is that, buried in the black earth, it 'does not see'. These contradictions between the Christian image of life in God and the bloodless

[24] Psalm 88 : 3–5, 10–1.

image of a life in the underworld are resolved over time, and how this happens is the subject of the next chapter. But still to be explained is the phenomenon of the vampire.

It has been said that, of all the customs at a wake, the one most urgently and most continually emphasized, until the Christian image of a good death is consolidated in burial, is the injunction: 'Don't cross over it [the body]!' This injunction, as has been shown, is critical in guarding the open space above the body, as it is in enforcing the cyclic movement around it; but these consequences do not appear in the rationale given for the prohibition, for this remains centred purely on the danger of 'crossing over' the body, and on the fear not only of an unconsidered action by the people but, especially, of being crossed over by a cat or a mouse. It is for this reason above all that a dead body is always 'guarded', as it is put, that is to say it is from death to burial never for one moment left alone.

In this context it is cats, being domesticated, that are thought of as particularly dangerous, and the need to guard the body from being inadvertently crossed over is typically phrased as 'so that the cats should not eat him', while the unguarded dead are thought of as being 'for the cats to eat'. The verb 'to eat' is in this kind of context normally used as a metaphor, but taken at face value it appears to hark back to the knowledge of a dreaded possibility where being 'crossed over' by an animal is associated with images of the body not as sacred relics but as something to be eaten, as prey. And in fact an ancient image of bodies exposed on the battlefield, torn and mangled by birds or dogs, or stripped by their enemies in an action likened to that of dogs tearing their prey, does lie in the background of this culture in the Greek past.[25]

It seems possible then that it is horror of the body as prey, neither living nor peacefully dead, which associates the crossing of these creatures over the body—and, by extension, any other careless movement of the same kind—with extreme visions of reversal and wrath. Such a vision is found in the image of the ancient Furies who pursued those who allowed the dead to be desecrated by animals;[26] and the Slav understanding of the pursuing vampire is remarkably

[25] Sophocles, *Antigone*, ll. 203–6, 696–9, 1016–22. Note also that in ancient Greek, *skýlax* (dog) is related to *skýllo* (mangle) and to *skýla* (arms stripped from a dead enemy).

[26] Ibid., ll. 1074–83.

similar.[27] The image of the vampire combines the corpse as victim with the corpse as avenger: an animal crossing over and thus threatening the body neglected by its relatives causes the dead to be reanimated by the blood shed in death, to 'become a demon', and to return to the living community to batten on its own kin.[28]

The idea that the corpse itself can in this way be reanimated, and become its own avenger, seems in turn to be associated with areas where exhumation is practised.[29] Exhumation and the gathering of the bones is common, though not universal, in Greek Orthodox practice, while cremation is to the villagers unthinkable, and this goes back to early Christian custom where the cremation practised in Hellenistic times was replaced by the Jewish practice of burial in caves or cemeteries. In Jewish tradition the buried body must decompose back into earth as expiation of the fall, and this is indicated for both Jews and Christians by God's words to Adam, 'Dust thou art and unto dust shalt thou return'.[30] Exhumation has a similarly ancient Jewish pedigree since exhumation was often carried out to allow the bones to be gathered into the family ossuary, and the dead to be 'gathered to their ancestors'.[31]

It follows that people involved in these practices would have a fairly extensive knowledge of the initial and final stages of decomposition, and probably also a sketchy and fortuitous knowledge of the middle stages. Thus it has been suggested that in Balkan regions where exhumation has been practised, accurate but unsystematic observations of these middle stages of decomposition have formed a basis for the vampire beliefs developed by the Slav people of these

[27] See p. 235 n. 7 above; the Greek word for vampire, *vrikólakas* (*βρυκόλακας*) seems to derive from the Bulgarian *vrkolak*, one of a variety of cognate Slav terms—see Oinas, 'East European Vampires', pp. 47–8.

[28] It appears that bodies subject to becoming a vampire are those in the village where relatives are at hand to carry out the due rites, as bodies dead on modern battlefields are said not to be subject to this risk. In the *Antigone* too, although the corpse concerned is on a battlefield, the plot turns on the sister who is nevertheless present to carry out the rites.

[29] P. Barber, 'Forensic Pathology and the European Vampire', Dundes (ed.), *The Vampire*, p. 132.

[30] Genesis 3 : 19.

[31] K. E. Bailey, Burial Customs, in Bruce M. Metzger and Michael D. Coogan (eds.), *The Oxford Companion to the Bible* (Oxford: Oxford University Press, 1993).

regions and borrowed by their Greek neighbours.[32] In other words, a folk theory has developed from these traumatic experiences which then shaped images only partially reconciled with Christian patterns of thought.

There is, however, a further layer of thinking which also appears to have helped to shape the image of the vampire as the antithesis of a good death, and this involves ideas of blood and kinship discussed earlier, for these emphasize the irreversible and auspicious movement of the blood onwards until, after a specific number of generations, death releases the descendants from the ban on marriage with each other. Thus the insistent theme of the bloodlessness of death is because blood is life, and the symbolic outpouring of blood shed by Charos at death, and the unidirectional dance of life around the body which enforces its non-return, ends also the need for vigilance to ensure the giving away of that person's blood to strangers in marriage. In this way the image of cyclic movement that protects the life in the blood as it goes out to strangers through the generations, insists also, at the moment of death, that the blood is given away for good, and thus protects the soul too from being trapped in a physical form which is neither alive nor dead.

In this way the vampire which images the return of the blood to the body has profound affinities with the 'turning back' of the blood in close kin who are joined in marriage,[33] and both are fatal. This connection is not directly spoken of by the people, but that it does not lie far below the surface of popular thinking is indicated by a discussion of the risks of second cousin marriage (allowed, it will be remembered, by the Church but disapproved of in folk thinking), during which the folk view that such marriages are dangerous was suddenly defended *sotto voce*, by means of a proverb about the vampire:

[32] The middle stages of decomposition include a stage in which the body appears as if charged with blood, and blood-stained fluid escapes from the mouth and nostrils (Barber, 'Forensic Pathology' pp. 118–19). In Slav cultures, observations of this kind suggested an explanation for epidemics of kin-related deaths or distress after a recent death, and had at least the advantage of scape-goating the recently dead rather than the living, after which the epidemics and the panic engendered often settled down (J. V. A. Fine, 'In Defence of Vampires', and J. L. Perkowski, 'The Romanian Folkloric Vampire', Dundes (ed.), *The Vampire*).

[33] See p. 222.

'The *vrikólakas* hunts down its kin' (*βρυκόλακας τὸ σόι κυνηγάει*).

According to the understanding implicit in both the prototype and the antitype of a good death therefore, not to move on is the true death, for the only other choice is to turn back—of which the fateful 'return' of the vampire is the most dramatic example. In contrast, the irreversible pouring out of the blood, together with, as will be seen in the next chapter, the dissolution of the body and the clean yellow bones which are left behind, are images of the soul's integration with eternity. Similarly, blood going to its own blood in marriage halts and doubles back, while blood going to 'strange' blood pours onwards in a life-giving spiral through the community. The movement of the soul into the other world and the movement of the living into marriage and the gift of new life are different aspects of an identical reality.

Thus in the immediate after-shock of death, negative images rise up which derive from pre-Christian understandings of death or from elements of the first-hand experience of death, burial, and decomposition which all villagers share; and these are ideas which Christianity sees as a distortion, a part of the fallen understanding, though in the face of the Christian understanding these images have not vanished but rather have shaped themselves as a reverse or shadow side of the correct management of death. And although in rare circumstances these feared images can overwhelm the bereaved,[34] at least for a time until they are exorcised, their normal course is simply to enforce a scrupulous enactment of the positive images which can lay the antitype to rest—the purification of the body and the gathering together of the community, the dance of life around the dead person which is an image of the re-birth of the soul into the hands of Christ, the willingness of the dead to let go and to move on, and the willingness of the living to allow the soul to depart and to hallow its progress with incense, candles, and the memorials of forgiveness.

The form taken by the correct management of death in the period between death and burial is, then, one which even in the midst of grief and lamentation relates the living and the dead to the unseen

[34] Historical examples are discussed in Juliet du Boulay, 'The Greek Vampire: A Study of Cyclic Symbolism in Marriage and Death', *Man* (N.S.), 19 (1982), pp. 223–4.

world which lies beyond this one. And through, in particular, the image of the dance, there runs a continuity of understanding which informs the processes both of life and of death. At the heart of the symbolism of death is a series of parallel images: the body in the priestly *sávano*, and the person made in the divine image, who is recognized, despite failure and wrongdoing, in the 'Blessings of the dead'; the sacred space above the body in the *sávano*, and the space in which Christ, in the Dormition icon, stands receiving the soul of his mother; the soul yielded up into this space, and the life of the living circling around the body, who will pass the blood on to strangers in accordance with the Church's law of marriage; the spiral of the *ísou* in which the soul's history is measured, and the journey which the soul makes with the angel reviewing its past life. This understanding insists at every moment from death to burial on the need for forgiveness, both of the dead by the community, and of the members of the community by one another. And it relates the need to accept death, and to give away the life blood of this world, to the same Orthodox symbolism which governs the mutual sacrifice in marriage which hands on life to children, which binds together the community in the giving of the kindred's life blood to strangers, and which insists on the blessed character of giving in hospitality, where it is Christ himself who is the guest. The central insight which this symbolism is meant to protect and preserve is the creative understanding of a profound set of meanings governing the whole of existence, which is to do with a continual giving away and giving on of life.

9
THE PROGRESS OF MOURNING

THE previous chapter, focused on the moment of death and its immediate aftermath, was concerned primarily with the images of violence in which even peaceful deaths are perceived, and with the intensity of the shock and rebellion which constitute the immediate response of the bereaved family. The twenty-four hours following a death constitute a highly dangerous period during which the violent transformation of the living person into a death-polluted corpse must be answered by a movement by which the transformation from life to death is continued but the pollution reversed: the corpse must become a sacred relic and the soul must be allowed free passage into its new existence. And because this negotiation is, until the moment of burial, so open to being overturned, the intensity of emotion surrounding the death is matched by an intensity of ritual activity whose end is peacefully to place the person definitively in the other world.

The direction of events set in motion by death must, then, be perpetuated. There is no turning back, and any such turning back finds dreadful expression in such images as the living death of the vampire. Nevertheless, for all the terror and the irreversibility of death, it is clear that what is being negotiated throughout these hours is not the deadness of the dead, but the deadness only of the body, and this is an insistence not on stasis but on movement. It is an insistence not on the end of life or love but on an altered centre for both of them, a transference of focus from the body to the spirit. So the movement which takes place in the newly-departed soul as it journeys from one realm to the other is one which takes place also in the hearts of the mourners as they struggle to locate their beloved dead in the spiritual realities of the unseen world. At the heart of the transitional rituals of the period between death and burial lies the mystery of the life surrounding death, and of the movement of the dead person through death into a new life.

Acceptance of these fundamentally altered realities is thus one of the chief ends to which the ceremonies of death are directed; but true acceptance is slow in coming, and the wake is the beginning only of a long process. The period which defines the limits of mourning is marked by strict practices and by a succession of memorial services which extend normally for three or five years—a period depending on the assumed accumulation of sins of the person who has died. This in turn, as noted in the last chapter, has been symbolized from the time of late Jewish and early Christian practice by the period which is needed for the body to go back to dust, in accordance with God's words to Adam in the Book of Genesis, leaving clean bones which after exhumation can be gathered to the ancestral bones in the village ossuary.[1] Children, relatively sinless, may be exhumed three years after burial, but older people, their flesh rendered dense by sins, are usually judged to need five or seven years. After this time, the exhumation of the bones brings to a conclusion the association of the dead with the darkness of the earth, and confirms finally the futility of any irrational and residual hope the mourners might harbour of regaining their beloved. At this moment even those shattered by the grief of an unacceptable death are said to 'take a decision' (*κάνουν ἀπόφασι*). Their acceptance is complete. The period of mourning thus follows through two concurrent dramas in the different situations of the living and the dead, among the living as rebellion converts to acceptance, and among the dead as the dissolution of the body within the earth ends finally the association of the physical person with the material world. The strands of these associations, however, are complex, and find a resolution not in a single logical scheme but in a many-stranded pattern of ritual and experience lived out in all sorts of particulars over a number of years.

The nature of death is thus portrayed in two sets of images. One set of images, seen chiefly in the laments, reveals the black underworld into which the mourners are plunged in the immediate aftermath of a death, and it is these images of darkness and loss which lie at the root of the passionate grief of bereavement. The other set of images—the rituals of purification, the candles, the incense, the *ísou*, the funeral service—form the overarching structure of the time until the burial, and these act to contain the passions released by death

[1] There are also other variations in what is done with the bones: see Margaret Kenna, 'Houses, Fields and Graves: Property and Ritual Obligations on a Greek Island', *Ethnology*, 15 (1976), pp. 21–34, for burial of bones in walls or on the family land.

and to provide a discipline within which the perceptions of the living may penetrate beyond the veil of this world and this world's griefs. At the time of the wake these two visions of the other world are held in suspension, as it were, side by side, though with darkness predominating. But the movement from the one perception to the other is already under way, and it is this that provides the dynamic of mourning in the gradually changing consciousness of death as the weeks and months pass.

There are two primary contrasts between these parallel imaginative worlds. Firstly, while the world under the earth is a dark place inhabited by disconsolate and bodiless souls, who 'don't see' and 'don't rejoice', drifting about in perpetual half-life, the Christian symbolism calls to mind a world entirely different—a greater light and a purer vision than in this life, a place, in the words of the funeral service, from whence 'all sorrow, sickness and sighing has fled away'—a place, in the words of the villagers, full of 'good things'. Secondly, while the world under the earth involves a relatively undifferentiated world of the dead where the virtuous and the wicked congregate without discrimination, at the root of the prayers for forgiveness and the rituals of Orthodox burial lies the very different theme of the soul's meeting with God, its accounting for the deeds of a lifetime, and its consequent allocation to its appropriate 'place'. The way in which the bereaved move between these two symbolic worlds constitutes the inner movement of the process of grieving, and it is this, governed by the steady progression of the mourning rituals, which brings it about over time that the contradictions between the two worlds of the dead are finally resolved, the passions of grief are purged, and the soul finally freed from its association with the earth and from all that holds it back.

In the period immediately following a death, each picture of the 'other world' finds its predominant expression in one of the two natural groupings which form at the time. While all share the same range of understandings of the nature of the other world, and all are involved to some extent in the expression of both pictures of it, the emphasis varies with the context, so that while the lot of the bereaved is to be the principal voice of rebellion and despair, that of the community is to be the principal voice of patience and acceptance. Similarly, the place of the priest in the rituals of death is as the foremost exponent of the Orthodox vision of the other world and the chief enjoiner of patience in the face of suffering. These complementary roles of the bereaved and the comforters are particularly marked at the wake, but continue after the burial in the less structured meetings of daily life. However, as time goes by, the forum where the two ways of thinking meet begins to shift, for ultimately it is not between the separate groupings in the community but in the hearts of the bereaved that the two visions of the afterlife must find their resolution.

One of the most significant distinctions between these pictures is that in contrast with the undifferentiated world of the dead, the Orthodox cosmology involves the idea of the judgement of individual souls, and of the existential states of heaven and hell.

Hell, although in popular thinking it is accepted to be a state of the soul only, is nevertheless portrayed in uncompromisingly physical terms, as a place of mediaeval torments, full of flames and devils with pitchforks, and ingenious penalties which aptly await the sinner. Gossips will be eternally hung up by their tongues; women who aborted children will be hung up by their breasts; those who lay in bed when the church bell was ringing will lie for ever on a flaming bed; thieves will be ridden by demons who will snatch away from them their memorial food and the candles lit in their name. This vision is of such literal force that contemplation of a mediaeval picture of hell can evoke a response of absolute immediacy in a woman talking to her son: 'Look at that, my child! Oh, Christ and the All-holy Mother of God, look how that demon has got him by the leg! Why do we give ourselves over into the hands of the demons the way we do? When I go and do something wrong it's the demon who leads me. When you mess around in the yard all day and get up to mischief and never come in out of the mud it's one of those who's leading you. Po, po, po, look what we'll come to. I don't want to go there, I want to be on the outside and watch!'

In contrast to this vivid portrayal of hell, the popular notion of paradise is much more vague, portrayed merely as a place of 'roses and good things', of greenery and abundant water, with a special place for children who play in a great plain full of flowers where they are looked after by a little old woman. Thus it seems that while pains worse than those experienced on this earth can easily be imagined, villagers have difficulty in imagining joys surpassing those of the garden of this world. Nevertheless, however ill-defined the vision of the kingdom of God may be, it is to the reality of this kingdom that many of the customs at a death are directed, and thus the constant reiteration of forgiveness in the words 'May God forgive him' is not a figure of speech but a perceived reality, as people accept that the life now ended has a reckoning to face, with a real outcome.

The funeral is a definitive moment in the inauguration of the journey of the soul after death, but it is only the first of a sequence of other moments marked by numerous lesser commemorations and five great memorials, or *makáries*. The term by which these great memorials are known derives from a vision attributed to St Makarios of Alexandria (died c.394–5 AD), already mentioned in the last chapter. This text describes the journey of the soul after death which lies at the heart of these great ceremonies.[2] According to this vision the soul feels grief at parting with its body, and accompanied by its angel it hovers around the earth, either over the coffin or around the places where it used to live. On the third day, the soul is comforted by its guardian angel who then brings it before God. Having paid reverence to God, the soul with its angel is sent until the ninth day to see the abodes of the saints and the beauties of paradise, after which period it is brought again to God. Finally, it is taken to hell, to be shown the different places of torment before on the fortieth day it is brought again before God, this time for judgement. Popular belief has conflated this more detailed account into the simple theme that the soul remains in contact with the earth for the full forty days, revisiting all the places and deeds associated with its life, until at its meeting with God on the fortieth day all its deeds are made manifest and it is sent 'to its place'. But the symbolism of the *ísou*, finally burned down on the third day after the death, provides evidence that popular imagination does make some differentiation between events over this forty-day period. Since, as has been argued, the *ísou* is closely identified with the past life of the person lying dead, its three-day burning must indicate some three-

[2] The earliest (14th c.) copy is of a Syriac version; it is edited and translated into French in Arnold van Lantschoot (ed.), 'Révélations de Macaire et de Marc de Tarmaqa sur le sort de l'âme après la mort', *Le Muséon*, 63 (1950). This text attributes the vision to Makarios of Egypt. The Greek text (earliest copy 15th c.) attributes it to Makarios of Alexandria: J. P. Migne, *Patrologiae cursus completus, Series Graeca* (Paris, 1857–66) 34, 385–392C.

day association of the person with the earth, as in the Makarian vision, even if these perceptions have become weakened in popular understanding. But in any event, the folk rendering does not contradict but only simplifies the ecclesiastical version, and both mark stages in the soul's enlightenment as it moves towards its definitive meeting with God and with the meaning of its past life.

It is clear that these ideas of heaven, hell, and judgement described above are of a different provenance from many of the ideas discussed in the last chapter which concern the half-life of the undifferentiated dead under the earth—ideas which have been mentioned earlier as related to the Jewish *Sheol* and the equivalent Greek underworld still referred to as *Ádhis* (*Ἅδης*), Hades, in the liturgical texts. This older conception has been overlaid by the vision of judgement and the contrasting destinies which it implies, yet from the behaviour of people during the wake it is clear also that although these two visions of the other world are philosophically discrete, they are nevertheless lived by the people as a single experience. Areas of contradiction and paradox are present and these can sometimes give rise to expressed concerns—the custom of requesting the dead to take gifts to other souls, for instance, can be seen as contravening the soul's own destiny in that it obliges the soul to 'search for them both in paradise and in hell'—and in this instance the collision between the unitary and the differentiated views of the other world is apparent. The logical contradictions between these two views are not often directly confronted however, for if they were they would force a resolution. The problem is resolved, rather, by the fact that while the two pictures coexist and interweave with each other, they are treated not as a single logically consistent picture, but as a multi-faceted reality whose different facets take on prominence for different people at different times. The combined resource presented by these two pictures is thus able to accommodate a great range of possible responses to death, which together provide a means by which people move, together with their dead, through rebellion, grief, and loss, to a country of the spirit in which death is accepted and overcome.

One thing which helps these two pictures interweave without their inherent contradictions being brought to light is the ease with which images are transferred from one picture to the other. Charos and the Archangel Michael have already been mentioned as having become elided into a single figure, with the pre-Christian figure of Charos, no less than the Angel, being understood as the rigorous executor of the will of God. Similarly, candles lit for the Christian dead have no difficulty in appearing before the souls in the world of the shades, and the invisible aroma of the memorial food and of the memorial bread reaches them in consolation and nourishment even in the underworld. It is this fusion of images which gives power to two of the lines in one of the laments already quoted, when in response to a widow asking her dead husband how he fares, he from under the black earth and with stones for company replies: 'The only thing you can do for me is to remember to burn incense and light a candle on my grave.'

The flow of images is not just one way however, and just as images from the Christian mysteries can appear in the underworld, so also may images taken from the disconsolate existence of the shades under the earth appear in beliefs relating to the Christian vision. Thus the problem of overcrowding among the souls in paradise is solved by reference to images taken directly from the underworld—the soul is a 'shadow', 'air', a puff of breath, and does not take up any room; and the answer given by Christ to the question asking which of a woman's seven husbands during life would be her husband after death,[3] is also understood by the villagers in terms of the world of the shades. This answer, 'In heaven there is no marriage nor giving in marriage', is so close a parallel to the picture of a world where there is no eating or drinking or sitting down, that the villagers have no difficulty in reading one in terms of the other: 'We see from this that things there are not as they are here.'

A final example of this theme lies in the folk tradition already recounted which speaks of the release of souls back to this earth for the forty days between the Resurrection and the Ascension.[4] The story itself makes this a period of release for souls in hell, but a further element is added to this tradition in the suggestion already mentioned that anyone going to a well after the liturgy of the Ascension and looking into it with a sheet over their head, will see all the souls trooping back 'into the earth, those to paradise and those to hell, old and young, in dresses, in costumes, with their ornaments and jewels . . .'. Even though paradise and hell are here distinguished, as in the Christian paradigm, both can be found in the world of the shades under the earth. Even souls in bliss can find joy in their return to the world of their physical lives.

[3] Mark 12 : 25; Luke 20 : 36. [4] See p. 75.

The ability of the village mind, then, to leap from the images of one way of thinking to those of the other, is one reason why innate paradoxes of the two visions of the other world are prevented from surfacing in too stark a manner. But there are in addition two other elements which work towards the same end. One has already been described and lies in the way in which the contrasting themes of rebellion and acceptance are expressed simultaneously in the community by discrete categories of people defined by their relative emotional distance from the death. In this way all the varied themes of death keep on surfacing and re-surfacing, not only as dissonance but also as symphony, the different voices of thousands of years of oral tradition flowing into one intricate but common understanding. Perhaps, though, the most significant element in the resolution of the two visions of the afterlife is one which does not merely contain, but virtually eradicates, the contradiction, and this is the passing of time.

In the context of death itself, where the violence of death and the contrasting sweetness of this life are inevitably uppermost, the 'other world' is associated purely with tragedy and with darkness under the earth. But when both death and life are seen from a more detached and contemplative perspective, as happens not only in the wider community at the time but also increasingly in the bereaved themselves during the years following the death, these tragic ideas recede and images of light gain in power, together with the assertion simply that the soul is now 'elsewhere'.

In these ways therefore, while the varying concepts of the 'other world' do not make up a single logical system, neither do they break apart experientially into a series of logical contradictions. Rather they flow into one another to make a rich and varied vision of the other world after death, and the complex imagery thus engendered, far from facing the people with irresolvable paradoxes, gives them instead a language for a wide range of emotions and states of being as they deal with the reality of physical death, the destiny of the soul, and the management of their own grief or the grief of those around them.

In contexts where the judgement of souls is uppermost, there exist in the local tradition numerous depictions of the tests faced by the departing soul on its pathway to the other world. There are two ladders in the 'other world', side by side, the one on the right leading to paradise, the one on the left to hell. There is a sieve through which the soul has to pass, pure souls slipping through the mesh while souls rendered coarse by sins are turned back. There is a bridge consisting of a single hair spanning a gulf of pitch, over which the souls must pass. The good souls manage the passage safely, while gross souls fall off and are swallowed up. Again, there is a pair of scales with Christ on the one side and the devil on the other. If the scales lean towards Christ then he takes the soul, but if towards the devil, then the demons rush forward and hale it away.

In all these instances the judgement of God is meticulous and just, and at the forty days' judgement people reap precisely what they have sown. More formidable still, together with this strict concept of justice according to works, is the view that paradise or hell are permanent states from which there is no redress. The consignment to one's 'place' at the forty days is final, and although at any time before death people can take a decision and change their ways, after death 'there is no room for repentance'. It is in harmony with this view of the judgement that folk tales telling of judgement or salvation nearly always end with words 'he went to hell' or 'the demons took him' or, in a happier outcome, 'he went to paradise'. These words have an undeniably final ring, and carry the clear inference that the story of that particular soul ends there.

In these cases, then, there appears to exist an absolute way of speaking of the judgement in which no intermediary state between paradise and hell is posited, and in which the ideas of heaven and hell are irremediably opposed. A soul may go to paradise or it may go to hell, but it cannot go from one to the other. It is in this life that change and repentance occur; heaven and hell are eternal states and the soul once passed into the realm of immortality is consigned in perpetuity to one or other of them.

Yet this is by no means the whole story, for a large body of additional evidence suggests that this belief in a permanent situation in the other world being allotted on the sole basis of the works performed in this one is an expression of only part of a much more complex reality. This complexity, and this refusal to limit the fate of the soul to a simple, permanent dualism, can be found both at a theological level,[5] and at the

[5] Ware, *The Orthodox Church*, pp. 254–5.

level of village thought and practice. In this reality, in addition to ideas of the tally of deeds committed and their just reward, other ideas of faith and works, charity, prayer, and forgiveness, the mercy of God and the impotence of the devil, all play a part, and the interplay of these forces is the theme both of the memorial services, and of many folk tales which provide a colourful backcloth of unpretentious hope to the otherwise apparently one-to-one relationship between sin and damnation.

Firstly, the constantly uttered prayer of the community, 'May God forgive him/her', is a real intercession made in the belief that such prayers are effective, and it is consistent with this that the memorial food given in the name of the dead is said to bring them not only comfort but, if they are in torment, some degree of release also. Thus each time such a gift is made in the name of any person in hell, that person will be drawn just a little bit out of the pitch, from the chin to the neck, for instance, or the neck to the shoulders. It is also said by some that by means of the memorials a soul may even be brought out of hell into paradise, since God would say, 'Look how they are loved, how good they were'.

However, a more detailed vision of the possibilities of movement in the other world is provided by folk tales. Two of these tales challenge the idea that the judgement is strictly 'according to one's works'. One runs that a baker, having never in his life given anything away no matter how minute, was one day visited by a beggar who pestered him, coming back again and again like a wasp, asking for a bit of bread. This man had been sent by 'the angel'—by implication the angel of death—the explanation runs, so that the baker should be saved. 'I haven't any,' the baker replied. 'You must give me some!' 'I haven't any,' 'You must give me some!' Finally the beggar went and settled down by the oven, at which the baker lost patience and threw a burned loaf at him, on which the beggar departed. A week or two after this the baker died, and at the judgement the devil said to Christ, 'This soul belongs to me, there's no question about this one'; but Christ, surprisingly, claimed the soul as his own. They argued it back and forth until Christ said, 'Bring the scales!', and when these were brought the devil put in all the baker's bad works, and it seemed certain that the soul would be damned. But at the last minute Christ tossed in the burned loaf, the scales came down on his side, and he took the soul himself. The second tale, related in an earlier chapter,[6] concerns the grasping woman who when she died was saved by the one gift she had ever given, the onion, and taken to paradise.

These, then, are deliberately worst-case stories, of people incorrigibly mean, badgered or infuriated into generosity, and they incorporate certain characteristic themes. One theme concerns the superiority of Christ over the devil, reminiscent of the story of the buffalo:[7] the devil is essentially helpless against the creative power of God. Another theme centres on the gift as the type of 'work' necessary for entry of the soul into paradise, specifically the gift which responds to need. Once again the fundamental spring of blessedness is hospitality. A final theme concerns the understanding of the free relationship between God and man—that God leaves man free to listen to him or not—and is taken a logical step further in the theme that God, for all his power, cannot act unilaterally to save, for man has to assist in the work of salvation. But that assistance can be small indeed. God can save souls through something as insignificant as an onion grudgingly given, or a burned loaf hurled in petulance.

A further folk tale, however, elaborates a new aspect of salvation. This tale concerns two brothers, one of whom did evil works all his life, the other, good. When the evil brother died, Christ contended with the devil for his soul. 'He's mine!' 'No, he's mine!' But in the end Christ could not find a single good work to put in the balance, and the devils took him. These devils turned him into a donkey and, loading him with wood, they drove him up and down the mountains from the lowest valleys to the highest peaks, beating him with axes and knives and sticks. Getting to the tops of the mountains they unloaded the wood and threw it all down to the bottom, and forced him to go down and collect it again, beating him with sticks and axes and knives.

But there came a time when the devils were led away by some distraction, and while the donkey was left miserably on his own, the good brother, coming down the path, recognized him: 'Hey, brother, how is it that you're like this?' To which the donkey replied: 'This is how I am now, I'm lost.' 'You didn't do good works in your life,' was the brother's comment; but he then told him to go quickly to the top of the mountain, unload the wood and lay every piece out to form crosses

[6] See p. 190.

[7] See p. 26.

circling the summit, and if there was one bit uncrossed he should take any piece of wood lying around and use it to complete the cross, and then he should go and stand in the middle of the ring of crosses. So the donkey did this, and after a time the devils came shouting up the mountainside looking for him, but when they found him surrounded with the wood all laid out in crosses, they made a great commotion: 'We can't get him now, he's superior to us!' And so Christ got the soul in the end, and put him in a 'lower place' in paradise.

Again in this story the familiar theme of good works appears, and with 'not a single good work' to argue for the evil brother, Christ is forced to relinquish him to the demons. But here there is a development, for after a period of suffering the dead brother is redeemed by three things: by the help of the living brother; by his own faith; and by fact that the victory of Christ over the devil is part of the structure of the world. In this story, even without works, the living can help the dead, and faith eventually save the soul. The judgement at the forty days is, in this case, not the end of the story.

It is thus in the light not only of the finality of a judgement between heaven and hell, but also of the folk tales which reveal a more subtle and sophisticated play of understanding, that the sending of the soul 'to its proper place' should be seen. For this 'place', it appears, is determined by mercy as well as by justice, and may involve only a temporary placing in a situation from which it is freed once it has learned what it needs to know. There is thus a gradation within the other world, rather than a permanent division, and this gradation exists also in paradise, described in the folk tale as having lower (and therefore higher) places, and in the Makarian vision as 'the varied and fair abodes of the saints and the beauty of Paradise', and 'the different divisions of Hell'.[8]

It seems, then, that this cosmology revealed in the folk tales involves a judgement which, though founded on the idea of due reward for good and evil works, is mediated by Christ's mercy, by the prayers of the living for the dead, and by the capacity of the soul to learn, and it is because of this that it is not judgement but forgiveness which provides the emotional context of both the wake and the funeral. There is indeed a moment when the soul is judged, but

[8] van Lantschoot, 'Révélations de Macaire'.

this judgement, it appears, does not preclude subsequent movement to different spiritual abodes, and is more about self-knowledge than about punishment. However, this ability of the soul to alter course after death has its own dangers, and two further tales illustrate that the progress of the soul need not inevitably be upwards. One story refers to a woman who, having done good works all her life, died, and was on the point of going to paradise. At this moment, however, she saw a great crowd of people going by, and stepping aside she said to herself, 'I'll stand here and see where they're going, and if they're going to hell, I won't follow.' But for that she was condemned: 'Why did you wait behind letting all the others go to hell, but try to escape yourself?' The other story cites two neighbours, one good and the other bad. Both died, the good woman first and the bad woman shortly afterwards, and the good woman began climbing the ladder to paradise. The bad woman, however, rather than taking the ladder which led to hell began following the first woman who, looking round and seeing who was behind her, remonstrated: 'Get away from me, you've got no business near me!' And straightaway all the bad woman's sins passed to her, and she went to hell while the 'bad' woman went to paradise.

These tales appear at first sight to contradict the earlier ones which illustrate the importance of only one act of grace in the life of an otherwise graceless person. But the character given to the 'works' in both sets of stories differs in one crucial respect. Those works which, in the stories quoted earlier, drew their authors into paradise, were works which were done, however grudgingly, in response to need, and without self-praise—even, it might be said, with a certain freedom from self-regard. The sin indicated in the stories of the women who fell from the gates of paradise, however, is the reverse of this, and is to do with self-congratulatory comparison with others. The woman who wished to watch where the others went does so in a kind of meanness of spirit, and in this there lies a hint that her motive in doing her good works lay in a basic self-congratulation; while those good works of the woman who despised her neighbour were shown to be, not a genuine response to the need of others, but to vanity. Works alone, in these tales, are not sufficient for paradise; they must be validated by faith, by a kind of simplicity, or, it might be said, by love. Lacking this they are empty of any real content, and reveal themselves, and their authors, in the end.

The existence of paradise and hell, then, and of consignment to either, is an integral part of the Orthodox vision of the other world; but the nature of the soul's relationship to these places has far wider parameters in village thinking than those which are initially apparent, and it appears that the judgement at the forty days is to villagers only a phase in the journey of the soul into the immortal world. And in fact the same tension between God and the devil and between a man's good and evil works which is seen after death, occurs through life as well. It will be remembered that on the shoulders of every man, to right and left, sit Christ and the devil, the one summoning to good, the other tempting to evil, and this theme is touched on in a tale which shows every minute of a person's life as caught up in an unseen spiritual dynamic, revealing the judgement as an on-going process in life as well as after death. In this tale a man was working in the forest and Christ and the devil were arguing over him, the devil saying, 'He's mine!' and Christ saying, 'No, he's mine!' At that moment the man left off his work and came out into a field to eat, so they decided to settle the matter. 'Well,' they agreed, 'let's see what he does when he eats.' And so they watched while the man sat down and ate and drank, omitting to make the sign of the cross. On this, the devil said, 'You see?' But Christ, knowing that hunger and thirst can cause a man to forget himself, said, 'Wait until the end of the meal.' But when the end of the meal came, instead of making the sign of the cross in conclusion, the man lifted up his leg and farted, and at this Christ made off saying, 'Yes, you were right, he's yours!'

It is in relation to stories like this that people quote the saying, 'you don't know what action you are punished for' (*δὲν ξέρεις ἀπὸ ποῦθε κολάζεσαι*), using a word which in Greek is also capable of being translated as 'be sent to hell' or 'damn yourself'—a conclusion which sounds arbitrary and permanent. But once again these stories have to be read in the light of the wider understanding presented above. Although sin and hell go together, and the expressions 'you have [committed] a sin' (*ἔχεις ἁμαρτία*) and 'you are punished' (*κολάζεσαι*) are virtually synonymous, this punishment clearly does not carry in these contexts the meaning that 'damnation' does in English; it is not necessarily a final state. Sin involves punishment, but the stark way in which this idea is often stated is mediated by the subtler intuitions expressed above which indicate that the sinner may encounter not a retributive punishment but rather a purificatory suffering through which the soul is healed.

It is perhaps because of this diffuse understanding of the nature of the judgement and the existence of hell—one that involves also mercy, prayer, forgiveness, and the possibility of movement in the soul's situation after death—that, in spite of the baldness of many of the references to hell, the village people are essentially balanced and often humorous in their relation to death, and mediaeval images of the punishment which on one level they feel is their due are not something about which they are greatly troubled. Death is so deeply accepted as part of the natural order that the imminent death of a man's wife can, when the future is being discussed, be rendered purely factually: 'She'll die, and after her, myself'; and an old woman, similarly, can say of herself, 'I will eat bread until I can eat bread no longer, and then I will die.' And after death? With a broad grin, and with complete detachment: 'Where? Into pitch, where I'll be hung up by my nails...!' Images of hell are only some amongst many intimations of the other world, and the same realism which allows the people to accept death with such clarity allows them also to let the morrow look after itself.

The first part of this chapter has been concerned with drawing together some aspects of the rich mythology which is present in the villagers' imagination when they meet the deaths of their relatives and of fellow villagers, and come face to face with the mystery of the lot of the departed soul in the 'other world'. The focus now turns to the perspective of the mourners as they travel imaginatively through the world of the dead, and to the way in which this journey is charted for them in modes of feeling, behaviour, and ritual.

The responsibility of caring for the dead is borne by the women, and thus the practices of mourning by which the dead are cared for is predominantly a feminine preoccupation and this can involve them in heavy restrictions for a matter of years. Men are not exempt from the general restrictions imposed on the household: they attend wakes, at funerals they carry out duties as coffin makers, grave diggers, and pall bearers, and after a death they grieve, of course, as individuals, and they are expected to wear a black arm-band and to refrain for a decent period from any obvious celebration. But in principle the men stand aside from institutionalized mourning; it is the women who are the guardians of the mystery of death and of the relationship of the household with their dead: it is the women who, as it is said, 'remember' the dead both of their own kin and of their husband's, they whose entire dress changes after a death, they who sing the laments and care for the dead body, they who observe the mourning prohibitions, and they to whom the welfare of the soul by means of the complex memorial observances is entrusted.

The degree of mourning in any individual case is determined by criteria to do with kinship and marriage. Non-related people may of course feel a personal grief for the dead—for a friend, a neighbour, or a young person tragically dead—but in these cases the sorrow and the loss is still, in a very real sense, the concern of others. It is the death of relatives alone, though that includes relatives by marriage, that defines those categories of people who are involved in formal mourning, and the degrees of mourning are closely tied to degrees of relationship. For the immediate family—parents, siblings, children—full mourning customs persist for up to the three or five years, mentioned earlier, which must elapse before the bones are exhumed. But for first and second cousins, and aunts and uncles, the mourning restrictions diminish proportionately, involving only the adoption of a dark headscarf, and an avoidance of public demonstrations of obvious gaiety, for a year or so. A widow's mourning is another matter however. Widows are expected to conform to a standard of mourning more rigorous than that applied to any other bereavement, and they are the only people for whom there is no prescribed conclusion to the mourning period.

Full mourning involves, firstly, a change of appearance. The traditional costume of a married woman whose husband is alive consists of two garments of unbleached white material, both hand-woven, the outer one, dense and tough, being felted by hand in water. The undergarment (*παλιαρούτα*) is a long gown of heavy cotton with flared sleeves; over it is a longish woollen jacket (*σεγκούνι*), sleeveless, intricately cut with triangular insets and long straight seams, flared attractively from the waist. The seams of both consist of deep close stitches of black silk which are not only functional in joining the pieces together but also ornamental, and the strong and graceful lines of the over-jacket mean that this contrast of black with white is strongly marked. On this basic black and white ground each garment has at various typical points tiny embroidered motifs in coloured silks, and the skirt of the gown in particular is bordered with solid embroidery which may run from a narrow band to a deep stiff hem many inches thick. To this basic dress is added a white neck-cloth, a white patterned headscarf (changed in the case of old women to deep yellow), and a patterned belt and apron. For work this apron is plain and serviceable, but for ceremonial wear the apron can be a glory of complex embroidery and silver thread, and is one of the great beauties of the costume. On these ceremonial occasions, silver or gold-plated clasps and buckles, earrings and tiered necklaces of gold coins, complete the ensemble.

At a death, however, this dress is dramatically altered. The headscarf, neck-cloth, belt, and apron are exchanged for black, all jewellery removed, and while the gown and the long sleeveless jacket remain fundamentally the same, only old, patched garments with a minimum of embroidery are worn, indicating that the wearer is no longer concerned with the vanities of this world. Thus the advent of death creates a change in the costume which results in a basic black and white scheme from which all or nearly all the colour has been withdrawn. In the case of a newly-bereaved widow the headscarf will not only be changed to black, it will be worn pulled well forward into a peak so that the face is in shadow, and under it she may well have cut off her long hair—'What need does she have of that now?' Accompanying the change of dress there is a similar alteration of behaviour. Celebrations of any sort must be avoided, dancing is not permitted, and nor is the singing of any songs apart from the laments, even in private. The traditional sweet refreshments may not be offered in the house, and although coffee and ouzo may be served, name days may not be celebrated. The house, also, will reflect a similar change—in many houses the wall hangings and the cloth under the icons will be dyed black, a black cloth will be hung inside the door and a broad black diagonal mourning band pinned on the outside, and the door itself and shutters painted dark. In cases of extreme mourning—the loss of a child or of a husband while the wife is still young—the walls may be painted dark blue or black, and the carpets dyed black as well. All these changes clearly indicate a required distancing of the mourner from joy, and it is this necessity that lies behind the otherwise surprising injunction that all mourners should refrain from attending the liturgy for the first forty days after a death, and that widows should abstain for two or three years. Such people at these times may come in quietly at the beginning, light a candle and leave, and they may also come at the end, if a memorial is being celebrated. But the liturgy itself is defined as 'joy', and as 'company' or 'people'; it is a celebration of life, and from such celebrations those in deep mourning must absent themselves.

There is no doubt that the wearing of black indicates, and is intended to indicate, the experience of grief. The outer dress, as it is said, 'resembles' the inner state. Nevertheless, the resonances in the culture concerning the blackness of Charos and the darkness of the earth extend the significance of mourning far beyond the boundaries of merely personal suffering. The account of the laments given in the preceding chapter has already illustrated that the grief felt by the bereaved is concerned not only with their own loss, but also with the cruel fate of the loved one now lying under the earth. And, in fact, however much the grieving expresses the loss to the living of the person now dead, the reference point of grief is not this loss of the loved one to the living, but the loss of life to the dead. 'He (or she) doesn't see' is the comment universally heard on such occasions, with the accent on the personal pronoun. And this customary phrase is put in context by the occasional explanation: 'The one who lives will eat and drink, will celebrate life again, will dance again; but that one [who is under the earth] doesn't see.' There is no sense here that the life in the spirit might be fuller than the life in the flesh, nor that any life in the flesh, however sorrowful, might be compared unfavourably with the lot of him 'who is under the earth and doesn't see'. The black of mourning reflects primarily the darkness of the grave, and the darkness of grief is derived from that. It is because of this that a typical line in the laments runs, 'You have dressed me in black, black earth!', and because of this also that, for all but widows, the mourning period ends and the black is laid aside only after the exhumation, when the darkness of the earth is exchanged for the light of the sun, and the bones are brought up 'into the air'.

Mourners enclose themselves in black, then, for as long as their dead are enclosed in the earth—a custom which expresses the reality of the grave before it expresses the reality of sorrow, and yet which links the two in a single experience. Thus the wearing of mourning does not merely conform outwardly to a behavioural stereotype, it is the analogy among the living of the power of Charos and the darkness of the grave, and evokes a concentration in the bereaved on some of the most fundamental images in the culture. And it is these complex symbolic associations which lie behind the connections between the death of kin, the wearing of black, and the depth of grief: 'You feel grief for kin, but for others you don't feel grief, you don't wear black.'

However, even though the prescriptions for mourning reveal the mourner as living, as it were, alongside the dead, participating imaginatively in his or her fate under the earth, there are limits to this participation. The last chapter mentioned how it was the function of the community at a wake to act as a counterbalance to the principal mourners, providing the antithesis to the absorption with the grave which grips, indeed threatens, the bereaved. It is a counterbalance echoed also in the role of the men, which sets them aside from the feminine preoccupation with mourning and places them in the freedoms and obligations of daily living. This counterbalance is vital in a culture which is prepared to encounter so unequivocally the first-hand experience of death, and it enters also into many of the customary actions which are part of the ceremonies of death. Leaving the door of the house open at the wake is so that Charos should not be kept within, smashing the water jar as the body is taken from the house for burial, and sewing a tiny red motif into a corner of the black headscarf, are all so that Charos should 'distance himself'; the numerous occasions of the giving of bread, not to mention the institution of the funeral meal itself, are all directed towards the same end, to ward off any further visitation of death, and to strengthen for life those still living. And similar checks to the uncontrolled invasion of the community by grief are the prerogative of those assisting the chief mourners, who may recall, for instance, with some asperity, a wailing widow to her role as host: 'People don't weep when they've got guests to entertain', or, as quoted earlier, repress in a bereaved daughter a threatened outburst: 'Don't beat your breast! Keep quiet!'

But perhaps most interesting of all these restraining instances is the custom of the close relatives of the dead refraining, for forty days after a death, from eating meat or fish, because 'it seems as if you are eating the dead'. Notably, it is this precise image which is used of the earth itself, which also is said to 'eat' or 'devour' the dead. So this refusal of the mourners to touch flesh, together with the reason given for it, is clearly a rejection of any parallelism between themselves and the action of the grave. The mourners, all removable colour in their dress replaced by black, and all flesh removed from their food, are indeed imaginatively associated with the underworld, but they participate not in the reality of death, the devourer, but of the dead, those now being devoured, who lie wrapped in the grave's 'black mantle'.

The mourner, then, identifies primarily not with her own sorrow but with the sorrow of that person now deprived of life, looking towards the dead while rejecting absolutely any association with death itself. But there is more to it than this, for, clothed in the colourless dress of mourning, deprived of joy, and carrying out the meticulous customs laid down by tradition for the salvation of the soul, the mourner's activity is not to identify with death but to overcome it in the name of the dead, and she does so by means of a doctrine which is central to the whole process of mourning—that concerning the dissolution of sins.

The effect of sin on the person who commits it has already been hinted at in the image of the pure soul able to slip through the sieve of judgement, while the gross soul, made fat by sin, cannot follow; and again in the parallel image of the light, balanced soul, able to cross the gulf of pitch by the bridge of a single hair. Sins, in fact, make the physical body dense and impure, so that the spiritual body of the soul is correspondingly coarsened. This teaching is intrinsic to the practice of exhuming the bones, for a body discovered at that time still to be in any way uncorrupt, is evidence of 'sins' and is hastily reinterred, while the 'clean yellow bones like candle wax' normally exhumed are evidence of a now purified and free soul. The dissolution of the flesh is thus linked with the dissolution of sins, and these ideas are intimately linked with the steady performance of the memorial services which mark the period from the burial to the exhumation.

It will be remembered that the explanation given in St Makarios's vision for the timing of the third, ninth and fortieth day memorials was that these times represented the stages of the soul's progress through its earthly recollections and the various abodes of the other world, and mark the repeated appearances of the soul before God.[9] This vision, mapping the path of the soul first through its own past life and then through the regions of paradise and hell, is thus a map of the soul's increasing enlightenment as it perceives more and more clearly the true nature of the life it has led, until it is ready to meet its own judgement. At the same time, however, in the body under the earth changes are being wrought, and a lament from Epirus, following the same time scheme, delineates these changes sharply:

> On the third day I begin to moulder, on the ninth I smell,
> And from the fortieth my limbs fall one by one.[10]

It seems a grotesque parallel, but there is nevertheless a precise and critical link between the judgement of the soul and the dissolution of the body, and it lies in the connection between sins and the flesh. This connection is made particularly clear at the exhumation, but it is not confined to it. In a related custom designed to 'save the soul' of a woman who died in childbirth, a girl, not yet at the age of puberty, should for forty days do forty prostrations at the grave on a piece of underclothing belonging to the dead woman, after which the garment is left on the grave to 'dissolve'. The impurity of the woman's death in a state of blood pollution is here countered by the prayers of a pure young girl, and the pollution itself, drawn from the dead woman into her garment, dissolves with the dissolution of the cloth. The stages of material or bodily corruption, then, are direct images of the stages of the purification of the soul, the 'melting' or 'dissolving' of the flesh (or the cloth) being a symbolic parallel for the falling away of sins, and it is because of this that in the lament quoted above, the stages of bodily corruption parallel exactly the forty days of the soul's spiritual initiation. The body as it begins to dislimb in the earth echoes the progress of the soul as it journeys towards its judgement, and both are united in a single spiritual movement

[9] Alexiou, *The Ritual Lament*, pp. 7f. and 47f., has pointed out that the timing of these memorials resembles ancient Greek practice which prescribed food offerings on the third, ninth and thirtieth day. The explanation for the timings given in the present paragraphs does not depend on this continuity, but is not incompatible with it either.

[10] Alexiou, *The Ritual Lament*, p. 48.

which concerns the release from sins. And it is here that is found a further detail concerning the 'unsorted' or 'uncleaned' wheat into which the candles at the wake are put, compared to the wheat for the candle used for the service of the *Trisághio* after the burial which is three times sorted over and washed. It has been said that the unsorted wheat at the wake is an image of the continuing association of the body with its sins, and that the clean, washed wheat used after the funeral service and the burial images the forgiveness both of the Church and of the people. The washed corn at the *Trisághio*, however, incorporates an additional strand of imagery, for it here signals not only the absolution of the dead by the Church and the community but also the beginning of the parallel process of physical dissolution in the earth which accompanies the process of the release of the soul from its sins.

A final association between the falling away of sins and the falling away of the body is found in the burning of the *ísou*. It will be remembered that the *ísou*—the symbolic representation of the person's life on earth—is only allowed to burn away completely on the third day after the death. This, it is clear now, is part of this same complex of meanings, for the burning of the *ísou* takes place over the identical period during which the soul remains in touch with its past life. Then on the third day all the changes coincide: the *ísou* is finished, the soul, in the Makarian vision, leaves the earth for its introduction to paradise, and the body begins 'to moulder'. By the ninth day, with the soul's initiation into the other world still continuing, this process of dissolution is accelerating, but it is only by the fortieth, when the soul's initial enlightenment is complete and it is sent to its 'place', that the limbs begin to fall 'one by one'. The process of bodily dissolution remains tied throughout the mourning period to the journey of the soul and the purgation of sin, and the link between these events and the activities of the mourners lies in the successive celebrations of the great memorials.

The sequence after a death involves in all—excluding the funeral which is not counted as a memorial—five great memorials or *makaríes*, but it also involves twelve lesser memorials, or as they are termed, 'soul liturgies' (*ψυχολειτουργιές*). These lesser memorials are simple services needing a minimum of preparation and expense, and they all need to be completed by the anniversary of the death. But with the great memorials it is a different matter.

The five great memorials, following the scheme laid out in the vision of St Makarios, mark the third, ninth, and fortieth days after a death, the anniversary, and the exhumation, although they need not be held on the exact day but on the nearest practical equivalent to it. Indeed, because of the immense outlay of flour for the baking—said to be 'like a wedding'—many poorer families have to delay the sequence to one a year in order to spread the cost. The exhumation of the bones is the final formal memorial, and is carried out one Friday on a date chosen from an uneven sequence of years after the death—three, five, or seven—by which time the flesh has 'dissolved' and the clean bones are ready to be committed to the ossuary.

At the heart of the celebration of all memorial services is the provision of memorial food for the dead. *Kóllyva* (*κόλλυβα*) is a generic term covering all the various types of food for the dead, and thus the word properly includes the two types of bread mentioned in an earlier chapter (*leitourgiés* / *prósphora*, and the *psychónia* and 'pieces' which are baked especially for the great memorials),[11] as well as the wine and the boiled wheat which is also offered to the community at such a time. However, since the most commonly made memorial food is the boiled wheat which is a prerequisite not only of the great memorials but also of the lesser memorials as well, the word *kóllyva* is also used to represent the boiled wheat alone. Wheat for the *kóllyva*, sorted and cleaned three times over of husks and little stones from the threshing floor, must then be washed three times. After it has been boiled and strained, a candle is lit and placed beside it and it is censed three times, and when it has cooled it is mixed up with pomegranate seeds, walnuts, sultanas, parsley and a little sugar.[12]

[11] See pp. 152–3 and 155.

[12] This mixture is placed in a bowl and covered with a layer of flour which has been browned in a frying pan over the fire. This again is covered with a layer of fine sugar and decorated with small silver balls which divide the surface into four segments with a cross, and then mark out the initials of Jesus Christ Conquers, or sometimes the initials of the dead person. The addition of the decorations, however, is relatively recent, and in the traditional way of thinking is described as 'vanities'. Everything is stirred up together before it is distributed to the people into the handkerchiefs which they have ready.

The woman who prepares *kóllyva* must not be menstruating at the time, and any woman who receives it when she is menstruating must take it with a spoon rather than with the fingers in the normal way. This *kóllyva* is distributed outside the church after the service, everyone taking a little into their handkerchiefs and eating it on the spot, with the children particularly crowding round and enjoying it because of its sweetness; and each person, as is the case with all other memorial foods, invariably replaces words of thanks with the words of forgiveness: 'May God forgive him.'

For the lesser memorials, the housewife must prepare two bowls of this *kóllyva* and one loaf of liturgical bread of the sort normally offered on Sundays for the eucharist. One of the bowls of *kóllyva* is taken to the church on Saturday evening and placed on a table set on the right hand side of the nave a little away from the iconostasis. A jar of wheat is set behind it into which three candles are put. At the end of vespers on Saturday the priest comes with the cross and the Gospel to this table to light the candles and chant longer or shorter versions of the commemoration service, and when this concludes he is the first to take some of the *kóllyva* and utter the words of forgiveness, while the rest is distributed outside the church as the congregation disperses. The same pattern, repeated the following day at the end of the liturgy—only this time with the addition of the gift of liturgical bread to the sanctuary before the liturgy begins—completes one lesser memorial.

The difference between the lesser and the great memorials lies less in ecclesiastical practice than in lay tradition. The same longer or shorter memorial service can be celebrated at either, and the only difference between the two types of memorial as celebrated in the church is that for the great memorials a few additional offerings are necessary. One *leitourgiá* and four *prósphora*[13] must be sent in to the sanctuary; and on the table, in addition to the bowl of *kóllyva* with a candle put in it, there should also be a bottle of wine, a jug of oil for the icon lamps, one further *prósphoro*, and two extra candles—one about two feet long (*λαμπάδα*) tied round with a purple ribbon—which are put into containers filled with wheat or, in the case of the

[13] The terms *leitourgiá* and *prósphoro* are normally interchangeable, but at the great memorials one *leitourgiá* should be sent into the sanctuary, accompanied by four *prósphora* which may be half size.

21. Between laments on a hillside: 'Ach! I pray the builder who builds the eternal home, / Ach! My little sister, ach! the house of eternity. / Ach! May it be wide, ach! for the dance, broad for companionship, my little Harikli!' (p. 242).

22. On a memorial day, after the liturgy: 'The priest...is the first to take some of the *kóllyva* and utter the words of forgiveness, while the rest is distributed outside the church as the congregation disperses' (p. 288).

unmarried dead, of rice. At the end of the memorial service these candles are blown out and the long one is taken away to be preserved for the next great memorial. Only at the exhumation of the bones is this candle lit for the last time, and left in church to burn away.

Nevertheless, in spite of these similarities in canonical ritual practice, there is a significant difference in the lay practice, and this lies in the enormous quantity of food which must be produced, the preparation of which is once again subject to strict rules of purity. Although a menstruating woman is permitted to carry water and light the ovens, she must not prepare or touch any of the food. Just as the boiled wheat has a lighted candle placed beside it and is censed three times, so exactly the same thing is done to every batch of bread as it is brought in from the ovens. As always, uneven numbers are auspicious, so great care is taken that, for instance, an uneven number of loaves should be sent into the sanctuary, an uneven number of objects placed on the memorial table, an uneven number of ovens fired when the bread is being baked, even if one is used only to bake 'hardly anything'. Similarly, if the group setting out from the house to the church, or vice versa, finds that it consists of an even number of people, either another person will be co-opted to join, or one person will remain behind and come separately.

However, chief among these observances is the by now familiar custom that all ceremonial movements should be right-handed. The group of women leaving for the church with the *kóllyva*, candles, bread, oil and so on, must leave the house by a right-handed path, and on departure from the church must take a different road home so as to complete the return following the same direction. Further, the journey both ways must be completed without deviation: not only must no member turn back, but also no one having set out must turn aside even briefly to any other house until they have completed their intended journey.

The irreversibility of this right-handed movement is particularly evident in a custom by which the advent of a great memorial is heralded to the community. On the evening before the memorial, three girls from the community—specified as 'grown', that is to say unmarried but over the age of puberty—having baked a great deal of the bread known as 'pieces', then take them round the community. One of the girls will take the 'pieces' in a basket, another will carry a jug of wine, and the third a bowl of *kóllyva*, and thus laden they go round the houses. At every house, one 'piece' is given for every person living there and one is left for anyone who is away, some *kóllyva* is offered, and some wine, although the wine is usually only received by one person who takes a little and perhaps keeps some in a glass for the householder if he is not present. Once again, this procession always moves 'right-handed', 'like the dance', and is on no account to turn back; so if the girls run out of anything before they have finished their distribution, they stay where they are while the woman of the house at which they last stop goes back to the original house for replenishments.

This procession of the bread, wine, and wheat is the beginning of a series of gifts which punctuate the memorial celebrations. Apart from the gifts of liturgical bread to the church, more 'pieces' and *kóllyva* are distributed both after vespers and after the liturgy to everyone as they emerge from church. After the liturgy the entire community in instalments passes through the house of the dead to receive a plate of hot bean soup, or beans and rice, together with more 'pieces'. And finally, everyone faced with a return journey to another village will be given as they leave a small loaf (*prósphoro)* to sustain them on their journey home. Again, thanks are in every case replaced by the words 'may God forgive him'.

The wheat which is the joyful climax of every harvest has already been described as the great link between the spiritual and material worlds, the grain which becomes Christ himself and, like Christ, 'must fall to the ground and die' if it is to bear fruit. It is this link which is at the root of the great abundance of bread and wheat at these great memorials and the extraordinary generosity with which it is given out, and which is itself the result of a further correspondence in which the eating of the memorial food on earth is answered by the feasting of the soul in paradise. This correspondence is exact—'What joy Katerini has now, since it was her memorial today and she has had enough to eat!'—and is enshrined in a folk tale where a mother, faithfully keeping the memorials for her son taken for dead in a landslide, in fact keeps him alive until he is discovered a year later. 'The aroma from the *kóllyva*', he says to the amazed crowd, 'and the steam from the [fresh baked] liturgical bread, kept me alive.' And the reverse also is true, so that those who are not commemorated sit alone and forsaken, while the old woman who looks after the souls of children is said to scold any who have no one to make the little circular loaves for them, and these children weep because they are forgotten. Due observance of these ceremonies, then, is vital for the wellbeing of the soul, and because for the first three days the soul is said to come 'like a fly' to drink from the water left out with the *ísou*, a fly in the room, circling round and around, is able to occasion the comment: 'That fly that comes and comes again, what do you say, is it hungry?'

These memorials, then, feed the soul; but they are effective with one important proviso. It has been said that at name days hospitality is offered to and received by the entire community without reference to on-going quarrels or bad feeling. The gift given in honour of the saint takes precedence over the expression of antagonism, even though this is no guarantee that the quarrels themselves will lapse. It has been said also that peace between two women on bad terms with each other is often restored when both meet at the laying out of a dead body. But it is the memorial celebrations which provide the most striking example of reconciliation as a primary focus within the social order, for the unstinting hospitality from the house of the dead, offered with tears and without joy, is hospitality offered in the spirit of grief and repentance; and the unanimous forgiveness with which it is answered brings about in the community, for however brief a moment, the experience of its own reconciliation. And it is in acknowledgement of this fundamental reality that, built into the memorial celebrations, is the belief that any quarrelling during the preparation of the memorials causes the memorial 'not to take', not to be effective: bad feeling and any display of hostility invalidate the memorial and deprive it of its healing power.

The effectiveness, then, of the memorial depends on charity and self-denial at a time, it must be remembered, when the protagonists are likely to be under considerable stress. And it is in relation to this theme of self-denial that the essence of the mourner's role is to be seen. It has already been pointed out that the denial of joy to the mourner is one of the corner stones of her role. Nevertheless, as has also been shown, the giving of joy to others is one of the primary consequences of what she does. The community, especially in hungry times, takes pleasure in the repeated gifts of bread and *kóllyva*; the soul is said to feel 'joy' as it feasts in harmony with the living, and the 'joy' of the children on eating the *kóllyva* is often commented on, and is of such significance that this joy is said to stand in the place of the prayer of forgiveness if the child forgets to say the customary words. The mourner is a person who, denying herself joy, gives it to others. More than this, it is only if the mourner does deny herself joy that she is able to give it to others.

The joy is the joy of hungry people being fed, of children receiving a treat, of a soul being comforted, of community and commensality. However, the true origin of this joy lies not in the gifts of bread and wheat themselves, but in the gifts of which the bread and wheat are the symbols. The gift to the soul of the *kóllyva* is more than its brief nourishment, it is the promise of the resurrection latent in the death of the seed corn whose body has first to fall to the ground and die. And this death of the seed corn, representing the death of the body which is the gateway to the resurrection, represents also in Christian symbolism the death of the ego and of all those elements in the person which stand in the way of the kingdom of God. So it is that behind the institutionalized denial of joy to the mourner there lies the doctrine of repentance (*μετάνοια*), or change of spiritual understanding, by which this resurrection is to come about. In this way the mourner's lack of joy is an image of her repentance and the repentance of her house, but it brings the consolation of the forgiveness which she receives on behalf of the soul and which she passes on to it through the piety of her actions and through the sacrifice involved in her mourning role. The real feast of the soul in the other world is the feast of communion and of forgiveness; the real feast of the community on earth is the feast of love and of freedom from the daily burden of grudges and resentment. The memorial service is beyond all else a great act of reconciliation negotiated by the mourner, and it is for this reason when any little group sets out together for the memorial meal they do so with those words already quoted which are never used in any other context but death: 'Let us go and forgive.'

This theme of reconciliation is critical in interpreting the custom just described in which the 'grown' girls inaugurate the great memorials by taking the memorial food round the community. The emphasis on the gift is immediately apparent, and the flow of *kóllyva*, bread, and wine right-handed through the village without doubling back recalls the onward movement of gifts given in hospitality where no return is sought. It is not, however, in the fact of hospitality only that the deep meaning of the custom lies, but in the choice of the 'grown' girls through which that hospitality is offered.

Daughters have already been described as the mobile element in society, destined from birth to leave the family of their birth and marry out. The 'grown' or mature (virgin) girls who carry the gifts of bread, wine, and the memorial food round the community, being on the threshold of marriage, are thus on the threshold also of leaving their family of origin and taking themselves, their fertility, their dowries, and their loyalties to bring life to the house of a stranger. In contradistinction, therefore, to the mourner, whose role secludes her in her own house, denies her joy, and places her apart from the communal life in the shadowy world between the living and the dead, these girls, full of promise but as yet uncommitted in marriage to any one group, represent the vital bond of blood and of life which flows between the separate households. And it is significant that this moment in the life of a girl is seen as one of particular innocence. For all that marriage is the good to which all aspire, it is realized also that 'if you marry you damn yourself', that is to say that marriage, in committing a woman irredeemably to the competitions and exhaustions of the social world, commits her also to its multitudinous sins, to envy, gossip, denigration of others, cursing of children and animals, quarrelling. Unmarried girls, therefore, innocent of sex, are innocent also of sins by which women 'damn themselves', and of responsibility for the social sins of the competitive family groups.

In this way these girls, on the threshold of marriage though not yet involved in its negative side, represent in their own persons the bond of blood and the promise of harmony between the different kin groups, and are thus supremely suited to carry from house to house the forgiveness of the memorial offerings. In this way one of the society's responses to death is to join the households in an unbroken and communal act of reconciliation, and to assert, along with the gift to the community of food and repentance, the life-giving progress of women *katameriá* through the households. And once again the unidirectional element in the passage of the gifts is significant, not only for the statement it makes about marriage, but also for the statement it makes about relations between the living and the dead. The memorials are carried out by the living on behalf of the dead, and in the trust also that the same grace will one day be granted to those who now offer them. So the gifts and the forgiveness which characterize the great memorials are acts of charity, as is the central principle of the gift of girls in marriage to 'strange' households. In the 'right-handed' distribution of bread and wheat and wine and in the onward-moving spiral pattern which accompanies it, the mourners take part in a ceremony which looks forward and not back, and is a living enactment of the cleansing of sin and the renewal of life.

In this nexus of customs, then, that accompany a death, themes of the tragic situation of the dead, the dissolution of the body, the progress of the soul, the continuity of life for the living, the repentance of the house of mourning, the forgiveness of the community, and the purgation of sin are all welded together into a single action, the memorial service, and expressed in a single figure, the mourner. The dark tones of mourning represent the darkness of the grave not as a final end but as a narrow way through which all must pass to the new and forgiven life that lies beyond. And the guiding principle by which this way is negotiated is revealed in the analogy between the mourners' prescribed absence from the liturgy and one of the ascetic practices of Great Lent, when the penitential character of the time denies to the faithful the consecration of the eucharist on all days of the week except for Saturdays and Sundays. During the weekdays even the reading of the Gospel must be foregone[14] as part of the greater good of inner purification and increasing self-awareness, and the spare, quiet Liturgy of the Presanctified Gifts (involving bread and wine consecrated on a previous Saturday or Sunday) takes place instead. The mourner's role, then, and in particular the role of the widow, is penitential, to live not for herself but for others: her business is not to receive joy—even the joy of the liturgy—nor, at the great memorials, is it even to receive thanks or the customary 'good-night' when people leave her house, for this, once again, is replaced by the formula of forgiveness. By symbolically renouncing her claim on life she becomes transparent, as it were, to communications from either world to the other and, neither wholly of one world or the other, is able to act as a medium between them, bringing the food of repentance to the living in the name of the dead, and forgiveness to

[14] The New Testament readings are replaced by readings from the Old Testament.

the dead in the name of the living. Dressed in black, fasting from meat, from society, and from 'joy', the mourner is the great intercessory figure of Greek society, a truly kenotic figure emptied of self. But her role, while eradicating her, as it were, as a social being, gives her in return a dignity so extraordinary that of this role it can be said: 'What is black? What is black? Honour!' (*Τί εἶναι μαύρο; Τί εἶναι μαύρο; Τιμή!*)

One theme with which this chapter began was the co-existence of ideas to do with hell both as a permanent place of punishment and as a temporary place of purification, and it has now become clear how through the complex meanings of the rituals of mourning the one converts to the other. For while the departing soul may indeed carry with it the burden of unresolved sins and be in itself deserving of perpetual judgement, the resolution of those sins is still a possibility, and in the dimension of the social world this resolution is undertaken by those it leaves behind. The means by which the soul does not suffer perpetually the reward of its sins does not lie only in its own efforts, even in its own repentance, but in forgiveness, both human and divine. Thus as well as marking the stages of grief, of decomposition, of the journey of the soul into the other world and of its release from sin, the sequence of memorials also maps the path of forgiveness, and thus maps simultaneously both the freeing of the departed soul and the healing within the social order.

A further theme was the tension between the two ways of thinking of the other world, and although this tension is accommodated in various ways from the wake on, certain ambivalences continue which are only finally resolved at the end of the mourning period. It has been seen that the theme of the decomposition of the body is pivotal in determining the staging posts in the process of mourning. The first two great memorials mark the stages in the wandering of the soul over its past life and its deepening experience of the other world, conveying to it the forgiveness of the community and hallowing the stages of physical decay. The third great memorial on the fortieth day marks the moment at which the soul is fully committed to its appropriate 'place', and the body increasingly caught up in the irreversible processes of dissolution. After this the twelve minor memorials or 'soul liturgies' must be celebrated within the year, before the fourth great memorial marks the anniversary, the completion of a period of time, an epoch, in the mysterious life of the soul. The fifth and last great memorial takes place an uneven number of years—usually, as has been said, five or seven—after the death, but the number of years elapsing is determined by the correspondence between the flesh and 'sins', and by the necessity that the body should have had time to decompose completely before the bones are exhumed.

At these events the natural pragmatism of the people is evident, as they dig for the bones with a certain rough tenderness, and in cases where grief is not extreme someone might, with a not irreverent sense of their own impropriety, be moved to a comment like, 'Look at the ribs, like chops that you put on the grill!' At the same time the exhumation is for all types of mourner a profoundly cathartic experience, for it is at this point that the agony of mourning reaches, as it were, a crisis from which there is nowhere to go but forward, into a stiller grief and a world made calm by acceptance. Although, therefore, there are all types of death and all kinds of grieving, there is a central pattern by which the people of this culture are led through its trauma, and in the following description of the exhumation of a man killed in his early twenties, the last act in the drama of mourning may be clearly discerned.

As always, setting out from the house with a little group of relatives, care is taken for the numbers of people in the group to be uneven, and for the path taken to the graveside to be right-handed. In normal cases, only the particular family group concerned is present, but for the young and tragically dead more people will come, and when the earth begins to be removed the horror of death is renewed and the chief mourner, accompanied from time to time by others, once again begins to fill the air with laments, ending each line with a shouted cry: 'My lovely young man!', 'My own George! My own George! My own George!', throwing back her head and beating on the ground with her hand. Keeping up a continual stream of song, the voice may break off occasionally to shout to the dead endearments or recriminations: 'Three years I waited to see you, and you didn't pass by my window!', or, 'Not even one night did you come to me in a dream!' The spade digs at the earth, chipping against the stones, with occasional instructions from the watchers as to where to dig next, and gradually the tension increases as the grave becomes deeper. With the discovery of the bones becoming imminent, the grave is censed, the laments become more and more frenzied, tears pouring down the faces of the singers, with 'Ach, my little George, so long a time and still you haven't appeared!' and, in a frenzy of grief, 'You haven't the strength to throw off the earth which covers you!' These laments can be utterly uninhibited, and indeed give licence to the chief mourner to vent to the world her grief and anger, to bang her hand on the earth or on the railings which may surround the grave, stamping her foot on the ground as she hurls her lamentations into the face of death. Then, without drama, the bones are discovered, the place where the head should lie pointed out, and the skull brought up out of the ground. It is the long awaited climax, the tragic meeting at which it is natural for a mother, stretching out her arms in longing, to cry out, 'Give me my son so that I can see him!' and, taking the skull, to hold it up at arms' length, momentarily, and, in an extraordinary gesture of horror and love kiss it quickly and put it from her.

With this, however, the climax is reached. The tension drains away, and the mourners, even the mother, look on with composure, occasionally talking and pointing things out. People watch that the full number of bones are found, remembering the money that they had thrown into the grave at the burial. The digger may look for coins which when found are kept as an apotropaic. They may find a bottle of ouzo, of water, or of wine, and smell them, and someone may perhaps take a sip. One by one as the bones are brought up they are washed with water and with wine, laid in a box already lined with a clean linen cloth, covered with flowers, and censed. When everything is complete, everyone leaving the graveyard washes their hands in the last of the wine, and the bones are taken to the church where they are placed on the right hand side of the iconostasis in front of the icon of Christ, with a lighted icon lamp on their right. Since the exhumation is always carried out on a Friday, the bones remain in the church throughout Saturday and the early part of Sunday so that they are present throughout vespers on the Saturday night, and throughout matins and the liturgy on the Sunday morning, in both cases concluding with the memorial office. The memorial meal is then held, and at some point after this the bones are taken from the church and laid with all the others in the village ossuary—a little stone building usually on the edge of the graveyard. After this, their period as objects of veneration is over. With the flesh purged and the soul no longer imaginatively placed under the earth but gone, as it is said, 'elsewhere' (ἀλλοῦ), all that can be done has been done. With the years the stones of the ossuary walls crumble and get dislodged, the boxes rot and spill out the bones, and no one worries that these once hallowed remains are now left to the mercy of any chance event, nor even that, as it can be put with a rueful laugh, 'the dogs eat them!' The physical remains have moved into a phase unrelated to sin or salvation, the soul gone elsewhere, and while an aspect of the soul may still 'wait' fifty years for memorials,[15] with the passing of the years this becomes weaker as the older generations—grandparents, uncles, and aunts—become increasingly marked not with an individual candle or a soul-liturgy but with a waxed strand in a candle twist, one among many, and merge quietly into the collectivity of the dead.

The emotional effect of the exhumation on the bereaved has already been hinted at, and indeed it does appear that this ceremony—sometimes deeply traumatic and sometimes filled with a kind of contemplative quiet—acts as a catharsis for those still in deep grief. During the years preceding the exhumation these people wait, in a sense, to see their loved one again, and to perform for the dead the last of the great institutionalized services where the evidence of purification from sin is also the terrible conversion of the remembered figure into 'a handful of little bones' (*μία χούφτα κοκκαλάκια*). The encounter once accomplished, however, the worst is faced, and it has already been noted that it is after this point that the greatly distressed are said to 'make a decision', and, turning from the self-destructive extravagance of grief, to create in themselves a mood of greater tranquillity and acceptance. It is, then, both emotionally and symbolically apt that the period of institutionalized mourning should end with the exhumation, and, for all but widows, this is in fact the case. For forty days after the exhumation normal dress is worn, except that the headscarf accompanying it is dark brown, which becomes dark green as the period comes to an end. At the end of the forty days the bereaved will enter again fully into the normal life of the community.

The case of a widow is somewhat different, for widows are expected, unless they marry again, to remain in mourning until death.

[15] See p. 218.

The point at which remarriage is ideally permitted to occur, however, is significant, for this point falls 'after the exhumation'. Although widows can and do re-marry before this point, particularly those too poor and with too many children to be able to survive on their own, it is the exhumation which customarily provides the pivotal point after which the bereaved wife may turn from a world which is ideally concerned with her dead husband to one which could legitimately contemplate a new marriage. At that point the widow's mourning changes from the 'deep mourning' of the years up to the exhumation, to the 'light mourning' which follows it, a relaxation which decrees no change in dress and deportment, but carries permission to remove the mourning band from the door, the black cloths from within the house, to lighten the colour of the walls and shutters, to begin to celebrate name days and serve sweets in the house. A widow's mourning before the exhumation is for her dead husband who lies under the earth and 'cannot see', while the mourning afterwards is more in the nature of the decent reticence of a woman whose husband has died, and whose life has not been re-validated by another marriage.

The picture which emerges from this description of the memorial customs is one according to which the situation at the exhumation of the bones is in many senses the reverse of that which is in play before it. Because the decaying of the body represents the loosening of the sins of the soul, dissolution becomes the pivot on which the mourning process turns; and because the medium of dissolution is the earth, and the memorials are tied to coincide with the completion of this process, the memorials which take place between burial and exhumation are revealed as little by little reversing the symbolism of death upon itself. Earth, the destroyer of temporal life, is now the destroyer of the sins which destroy eternal life, the means of destruction becomes the means of salvation, and that dark force which plays so terrible a part in the grief and despair of the newly-bereaved becomes that very aspect which, in loosing the flesh from the body, images the loosening of the sins from the soul and enables the passage of the soul to its final spiritual home. With the exhumation the transition is successfully negotiated, the sins of the dead have vanished, and the soul is released, and it is consistent with this that at the last great memorial meal when the community go to the house of the bereaved on the Sunday after the exhumation, for the only time in the entire sequence of memorial services 'it doesn't do' to say the customary words, 'May God forgive him'.

In this way the exhumation bears, in more ways than one, the stamp of finality, and it is awaited with a kind of quiet anticipation. The ceremony itself is universally described as the time when the bones are brought up 'into the air' (*στὸν ἀέρα*), and this is an essentially joyful image made all the more significant by the contrast between air—which also means light and the act of seeing—and the darkness of the earth where the dead 'don't see'. The exhumation is thus an act of extraordinary importance, while to neglect it is to consign the dead person to perpetual imprisonment: 'it is as if the body is in hell (*στὴ κόλασι*) if it stays in the earth'. Thus the bringing up of the 'clean yellow bones' from the darkness of the earth into the light of day completes the work of the entire mourning period, and sets the seal on the complex patterning of transformations which involve both the bereaved and the dead. At this point the mourners are freed from their ascetic role and even widows may think of remarriage. And as for the dead, darkness is exchanged for light, earth for air, flesh for bones, sins for forgiveness, confinement for freedom, the process of purgation of the sins of this world for a destiny definitively 'elsewhere'. In this way, taking into account all the associations outlined above, it seems that this moment which takes the bones from the earth and from its associations with the underworld, and returns them to the air, to society, and to the 'joy' of the liturgy, is seen as bringing also the forgiven soul into a corresponding state of blessedness in an incorporeal world of light. These connections are intuitive only, for the villagers are sceptical of a world they have never seen and too good theologians to be anything other than apophatic about the nature of the eternal world and who is where in it; but there are indications here, at any rate, at the completion of the exhumation, of one last transformation, which is the exchange of death for life and of hell for paradise. And it is in the context of these intuitions that one further connection can be made, and a question about why Greeks practise exhumation can sometimes receive the answer: 'Because Christ is risen!' The exhumation is not of course itself a resurrection—for villagers, that is something only Christ has accomplished, and exhumation is too mixed with renunciation of the dead, and with reflection on the handful of little bones which death presents as our real selves, to be an uncomplicated symbol of hope. But notwithstanding all the renewed sadness of parting, the exhumation does also appear to be a sign for the villagers that the resurrection of Christ, which opens the gates of the underworld, opens also, in the words of the Orthodox memorial service, 'a place of light, a place of refreshment, a place of repose'[16] to which the forgiven soul goes as it passes beyond the knowledge of those who mourn.

In the processes of death as in life, then, there is a movement, and yet another turn of the cycle is completed when the body, put into the earth with the desperate grief of loss, comes out changed. The continual right-handed movements observed at the memorials themselves are an image of another turn of the cycle of dance which will take the dead through the grave and into the sunlight once more, though once again the circle does not end where it began but at a new point of relationship both with the living and with the 'other world'. Death, itself a transformation, is only the beginning of a long series of further transformations which are not primarily about loss but about forgiveness, and end with a sign of the resurrection occurring on three levels: of the bones from the earth, of the mourner from her grief and from her exclusion from social joy, and of the soul from its sins and into the freedom of its spiritual life.

[18] See *Memorial for the Departed*, Great Litany for the Departed, p. 6.

10
THE GOD-BEARERS

THE process by which the death of the body is transformed into the life of the soul is a process which is attested by the evidence of the clean bones dug up at the exhumation, brought again into the church and received into the mystery of the liturgy. And yet this is not the whole story, for while the transitional period between death and the exhumation is the dissolution, or the washing away, of sins, there are those who in this life have already conquered these negative impulses in themselves, and having already purified their flesh need no further purification. For these people—the saints of the Church—the story after death is different. Saints of the Orthodox world are in the course of time recognized by the Church, but initially they are disclosed by the spontaneous verdict of the people, and it is to the people that they appear in dreams and visions, and to the people that they are revealed, sometimes by the sweet scent which hovers around their grave, sometimes by the fact that their relics are found to be uncorrupt or exude sweet smelling myrrh, always by the miracles that flow from them after death and by which they become more and more widely known. In the case of ordinary mortals, who after death need the intercessions of the community to help them disengage from the sins that hold them back, the process of working through the dross unpurged in life is only achieved by degrees. The saints, however, are revealed after death (and sometimes before it) as people who have in life achieved this freedom and who, already with God, can themselves intercede for the people, guarding and protecting them from harm.

In the figure of the saint, then, death has its moment of power in bringing about the severance of the body from the soul, but thereafter its action is reversed, and this reversal is often expressed by incorruption. It may seem strange from a purely conceptual point of view that lack of corruption is one sign of a saint, when it has already been emphasized that it is also a sign of a vampire and, in less extreme cases, indicates at the exhumation the presence of 'sins'. But the villagers, living by experience rather than by theory, do not find it difficult to distinguish the uncorrupt and holy from its mirror image, the uncorrupt and demonic dead: 'Of course you know whether someone was a saint', or, again, 'A saint works miracles'. And the underlying rationale is similarly secure, for while most of humanity dies still full of sins—fat, gross, opaque, as it were, to the spiritual world, needing still the long process of purgation and forgiveness before their soul is truly free—the flesh of the saint in whom the spirit has already taken up its abode, having already achieved purgation, has no need of this process. The vampire's flesh betokens the presence of such evil that it cannot decompose; the saint's flesh betokens such a presence of holiness that decomposition is no longer necessary.

To these people, then, is given the term *Theophóroi* (*Θεοφόροι*, sing. *Θεοφόρος*), 'those who carry God [within them]' or 'carriers of God', a term that translates into 'our God-bearing fathers',[1] or 'God-bearers'. But this term 'God-bearers' as it relates to the saints must be understood in a way which distinguishes it from the 'God-bearing' nature of the 'ever-virgin and God-bearing Mary', who in the flesh carries God in her womb and gives birth to him. The distinction in Greek is clear, for in relation to the Mother of God, the term *Theotókos* replaces the term *Theophóros*, and the suffix 'tokos' is derived from *tíkto*, to give birth to, a word which is the root also of *téknon* (*τέκνον*), offspring, or child. While the English word 'God-bearing' therefore elides this distinction between *Theophóroi* and *Theotókos*, it is important to keep in mind the qualitative difference between the two: the *Theophóroi* have followed the path of Christ, but the *Theotókos* has given birth to Christ; the *Theophóroi* have gradually been freed from sin, but the *Theotókos* has given birth to the one who is without sin; the *Theophóroi* receive God in their hearts, but the *Theotókos* enables God to be born whole in the flesh. Because of this the Mother of God is looked to as the protector and guide of all those who follow after her. She is the All-holy or *Panaghía*, their Mother, guide and exemplar, but in her God-bearing she is also qualitatively different from them—'ever-blessed and most pure and the Mother of our God, more honourable than the

[1] e.g. *Divine Liturgy*, Liturgy of Preparation, p. 16; cf. Hapgood, *Service Book*, p. 73.

cherubim and incomparably more glorious than the seraphim'.[2]

Following the Mother of God, then, saints are people who have become able to stand as intermediaries between the seen and the unseen worlds and able themselves to act as guides and exemplars. Critically, also, they are, like the Mother of God, not an exceptional but a normal part of people's lives. The saints are an extra dimension of an already many-dimensional world, and the people keep their icons in their houses, pray to them, see them in dreams, celebrate their feast days, venerate their relics and visit their holy places as a regular part of daily life. They also give their names to their children, and in this act individualism is renounced for incorporation into the communion of saints, so that the child's personal celebration thereafter is not his or her own birthday but the 'name day' or feast day of the saint. The saints are part of everyday reality, venerated for their holiness and loved for the simplest of reasons—because they have suffered for the sake of truth and because it is in their nature to 'help people'.

Saints are thus living testaments to the incarnation of the divine life in the human person; and they appear throughout the Orthodox world at all times and in all places as the authentic witness of a tradition going back to the early centuries of Christianity. By no means confined to a historical or mediaeval past, the saint in this tradition is a fully contemporary phenomenon, and there are always a number of elders (m. *γέροντες*, f. *γερόντισσες*) in monasteries and hermitages scattered throughout the Orthodox world becoming imperceptibly more and more known as holy men and women, of whom some may well in the end be recognized as saints.

Except in times of martyrdom, the making of a saint in the Orthodox tradition lies in the embracing of the ascetic way—thought of as another kind of martyrdom—a way of great cost in that it involves the death of the ego and of all that obscures the image of God in the person. Thus saints are people who, encountering life in all its severity—whether in voluntary asceticism, in prison camp, in persecution, in poverty or privation of any sort, in self-giving, in providing for the poor—have come to know the depths of their own nature and thus of human nature, and they find their touchstone

[2] *Divine Liturgy*, p. 62; cf. Hapgood, *Service Book*, pp. 107–8.

23. Baking for one of the five great memorials: 'The immense outlay of flour for the baking—said to be "like a wedding"...' (p. 287). While the woman behind uses a long paddle to place prepared loaves in the hot oven, the two in front, having stamped their dough with the seal on the left, are pricking features of the pattern.

24. Fr Iakovos Tsalikis, Monastery of St David in Evia: 'There are always a number of elders... becoming imperceptibly more and more known as holy men and women' (p. 304).

for these experiences in the Scriptures, in the liturgical life of the Church, in prayer and fasting. Sheer suffering on its own does not lead to this sanctity, for it is not suffering which is the point but self-knowledge and the acquisition of, as it is put, the mind of Christ; but such self-knowledge is not gained without suffering, for suffering is indivisible from the encounter with the great reaches of human experience and human weakness. It is this encounter, both with the self and with God, interpreted within this particular way of spiritual illumination, which brings into being the holy men and women of the Orthodox Church, people who in their lifetimes are sought after for their comfort, prayers, and guidance, held in reverence for their knowledge of the human condition, loved for their extraordinary wisdom and compassion, and after death recognized as bringing healing and enlightenment to those who ask their help. In spite of all this, however, saints are drawn from the people; they are ordinary people become extraordinary.

It is clear from what has just been said that life itself provides the testing ground by which the human spirit is refined and purged, and because of this the saints of the Orthodox tradition may be found in any walk of life—they may be married or celibate, men or women, monastic, clerical, or lay, old or young, intellectual or 'fool for Christ' (that is to say, someone who forswears ordinary social norms in order to follow his or her spiritual way). Nevertheless, the typical route to sanctity is the ascetic way of the monastery or the hermitage. This is well understood by the village people to whom, in the context of social life and the competitive nature of social relations already described, the temptation to sin is virtually irresistible. The unredeemed desires of the fallen human being, which life in society in many ways exacerbates rather than controls, can in village eyes be best, if not uniquely, brought under control by removal from the comings and goings of village life, and the people in talking of the making of a saint rarely divorce it from the strictly ascetic path lived in the context of the monastery or the wilderness: 'He became an ascetic,' they say, 'and a saint' (*ἀσκήτεψε καὶ ἁγίασε*).

This picture also accords with the texts of the ascetic tradition,[3] for these assume that it is in the spiritual discipline of the monastery and

[3] For a summary, see e.g. Ware, *The Orthodox Way*, pp. 105–7, 112–17.

in the struggle with the demons of the wilderness that, having abandoned all social aspirations and the cares and comforts of this world, the ascetic is free to face himself: to endure hunger, thirst, lack of sleep, privation, fear, solitude, to practise self-discipline and to engage in a life of continual prayer. As mentioned earlier, these abstinences are by no means undertaken in the spirit of self-punishment—quite the reverse. They are part of a testing ground in which the ascetic comes into naked encounter with the demons—that is to say, he engages with the radical weaknesses and temptations which lie within himself. It is this confrontation, dangerous in itself but contained by being brought by prayer into the protection of the heavenly powers, which puts him in touch with the divine life that also lives within him, and which after many years gives him freedom from his passions and union with God. At the same time, biographies of many Orthodox saints presuppose that the person who carries this encounter through to its end becomes a solace to thousands. Since the self that has not been enlightened and purified cannot enlighten or purify others, the solitary life plays an essential part in this movement from inner to outer, from the self to the multitudes. But while the holy life is in this tradition characteristically marked, particularly at the beginning, by withdrawal from the world, it is also marked by an extraordinary compassion for suffering humanity, and the direction of the struggle is epitomized in the words of St Seraphim of Sarov: 'Acquire inward peace, and thousands around you will find their salvation.'[4] The search of the ascetic for inner peace is not a selfish task; it is a task which saves the world.

The path by which the ascetic becomes known to the people follows the way in which the monastery is related to the outside world, for throughout the Orthodox world the monastery acts as a centripetal force, a living presence in the locality actively drawing people to it. From town and village people will visit their local monastery at its patronal festival, for instance, or at some other great feast, they will make a vow to provide the *prósphora* for the liturgy on some day special to themselves, and they will seek out its holy men as healers and confessors. In the monastic life devoted to self-knowledge and self-giving people see the fulfilment of their own longing, and this longing is met also by a reciprocal movement by which the monas-

[4] Quoted by Ware, *The Orthodox Way*, p. 89.

tic will move into the outside world, bringing the liturgy to those villages which have no priest, visiting the sick, celebrating marriages and funerals, and, where there are relics of a local saint, bringing these relics to them for special occasions. In this way the future elder will gradually come to know, and be known by, the surrounding area, so that long before the outside world hears of his quality, the elder will already be a revered and loved figure among his own people.

A number of contemporary examples illuminate in detail the path of an Orthodox holy man or woman, including one in the area which is the focus of this book, and the life of this elder is of particular interest, since it provides an image of the way in which the local attachments and personal qualities recognized in such a man are essential to his embodiment of the universal character of holiness. Father Iakovos Tsalikis (1920–1991), a monk of the monastery of St David in northern Evia, had in the years before he died become so widely renowned that huge numbers of people from throughout the Greek Orthodox world both in Greece and abroad were present at his funeral. But decades before he became publicly recognized, he had been trusted for confession by the villagers of his area—a trust not given lightly—and referred to universally as a 'good' man. Given the scepticism, discussed below, with which the Church as an institution tends to be regarded by the villagers, this was praise indeed.

The life of Father Iakovos,[5] as compiled from accounts of monks and villagers who knew him, is paradigmatic of the path by which the figure of a great elder comes into being, demonstrating both the close links that exist between the monasteries and the villages, and the path of heroic sacrifice that characterizes the life of those on the ascetic path. First of all there is the necessity to forswear individual family bonds in favour of obedience and communal loyalty, and this is illustrated in the following story. Early in his monastic life, immediately after the civil war and during days of extreme austerity in the 1950s, the young monk Iakovos had been put in charge of the monastic supplies, and at the same time put automatically under obedience not to use them to assist his kin. After the death of his widowed sister, her two orphaned children attached them-

[5] Sylianos G. Papadopoulos, *Ὁ μακαριστὸς Ἰάκωβος Τσαλίκις* [*The blessed Iákovos Tsalíkis*] (Athens: Ἱ. Μ. Ὁσίου Δαβὶδ τοῦ Γέροντος, 1992); *Ἕνας ἅγιος Γέροντας, Ὁ μακαριστὸς π. Ἰάκωβος* [*A holy Elder, the blessed Fr Iákovos*] (Rovies, Evia, Greece: Ἱ. Μ. Ὁσίου Δαβὶδ τοῦ Γέροντος, 1993).

selves to a group of villagers going to the monastery, and walked with them barefoot for miles across the mountains to seek the care and comfort of their uncle. Exhausted and hungry, they found him, but he, with tears running down his face, was forced to give them nothing but his blessing before sending them back over the hills again. Father Iakovos had a penniless boyhood in an impoverished refugee family, a monastic life of great privation and, in his last twenty or so years, continual pain and illness; but recounting this story many years later he more than once said that this incident caused him the greatest pain of his life.

This rule of non-assistance of kin has a precise spiritual logic. In the social world all significant relationships are, as has been described, with kin; but to the monastic there are no exclusions, and all, without exception, are to be loved, helped, comforted, enlightened. Thus contrary to village life where customary giving is largely confined within the house and family, and where hospitality to strangers breaks into this circle only at critical points, in the monastery the dynamic is reversed and the principle of hospitality to all is the norm. To achieve this, however, the monk must forswear individual personal loyalties, for only by doing this can these loyalties be freed for the whole world—a spiritual economy which is summed up by another elder as follows: 'The moment the monk takes his vows, he gives his loved ones to God and he forgets them. Then God is obliged to help them. That is how the monk emerges from his own little family and enters the great family of Adam [i.e. mankind].'[6] The divine end of this covenant is also illuminated in the case of the orphaned children, told above. They encountered another monk who, unprompted, understood their plight and gave them some bread, and passed on to them a little money that he had received from elsewhere. This story is rounded off by the fact that although their uncle, Father Iakovos, was not able at that moment to give anything to his own kin, it was to become a feature of his life that the money which, unbidden, flowed in continually to the 'little bag' in which he received gifts, flowed out continually in alms to the sick and destitute, and that all who came to him in need were the recipients of his care.

This uncompromising reversal of the ordinary norms of society, while it is clearly a source of benefit to the people, means, however,

[6] Elder Porphyrios in Kleitos Ioannides, *Ὁ Γέρων Πορφύριος: μαρτυρίες καὶ ἐμπειρίες* [*Elder Porphyrios: testimonies and insights*] (Athens: Ἱερὸν Γυναικεῖον Ἡσυχαστήριον ἡ Μεταμόρφωσις τοῦ Σωτῆρος, 1995).

that as well as this symbiosis between the outside world and the monastery there is also a certain tension. Notable holiness is recognized by the people, but corruption in the Church and lapses from chastity among many sworn to the ascetic life are also known about, or invented, and the villagers, skilled in gossip and innuendo and with a cultural conviction that men 'cannot contain themselves', have no problem with scandal-mongering about monastics and are not above treating a monk who is out of his monastic context as the butt of sly humour. In addition, somewhat naturally for a people whose social destiny is seen in terms of marriage and children, there is a sense in which serious concern for the holy life is seen to be appropriate to age rather than to youth, and in which the departure of a son or a daughter for the monastery is taken as a disaster. Nevertheless, this step, once taken, is said after a time to be accepted, and even to bring with it a certain pride, for however obvious its failings and whatever the opportunities for gossip—deserved or undeserved—that it provides, the Orthodox Church is a part of village life, and its expression in the monastic life is an indispensable element in village consciousness.[7] From this outside world the monastery draws each new generation of monastics, and from it also come, for a few hours, lay people in great numbers, drawn to a society which exists in order to put into practice the values whose deficiencies in their own lives

[7] A distinction has to be drawn here between the Church as an institution and the Church as a repository of sacred wisdom embodied in liturgical offices and spiritual practice. The two meanings go together, of course, in so far as it takes the institution to pass on and sustain both offices and practice, and to root them in the lives of the people. Nevertheless, the institution, like all public institutions, is the object of much scepticism and gossip, attracting accusations ranging from betrayal of confidences and sexual immorality to financial greed and corruption of every kind. In the village these accusations contrast with the reverence in which the liturgical offices and particularly the eucharist is held, and this tension is behind the defence of a notoriously unpopular priest in the area in words which insist on the respect due not to the person but to the office: 'We know what he is, but…he is a priest.' And the reverse side of this relationship has already been quoted in the story of the shepherd boy who saw that all the congregation had a saddle of sins on their backs while the priest had two. The priest is a sinner like everyone else but, precisely because he is a priest and consecrates the holy mysteries while still being a sinner, he is a greater sinner than anyone else. It is this that gives rise to the otherwise surprising saying that 'the priest is a demon' (*ὁ παπᾶς εἶναι δαίμονας*).

they so deplore. The villagers' inevitably partial living of the precepts of the Gospels, their inevitable proneness to gossip and quarrels, the necessary inflation of an egoistic and combative stance in men and of competitiveness and tendency to gossip in women, means that the villagers come to the monastery with a particular awareness of these burdens and a longing to be released from them. In the monastic life they see the enactment of all the virtues which the sin of the world prevents them from emulating in their own lives. And it is because of this that throughout the Orthodox world the monastery acts as a living presence in the locality, actively drawing people to it.

It is in this way, then, that the initial separation of the monastic from his kin and of the monastery from the outside world is overcome, and it is typical of those elders who in the course of time become spiritual guides that they never lose touch with their roots, keeping their sense of humour and simplicity, understanding the pressures on the people who come to them, knowing about severe economic conditions, poverty, hardship and anxiety, temptations to gossip and sharp practice; taking part with them in the love for family and children, the delight in life, and the desperate grief of death. At the same time the monastic has also been through the hard school of humility, vigilance, discernment, obedience, and purity of thought, and on this path gained equilibrium and control of the passions that threaten it. Thus the great elders and saints are made, not born. They come often from very simple homes; indeed, after the transfer to Greece of the Greek populations of Asia Minor in 1922 following the Greek military disaster there, some have come from refugee families. But all by example and through experience transmit a wisdom which refuses abstractions and academic pretensions but deals in the realities of the human heart, and it is this that lies behind a typically pithy riposte delivered by a noted elder on Mount Athos: 'You say theology—I say stupidology.'[8]

These elders, or elders-in-the-making, then, become known simply through modest contact with ordinary people, being revealed secretly as it were, by word of mouth, through stories and anecdote. By such people fame is regarded as a spiritual danger, which risks de-

[8] Conversation with Elder Paisios, personal communication from Fr Alexander Williams.

flecting them from their goal, and one of the many stories told of Father Iakovos relates how, singing one day a part of the office with extraordinary beauty, he was noticed to stop suddenly and ask the cantor to take over. To enquiries later as to why he should have stopped when he was singing so beautifully, he replied: 'The devil put it into my mind that I was singing well.' Vigilance over the ego is a capacity stressed by ascetic texts, and this is one instance of it. Again, when Father Iakovos, by this time the abbot of his monastery, was pressed to build a residence for himself more suitable to his estate than his tiny cell, his reply was of the same order: 'Listen. I never wanted an abbacy, or fame, or buildings, or honour. I wanted paradise! St David, who lived in caves in the wilderness, and lacked all those things, what did he do? With simplicity and humility he attained paradise. Did you ever read in the life of any saint that he built such and such an abbot's residence [for himself], such and such a building, and got to paradise? Rather, they made sacrifices, they prayed and fasted, they kept their eyes on the ground, and things like that. They were virtuous, with these things they gained paradise. I want at least a corner in paradise, right on the very edge...'.[9]

In this manner, the ascetic way which the elders embrace is initially the way of sacrifice—whether of passions, or pride, or possessions, or comfort, or personal ambitions, or house, or self, or kin. The tendency according to which material and emotional wealth is kept largely within the household and the close kin group must be broken, so that the treasures of the family can move outwards to the community. Thus the greatest good of social life, marriage and children, is sacrificed for celibacy and childlessness; the locus of identity in the social world—kin—is sacrificed for service of the community; the normal pleasures of food, sex, sleep, are exchanged for fasting, celibacy, vigils. In the context of social life, such abandonment of customary norms is seen as a form of self-indulgence which results in people who are deviants or drop-outs, people who have wilfully abandoned their honour, forfeited their future, and are 'out of the common life'. In the context of the ascetic way, however, the entire picture is transformed, for these things are sacrificed for

[9] Papadopoulos, *Ὁ μακαριστὸς Ἰάκωβος Τσαλίκης*, p. 135; for the incident with his sister's children see pp. 97–9.

a greater good in which the reversing of the social norms is again reversed. In the place of biological offspring are given numbers of spiritual children; in place of the love and support of kin is given the affection and respect of the people of the area, even of the Orthodox community at large; in place of the normal pleasures of life is given the hunger for paradise. For the true monastic, although the denial of self which is involved in the ascetic life is so hard that it is known in the tradition as 'spiritual warfare', the end result is the realization of the true self, united with God and freed from the tyranny of the ego, and to live in this region of oneself is to live in paradise.

So it is that an Orthodox monastery with its celibacy and asceticism has a precise relationship to the village life of marriage and children which surround it, in many ways opposite and in many ways similar.[10] This local relationship between monastery and village, however, is not contemporary only, but has roots which go back deep both in time and place.

Stretching back in time, the known saints of the Church are the spiritual ancestors of those who are living now. The kind of sanctity which is outlined here is a continuing phenomenon down the ages, and indeed the very use of the term Father implies a line of descent from elder generations to younger ones by which sacred wisdom is transmitted. This line of descent, however, reaches further than that described above where people seek guidance from the great elders of their time, and once again Father Iakovos provides an illustration. The young monk, who carried the relics of St David to the villages and looked after St David's monastery with scrupulous devotion, is a graphic picture of the relationship between the saint himself and the saint-in-the-making. It was for the sake of St David that the young monk Iakovos took up the monastic life in the dilapidated and war-torn monastery, and it was the saint himself who, as Father Iakovos related, greeted the young man when he first arrived at the monastery, letting him in through the great door when no one else was there. It was knowledge of St David, praying every night in his cave in the mountains, which inspired Father Iakovos to go to the same cave by night and carry out the same ascetic discipline, sur-

[10] Iossifidhes, 'Sisters in Christ' and 'Earthly Lives and Life Everlasting'.

viving with very little sleep and returning in the early hours to a day of continuous work. Between Father Iakovos and St David there was a close relationship, the saint becoming an accustomed and familiar presence to Father Iakovos, Father Iakovos in his turn addressing him as 'my saint', 'my holy one', serving him and his church, caring for his reputation, his relics, his property. Father Iakovos would beseech the saint to hurry and befriend someone in need, and also on occasion take him to task, for instance for not paying enough attention to his land, allowing an unknown wood-cutter to cut down some olive trees and leaving the young monk to run hither and yonder trying to keep things right.[11] This paradigmatic example of the relation of elders with saints teaches others in their turn what their relationship with the saints should be, a relationship with someone who is alive in Christ, not dead, fully present and always at hand to help. This is the spirit in which the memory of the saint is kept and his relics guarded, and thus there is a direct line of descent from the saint to any maturing spiritual father, and from him to the villagers who in their turn, tellingly, know the saint as 'Grandfather' (*Παπποῦ*), so that the terms 'the saint', 'the relics' or 'the holy relics', 'the holy Elder', as well as the term 'Grandfather', are used freely and interchangeably. 'Have you been to Grandfather?' is a familiar way in which someone may be greeted on return from a visit to the monastery to venerate the relics.

This spiritual ancestry through time is also linked with the history of place. St David, though coming originally from Roumeli on the mainland, is thought of in northern Evia as a local saint since it was there that, as people say, 'he became an ascetic and a saint'. Stories have proliferated around St David which bind him to the place and make him live in the minds of those who come after, prominent among which are the archetypal tales of his finding water by tapping on a rock with his staff. The saint is indeed welded to the landscape, a fact which finds concrete illustration in the story which relates that when the saint died his blanket was spread out over a rock, and this has now fused with the rock and may still be seen.

Perhaps because of St David's association with water, his relics

[11] For St David opening the door, *Ἕνας ἅγιος Γέροντας*, pp. 33–5, Papadopoulos, *Ὁ μακαριστὸς Ἰάκωβος Τσαλίκις*, p. 61; for the cutting of the olive trees, *Ἕνας ἅγιος Γέροντας* , p. 73.

have a particular reputation for bringing rain, and local stories relate how after a prolonged drought they were requested, and hardly had the service finished when big thunderclouds bubbled up and there was a downpour. The miracles related, however, are not limited to rain. The relics were brought one year to a village when a plague of locusts was devouring everything, and the next day all the locusts died; another time a disease which was killing the mules and goats never struck again after the relics had been sent for. And while the relics are often requested in times of drought or other need, they are also by some villages requested two or three times a year simply 'for the sake of the people' or 'to bring good fortune'.

These occasions on which the relics are brought to a village are times which reveal that the relationship of the devoted elder with the saint is indeed echoed by the people, for it is clear that to them also he is the object of an unusual affection. The relics, sometimes brought by a monk from the monastery, may also be collected by a small group of trusted people who go for them on foot over the mountains, singing simple liturgical chants as they go. On arrival back at the village the relics are taken straight to the church, and the people, alerted by the bell ringing for vespers, begin to gather, bringing gifts 'for the saint'—money, wheat which people pour into the waiting sacks or present in woven goat-hair bags, bottles of oil, home spun blue and white napkins—after which they venerate the relics by kissing them and doing three prostrations. After vespers and the singing of the *Paráklisis* (*Παράκλησις*)—a service of prayer to the saint—a large number of the women will settle down on rugs to spend the night in the church, for just as a body before burial must always be kept company, and as the body of Christ between the laying-out and the burial service is never left alone, so the same custom is invoked at the all-night vigil guarding the relics of the saint.

The following day early in the morning almost the entire village will be at the liturgy, after which holy water is blessed and distributed, the relics venerated again, and at the end the church bell will be rung to signify that the saint is leaving. The sacks of corn, their mouths now tied with string, together with the woven bags and all the other gifts, are loaded onto mules, while the relics themselves in their casket are carried in a villager's arms. Then, with a great crowd watching the departure, the little cavalcade sets off, accompanied by many people who go with it some way down the path, detaching themselves one by one, holding the casket with the relics for a moment, kissing it, and then standing there, crossing themselves and making prostrations as they watch the saint out of sight. There is in this scene a powerful sense of a much loved and honoured visitor taking his departure, and a real feeling of loss as the little procession vanishes between a fold in the hills.

The saint of the local monastery thus brings into being both a spiritual family in which the people of the area are included, and a landscape touched by his blessing and sanctity; but no place belongs to one saint alone, and imaginative sympathies with saints of other places, through family history or naming patterns, or through dreams or other significant experiences, lead to dedications of wayside shrines or small churches in remote places to various saints which then acquire their own local history, so that every area is populated with several such local presences. Collectively the whole village keeps the festival of the saint to whom the village church is dedicated. At the same time any area of mountainside will be dotted with tiny churches perched on the peaks or hidden in forest and valley, and anyone working or walking in that area will relate particularly to the patron saint of that place. Thus gratitude from someone cured by a local healer can find a natural expression—'Who sent you? Did St John send you?'—an encounter related with the explanation: 'They have St John resident there, as we have the Mother of God.' In this way the residents of a village include not only its customary population but also the saints and divine presences who are commemorated there, and who live in the same place, keep guard over the same mountains, care for the same fields and pastures as the villagers do. Thus an obvious recourse in extremity is the saint of the place, so that a person fighting a fire on a hill-top near the church of the Prophet Elias, for instance, instinctively calls on the prophet to help because it is his place and he is present in it. The dedication of a church celebrates not a memory but a living person who becomes one of the inhabitants of the place, and can be listed in much the same way: 'We have here St Dimitri, St Paraskevi, the Prophet Elias, the Mother of God . . .'. The attribution of sacred presences to a place is no mere abstraction, it is a living relationship between that sacred person and that particular patch of earth, and it is because of this it is said: 'The *Panaghía* goes first, but one honours the saint of the place' (*Η Παναγία πάει μπροστά, ἀλλ' ἐκτιμᾶς τὸν ντόπιο τὸν ἅγιον*).

The key to the value placed on locality lies in the emphasis within Orthodoxy on the continuing penetration into the material world of the energies of God, without which the entire universe would collapse in on itself and cease to be. God did not merely create the world, he actively sustains it and makes it new from moment to moment. Thus the spiritual task of fallen man in a fallen world is seen by the Orthodox Church not in terms of a struggle of spirit over matter but in terms of the redemption of matter by the spirit, and in this process it is the destiny of the entire material world, and not of man alone, to become transfigured. This divine potential inherent in the natural world only at times becomes fully manifest, and then only through the saint who, purified by the ascetic struggle, is able fully to restore the defaced image of God within man, and thus to reintegrate the fallen creation with its divine archetype. It is only the God-bearer who can see the world as God-bearing.[12]

This redemption of matter by the spirit also lies behind the icon, for the existence of the icon in Orthodox worship and liturgy is based on the theology of the Incarnation and on the understanding that God has been manifested in time and space and clothed in the fabric of the incarnate world. Put shortly, an icon can be painted because God has manifested himself in Christ, and Christ is manifested in his saints; and what the icon paints is the light and form of the spirit of God revealed in the flesh.[13] The icon therefore is a painting which represents a sacred person according to universal qualities of transformed and enlightened humanity, as well as according to lineaments traditionally attributed to the particular person in the sacred memory of the Church and passed down in the canons of iconography. Thus the icon is more than a pictorial likeness of someone who is absent or has died; it is more too than a conventional sign of qualities of holiness. It 'mysteriously mirrors and enshrines'[14] the person portrayed, though it is less than the person; in the Platonic language of the Fathers of the East-

[12] For the theological and moral basis of this way of viewing the natural world see Ware, *The Orthodox Way*, pp. 21–3 and 117–21.

[13] See Ware, *The Orthodox Church*, pp. 30–5.

[14] Philip Sherrard, *The Sacred in Life and Art* (Ipswich: Golgonooza Press, 1990) p. 74.

ern Church, it partakes in the nature of a spiritual archetype, although it is not the archetype itself. It is because of this that icons, like relics, are venerated with the sign of the cross and a kiss rather than merely being viewed with respect, and because of this that certain icons are credited with miraculous powers. But the reason for this power of the icon does not lie in the skill of the painter, nor yet in the faithfulness with which the traditional forms are represented, although both of these are vital. The reason is antecedent to these things and lies in the fact that in Christ and in his saints, the living and eternal forms of the Spirit have been realized in the local particulars of the flesh.

This theology is well understood by the villagers, though they understand it not in terms of texts and their interpretation, but through a structure of attitudes handed on by older generations in axioms and precepts and stories, and in the customs and beliefs which everyone learns from childhood up. The way the people understand icons is apparent simply from the way they behave towards them, crossing themselves, kissing them, and being shocked at any irreverence towards them, though they know well the difference between veneration (treating an object as partaking in the qualities of the holy person it represents) and idolatry (treating an object as divine in itself), the latter being a notion they indignantly reject. Thus what is particular, limited, and material, can partake in what is eternal, unlimited, and spiritual, and it is because of this that the places where saints have walked, the monasteries they founded, the relics they left, are all instinct with the power of their presence, and because of this that certain icons can become known as 'wonder-working', and churches and wayside shrines become places of veneration.

One consequence of this understanding is the idea already mentioned, that the saints of a place, or perhaps a special icon in a place, have a particular potency and a particular ability to guard its inhabitants, for they bring the sacred into the same natural order as the inhabitants and share with them the same physical world. To perceive in this way the sacred in the social world, however, is to render the sacred liable to the ills of the social world and, society being what it is, arguments can break out over the relative virtues of the icons of various villages, and a man can find a way of defaming his antagonist by blaspheming, for instance, 'his' Mother of God. This does not, however, indicate fragmentation of the divine world so much as fragmentation in people's perceptions of each other's beliefs. To live under the protection of the divine powers a person has to be in relation to them; thus any protagonist of a dispute finds it easy to assume that his opponent has, unlike himself, broken this communion with the source. The opponent is therefore in error and the Mother of God that he venerates, the Christ that he worships, is a false Mother of God, a false Christ. The division, for the speaker, lies not in the sacred world, but in the material world where there are false images as well as true icons, and where the false images are, naturally, those of one's enemy. Personal passion does not obscure the fact that, as the villagers often say, 'God is one'; rather it extends the field of battle from that concerning the antagonists' social reputation to that concerning their spiritual integrity and their individual relationship with the sacred presences.

If the saints lend themselves to be seen in their local aspect, and if villagers can occasionally lapse into a potentially fragmented view of things because of local allegiances, this nevertheless is continually corrected by that other aspect of the saints which is their universal nature as saints of the whole Church. This is articulated in the liturgical year already discussed, in which are set the great cycles of Christ and the Mother of God and in which each of the saints finds his or her time. And as we have seen, the sacred resonances of this liturgical cycle penetrate the agricultural year, so that this year is punctuated by the rhythms not only of seed-time and harvest but also of periods allotted to work and rest, fast and feast, and in this way the holy persons inform the daily labour which all villagers carry out season by season. The local and particular is thus held always in balance with the universal, a balance which is expressed continually in the litanies of the Orthodox Church as they pray 'for this countryside' (or in a city 'for this city'), 'and for every city and countryside'.[15]

The communal relationship of a village with its local saints is thus one way in which villagers perceive themselves to be part of a God-bearing world; but there exist also individual relationships with saints which illuminate further some of the consolations and perplexities of the villager's relationship with God. What kind of relationship man has with God, how to co-operate with God and receive

[15] *Divine Liturgy*, Great Litany, p. 26.

his blessing, how to understand one's own failings and responsibilities in the relationship, and how to cope with what at times appears to be God's rejection of the relationship, are all questions which village responses and axioms implicitly and incidentally address; but such questions can be illuminated with special clarity by relationships with saints, because saints are familiar and close at hand, and can be spoken to with frankness.

The initiation of the relationship is made easy by the fact that saints, as has been said, are typically thought to 'help people', and indeed the fact of incorruption where it occurs is seen by some as evidence that the saint has prayed that he should remain with his body for the sake of the people, as in the case of St Spyridon who is said to wear out three pairs of shoes a year walking about doing good. Thus the love, trust, and veneration shown to the saint, and the gifts given to his monastery, are the villagers' answer to the love which the saint has already shown to them by his presence amongst them and by the asceticism which brought him to sanctity in the first place; and it is this mutual giving and receiving which is the hallmark of the popular understanding of the proper relationship with the saints. The person who expects to live under the protection of the saints must 'honour them'. He must venerate the icons, lighting candles before them, and should ideally accompany requests with prostrations and pray 'with fervour'. Of such a person the saint will say 'Here's someone who honours me', and such a person may legitimately appeal to the saint for assistance in time of need—'If you keep the faith, and fast, and observe the saints' days, then when you are in trouble you can call out "Help me!"' It is of course not expected that this help will automatically be forthcoming in the terms requested; but it is fair to say it is believed that gratitude and affection given is answered at least by a listening ear.

This sequence of love being returned for love, of honour being returned for the readiness to help is, however, not direct reciprocity, for inbuilt into the villagers' relationship with the sacred world is the essential asymmetry pointed out at the beginning of this book. God is the Almighty, the Maker of All, on whose will all depends. The phrases 'If God wills', 'Whatever God wills', 'This is how God has ordained us', are phrases so often repeated as to make it clear that the villagers perceive the superiority of the sacred world to be beyond a doubt, its reality of an order quite different from other realities, and one before which all other realities must bow. Thus in times when there is a perceived lack of miracles, this lack is not seen—as it is by the secular mentality—as indicating that such miracles were always only a figment of the imagination; it is universally taken as evidence of man's lack of faith. If the miracles worked by the saint have ceased it is because people have become wicked, and this argument is clinched with the explanation: 'Look, since he doesn't work any miracles now, it follows that people are wicked.'

The relationship, then, between men and the saints is not one between equals: if something goes wrong in the relationship it can not, in the nature of things, be the fault of the saints. Men sin, the saints do not; men depend on the saints but the saints do not depend on men. That element of reciprocity which does exist, though, is vital, for the saints, like Christ himself who 'goes with glory', cannot operate by force. They are at hand to help, but, unlike the devil and his emissaries who work their way under a 'layer' or 'leaf' of the human heart by stealth, they have to be invited in. The element of readiness in the human heart is therefore the vital implication of the 'honour' which is said to be due to the saints, for without it they are powerless to help. With it, however, 'they conquer'.

Out of the great numbers of saints in the calendar, there are some who are particularly important to a particular household. People, as has been said, bear the name of a saint and celebrate their saint's day rather than their own birthday as their personal feast, and women—who are often known by a feminine variant of their husband's Christian name, Christina from Christos, Ioannina from Ioannis—are implicitly involved in the celebration of their husband's saint's day and with him fall under the protection of the saint whose name he bears.

However, there is a further way of honouring the saints which is specific to individual intent, and this lies in the vow. The word 'vow', *táma* (τάμα), together with its verb *tázo* (τάζω), denotes the making of a promise to a saint, and is only used in this sense; for any other kind of promise another word is used, *yposchethó* (ὑποσχεθῶ). *Táma* is also the word used for the votive offerings which, in the form of miniature replicas of parts of the body for which the saint's help is sought, or precious pieces of jewellery, if the donor is wealthy enough, are hung around the icons of particular shrines in prayer for a favour sought or in thanksgiving for one granted.

A vow is of two kinds, unconditional or conditional. The unconditional vow most often takes the form of an undertaking to go to a particular monastery or place of pilgrimage, and is usually the business of women who thereafter are under an obligation to make good their promise, even if it takes years. The expression 'I vowed' here seems to have the meaning simply of 'I said I would', and does not necessarily involve a formal address to the saint concerned. The vow which promises a favour in return for a favour is a different matter, for it is evoked by need and takes the form of a face-to-face conversation with the saint. This need ranges from simple anxiety to extremity of suffering, including illness, childlessness, the death of children, poverty, imprisonment, danger, worries over the marriage of daughters, and so on, and takes the form, 'Please do "x" for me, and I will give you "y".'

In these cases in which a prayer for something is accompanied by a vow to give some gift to the saint, and where the request is granted, the necessary response of the recipient is clear. It is in those cases where the request is not granted that the more subtle connotations of the vow are revealed. There are, of course, cases of real impropriety in which, once the prayer is answered and the tension released, the suppliant gives to the saint a lesser gift than the one promised—a temptation particularly strong in cases where the gift promised is substantial. But not only is this kind of response which attempts to deceive the saint thought to be improper; more interestingly, so is the one which reciprocates the saint's denial. There are some cases in which a vow literally cannot be fulfilled unless the request is first granted—such as, for instance, the vow to name a baby after a saint if the baby lives, or to go on a pilgrimage if health is restored. However, even those cases in which the prayer is not granted, provided that the return gift is not linked with the thing asked for (such as the naming of a longed-for child after the saint concerned), this return gift should still be given: 'A vow is a vow and you must carry it out even if you don't get what you want.'

This apparently unequal conclusion can be rationalized in the notion that 'the saint can be testing you, for that matter', and would give some other gift if he didn't give the one requested. But whatever the logic behind this sense of obligation, if the suppliant's vow can be carried out, it should be carried out. The suppliant's gift should be forthcoming even if the saint's is not, and this behaviour is spoken of as the norm. Thus the original reciprocity built into the request, 'If... then...', is in the event translated into, 'Do this for me, but anyway I will give you "x".' It is an understanding of a vow as essentially non-retractable, whether it is phrased as conditional or not.

What emerges from this is an understanding of the vow which sets it qualitatively apart from the secular contract. A secular contract involves a negotiation in which default by one party can justly be countered with default by the other. The relationship with the saint which is set up by the vow is quite different, for though it involves the offering of a gift simultaneously with the request for assistance, the fulfilment of one is not, ideally, conditional upon the fulfilment of the other. The fact that the negotiation is with a saint rather than with another villager converts an apparently conditional offering into a 'vow' in which although the saint is free to default, the suppliant is not. 'If you vow something,' people say, 'you have to give it.' Any element of calculation is unfitting to the relations between the believer and the heavenly world, and loyalty to the vow and faith in the saint should take the place of an insistence on the strict reciprocity of a commercial bargain.

The effect of this understanding of the vow is profound, for at one stroke it releases the saint from obligation and the suppliant from calculation, and allows the gift of either to be given in freedom. To treat the vow as an occasion of barter rather than as a mutual exchange of unconditional gifts is to violate the ideal love and trust which should flow from the suppliant to the saint, and to interpose between them the calculating and corrupted relations of the world of men. And though the temptation to fall into this secular mode is clearly at times irresistible, and people can and do answer a saint's refusal to give with a similar refusal of their own, such bargaining is seen to be in defiance of the true nature of things. The vow sets up, in fact, a relationship which is in essence innocent, free from guile, and it is perhaps this element predominantly which is reflected in the saying: '[As] a child [waits for] a bread ring, a saint [waits for] a candle.' The vow, like the simple gift, is ideally not so much a conditional demand for patronage as a way of keeping the relationship open, thus permitting the saint's power to operate when the time is ripe. The saint is not constrained by the gift, but the believer must be bound by his own promise to give, and must keep faith, and patiently await that 'good thing' which will in due course be his. The vow, then, illustrates once again that relationships between the human and divine worlds are asymmetrical—the standard is set by the saint or the holy person, not the suppliant. It is a principle by now becoming familiar, and one which also informs the complex attributions of spiritual causation which can lie behind the simplest events in the social world.

If the suppliant is responsible for keeping the relationship with the heavenly powers in their pure form, this provides a partial answer to the attribution of responsibility for misfortune in cases where this misfortune can be linked to any ritual failure. It has already been said that ritual observances and abstinences fall particularly on women who, as keepers of the house, are also the guardians of the mysteries that preserve the house, and the rhymes quoted earlier which encapsulate this aspect of the women's role testify to the seriousness of the woman's ritual responsibility for those within her care. The blame attaching to the wife whose husband cut his hand on an axe after she had been weaving all through a saint's day has already been mentioned, and the admonitory moral drawn at the end of one description of this event makes the point neatly: 'Fridays protect your husband and Wednesdays your children.' Even so, it is not only women who can fall foul of the sacred law, for the same understanding of causation can provoke the judgement on a man newly returned home who insisted on sleeping with his wife on the eve of the Annunciation: 'The wild beast! And the next day her goat strangled itself [on its tether]!'

It would be easy to give the impression that the villagers in their focus on spiritual realities pay little attention to rational sequences of cause and effect, but no people who live from and with the land could possibly be anything other than close observers of natural processes and extremely practical in their response to them. A discussion about direct spiritual causation behind, for instance, a woman falling off her mule, or a boy killing himself in an accident on his motorbike, can both prompt the robust comment that in both cases the people concerned had not taken enough care. Yet in a world governed not only by natural causation but also, and antecedently, by the play of the forces of good and evil, the attribution of a metaphysical cause to a material event is also a natural response, and which of the two is cited as a primary cause of any event is a matter of the context and the individual perspective at the time. Thus it is inevitable that a catastrophic event like the death of a small boy, shot by accident during a game with his brother on the feast of the Three Hierarchs, should be universally attributed to a notable ritual lapse on the part of the mother, who had been knitting the whole day.

This event, however, highlights a further aspect of spiritual causation, because even here, where the cause and effect is held to be conclusively linked, the memory of the event does not portray the Hierarchs as child slayers: rather it simply sees their day as highly ritually charged and one that necessitates caution. It is not the Hierarchs but the ritual lapse which is thought to precipitate the evil. Thus it is not that the saints call down retribution for trivial sins; it is more that any lapse of attention on the human level can upset the balance between the sacred and social worlds and set in motion a sequence of cause and effect which the saints are powerless to frustrate. Though the saints protect the people they cannot do it all, and it is the voice of experience that adds a cautionary note about the power of the saints to keep people safe: 'They protect one, but…'. Ritual infringements by no means always result in harm, but such infringements are capable of putting a person outside the sphere of divine protection, making them or their family vulnerable to evil.

The question then arises as to why some actions incur such terrible consequences and other actions, perhaps much more grave, do not, and the answer appears to lie in the idea of the peculiar receptivity of certain times which was referred to earlier. The word 'hour' which is used here can, as in the concept of the 'evil hour', or in the farewell greeting, 'A fortunate hour!' (*ὥρα καλή*), be interpreted as 'time' or 'moment'. Thus the critical phrase, often used, invokes the idea of evil striking 'if the time is ripe' (literally, 'if the hour finds it' (*ἄν ἀνταίνει ὥρα*)), or, more rarely, 'if the hour takes effect' (*ἄν πιάνει ὥρα*). Explained as indicating a sudden fortuitous conjunction of circumstances, the verb translated as 'finds it' is described by the villagers as being related to the word 'meet'(*ἀνταμώνω*), and is paraphrased as 'if it happens' (*ἄν τυχαίνει*)—a word involving both chance and fate. This meeting of spiritual possibilities which can suddenly let an effect through seems to imply that ritual danger is in fact crucially determined by the time and only secondarily by the person or the act, and that it is because of this that not every similar act calls down a similar response. Although the prescriptions and prohibitions are so widely observed as to form a firm foundation to village life, there exists also a kind of flexibility which, where it becomes an issue, allows a negotiation between spiritual and material needs. The keynote here is necessity, and a woman who is mindful of the sacred time but who for some overriding need neglects a particular prescription, feels herself justified. And in cases in which rain, for instance, has prevented the washing being done for overlong, the entire village will be seen washing on a Wednesday or a Friday if that provides the first opportunity.

Thus all women, for good reasons or bad, neglect the ritual prescriptions from time to time, or observe them only in a partial manner, and even in cases where neglect is followed by misfortune the other villagers are not inclined to blame unduly the person concerned. They comment on the connection however, and, in dramatic instances, take greater care themselves. Nevertheless, whether or not they see responsibility as lying in the human realm, they do not see the saints as being guilty in any way. The saints are in fact the only participants in this kind of event entirely free of implication in its evil, for the active agents are the powers of evil themselves which take their moment and irrupt briefly and devastatingly into human life, and any residual responsibility lies at the door of the woman who, although she cannot avert evil if it is to come, nevertheless needs to do what she can to keep those in her care under the protection of the powers of heaven.

Within this overall attribution of responsibility there are, however, a few exceptions. A more threatening figure, for example, is St Paraskevi. Paraskevi—meaning 'preparation' and therefore 'Friday' because of the Jewish day of preparation on the Friday before the Sabbath on Saturday—in the Christian era became a name given to girls because of Holy Friday, the day of the crucifixion. The saint of that name has her feast day on 26 July, but in village thinking she is naturally associated also with the Friday fast which acknowledges the crucifixion. Seen always as an old woman dressed in black, sometimes with two teeth 'one above and one below', she appears in dreams and strikes fear into the hearts of the disobedient. Thus housewives who, for whatever reason, have kept on working on a Friday evening, or may have forgotten to light the icon lamp, tend to have dreams of waking up with a suffocating sensation, or of having had some visitation by a black-clothed woman whose very presence is a reproof. Around this saint in particular, various tales congregate which center on the retribution falling on those who neglect the Friday prohibitions on handwork. In one tale a woman had been spinning continually during the evening, making the saint's bread uneatable with the dropped bits of fluff. Eventually the saint, pulling yet another clump of wool out of her bread, is said to have lost patience and, leaning forward, to have picked up a poker and jabbed it into the fire, saying, 'Take that!', whereupon the spinner was seized with violent pains in the stomach and abandoned her work forthwith. In another, St Paraskevi loses patience with a woman doing the same thing, and takes her child. Searching in the forest for her child the woman eventually finds her safe with the saint, who says she can have it back, but first offers her food. However, as she eats she keeps having to pull out clumps of wool, and hairs, and bits of rag rugs. The subsequent exchange concludes with the saint saying, 'Why do you keep washing and weaving and spinning on my day so that my bread is full of bits and I can't eat?', and receiving the woman's promise to abstain from work on that day thereafter. These stories do reveal the saint in a punitive light. But even here no permanent harm results and it is the woman's behaviour, not the saint's, which is found wanting.

Customary wisdom on the freedom of the saints from blame is, then, unequivocal; but even so the people's acceptance of the unaltering beneficence of the holy world is not without its fault lines. One such fault line is shown up when moments of extreme passion sweep a person into open rebellion and when grief or despair, on this occasion at the death of a young son, prompts an outcry of the sort, 'I spit on you, God, look what you've done to us!' But the norm in such cases is immediately re-established by the admonitions of bystanders, and by the judgement that such behaviour is appropriate only for 'those who are stupid'—that is to say, those who do not understand the way things are. There is, however, a much more prevalent fault line, and this lies in the way in which blasphemy figures so notably in male vocabulary. At the least thing, whether tripping over a stone or racing after a bolting mule or trying to shut a henhouse door, the male reaction is to blaspheme the cross, the faith, the Mother of God, Christ, in a series of colourful expletives, predominantly sexual. So customary a part of everyday use are these expressions, however, that they almost entirely lose the connotations which, even today, any literal translation into English would carry. Indeed, they can on occasions be uttered simply as an expression of wry admiration and amazement, and with the utmost good humour. So it comes about that while this form of expression is not considered 'good', and while women—tempted as they are to come out with a wide range of eloquent curses—do not have recourse to this kind of blasphemy, and while men may be criticized for the way in which they take the name of God in vain, nevertheless such language does not appear to rest on any challenge to the basis of their faith. Constant reiteration of the divine names in this context is an instance in which people take their ill humour out on the things they love; it is evidence not so much of an overthrowing of God as of the ubiquity of the things of the faith and the familiarity of the people with them. Male oaths are not somehow taken seriously, either by those who speak or those who hear; and if they are, they are repudiated: 'How are the Mother of God and Christ to blame?'

Once again, therefore, in the cool light of day and with the clarity of true understanding, the heavenly world is guiltless for the ills that humanity heaps on itself. The heavenly world is beneficent, evil comes only from the devil and through those human beings who listen to him. The only logical stance is always, no matter what the circumstances, to give honour to Christ and to his Mother, and to those who in their lives became bearers of God to the world. All the ritual customs and avoidances to do with holy days, together with the perceived consequences of their neglect, are to do with maintaining this understanding. It is a view of the world in which, although evil exists, love calls to love, the love of these divine persons for men and women calling for a response from them which, once evoked, allows a circulation of those divine energies with whose aid alone the community is able to live.

The distinction between the saints as God-bearers (*Theophóroi*) and the Mother of God as God-bearer (*Theotókos*) has been mentioned already, in that while the saints through a process of ascetic endeavour become filled with God, the Mother of God actually gave birth to God in the flesh. It is with her, therefore, that this chapter on the God-bearers must end, showing those ways in which she comes first in the household of 'our holy and God-bearing fathers',[16] for her importance can hardly be over-emphasized. Addressed in the liturgical context as Mother of God, All-holy and Ever-Virgin Mary, and referred to by the people as the *Panaghía*, the All-holy, she is a person always at hand, a constant point of reference to whom they turn in need, for help, comfort, and guidance. 'Second' to Christ and 'first among the saints', the *Panaghía* 'goes in front' of all the other saints and is the one to whom the people chiefly turn. 'Just as one calls out "Mother" in time of trouble,' they say, 'so one calls to the *Panaghía*'; 'We have the *Panaghía* as our mother', 'The *Panaghía* feels pain for us', '[Just as] a mother agonizes for her children, [so] the *Panaghía* is a mother to us'. She is a living and compassionate presence watching over the people and saving them from harm. For villagers this pre-eminence of the Mother of God among the saints turns especially on her importance as an exemplar for men and women in the family.

There is a sense in which the Mother of God is the archetype for all humanity, for men as well as women, for all are called to become God-bearers after her, and to men as well as women her icon speaks, gesturing towards her son and showing them that their way, which is also hers, is to give birth in their hearts to Christ. But in addition to this universal aspect of the Mother of God there is a particular sense in which she is the feminine archetype for women, and from this archetype are derived those ideas of motherhood, chastity, honour, diligence, obedience, compassion, and fidelity which lie at the basis of the woman's ideal role as married wife and mother of children, and which therefore are at the basis also of the possibility for man's ideal role as the loyal protector and support of his family as well.

The customary perceptions of men and women are, as has been mentioned already, based on the idea of the fall, and this symbolism recurs throughout village conversation in a series of typical epigrams. Men carry 'responsibility' but women are 'the weak link'; 'men are intelligent but women are gossips'; men are on woman's 'right hand side' but women on the left are 'from the devil', men's work in the fields 'has a blessing', women's work 'is cursed'. Man, in a word, is 'Adam', woman is 'Eve'. However, along with this consis-

[16] See p. 303 above and n. 1 there.

tent range of definitions there is a parallel set which gives a different picture—'A man is a guest in the house', it is said, and, 'What has a man to do in the house?', and these phrases are thrown into relief by contrasting expressions affirming that 'It is the woman who holds the house together', and 'Without the woman the house cannot exist'. When it is remembered how the house and family stand at the heart of village life, and how not only the material but also the sacred life of the villagers is centered within its walls, it becomes clear that between the woman as Eve and the woman as housewife there has been a radical change. The way in which women redeem themselves from their disruptive potential has been described previously as lying in the self-discipline with which they are required to order their time and their work. But the inspiration behind this has not yet been touched on, and this lies in a greater pattern. The way in which women cast off their associations with Eve, and become instead the wives and mothers who hold together village life down the generations, is founded on the parallels between the married woman and the Mother of God.

That the motherhood of the *Panaghía* resonates with the villagers' own experience of motherhood has been amply illustrated, but there is more to it than this, for there is both in the liturgical texts and in popular wisdom a value put on feminine nature which lifts its capacities from the level of human nurture to that of divine destiny, and draws an explicit opposition between the Mother of God and Eve. Liturgical examples of this are many: 'Of old [the serpent] deceived the woman in Paradise, but now he sees a woman become the Mother of the Creator'.[17] 'The sinful vessel that brought death upon all flesh has through the Theotókos become the first fruits of salvation for the whole world'.[18] 'O Theotókos Virgin who hast borne the Saviour, thou hast overthrown the ancient curse of Eve',[19] and these ideas are exactly reflected in the folk tradition in the sayings, 'From one woman all evil comes, and from one woman all good comes', and 'From woman sin was born and from woman salvation was born'. Thus just as the action of Eve involved the downfall of women as a whole, so the action of the Mother of God reverberates through the whole of feminine nature:

[17] *Festal Menaion*, Matins of the Nativity of Christ, p. 265.
[18] Ibid. p. 265. [19] Ibid. p. 285.

while it is said in the village that, 'Women became sinners through Eve', they also 'became honourable through the Mother of God'.

There is, then, a close symbolic relationship between the ideal wife and mother and the figure of the Mother of God. The virginity that is a prerequisite for an honourable marriage is analogous to the virginity of the Mother of God; the prototypical relation of a woman with her husband is seen perfected in the obedience of the Mother of God; the care and protection that a mother lavishes on her children and husband, and the constant ritual acts by which she preserves the integrity of the house, echo the role of the Mother of God as the bearer of Christ and the vessel of the Holy Spirit; in giving birth, a woman reflects the divinely appointed mission of the Birth-Giver of God; and in bearing the task of mourning with all the particular weight of grief which is the lot of women in this society, she reflects the figure of the Mother of God who saw her son on the cross and who grieved over his body on the bier. It is marriage which, bringing a girl from innocence into her full sexuality, and introducing her to the range of temptations which are inseparable from a mature social life, renders her accessible to the archetype of Eve. But it is marriage also which brings her into the realm of the *Panaghía*, giving her the context in which to develop the qualities mentioned above by which she 'sets everything in order' and becomes a true wife and mother. For above all, the *Panaghía* is mother in a family. And there is an interesting correlation here which goes further than the fidelity demanded of a wife to a husband, for the critical relationship in the Greek world is between mother and child, and this is archetypal, pure, and therefore in that sense a virginal relationship. Thus the virgin mother is the inspiration which lies behind the chaste wife and nurturer of her children, the Bearer of God is the inspiration behind the bearer of children who carry on the line. It is this complex symbolic association which relates the *Panaghía* to the woman so closely that the *Panaghía*, typically depicted in the folk tradition, as already noted, as carrying a distaff, does so 'because she is a housewife'. The *Panaghía* as the housewife enables the housewife to become the *Panaghía*, and it is this understanding that lies behind a woman's comment, on the death of her married sister and the consequent closing of the family home, that 'The woman is the *Panaghía* in the church. The woman is the *Panaghía*. She is the church.'

This transformation of Eve into the *Panaghía*—or correctly speaking, of woman into an icon of the *Panaghía*—is, however, a gradual process, inaugurated on marriage, blossoming with the birth of children, and finding fulfilment only with the passing of the years as grown sons bring new brides into the house and as decreasing sexuality and increasing maturity are accompanied for the mistress of the house by decreasing exploitation and increasing respect. But however slow the coming and however partial the attainment of this transformation, it is this transformation which is at the basis of the honour given to the married woman, and it is because of this too that it is accepted by all that the spiritual as well as the social destiny of every woman is to 'marry and have a family', 'marry and become a housewife'. Further, if the role of mother is formed after the archetype of the Mother of God, so is the role of mourner. For the role of mediator between the living and the dead and intercessor for the forgiveness of the dead, which is supremely the feminine role at a death, is formed in the image of the Mother of God who is the 'bridge' or 'ladder'[20] mediating between heaven and earth, who as the link between earth and heaven is 'our fervent intercessor',[21] and who herself knows the grief of a mother for a murdered son.

It has already been indicated that the position of men in the redemptive scheme of marriage is somewhat different from that of women, even though marriage for them too is vital if they are to 'make progress' in life. And while it might be thought that the same relationship between woman and the *Panaghía* would be repeated between Christ and man, in fact the villagers, who know that 'Christ is God', never directly draw this conclusion. Nevertheless, there are a number of connections here which, implicit rather than explicit, are suggestive of this relationship. Firstly, a parallel between the two figures lies in the saying, already noted, that 'just as the family is eating on earth so Christ and the *Panaghía* are eating in heaven', for this saying represents the earthly family as an icon of the Holy Family, and the Holy Family is implicitly identified with the icons on either side of the Holy Doors in the centre of the iconostasis, that is the icon of Christ in his full manhood, and the icon of the Mother of God with the infant Christ in her arms. Secondly, at the beginning of the mar-

[20] *Lenten Triodion*, Akathistos Hymn, p. 424.

[21] Ibid. Saturday of the Akathistos, p. 428.

riage ceremony, when the bride and groom enter the church, they are led forward, the man to kiss the icon of Christ and the woman to kiss the icon of the *Panaghía*, thus confirming the archetypes to which each should aspire to conform.[22] Thirdly, this action at the beginning of the marriage ceremony corresponds to what is said in the wedding epistle: 'For the husband is the head of the wife, even as Christ is the head of the Church: and he is the saviour of the body. Therefore, as the Church is subject unto Christ, so let the wives be to their own husbands in everything. Husbands, love your wives, even as Christ also loved the Church, and gave himself for it. . . '.[23] This passage defines two complementary acts of sacrifice: the wife sacrifices her independence to her husband's understanding and capacity to protect her, and the husband his independence so that he can give himself to her as Christ gave himself for the Church (a reference to his sacrifice on the cross).

Although, therefore, the villagers are silent about any explicit connection of the man with Christ, it is the case that the pattern described in the epistle reading exists both in village conceptions of marriage and in those marriages which are typical of these conceptions. Wives think they should, and for the most part do, accept their husband's protection and his more rational understanding; and husbands think they should, and for the most part do, sacrifice themselves to sustain their wife and children.

In fact, in the villages, the work of the man on the land does indeed carry sacrificial overtones. These connections centre on the eucharist, for the corn which becomes Christ's body is produced by toil in the fields, and this is characteristically the work not of the woman, which is in the house, but of the man, which is on the land. In spite, therefore, of the fact that the women will help on the land in tasks such as weeding, breaking up clods with a mattock, or reaping, the understanding that men are responsible for the land has been shown as unvarying, and apart from this general responsibility, particular tasks such as ploughing, and sowing any seed which has to be scattered broadcast, have been shown as exclusively the province of the men. It is the men, then, who are responsible for the

[22] This custom is observed in some villages of the area, though it is not ubiquitous throughout Greece.

[23] Ephesians 5 : 23–5; the entire wedding epistle reading is vv. 22–33.

production of the wheat which becomes both the staff of life for the house and the body of Christ in the eucharist. In the conditions of subsistence agriculture this is a work to which men have to give themselves wholeheartedly, and it is a terrible struggle—an 'anguish', a 'torment'—to win through to the harvest.

In general, the use of these words by the villagers in this context point to physical toil and the living through of the punishment of the sin of Adam to which it is so often related; but the symbolism of marriage (the wedding epistle's injunction to the man to give himself for his wife as Christ gave himself for the Church, and the custom that the bride and groom kiss the icon of the Mother of God and Christ respectively at the beginning of the ceremony, together with the relation of these icons to the village conception of the Holy Family) also points to the way in which the tribulation of man in the fields, whose suffering is the precondition of the harvest and the offering of the liturgical bread, echoes at a lower level Christ's offering of his own body on the cross, whose suffering is the precondition of his saying of the bread, in words repeated by the priest at every consecration: 'This is my body which is given for you...'. According to this symbolism, it is in imitation of Christ's gift of his body for his people that the farmer toiling in his fields gives his body for the life of the house and for the holy mysteries in the church.

In this way, even though the man as *ándras*, a person of the male sex, is in the village explicitly connected with Adam—'*ándras*, Adhám; *ándras*, Adhám'—there is, according to the marriage symbolism just described, more to man's labour in the fields than the bearing of Adam's sin, and more than the annual fulfilment, discussed earlier, of man's labour in the fields. For if the tribulation of the man in the fields, fulfilled in the wheat harvest, is parallel to the self-offering of Christ, fulfilled in the liturgical bread, this gets to the heart of why it is the man's labour which, in spite of its being universally portrayed as the punishment for the fall, has at its heart 'a blessing'. These mediating ideas are not openly expressed, but they surface in intuitive conclusions such as the final words in a discussion about whether or not to buy bread ready-made for the eucharist: 'I don't know. I'm just a stupid toothless old woman, but *I* say that the farmer himself should produce the corn from his own land to make the liturgical bread. That is what is good.'

The liturgical order thus brings in a series of transformations which overturn the fallen world, not only moving from women's work being 'cursed' to the housewife being an icon of the *Panaghía*, but also from man's work being the punishment for sin to its 'having a blessing' in bringing forth the bread which is the body of Christ. In both it is unremitting fidelity which allows the transformation of one into the other, the fidelity of the woman to her husband, and the fidelity of the man to the land, to the house, and to the eucharist which he makes possible by his work on the land. Through the discipline of these exacting callings both man and woman are ultimately likened to their divine archetypes, and a tacit and deliberately understated association can be understood between the man in his toil and Christ, while a much more explicit association can be made between the woman in her obedience, motherhood, and self-discipline, and the *Panaghía*. Nevertheless, it is still the case that while the *Panaghía* is a woman, Christ is not only man but God. Thus while the assimilation of woman to the *Panaghía* becomes in many contexts openly expressed, the assimilation of the man to Christ remains muted, buried in a symbolism which dignifies man's suffering on the land and subsumes the entire earthly family into an iconic relation with the heavenly family, but which refrains from too close an identification between man as a gendered being and Christ, for Christ as God is not so much man (*ándras*) as human being (*ánthropos).*

It is woman, then, who in the *Panaghía* has the more explicit spiritual archetype; but to the woman as *Panaghía*, the man can stand as Christ—indeed it might be said that in this role she brings into being the man as Christ—and since the ideal marriage relationship is thought of as 'a symbiosis', it follows that what the woman does for the man the man does for the woman, either calling into being the divine archetype in the other, the woman drawing her husband into becoming like Christ, the man drawing his wife into becoming like the *Panaghía*. The true marriage is in fact one in which both husband and wife help each other to realize their divine potential, and it is this understanding which lies behind the action at the beginning of the marriage service described above where the groom venerates the icon of Christ and the bride that of the Mother of God; and it is this understanding of mutual sacrifice also that inspires the words which accompany the central action of marriage where each is crowned 'to' the other, the priest saying three times for each of them: 'The Servant of God [name] is crowned to the Servant of God [name], in the name of the Father and of the Son and of the Holy Spirit'.

It appears from this that for both sexes their identification with the Holy Family comes into being as the meaning for the man of his relationship with his family and his land, and for the woman of her relationship with her husband and children. It is an inspiration which runs deep within family life and is capable of a profound transformation of these relationships over time. But though this is the case, it is in the fallen world rather than in paradise that the people habitually dwell, and therefore it is the fallen archetypes that are emphasized: man as Adam, woman as Eve. As Adam, man is a curiously noble figure, less in need of redemption than woman, but redeeming nevertheless the consequences of his fall through his obedience to the law of the natural world, and through his care for the family and household which in their turn sustain him. As Eve, women live under the consequences of the weaker nature through which they precipitated the fall, but in spite of this they are capable, through the redemptive process set in motion by marriage, of gaining over time an explicit spiritual stature as *Panaghía,* through which they bring into being a household in which the analogy of the man with Christ can begin to be intuitively perceived.

This is a world, then, in which villagers in a harsh subsistence economy nevertheless can have a sense of kinship, relationship, and even identification with their holy figures. And this possibility comes about in several ways: communal, individual, and in the household of marriage. In the first part of this chapter, the devotion of villages to their local saints was seen to be connected with a sense of inclusion into the spiritual family of the saint. Prototypical local saints often arise in a tradition which has generated successive elders of the local monastery, who play their part in the wider community by attracting gifts from the villages and by redistributing them, together with confessional counsel, to those in need. At the same time this sense of local kinship is enhanced by a consciousness that the saint lived in (and in some cases left his mark on) the same mountains, rocks, caves, and springs as form the landmarks of the contemporary village; and even saints to whom a wayside shrine or country church has been dedicated are felt to keep watch over the place where they reside. This intensely local character of the saint is in turn related to the Orthodox sense that the energies of God uphold the particulars of this physical world; that a holy man or woman can become an icon of these invisible energies; and that this is so because of the doctrine of the incarnation, whereby the eternal and unlimited God could become revealed in the limited and local particularities of the flesh.

Villagers' individual relationships with saints reveal in turn some of the ways in which they seek to co-operate with the divine world. In this world, unconditional giving is upheld as the model for initiating relationships, and unconditional trust must be placed in what God or the saint will give on their side, even if human nature is sometimes too imperceptive or too selfish to manage this all the time. And though disaster may occur and longed-for help be withheld, any evil in these experiences comes not from the divine world, which works by love and trust and sends only good, but from the inherent dangers of this world in which circumstances can combine at certain moments to allow the demonic powers a pathway. To keep the path always open to the powers of heaven, the protection from God and the saints must, so far as is possible, be steadily sought and sustained in the ritual pattern of village life.

In the shaping of this ritual pattern in the villages, and in living out the sacred order in the flesh, marriage is central; and in marriage the figures of man and woman become involved in a union which is to do with far more than the need to live and to procreate in a difficult environment: it is one in which the sexes become linked with the fundamental archetypes of their sacred cosmology. Through the woman's relationship with the Mother of God and the man's participation in the sufferings of Christ, the fall can be overcome and a transfigured order of nature reinstated. There is more than an echo here of the pattern which inspires the ascetic endeavours of the monastics, and it casts further light on the relationship between the villages and the monasteries discussed earlier.

Between village and monastery a series of contrasts has been described in which the monastic life appears to be in many ways antithetical to life in the villages. The exclusive kin relations in the village are exchanged in the monastery for impartial love for all, sexual fulfilment in marriage and the birth of children are exchanged for celibacy

25. The bones of the saint: Above, 'The church bell will be rung… The relics themselves in their casket are carried in a villager's arms.' Below, 'Then, with a great crowd watching the departure, the little cavalcade sets off' (p. 314).

26. "The woman is the *Panaghía*": 'The *Panaghía*, typically depicted in the folk tradition…as carrying a distaff, does so "because she is a housewife". The *Panaghía* as the housewife enables the housewife to become the *Panaghía*' (p. 330). (See icon of the *Panaghía* with spindle and yarn facing p. 352.)

and childlessness, the customary pleasures of life are exchanged for a life of ascetic self-denial. These oppositions account in part for negative village attitudes to the monasteries—expressed in gossiping about the probity of many in the monastic life, and the fear of monastic vocations taking their children away from marriage. Nevertheless, in spite of these attitudes the relationship has also been described as being an attraction of opposites—the people visiting the monastery for a glimpse of a life in which competition, hostility, suspicion, and self-seeking have been laid aside, a world which belongs to Christ, the Mother of God, and the saints; the monastics opening their arms to people in need and giving them the treasures of their experience. But it has now become clear that the element of contrast highlighted earlier is less than might appear, for it is not only in the strict dedication of the monastery but also in the households of the villages that Orthodox culture seeks to attain a transfiguration of human nature. Monastics choose the path of uncompromising espousal of spiritual values in their purest form, but the institution of marriage is the bedrock by which the villagers also work towards their redemption. The role of woman in the house and the role of man in the fields is, even within the tormented world of unregenerate humanity, infused with a life as sacred in its way as the life of the monastics in the monastery. The demons are not absent from the struggle of the monastics in the monastery just as they are not absent from the struggle of ordinary people in society; in both worlds—except for those great elders who become saints—the realization of the divine potential is partial only. So in the end the apparent opposition between life in the monastery and life in the world is not one of opposition but of complementarity. Man as Adam, in the fields, bearing in his body the crushing consequences of fallen human nature for the sake of the wheat harvest, and through this being tacitly linked to a form of crucifixion and resurrection; woman as Eve, in the house, living the difficult necessities of obedience and dedication to become assimilated to the figure of the Mother of God; both parallel in their way the ascetics who through the heroic reversal of social norms and the sacrifice of ordinary human consolations are seeking a share in paradise, the entry of the divine world into the temporal. The way of marriage and the way of the ascetic share the same inspiration, and seek the same transformation of those who undertake them into God-bearers.

11
THE INCARNATE GOD

IF the familiar world of the saints and the Mother of God reveals an intimate and kindly side of the village relationship with God, there are also other sides to the relationship which engage with the bleak questions of the human predicament and do so with unflinching pessimism. This is the level of experience in which sin and disobedience bring on themselves the curse: the fall from grace, the loss of paradise, and the sentence of relentless toil for survival concluded by death—the pouring out of the life blood and burial in the 'black earth'. Yet running through this understanding of the world as fallen there has also been seen a countervailing set of perceptions to do with the world as redeemed. The fall can be remitted, paradise attained, and the consequences of disobedience set aside as a new order of forgiveness and healing takes its place, with Christ standing at the heart of these transformations, accompanied by the Mother through whom he became flesh and took into his own nature the fabric of the world.

Two levels of experience are in this way carried simultaneously in the stream of the tradition, and this allows for a variety of perceptions of the great questions about the relation between God and man. On the one hand, in a context where the world as fallen and human nature as sinful is uppermost, God is seen as stern, even tyrannical, a distant and omnipotent figure who sets the conditions in which men live, answering sin with punishment and permitting or allotting suffering without apparent reason. On the other hand, in the context of the world as redeemed, God is seen as accessible to prayers, as close to each person, and as offering the hope of undeserved mercy. These two dimensions of experience, both real enough on their own level, are different aspects of the same reality, and together they provide the key both to the villagers' endurance and stoicism in the face of long suffering, and to the joy with which they recreate their traditional patterns of living in generation after generation.

The word *Theós*, God, is the one commonly used in customary expressions already quoted, such as 'If God wills', 'God is great', 'God doesn't lose you', 'Whoever goes with God makes progress', and so on. In this usage the word seems to be often involved with the moral order, with God's relation to man and to the social world. However God in his aspect as majestic creator of the heavens and the earth, as cosmic deity, also finds expression, and here he is the *Pandodhýnamos* (*Παντοδύναμος*), the Almighty, or 'the great Almighty' as it is sometimes put, and the vast sweeps of sea and mountain, the great plenitude of 'living things' in the natural world, the moving air and the burning sun, are taken in themselves to be evidence of the working of God in his aspect of divine energy. While these two terms have different connotations however, they are not distinct, and 'God', '*Theós*', is inclusive of both these meanings and is the power behind both orders of reality mentioned above—the order of fall and repentance, and the order of salvation and paradise. In the first part of this chapter the order of nature in the fallen world is considered in detail, so that in the second part the order of salvation can be more fully understood.

Fallen nature is conceived in terms which echo the village account of man's banishment from paradise, where God is seen as coercive and authoritarian, punishing sin, making both man and woman suffer in this life—man subject to the hostility of nature, woman subject to man, both subject to death. The fallen view of death has already been described; but life must also be lived in this same fallen world, and the charter for man's predicament in living is elaborated in terms of two primary ideas, sin and fate, both involving subjection to a law of suffering. The idea of sin involves man as actor, invoking with his choices the working out of the law with consequences for good or ill. The idea of fate, together with a range of vaguer cognate perceptions, involves man as acted upon rather than acting, the object of the law, relatively powerless in the face of impersonal forces far greater than himself.

In the mode of thinking according to which man is subject rather than object, actor rather than acted upon, man has both freedom and responsibility. Here he understands himself to have free will and the power to set in train a series of consequences which then bear upon his life. God is here the author of a justice which gives man the power to act for good or ill and makes him responsible for the consequences attendant on his choice. A pattern of cause and effect is thus built into creation by the divine will, and responsibility for the pattern invoked lies with the man who invokes it, so in this way of looking at things there is the idea of merit and reward, and of sin and punishment. 'Whoever goes with God makes progress', it is said, but this carries the correlative already seen: 'Sins are paid for.'

In this way, responsibility for choices becomes a fundamental element in the social order and contrasts with the sheer stoical acceptance already discussed. And once again the blueprint for this responsibility is found in the story of Adam and Eve who, as the ancestors of the human race, stand as embodiments of the idea that if man follows the devil, or the diabolical element in his own will, he loses his sense of the divine presence and is excluded, or excludes himself, from paradise. Man is responsible for his own predicament.

According to this perspective, then, the divine law is not arbitrary but operates with strict and relentless justice. God, it is said, has a 'great belly'—that is to say a long memory, storing things up in patience, receiving sins and insults, but in due course saying, 'You did this and this', and sending the sinner off to sit in boiling pitch. 'Sins bring death' is the storyteller's judgement on the story of Adam and Eve, and the classic sayings, 'sins must be paid for', and, 'the sins of the fathers are visited on the children'—often quoted as explanations for misfortune—leave no doubt of the place in village thought for this kind of retributive justice. Thus it becomes logical for an old man, living in squalor and with his wife and two of his three children all more or less out of their minds, to reap the judgement from neighbours acquainted with a dubious history that these things are the result of 'sins'. In the competitive reality of social life this evaluation of responsibility is of course subject to the memory of past injury and present hostility, but even so such proverbial judgements are not necessarily lacking in compassion, not only because no one is free from the awareness of their own sin, but also because the sins being suffered for are understood to be not necessarily one's own but may be consequences inherited from the past.

This pattern of responsibility for sin is the first of the modes of man's relationship with the divine law. The second mode, however, presents man not as the subject but as the object of the law, where the freedom and responsibility discussed above are replaced by constraint and necessity. The structure of the world is seen as a given, with man himself able to operate only within strict limits, an object of external forces which have made him as he is and which will do with him as they please. Thus man, acted upon by irresistible external or internal forces and in some way exonerated from his own fallibility, must suffer and accept rather than attempt to control or innovate, and the depth of this experience is apparent in the frequency of the expression, uttered not as question but as answer: 'What [else] can I/we do?' On this level, then, man is seen to act for much of the time under *force majeure*, experiencing the constraints of both the world and his own (fallen) nature as total, and dealing with them as he may. 'That's how God has made us—to suffer', people will say of the evident hardships of their lives, and fallen human nature itself is, with all its irrationality and ironies, passions and self-interest, accepted also as being, along with all else, ordained by God. 'That's how God has made us' or 'That's how we are created' are also common reactions to stories involving quarrels and egotism, and are nicely illustrated in the comment: 'One goes to church and makes the sign of the cross—and then one goes and makes mischief. That's how God has made us.'

One effect of this view of things is to promote a philosophic acceptance not only of the tribulations of human life, but also of human failings—one's own and others'. If wars, as was said earlier, are 'from God' and illnesses 'thrown' at man by God, these things are to be expected as a part of life. And even qualities such as laziness are a given, so that people will say of themselves, 'Where is laziness to go? To us!' or 'To the villages!' So misfortunes, whether deriving from other people or simply from ill chance, are accepted under the same rubric—'This is how God has made us—to get ill', or 'to quarrel'; and the saying, 'There are people and there are people' (*εἶναι κόσμος καί κοσμάκης*, or, *ὁ κόσμος εἶναι κοσμάκης*), roughly translatable as 'people come in all sorts', is not just an observation but also an explanation of minor trouble between people, for that is how we are made.

There is this sense, then, in which even man's predilection for wrong-doing is seen to be something he is a victim of rather than responsible for, and the result is a certain freedom and a notable lack of guilt even alongside the clear recognition of sin: if we are made sinful we cannot be blamed if we sin, there is a place for everything, everything has to go somewhere, wars, illnesses, laziness or whatever else, for God has ordained it like this. And it is consistent with this that spells against illness and demonic attack do not seek the eradication of these agents of misfortune but merely their banishment, exiling them to the 'wild places' and 'wild woods' or 'scrub' of the wilderness. They are a part of creation, they have to go somewhere, so they are sent to places where they will do no harm. And this tolerance of things inimical to human well-being lies behind a real charity as people accept their own misfortunes and feel compassion for the sufferings of others, and of all the creatures of the world, as something to which they themselves are prone; and it is this understanding of a common situation under God that lies behind the indulgent comment on, for example, the need of a dog for affection, 'Look at him, the shameless one', or the mice raiding the corn bins, 'They also have got to eat, the little creatures'.

In this view of things, then, of man as acted upon rather than as actor, man is subject to the all-powerful God who as absolute disposer of all things seems to exercise a somewhat arbitrary rule in a life which inevitably involves suffering and danger. Yet the same rule gives to everything its place and fills creation with beauty and fruitfulness. God's ways are inscrutable, his rule both tyrannical and merciful, so that while people feel themselves to be surrounded by hardship of all kinds and with only limited freedom of action, they feel also that they are living in a world whose structure is ultimately beneficent. Moments of passionate rebellion do indeed occur, as in the case already quoted of the woman who shouted out in church, 'I spit on you God, look what you've done to us!' But this behaviour is remarked on as the action of someone who is 'stupid'; those things which are from God must be accepted since God is the absolute arbiter of the world and the only recourse for man. It is not, however, resignation which is at issue here—the loss of hope and the abandonment of personal action. What is called upon is an acceptance which seeks to be creative within the limitations of what is given, and in this acceptance the people find a genuine comfort because, at bottom, 'God is great, everything will be fulfilled', 'God will not let you be lost'. At a level deeper than the reality of suffering lies the reality of the Creator who holds all things in his hand and, ultimately, orders all things for good.

These two views of man's relation to the *Pandodhýnamos* or Almighty thus combine the idea of responsibility for choices with acceptance of powerlessness in a world whose nature is pre-determined and necessarily involves a degree of sin, and much of social life is worked out by the tension between these two ideas. Although polarizations, they are parts of the logical working-out of a single mythological intuition, and both come together in the typical statement: 'That is how God has made us—to struggle. Because of Eve we are all cursed.' Man, in fact, is both acted upon and actor at the same time, he must suffer his lot as well as try to change it, he is free from guilt but must accept responsibility; his God is a God in whose world there is often little room for manoeuvre, but who yet gives his people freedom to choose between right and wrong. The Creator of all is a God of mercy who made and sustains all things, and yet also a God of inscrutable purposes and of sometimes harsh retribution, quite capable of acting in a purely imperative manner. The Creator is the God who 'accomplishes all things' and who 'doesn't lose' the faithful, but he is also the God of the unanswered prayers and who, keeping his own counsel and listening to the beseeching of the faithful, sends them in return 'a bum fart' (*ὁ Θεὸς μας κωλοπορδάει*).

The understanding of the divine law is based, then, on two ideas, both perceived within the limits of the fall. One is that there is an inner dynamic in which sin reaps an external punishment, and where God deals with man in a remorseless manner: 'Is that what you're like? Take that!' It is when caught up in this situation that men deal with their women in much the same way, applying the rule of superior strength and an *a fortiori* requirement of obedience. The second idea of the nature of things within the fallen world is that the world is ordered for good but involves also an inevitable degree of apparently random suffering, for which man is not personally responsible. This second view of things is extraordinarily potent, and has a yet starker elaboration in terms not of God but of fate or *moíra* (*μοῖρα*), literally the 'share' or 'lot' of man, or 'what is ordained' (*τό πεπρωμένο*).

Fate is commonly referred to as *týchi* (*τύχη*) or luck, but used in the contexts described below it is synonymous with the word *moíra*, and to describe anything in these contexts as *tycheró* (*τυχερό*, adj.) does not mean 'lucky' but 'fated'. The 'Fates' (*Μοῖρες*) feature in the symbolic imagination of the villagers as three old women who sit around the cradle of a newborn child for the three days that the mother and child remain uncleaned from the blood of childbirth.[1] All this time they 'fate' (*μοιράνουν*) the baby, laying down all the things that will happen in its life, determining its future down to the last detail. Their talk may on occasions be overheard by the mother and the mother-in-law, or, in particular, the 'grandmothers', who are all people attuned at that moment to the liminal world within which these things happen; but whether overheard or not the fate becomes written into the crabbed, irregular lines found on the skull, and these words once uttered can never be erased. 'What is written cannot be unwritten', 'What is written never becomes unwritten', 'What is written cannot be erased', are continually recurring sayings, and neither the Fates themselves, nor the saints, nor the Mother of God, nor yet God himself, can overrule this once-written decree. This idea provides, then, one primary way in which the villagers make sense of their lives, and it is a message which is conveyed with enormous insistence, both in daily talk and in the great number of folk tales based on the theme.

These folk tales occur in an infinite number of ingenious permutations, but the central theme is always that what fate decrees inevitably comes to pass. Thus they tend to dwell in particular on the archetypal theme of love of parents for children, and to play on their efforts to save children who have a bad fate, or 'a bad word' in their fate, from 'what is written'. A father, for instance, learning that his son is fated to die through a tortoise, sends him to sea thinking, 'How can he find a tortoise at sea?' But when at some point the ship comes to land and the boy gets off with his mates, on the road where they pass they find a tortoise. Seeing it the boy kicks it, saying, 'That's the thing my father says I will die from.' But a splinter from the shell gets into his foot, gives him blood poisoning, and he dies. Again, a girl fated to die through a snake-bite is shut up in a cupboard by her parents, to keep her safe. They pass her in food through a little opening, and there she sits and eats, and there she lives. One day, though,

[1] See p. 37.

they send her in some grapes, not knowing that there is a tiny little snake hidden amongst them. Inevitably, the snake bites the girl, and she dies. And again a king, learning that his daughter is fated to give birth to a black baby, vows: 'What is written I will make unwritten!', and, building a tower in the middle of the sea, he immures her in it. But even so, one day a black man appears at the foot of the tower and, conceiving an inordinate passion for him, the girl insists on him being hauled up. In course of time she duly gives birth, and the rest of the story is concerned with her efforts to conceal her action by the murder of the baby, her subsequent efforts to conceal the murder, and her consequent grisly death when all is discovered. Irony is thus a chief element in this category of tales, highlighting the inevitable outcome when man's desire to act for his own good clashes with the decree under which all his action is subsumed.

These stories tell of evil fates, but a fate can be good as well as bad, and thus there are tales also of penniless men being chosen by rich families to marry their daughters, or of girls with unfortunate beginnings unexpectedly striking good fortune, such as the virtuous but poor and unsought-for girl, who unknowingly receives God into her house and then 'spoke pearls, spat pearls'. Tales are also told of marriages foreordained from which one or other party tries to escape, but to which they eventually bow. And tales are told to illustrate the workings of fate which do not feature any foreknowledge but stress rather the apparently inconsequential nature of the events that can lead a person to crisis. One such is that of a boy who grows up to play the flute so well that the leaves on the trees dance at his playing. Coming back from a wedding he goes to a spring to drink, and in the great tree over the spring a snake, entranced by his playing, beseeches ever more tunes to dance to, in return for golden coins which he fetches in his mouth from his tree. The idea then enters the boy's head that it would be better to kill the snake so as to get everything. He swipes at the snake with his knife; but missing his aim he cuts off the tail only, enabling it to take revenge with a fatal bite. The boy's grieving father finds his body, but on being told by the snake not to look further for the murderer, for the boy had brought his death on himself, he returns home. In this story as in all the others, the explanation is constantly interpolated—'It was fate, you see'.

These stories reveal that, although the Fates are said to determine every last detail of peoples' lives and characters, the area in which the Fates impinge most significantly on people's lives is that of great life events, particularly birth, marriage, and death. And this is in fact a precise reflection of the way people actually experience the workings of fate in their lives and in the lives of others, for it is in the great rites of passage that they see incontrovertible evidence that only in this realm can be found the explanation of why things turn out the way they do. At birth, as has been said, as the vulnerable mother and child hover between the visible and invisible worlds, the fateful first three days set the scene for the rest of the child's life; at death, people for the first time are able to see the life laid out before them as a completed story, and thus are able to map its contours in terms of a patterning laid down by some force other than personal intention and personal deserts; at marriage, imbued as it is with the uncertainties of an alliance with 'strangers', the idea of fate is so prominent that during any discussion of marriage someone or other is bound to make the proverbial utterance, 'Wherever you go, it is fate', and to cite the universal axiom, 'Marriage is a matter of fate'. A girl will refer to her prospective bridegroom, as yet unknown, as the person who is 'in my fate', and the idea of fate is so powerful at these times that it may be applied to cut through normal hesitation, or used as a lever to circumvent doubt in a marriage negotiation: 'I'll tell you this. Marriage is a matter of fate, and if it is for Nikos to marry Vassilo, tak! it will happen, no matter what you do.'

Belief in the power of fate, then, is pervasive in village belief and experience, and an inescapable part of this belief is the conviction with which it is insisted that God himself cannot alter a man's fate, and that in this respect prayers to the Mother of God and the saints avail nothing. On this level, then, there is a clear contradiction between belief in fate and belief in a God who himself ordains the patterning of events, and who at the same time offers choice and tests the righteous. This contradiction is taken seriously by the Church, and members of the clergy commonly react on this level, insisting on the responsible and free relation of man to God, even driving their point home with the comment, 'Fate is nothing!' Such an attitude evokes, however, in the village interlocutor, a furious response as at a real blasphemy, and in fact any direct challenge to fate, even the much milder objection that surely people have freedom to choose between the good road and the bad road, elicits the same reaction —one not just of shock and anger but of alarm—'You mustn't say that!' To question the role of fate then is to blaspheme, and the role of foul language is illuminating here, for while, as has been said, men curse the Mother of God, the cross and the faith with fluency and a certain reiterative obscenity, they are said only very rarely to curse their fate and if they curse it at all, to use a politer terminology: 'Anathema on my fate!' It is the Fates above all that people must not offend.

There is a story said to be known by all villagers, though as part of esoteric lore and never spoken in a public context, which throws some light on this matter. This story relates how all the people's different fates live in separate rooms in a great house by the sea and how, a long time ago, a man whose lot had been persistently bad went to seek out his Fate, finding her eventually in her room 'upside down', in which position she remained, refusing to speak to him. For some time he questioned her but eventually, still being refused an answer, he lost his patience, 'did the work in the rear end', and departed. Since when people, at a persistent run of bad luck, are said to comment, 'Is your Fate upside down?' The full significance of this story is obscure, but it is clear that it relies on the shock created by an all too literal interpretation of the terms of customary blasphemy. When it is remembered that sexual blasphemy is freely used, by men, of the holy things and holy people of the faith, though excluding God himself, this story highlights a distinction between people's attitude to the *dramatis personae* of the holy world, and that used to the Fates. The former are familiar, loved, and loving, and not being feared they may be sworn at with a kind of familiarity commonly used throughout village life; the Fates are distant, recalcitrant, intractable, and instil fear, so that even to mention them in uncomplimentary terms is done in a hushed voice.

Fate then is an awesome and autonomous force, ruler of people's lives, immutable arbiter of all that happens to them, unchangeable even by God himself. This having been said however, there is another level on which the dividing line between God and fate is more permeable. In one folk tale a woman, said to have every day 'gilded', or praised and honoured, her Fate, is described as crossing herself as she addresses her Fate, with the story-teller at one point replacing the words 'my golden Fate!' (*χρυσή μου Μοῖρα*) with the term of address normally used for the Mother of God, 'my All-holy One!' (*Παναγία μου*). In the story of the parsimonious baker saved from damnation by the ungracious gift of a burned loaf to a persistent beggar,[2] the teller of the tale interjects a comment equating fate with the Angel (of death): 'His fate sent him [the beggar] so that he should be saved: the Angel sent him.' Finally, in the story of the princess destined to become pregnant by a black man, the black man appearing at the bottom of the tower is explained as coming 'from God'. He was sent from God, because the king had said, 'What is written I will make unwritten!' And there is a hint that God not only caused the black man to arrive at the tower, but created him especially for this purpose, for the same phrase is used of the appearance of this man as is used in stories of the original creation of the animals, 'God prepared (*στόρισε*) him'. These illustrations—together with the fact that in their experience and in their conversation the villagers' belief in God coexists quite easily with their belief in fate—point to a factor which mediates in the apparent contradiction between the two, and this factor is revealed in the general explanation that it is God who tells the Fates what to say, and in the *ad hoc* interjections in some of these stories that their fateful conclusion was 'from God'. In some way, therefore, the God who creates free choice is the same as the God who subjects people to an immutable fate, and the key to this lies in the contexts within which fate is customarily perceived to be at work.

It is clear from the stories about fate which have been cited above that they represent a particular way in which people account for the unexpected, dramatic, and ironic elements in their lives. Of marriage, that most uncertain negotiation, the knowledge that 'you take a man as a good man and he turns out bad, while a bad man turns out good' finds its explanation in the gnomic comment on the nature of marriage: 'Marriage is a matter of fate.' And in fact kings immuring their daughters in towers at sea to no avail, or parents shutting up their daughters in a cupboard only to find that they themselves are the unwitting agents of her death, are no more than dramatized versions of parallel events in real life, as when people who long for their children, wives, or husbands to live, find that death has claimed them, or when parents take infinite pains to marry their daughters to a diligent and

[2] See p. 274.

kind man, only to find that they have chosen a wastrel or a wife-beater. Thus a true story of a man who made money but died unmarried reaps the comment, 'Wasn't it fate that made him make a pile of money for another to take?' And a long story from an old herdsman telling of the failure first of his herd of goats and then of the sheep with which he replaced them, culminating in his buying—at his wife's behest and simply to provide wool for his daughters' dowries—a few sheep, which then multiplied unexpectedly into a fine flock, is concluded with the self-evident moral, 'It was fate. What else was it?'

Characteristically, then, the interpretations offered by the idea of fate are retrospective rather than predictive, allowing people to look back over their own life or the lives of others and see with clarity the twists of circumstance which brought them to this point. And while in the folk tales the stories of the 'grandmothers' in the shadowy world of birth overhearing the talk of the Fates do allow for prediction, it is significant that this prediction gives the few who overhear it no greater control over their lives than they would have had anyway. Life will unfold for each person according to its own pattern, and in the final analysis it is only at the hour of death that those left behind can look over the life of the dead and see its pattern laid bare with its ironies, its triumphs, and its sorrows, and celebrate its summation in the laments—the 'words of fate'—which is the literal translation of the Greek word *moirológia*.

At birth, then, a person's fate is laid down, and at death it is summed up. Fate is in fact the people's way of understanding in retrospect the working out of individual lives, in a world which is greater than they are, whose parameters are wider than they can comprehend, and whose laws interact to produce unpredictable consequences. Belief in fate is a way of living in a world which the people accept, wisely, is beyond their control. But it is also a way by which the people understand their place in the world, and accept with grace and fortitude the uncertainties and tragedies, the griefs and joys, whose unexpected interplay is the lot of human beings on this earth. It is because of this that belief in fate is to these people a real consolation in time of trouble, and because of this that a tale of fate can in the most active sense prevent a man caught by sudden catastrophe from falling into despair. One man, with his son having murdered a fellow villager and with himself and his family facing flight from their ancestral house and lands, was told as comfort the story of the flute-player who attempted to kill the snake and was killed in his turn. This fantastical story of the convolutions of fate was understood by the story-teller to apply quite precisely to the current catastrophe, and it did in fact figure as a kind of comfort and pave the way to a kind of acceptance: 'Almost you persuade me that this is true.'

The retrospective nature of the understanding of fate has another important consequence in that belief in fate by no means makes the people 'fatalistic': they are very far from abandoning effort and letting blind forces unravel as they will, in the case of marriage or anything else. In the stories, people struggle for good marriages for their children, for life and prosperity. In life, the efforts, for instance, of the herdsman to buy sheep, to buy goats, to labour for their increase, were clearly unremitting. Marriages are focuses of hopes which begin, particularly for girls (who need a dowry), at the cradle, and are subject to the most intense enquiry, assessment, speculation, and negotiation. But in the end 'you take a man to be a good man and he turns out bad; and a bad man turns out good'. Fate does not free people from effort, but it frees them from the plague of self-recriminations if things go wrong. Getting things wrong may be a matter for grief, but not for guilt, for it is a natural part of our life on earth.

It is in this way that the gulf is bridged between God and fate, freedom and predestination. Posed as philosophic statements, the two theories of life are in contradiction and the Church treats them as such. But for the people who hold them they are ideas which are lived, not conceptualized, and as experiential realities they form a single complex weave in which the belief in fate by no means excludes personal endeavour or a creative interplay between man and the spiritual world. Fate and God are not mutually exclusive, and the intuitive fusions of fate, God, the Mother of God, and the Angel, which occur in the story-teller's mind, are natural consequences of this inner reconciliation between the two sets of ideas. And it is in the end a reconciliation which is extraordinarily simple: 'Everything is written, but you have to take care.' The idea of predestination has in fact no power to stifle the imaginations of the people as they struggle with their present and their future, as they pray and toil, fast and feast, honour the saints, arrange their marriages, and care for their creatures. And in retrospect it has a healing and a freeing function, for it enables the people to see that sometimes as a result of and sometimes in spite of their endeavours, a certain pattern was all the time being unfolded which was ordained by another hand than theirs. *Moíra*, in fact, means exactly what it says—a person's 'share' or 'lot'. A person's 'fate' is his share or apportionment of good and evil in his life, and as such it is a part of God's law, given by God.

The fallen order of sin and death which Christ comes to renew involves, then, first, that sins draw down punishment, whether on present or future generations; second, that God, though creator of a beneficent world, is an authoritarian figure who distributes to each a share of suffering on a random basis, and whose ultimate power over the life of every man is dramatically expressed in the idea of fate; and also, third, that death in its violence and finality has the last word, revealing in the end the life of man to be 'deluding' or 'false'. Death shows life to be but a brief interlude under the sun before the soul is banished to a shadowy existence in the underworld and the body becomes a handful of bones.

In Orthodox tradition the renewal of this fallen order involves repentance or *metánoia* (*μετάνοια*), a change of perception which enters into God's way of looking at the world and transforms a relationship of subjection to power into one of understanding. In this altered way of looking at the world the figure of Christ is central, because he is seen as both human and divine: as human, he inspires understanding, empathy, and affection; as divine, he reveals the mind of God. Not only in the Church tradition though, but in village understanding too, the changes of perception which soften and illuminate the harsh experiences of the village predicament centre on images of Christ, and the village perspective thus reveals suggestive echoes of this Orthodox view of the fall and the way to restoration.

The divinity of Christ is a simple fact to the villagers to whom 'Christ is God', and it is consistent with this that it is 'Christ', rather than 'God', who springs most easily to people's lips when they refer to the creation of the animals, such as in the stories of the cat, the pig, and the buffalo, and Christ also who, as 'the son of God who could do anything he wanted', created light to dispel the darkness. Sometimes he is portrayed as going to his Father to ask for something to happen—a request always granted. In these essential creative acts the village Christ reflects the Logos, the Word of God who 'is before the world was',[3] and brings the world into being. Here, therefore, Christ is none other than the Almighty who made and rules the heavens and the earth, and who is the son of God—the Word who expresses the will of his Father.

If the divinity of Christ poses no problem to the people, however, neither does his humanity. In the stories of his wandering the world in various guises as an old man or a young gallant, sometimes as a child, demonstrating by his mere presence in a place the extent to which divine love resides in it, he is the incarnate Christ of the Gospels, God who took on our life. And as this figure he features in the people's conversations and imagination as the Christ who came into the world as a little child, whom they sometimes refer to with extraordinary affection in the endearment '*Christoutzikós mou!*' (*Χριστουτζικός μου*), 'my little Christ!', the innocent one who died 'for us', the Christ who 'came to save us' but whom 'we killed'; and the Christ who, betrayed and put to death on the cross, nevertheless, as the Easter hymn constantly asserts, 'trampled down death by death' and rose from the grave. Thus the villagers' Christ is both God and man, both the Almighty and maker of all, and a deeply loved and deeply-loving figure with whom is possible a relationship altogether more personal and intimate than that offered by other modes of the divine.

The villagers' relationship with this divine and human Christ derives from the Church's liturgy, but it is also, as has been seen, expressed in stories, songs, and practices of their own, and both means of transmission act to transform the village understandings summarized above: the understanding of the law of punishment for sin, the law of apparently random suffering, and the law of death. All three laws surface again and again in the liturgy and receive liturgical answers throughout the sacred year, but it is the liturgy of Holy Week, the week of Christ's Passion leading up to the morning of Easter, which expresses their quintessence. This second and last part of the present chapter discusses these themes as they appear in the last days of Holy Week, and points to the way in which in each case confirmatory folk practices have grown up to interpret and elaborate their meaning.

It is on Holy Thursday, the Thursday immediately preceding Easter, that the issue of sins being paid for comes face to face with a God

[3] John 17 : 5.

27. Figure of the *Panaghía* from an icon of the Annunciation: the spindle and spun yarn on the right of her upraised hand has jumped away as she throws the hand up, indicating surprise and shock at the arrival of the angel. With her left hand she has been winding a ball of yarn from the spindle, the last stage after spinning from a distaff.

28. The story teller: 'It was fate, you see' (p. 345).

who acts quite otherwise. On the Thursday evening the Passion Service is held which recounts in twelve readings from the Gospels the story of the crucifixion. The twelve readings include virtually the whole account of John[4] and Matthew[5] with additions by Mark and Luke, and these form the predominant part of the service, with the addition of some sung commentary after each reading. The crucifixion itself is imaged at the mid-point of this service, when, in one of the most dramatic events of the whole liturgical year, the priest emerges from the north door of the sanctuary bearing a great cross, often twice his height, which is carried in procession right-handed round the church before being set upright in the centre of the nave. On this the priest then fixes an icon in the figure of the crucified Christ, or drapes around it a white cloth in representation of the figure of Christ. This is the moment of the crucifixion itself, and for it the people wait in awe, crossing themselves and prostrating when the cross appears, and it is characteristic that of this moment a newcomer should be told: 'You wait for the moment when the cross is brought out. Your hair will stand on end!' Both the liturgical and the village commentary on the death of Christ thus focus on this moment.

The crucifixion is an event which villagers sometimes, consonant with habitual village patterns of asserting the honour of one's own behaviour and denigrating that of others, describe as an alien act—it is not an act of shepherds, for instance, since it was a shepherd who took the three nails first made for the crucifixion and hid them in his *tsournás* (*τσουρνάς*),[6] but it can be described as an act of the Jews, and on occasion of the gypsies too, since a blacksmith was needed for the nails and he then made not three but five nails, one each for the hands and feet and the fifth for the heart.[7] Blaming

[4] vv. 13 : 3 to 19 : 42. [5] vv. 26 : 57 to 27 : 66.

[6] The *tsournás* is a bass woodwind instrument which carries long distances in the open air, and in the mountains can be used to powerful effect for laments, which may be the allusion here. Sometimes described as a bass clarinet, it is according to Jane Cowan (*Dance and the Body Politic in Northern Greece,* Princeton: Princeton University Press, 1990, p. 97) a Balkan double-reeded shawm (hence an ancestor of the oboe, or in terms of its register, of the cor anglais).

[7] For claims to honour and denigration of others, see p. 178. The narrative details which express this pattern in folk tales of the crucifixion derive from an ancient ballad tradition, see Alexiou, *Ritual Lament*, pp. 65, 73.

others, primarily the Jews, for the crucifixion, has also been a tendency in Christian liturgies; and Oriental liturgies like the Orthodox, which often draw on texts from the first centuries after the painful break with the Synagogue, are liable to fall into this.[8] But an attitude of blaming others is, in these liturgical texts, constantly undermined by an inward shift of perception, a change of heart, in which such images of 'we' as honourable, and others as suspect, fall away.

In this second more serious and intimate perspective, which is at the fore in Holy Week, the villagers speak of the crucifixion as their own act. Moving into this second way of seeing it, they will say with the utmost simplicity, 'We crucified him'; with the addition, sometimes, that this did not need to happen, that we could have acted otherwise, and that God meant it to be otherwise: 'Christ came to save us, but we crucified him.' The crucifixion of Christ is here therefore a shared human responsibility, 'our' responsibility, and not in any way an act of 'others' or an act of God; and it is apparent that in saying this the people can only be speaking from within the understanding of their liturgical tradition referred to at the end of Chapter 4, where the 'I' of all the people present speaks with the voice of Adam of things which are happening 'today'. The people are Adam and Adam is the people in a timeless present; so likewise in the matins of Holy Thursday, the words of the high priest Caiaphas, as he advises the secret arrest and rapid execution of Jesus as the best way to avoid 'an uproar among the people' and a Roman decision to crush the fragile Judaean state, are marked out as having a timeless significance for human society which is beyond the understanding of Caiaphas himself:

> Today the evil Sanhedrin has assembled against Christ
> And devised vain things against him,
> Plotting to deliver him, though innocent, to Pilate to be put to death…
> Today Caiaphas prophesies against his will, saying:
> 'It is expedient that one man should perish for the people.'[9]

[8] Charlotte Klein, 'The Oriental Liturgy and the Jews', *Sobornost*, series 6, number 7, 1973.

[9] *Lenten Triodion*, Holy Thursday Matins, Aposticha, p. 555, commenting on Luke 22 : 1–2 (just previously read at Matins, p. 548, cf. Matthew 26 : 3–5 read at the Vesperal Liturgy that follows it, *Lenten Triodion*, p. 559) and John 11 : 47–52.

It is this people, this Adam, whose kinship to themselves the people in the village recognize when they say 'we crucified him' and 'he died for us'.

The service of the Twelve Gospels which follows on Thursday evening continues at this level of consciousness; and the event of the crucifixion is thus presented as a typical collective process of the whole of fallen humanity, involving not only those who decide the deed—the Sanhedrin—but also those who support it, those who obey orders, those who stand aside and let it happen, and those who (like the disciples) run away or (like Peter) deny their involvement. Although responsibility is differentiated, and the Judaean authorities, the disciple who betrayed Jesus, and the crowd which calls for the death of Jesus are held most to blame, the service of the Twelve Gospels comments on the part played by every participant in turn, and the constant reference to the need for the worshippers at the service to recognize, as their own potential or actual temptation, each sin that is identified, and to pray to be saved from it, implies the complicity of the people not only of the place and time of the crucifixion but of all places and all times. It is these universal and differentiated but interacting faults of humankind that engender violently conflicting responses to Christ's message; and these violent passions, which in the Sanhedrin are expressed as fear of an 'uproar' and a crushing Roman response, are diverted by Caiaphas onto Christ.

In both the villagers' and the liturgical view, therefore, 'we' have generated and are responsible for the violence, and would normally receive its effects; but in fact it is Christ who 'though innocent' receives them. Thus it is not just that he dies at our hands —'we crucified him'—but also that he dies in our place, which the villagers render by saying 'for us'. Furthermore, he dies 'for us', not only because he dies in our place, but also because he understands what is happening, and, though he could act otherwise, he accepts to suffer in order to free the people from the consequences of their actions. For villagers it is obvious that Christ could act otherwise because Christ 'is almighty'; but the service too is at pains to underline the active choices of Jesus in the detail of the Gospel story. That Jesus could resist and escape his enemies, but has renounced the use of force, is indicated by his rebuke to Peter for drawing his sword, and this is underlined by the liturgical commentary.[10] That he accepts his death and forgives those who bring it about is indicated in his words from the cross, 'Father, forgive them, for they know not what they do,' also underlined in the commentary.[11] As a consequence, he is seen to 'lay down his life for his friends',[12] praying for the sanctification of the disciples who have been saved through his death, and for the sanctification of all those who will believe through them thereafter.[13]

Thus both the village and the liturgical picture shows Christ deliberately acting so as to accept on himself alone the violence generated by the collective faults and deficiencies of the people as they react to him, and in doing so he frees the people from experiencing these violent consequences themselves, at the same time saving his disciples and his future Church. And from this follows the response expressed in verses which come straight after the moment of the crucifixion, which both echo and sharpen the 'for us' of the villagers by saying that Christ died 'for me':

> For my sake thou wast crucified, to become for me a fountain of forgiveness.
> Thy side was pierced, that thou mightest pour on me streams of life.
> Thou wast transfixed with nails, that through the depth of Thy sufferings
> I might know with certainty the height of Thy power,
> And cry to Thee, O Christ the Giver of Life:
> O Saviour, glory to Thy Cross and Passion.[14]

Thus far Christ is being seen chiefly as man, put to a human death. But in village and liturgical thinking Christ is also God, and so it is possible, finally, for the liturgical commentary on the crucifixion to declare that it is God who, in this event, suffers and dies:

> Today He who hung the earth upon the waters is hung upon the Cross.

[10] *Lenten Triodion*, Holy Friday Matins (Service of the Twelve Gospels), p. 578 commenting on Matthew 26 : 53–4.

[11] Luke 23 : 34 in the Eighth Gospel, *Lenten Triodion*, p. 592, and Lauds, first sticheron, p. 596.

[12] John 15 : 13 in the First Gospel, *Lenten Triodion*, p. 568.

[13] John 17 : 19–20 in the First Gospel, *Lenten Triodion*, p. 571.

[14] *Lenten Triodion*, verses between the Beatitudes after the Sixth Gospel, pp. 589–90.

> He who is king of the angels is arrayed in a crown of thorns.
> He who wraps the heavens in clouds is wrapped in the purple of mockery.

And as it continues this imagery moves seamlessly to include the human biography of Jesus:

> He who in Jordan set Adam free receives blows upon his face.
> The bridegroom of the Church is transfixed with nails.
> The Son of the Virgin is pierced with a spear.[15]

Thus it is God in the person of Christ who dies in our place.

The effect of this conclusion on the way these events are understood is profound, for if it is God who dies 'for us' and thereby saves us, then the perception that God exacts retribution for our sins—that 'sins are paid for'—is transformed, and this is why the liturgical commentary can go on to say:

> Thou wast lifted up, O Lord, upon the cross and hast destroyed the power of death,
> And as God thou hast blotted out the record of our sins that was against us.
> Grant to us also the repentance of the thief,
> O Christ our God who alone lovest mankind.[16]

The suffering of God in Christ, and the forgiveness of our actions which it reveals, has 'blotted out the record of our sins', and combines with the repentance of the sinner to mark the abandonment of the fallen perception that sins inevitably draw down punishment from an authoritarian God.

The representation of the crucifixion, then, both in this service and in village comment, is to do with a change in how God is seen and understood, with a God who in a direct encounter with humanity is seen not to enact the 'curse of the law'[17]—to answer sins with punishment—but instead to pay the cost of sin himself and to give undeserved mercy. The villagers, who do not grasp all the details of the high liturgical language in which these texts are written,

[15] Ibid. Antiphon 15 before the Sixth Gospel, p. 587.
[16] Ibid. verses between the Beatitudes after the Sixth Gospel, p. 590.
[17] Ibid. Sessional Hymn immediately before the Sixth Gospel, p. 588.

nevertheless understand that at the moment of the crucifixion God, rather than causing the law of sin and punishment to take its ordinary course, willingly dies 'for us'.

This understanding of the Christ who dies in this way, and this awareness of the forgiveness which flows from his choices, thus runs deep in the consciousness of the people. However, it is gained not only from liturgical poetry but also from its echoes in popular mythology.

The villagers' everyday awareness of their own sin and their sense that they cannot avoid it has already been commented on,[18] together with their ability to accept this as their natural state rather than being plagued by remorse and guilt. But the inner pattern of this awareness changes in certain contexts, and in the context of the crucifixion, instead of the wry, self-excusatory tone in which man's treatment of his fellow man can be commented on—'that's how God has made us'—people will react differently, taking the responsibility squarely on themselves—'Christ came to save us but we crucified him'—and saying also, in discussions about sin and forgiveness, things already quoted such as 'whatever we do, we sin', and 'can our sins be forgiven?' Their sins are no longer those inevitable peccadilloes that flesh is heir to, they are part of the failures of humanity that lead to Christ's death. Yet, rather than blasting the sinner, he saves us.

This paradox of a Christ who is rejected yet who saves is also a recurrent theme in village stories, especially in the hospitality stories already recounted.[19] In the tale of the meat turning to human flesh after the householder fails to answer the knocking of Christ, the irony of the prized meal becoming a cannibal act represents in dramatic form the cruelty implicit in the denial of hospitality. In the householder's refusal to give to the unknown suppliant he is in fact sacrificing this unknown other—Christ—to his own self. And the same theme is extended in the story of the village which mocks the disguised Christ and brings on itself the sorrowful prophecy that it will never increase beyond nine houses. The inner dynamic revealed here is again that failure to give is failure to let live, and so in itself condemns the population level of the village always to remain below that of a thriving community. In both cases the denial of the divine command to

[18] See p. 188.

[19] See pp. 189–91.

give is revealed as the destruction of human life, the life of Christ.

A further story, not yet recounted, falls also into this category, and concerns a woman who asked Christ to visit her house. The day he was expected she was in a frenzy of cleaning and preparing, and at the critical moment along came an old beggar to her door, whom she abused and sent away, saying she was awaiting an important visitor. The day passed, and Christ never came, and the next day she reproached him: 'All day I waited and you never came.' But he replied: 'How is it that I never came? I came, but you shouted at me and beat me black and blue.' Once again, the refusal to give to the unknown, the poor, the disreputable, is revealed as synonymous with the rejection of Christ and the denial of human life.

Parables of the rejection of Christ implicit in the refusal to give hospitality thus represent one type of hospitality story; but linked with these is a further type, which may be described as parables of uncovenanted forgiveness,[20] when at the last moments of a lifetime of selfishness Christ wins the battle for an imperilled soul by casting into the scales an onion grudgingly offered, or the gift of a burned loaf hurled in fury. The first type of story reveals that the cause of destruction lies not in God as an external agent but in the sinner himself; the second type shows that Christ nevertheless forgives, provided the soul gives him the remotest reason to do so. But even the mercy of Christ must have something to work on, and the key that unlocks this forgiveness is in both tales the act of giving. Such repentance is also exemplified in the tale of the man who after death became a donkey and was tormented by demons, for when he understands the consequences of his bad deeds and turns to Christ, witnessing this by laying out wooden crosses, he is saved. In all these examples, some change of heart is needed from the sinner, but in return for the smallest generous movement in an otherwise graceless life, Christ takes the soul to himself.

These stories faithfully portray the Christ of the texts of Holy Week, rejected, suffering, yet merciful, the Christ who is, in the liturgical phrase, 'the life of all', turned away by those who sacrifice others to the self, but ready to forgive and save the soul at the first sign of repentance, or of the soul's willingness to sacrifice itself even to a minute extent for others.

[20] See pp. 275–7.

One final story brings together the theme that sins are paid for with the theme of unexpected forgiveness. This is the story of the lazy man and the industrious girl. The lazy man was the one who, asked by Christ for water and in answer pointing wordlessly to the well with his foot, found his formerly placid cows plagued by gadflies, while the industrious girl, who left her unruly goats to fetch water for Christ, returned to find her previously recalcitrant flock docile and obedient. But a sequel not yet related gives an unexpected ending, for Christ then comments to his disciples: 'Nevertheless, the lazy man will marry the industrious girl.' This is greeted by indignant expostulations from the disciples, but he counters these with the argument: 'How else is the man to live?' Here, then, the refusal to make even a small act of sacrifice is self-destructive, but still the hard-working must go on giving to the lazy, because in the end what is important is not that strict justice should be observed, but that all should live. Those who are willing to sacrifice themselves must give to those who withhold from giving, the undeserving must 'live off'—as a comment on the story puts it—the deserving, and it is because the dispensation of Christ finds a place for both that the saying has arisen that 'one good person can save a whole village'.

In this way the remorseless logic of a God who in the fallen order is perceived to see the wicked act and say, 'Take that!', is transformed not only in the service of the Twelve Gospels, but also in the folk portrayals of Christ, into a picture of a God who himself pays the cost of human sins and continues to offer undeserved mercy.

The second characteristic of the fallen order as defined above involves God, though creator of a beneficent world, keeping to himself his inscrutable purposes and ordaining to man an immutable fate, allocating apparently randomly to each person before birth his or her meed of good or evil fortune against which there is no appeal. Counterposed to this in Holy Week, however, is the idea of God who suffers with us, the Christ who took on our humanity and who was himself destined to die a cruel death.

This Christ also is intimately known to the villagers as the God who left the glories of paradise to be born in this world, the innocent one put to the worst of fates, whom they mourn as their friend, 'my Christ', and care for and grieve over as their child, 'my little Christ'. Thus Christ, the son of the God who ordains the edicts of fate, is balanced by Christ as a child, their child, the innocent one done to death. And just as Christ as the God of forgiveness for sins has his paradigmatic moment on Holy Thursday, so does Christ as the suffering servant have his moment in the vespers of Holy Friday, which commemorates the taking down of the dead Christ from the cross.

At the end of the Twelve Gospels the previous evening, the younger people and the men will have venerated the cross and left the church, but, just as a dead person is never left unattended from the moment of death until burial, so in the case of the dead Christ the old women stay to keep a vigil in the church until the Lament at the Tomb (at the Burial Service which follows Holy Friday vespers) twenty-four hours later. On Friday no food is taken and only a cup of black coffee drunk until after the Burial Service in the evening. Only after the service will a meal be eaten, consisting of the traditional Holy Friday fare of bread and young bracken fronds boiled and served with vinegar, eaten standing up. Vinegar recalls the sponge of vinegar offered to Christ just before he died, and the importance of this meal being eaten standing rather than comfortably seated at the table is because, as people say, 'Christ died today so how can I sit down to a meal?'

On Holy Friday the same prohibitions are followed as for all the great feasts: no one works in the fields or the forest, and no handwork or washing is done in the houses, and although a certain amount of housework such as whitewashing the sooty fireplaces is permitted, the day is for the most part given over to the preparation for the vespers of Holy Friday. At this season all sorts of meadow and woodland flowers are abundant, and there may be a special place where white peonies bloom in the mountains, or where hyacinths and anemones carpet the ground, and from early morning the younger women and children go out scouring the hillsides looking for them to adorn the bier on which the *Epitáphios* (Ἐπιτάφιος) is laid. The *Epitáphios* itself specifically (as the term is used here) is a rectangular cloth on which is embroidered or painted the icon of the dead Christ laid out for burial, though in cases where this is lacking a wooden icon is used instead. Further, though, the bier—the table-like structure surmounted with arched wooden struts like a crown in which this icon is laid—is by extension also popularly known as the *Epitáphios*. It is this bier which, on the return of the women and children from the hillsides, is decorated on every surface with flowers and set ready.

Holy Friday Vespers, which begins in the early afternoon, retells, mainly in the words of Matthew, the last part of the story of the crucifixion, beginning with the morning of the crucifixion, and continuing with the taking down of the body of Jesus from the cross and its laying out. The Gospel reading recounting this moment occurs in the middle of the service and is immediately preceded by readings from Old Testament prophecies and an epistle. Up to these readings, the service continues the themes of the Twelve Gospels; after the readings, new themes enter, clustering round the taking down of Christ's body from the cross which is enacted as the service nears its end.

The enactment begins as the priest takes down the icon or the cloth representing Christ crucified from the great cross standing in the centre of the church, and carries it from the nave into the sanctuary through the Royal Doors. The flower-decked wooden bier is then brought into the church and set before the cross, and the priest, now having fully robed himself, censes the *Epitáphios* imaging the dead body of Christ, which has been laid ready on the altar, and it is then carried ceremonially from the sanctuary and, as the people kneel, taken in procession right-handed round the church, and laid in the bier. During this procession verses are sung commemorating Joseph of Arimathaea and the women who laid out the body of Christ, and, once the procession has come to rest, one by one the congregation come to venerate the tomb of Christ, crossing themselves with deep prostrations, and kissing the *Epitáphios*. Once again this service is represented as occurring in the 'today' of the eternal mysteries, and the participants in this vespers behave not as spectators at a memorial ceremony but as mourners at a death; and it is the body of the dead Christ itself which lies before them as they approach the bier in real grief and awe, sometimes in tears.

This is the service at which questions of suffering and an unavoidable fate are most clearly addressed, and it is the readings from the Old Testament, in particular the story of the suffering servant from Isaiah,[21] which bring about this new focus. This prophetic writing of the sixth century BC, about the man who, despised and rejected, bears our griefs and carries our sorrows, is frequently referred to in the liturgical commentaries of Holy Thursday and Holy Friday as a 'scripture' (literally, something that is 'written') fulfilled in Christ,[22] and when juxtaposed with the history of the crucifixion, it is strangely reminiscent of the village understanding of fate which, also referred to as 'what is written', is also thought to govern the outcome of the life story which is told at a death.

It is apt, therefore, that at the moment when the priest censes the *Epitáphios* before bringing it out into the nave, the lament, the 'word of fate' (*moirológi*), re-appears; but it appears with important differences. The first difference is that physical decay and the ending of earthly companionship is no longer the focus, as it is even in the lament voiced in the Orthodox funeral service. The song is not for the ending of the one life given to each, but for the death of the 'Giver of Life' to all, and it engages unflinchingly with the paradoxical conclusion that God himself can die.[23]

This lament is one of a series of laments, and it is preceded on Holy Thursday by that of the Mother of God at the cross:

> Beholding Thee hanging on the Cross, O Christ,
> Thy Mother cried aloud: 'O my Son,
> What is this strange mystery that I behold?
> Nailed in the flesh, O Giver of Life,
> How dost Thou die upon the tree?'[24]

That it is not a hapless individual but the 'Giver of Life' who meets this end indicates that this is more than the unlucky draw of some in

[21] Isaiah 52 : 13 to 53 : 12.

[22] Paradigmatically in Holy Thursday Matins, *Lenten Triodion*, p. 555, 'The Lamb whom Isaiah proclaimed goes of his own will to the slaughter...', but also at pp. 554, 562, 584, 595, 601, 612, 623, 624, 636.

[23] Alexiou, *Ritual Lament*, pp. 62–9, gives the early Christian (and some possible ancient) sources for the lament of Holy Thursday and Friday, under the general heading 'The Virgin's Lament' (but note that most of the laments during these services are actually put in the mouths of the congregation, and some in the mouth of Joseph or Joseph and Nicodemus).

[24] *Lenten Triodion*, Theotokion before the Sixth Gospel, p. 587.

life's lottery; rather it is something essential to the nature of life, and must partake in the sacred qualities of the God who gives life. In the vespers of Holy Friday, at the time of the censing of the *Epitáphios*, the lament of Joseph of Arimathaea takes the difference a step further by insisting that this death is not inflicted by force, but (unlike the typical response in the folk tales) accepted with consent:

> Woe is me, my sweetest Jesus!
> When but a little while ago the sun
> Saw Thee hanging on the Cross,
> It wrapped itself in darkness:
> The earth quaked with fear
> And the veil of the temple was rent in twain.
> And now I see Thee for my sake
> Submitting of Thine own will to death.
> How shall I bury Thee, my God?
> How shall I wrap Thee in a winding sheet?
> How shall I touch Thy most pure body with my hands?
> What song at thy departure shall I sing to Thee, O compassionate Saviour?
> I magnify Thy sufferings;
> I sing the praises of Thy burial and Thy resurrection,
> Crying, O Lord, glory to Thee.[25]

Finally, after the procession bringing the *Epitáphios* from the sanctuary to the bier, the prostrations of each villager in turn before the bier are accompanied by a hymn which, returning to the theme of the death of the Giver of Life, recalls that the destiny of Jesus was foretold when as a young child he was brought to the temple, and Simeon receiving him into his arms prophesied to his mother that through this child a sword should pierce through her own soul also:

> Come, let us bless Joseph ever memorable,
> Who came by night and begged for the Life of all:
> Give me this stranger who has no place to lay His head.
> Give me this stranger whom His evil disciple delivered up to death.

[25] *Lenten Triodion*, Holy Friday Vespers, lament at the censing of the *Epitáphios*, p. 615.

Give me this stranger whom His Mother saw hanging on the Cross.
And with a mother's sorrow she cried weeping: 'Woe is me, my Child!
Woe is me, Light of mine eyes and beloved fruit of my womb!
For what Simeon foretold in the temple is come to pass this day:
A sword pierces my heart.'[26]

The reference to this prediction and the reading of the prophecy of the suffering servant noted above, together with the particular fulfilments of Scripture to which the long Gospel story of the crucifixion draws attention at several stages,[27] thus underline the similarities and differences between the idea of fate and the sense in which the death of Christ has been foretold.

The similarity with the idea of fate obviously lies in the way the destiny of Christ is seen to be foretold or 'written' in the Scriptures from the beginning, and must come to pass. But there is a telling difference in that these three laments declare that this death is God's, accepted by him of his own will, so that it cannot be seen as a random share of bad luck confined to the individual and vainly resisted by him, but must be seen as something in the nature of things which carries a divine purpose.

This, then, is the liturgical form taken by the lament on Holy Friday, and the liturgical response to the issues raised by village conceptions of fate and suffering; but immediately after vespers there is a spontaneous village counterpart which makes its own statement. During the time intervening between the two Friday services, that of the taking down of Christ from the cross and the burial service, the dead Christ is accompanied, now not only by the old women who have remained in the church since the end of the service of the Twelve Gospels, but by young women and children also, and this period, like a wake, is a loosely structured event during which people can come and go and conversation can range over different topics and children can misbehave. But during it there are periods of deep seriousness, chiefly when the people sing the folk lament on the death of Christ, or as much of it as they know. This powerful

[26] Ibid., lament during the veneration of the *Epitáphios*, pp. 654–5, commenting on Luke 2 : 35.

[27] e.g. John 15 : 25, 17 : 12, 18 : 9, 19 : 36–7, Matthew 27 : 9, 27 : 35.

ballad[28] begins with references like those of the laments to being covered by the earth's 'black mantle':

> Today black is the sky, today black the day,
> Today everything is grieving and the mountains weep.

It briefly describes the conspiracy against Christ, then continues as the Passion Gospels begin, with the Last Supper, in a couplet which achieves an extraordinary degree of compression:

> The Lord wanted to go into a garden,
> To receive himself the mysterious supper in order that all should receive it.

The garden here can be heard as both Eden and Gethsemane, for the mysterious supper is both the drinking of the cup which Christ prayed to be taken from him in Gethsemane—his giving of his body and blood in death—and the mystery (that is, sacrament) of the body and blood of Christ received by all in communion, which intimates the restoration of Eden. A link is thus made between the fate of Christ and the communion of humankind in him which in this way is made possible, for which there are liturgical parallels.[29] The achievement of this communion is here presented as the inner purpose of Christ's death, in spite of all it costs him; and the cost and the forsakenness of suffering is not shirked in the lines which follow:

> The Lady, the All-holy One, sat on her own.
> A shout came out of the sky from an Archangel's mouth,
> 'My Lady, the time for your prayers has come to an end,
> The time for your prostrations too.
> They've taken your Son and sent him to the blacksmith,

[28] Alexiou, *Ritual Lament*, pp. 69–76, describes the wide range of variant themes in this ballad tradition. The version cited here was taken from Ambeli.

[29] Especially in the Matins of Holy Thursday, focused on the last supper—see e.g. Canticle One of the Canon: 'Instructing His friends in the Mysteries, the true Wisdom of God prepares a table that gives food to the soul, and He mingles for the faithful the cup of wine eternal', and Canticle Three: 'Filling thy cup of salvation with joy, O loving Lord, Thou hast made Thy disciples drink from it. For Thou offerest Thyself in sacrifice, crying: 'Drink My blood, and you shall be firmly established in the faith', *Lenten Triodion*, p. 549.

Like a thief they've taken him, like a murderer,
And in the court of Pilate they torment him.'

The nails placed by the blacksmith are described, and the Mother of God is depicted as falling into a frenzy of grief, and after she is revived she goes to find her son, but he is not able to comfort her: 'What can I say to you, little mother, since things are thus and not otherwise?' Just as in village grief, no superficial consolation is offered.

With this ballad, then, and with the liturgical materials which precede it, a deep and complex link is suggested between Christ's acceptance of self-sacrifice and the communion of all in him and with him. The poem alludes to the sacramental meaning of this link, but not to its meaning in communal life; and yet experience of village life suggests a number of communal resonances. First, in spite of all the competitiveness of day-to-day relations within the village, any situation of critical harm or threat to one villager tends to bring about an immediate unity of all. The wake was described earlier as an event to which, except in the most unusual circumstances, everyone will come, and the funeral also, and all will give their forgiveness with the eating of the memorial food. Similarly, 'everyone', it is said, will 'run, with methylated spirits, with water' when a villager collapses in the heat, or when accident or injury occurs to man or animal in the forests or mountains. It is acknowledgement of hardship and danger which forces this abandonment of individual grievances for the sake of a common cause, summarized in the comment quoted earlier: 'What can we do but help one another since we live in such a harsh place?' In these circumstances a common spirit is evoked by the suffering of one which acts as a force for self-giving among the rest.

And it is not only crisis which brings people to a communion or solidarity of one with all, for it can occur on any occasion in which people meet not in the arena of neighbourly grievances but in the context of mutual understanding of the hard terms of life. Thus when two women, previously unknown or only distantly known to each other, fall to talking, they will almost immediately be joined in an extraordinary intimacy by their knowledge of a common experience of living, common griefs and joys, so that the talk is incessant and interspersed with agreeing and compassionate comments

—'don't we know that?' (*δὲν ξέρεις*), 'that's how God has made us' (*ἔτσι μας ἔφτιαξε ὁ Θεός*), 'what else?' (*τί δά*).

It is, then, in a vivid response to another's suffering that a solidarity or communion can arise spontaneously in village life. There are on the whole no professionals to turn to, for even the priest is a villager, and in these contexts what is evoked is not just the mutual self-giving of family members enclosed within one house, but the mutual self-giving of members of a far wider community to those with whom they recognize a common bond of experience or, at its widest, a common humanity.

There are thus times when individual suffering evokes a solidarity among all, and when a tragic and yet positive acceptance of one's own suffering can be envisaged which is different from the outcry of the village laments against fate. It is this side of village life which resonates with Christ's acceptance of his own suffering 'for us', and with the solidarity which this evokes. In this way, because the cup that Christ drinks becomes the mysterious supper of all, and because the unalterable experience of evil and death which at some point overtakes all is seen to be shared by the 'Giver of Life' himself, 'what is written' can be worked out, by man as well as by God, not as fate but as a sacred destiny, and a way to human communion and communion with God. The whole conception of 'what is written', and of the fate which is the share of evil that each undergoes without any apparent reason for deserving it, is thus encountered and transformed in a similar way in the story of Christ as it is told both in Orthodox liturgy and in folk poetry.

The offices of Holy Thursday and Holy Friday, then, and the folk practices which accompany them, following through the mystery of the Giver of Life suffering and dying at the hands of his own creation, mark the transposition from the idea of an Almighty God who rules imperiously from the heavens and allocates suffering to others, to the Almighty God who voluntarily suffers both for and with his people in order to restore them to communion with him. The understanding of the people, weeping over the *Epitáphios*, singing their lament and guarding the body between death and burial, is part and parcel with the understandings in the liturgical tradition, and it is striking that the village mourning endearment '*Christoutzikós mou*', 'my little Christ', like those used to a child in ordinary speech, is paralleled in the liturgical context by the words put in the mouth of the Mother of God: 'O my sweet springtime, O my sweetest Child.'[30]

The third characteristic of the fallen order which Holy Week confronts is death—the categorically violent death of village symbolism which in the end makes of life with all its joys and griefs a mere 'deluding world'. Intimations of the victory of Christ over death recur again and again in the Holy Week services, but the pattern that emerges may to western eyes not be immediately apparent. For example, Holy Week is inaugurated in village practice by the raising of Lazarus, and this story is passed down from year to year by the children who on the eve of 'Lazarus Saturday' go round the houses with a little effigy of Lazarus dressed in white which they jog up and down, while they sing his story:

> Today Christ arrives, God from the heavens,
> From the town of Bethany, with branches, with bay leaves.
> Please may we show you and let you learn
> What is happening today in Palestine where Mary and Martha are weeping.
> They are weeping and lamenting the death, weeping and lamenting
> The death of Lazarus their sweet brother, close to their hearts.

The story then follows the account in John's Gospel,[31] but makes Mary rather than Martha meet Christ, and she expresses her faith in the resurrection in a simplified form which omits Martha's reference to the resurrection at the last day.[32]

> 'Had you been here, my Christ, my brother would not have died,
> But even now I do believe, and well indeed I know it,
> That you are able if you wish to raise even the dead.'

When he hears this Christ weeps, and 'puts fear' into Hades: 'Hades, Tartarus and Charos, I will take Lazarus!', and the story then adds that Lazarus, when he emerges from the kingdom of death, is asked, 'What did you see?', and replies in the words everyone knows: 'I saw

[30] *Lenten Triodion*, Holy Saturday Matins, p. 641.

[31] John 11 : 1–44.

[32] John 11 : 24: 'Martha saith unto him, I know that he shall rise again in the resurrection at the last day.'

trembling, I saw fear, I saw torments and pain.' The song ends with the household being wished good health and joy until the children come again to sing the following year, after which they are rewarded with eggs (to be dyed red for the resurrection) and move on to the next house. This theme appears again at vespers in the evening and at the liturgy next morning, when the hymn or *tropárion* of the feast is sung, adding the Church's interpretation: 'Giving us before Thy Passion an assurance of the general resurrection, Thou hast raised Lazarus from the dead, O Christ our God.'[33] The raising of Lazarus as an intimation of the resurrection of all, and a foretaste of Christ's power to deliver people from death, is thus the first statement of Holy Week.

Nevertheless, although this is how both village and Church begin the week, the villagers see Christ in Holy Week less as the one who raises the dead in the day of judgement at some time in the future, than as the hero who himself defeats death on our behalf in the hour of his resurrection. This may be in part because the icon of the resurrection shows Christ bursting the locks of Hades and in the same moment, with one sweeping movement, pulling Adam and Eve from their tombs. This dual statement implies a synchronicity which is another sign of the Orthodox view of time, and the icon of the resurrection has achieved a dominance in the Orthodox tradition which has made icons and frescoes of a separate last judgment, though they exist, more marginal. But in any case, in the Orthodox liturgical understanding, the end of time exists already in eternity—the 'today' where time has ceased to exist—and in spite of the people's knowledge of the idea of the Second Coming, the thought that their own village dead might rise in this world in the same way as Christ tends to be answered by a statement of simple disbelief, or a disclaimer of the order, 'Are we all gods?' Rather, the village emphasis is on a dispensation which, out of the darkness of Hades, brings all the dead back into contact with God, each in their own 'place' in the other world, and brings the Mother of God and the saints into eternal life and active help and intercession for both this and the other world. It is this dispensation which is the fruit of the resurrection, accomplished through Christ as the one who suffered every indignity and then broke down the doors of death.

[33] *Lenten Triodion*, p. 492.

The village Easter thus emerges as a constantly recapitulated overturning of the concept of Hades or Sheol as the receptacle of shadowy souls—an overturning which began in the last centuries before Christ with new notions of resurrection and the immortality of the soul, but was given a decisive impulse by the spread of Christianity.[34] Enfolded in this event is all that will spring from it—the raising of Adam and Eve and of all mankind, the judgement of each person, and life in the eternal world, as things already present beyond time. Nor is this a peculiarly village view. A recent summary of Orthodox eschatology[35] points among other things to a strong emphasis on the eucharist as already beyond time, in a space in which 'the boundaries between life and death have been broken down'; on the dead in general not being asleep but passing through a range of experiences; on the Mother of God (and perhaps the saints) having already 'passed over into life';[36] and on the resurrected body being different from human bodies as we know them. Even the distinction between the particular judgement (of each individual after death) and the final judgement is 'an issue on which the Fathers of the Church do not speak with a single voice'.

Village belief, though it relies on symbols and images more than dogma, seems to reflect these emphases in ways which have already been described. Crucially, when exhumation is the rule, the dead are only under the earth until the sinful flesh dissolves and forgiveness is complete, and then the bones must come up 'into the air'—an action which is itself its own pre-eminent justification, but whose origins, in the minds of some, lie deeper, 'because', as they say, 'Christ rose again'; and thereafter the dead find their 'place' 'elsewhere', in the 'other world', unknowable to those in this world, though imaged, in that liminal period of forty days after the Easter Vigil, in the story of how at this time the village dead walk this earth again, and can be seen in their costumes returning to their 'place' by those who look down into the wells on the eve of the fortieth day.[37] Otherwise, though, it is Christ, the Mother of God and the

[34] For a summary of the evidence see e.g. W. T. Pitard and S. A. White, Afterlife and Immortality, in *The Oxford Companion to the Bible*.

[35] Andrew Louth, Eschatology: An Orthodox View, in *The Oxford Handbook of Eschatology* (Oxford: Oxford University Press, 2007).

[36] Cf. John 5 : 24.

[37] See pp. 271.

saints who are the real link with them, bringing mercy to all, especially those who on their journey through the other world can be lured into a generous or repentant act; and this link is additionally expressed in the idea that a candle lit for the dead is a comfort to them and appears before them.[38] Christ and the saints likewise encounter, in ways which are concrete and yet mysterious, those who remain in this world: the saint comes to the village when his bones come to it, but also he is present simply when he is thought of in prayer; St David's skull lies enclosed in its casket while at the same time he protects his monastery and meets the young Iakovos at the gate, and a saint like St Spyridon can 'wear out his shoes' helping people even while his uncorrupt body lies in its glass case.[39] Here, space is transcended as well as time; and this is why it is possible for saints to give help to people through their lives, and why the resurrection of Christ celebrated at the Easter Vigil can be simultaneous with the raising of the dead and the judgment of all in the 'today' of the eternal world.[40]

From the end of vespers on Holy Friday in the afternoon and throughout the last service on Friday evening this changed dispensation begins to be anticipated. Both liturgical texts and the folk lament reveal that something new is happening in the darkness of death, and it is an indication of this changed nature of death that this service, known formally as the 'Lament at the Tomb' (*Ὁ Ἐπιτάφιος Θρῆνος*), is also known more familiarly as 'The Praises' (*Τὰ Ἐγκώμια*).

[38] See p. 271. [39] See pp. 312, 319.

[40] This may help to explain a difficulty encountered in previous studies of Greek views of death. Danforth, *The Death Rituals*, pp. 67–9, and Alexiou, *Ritual Lament*, pp. 71–2) both contrast Greek village belief about the resurrection with an aspect of what they take to be the theologically 'correct' account, that all humanity will be resurrected bodily in a distant future at the Last Judgment. As a result they interpret village scepticism or amnesia when presented with this account as evidence either of an ultimate rejection of Christian belief about the resurrection (Danforth), or as the reassertion of pre-Christian beliefs (Alexiou). But in a culture where exhumation is the rule, the emphasis is thrown more powerfully than otherwise on the life of the soul, and in the case of the saints on those mysterious correspondences between the life of the soul and the body of the saint which indicate the presence of a world beyond space and time. So, too, the resurrection of Christ, the raising of Adam and Eve and the whole company of the dead, and the progressive judgement of the individual can all happen synchronically, or without a strong insistence on a temporal order.

The Praises are divided into three long sections, sung in separate verses and intercalated into verses from Psalm 118 (119 in western numbering). For the most part these verses are the voice of the people and they begin with the cosmic despair which has already been confronted in the earlier laments: 'Thou who art the Life wast laid in a tomb, O Christ.' However, the figure of the Mother of God enters from time to time, either in a single verse or occasionally in a series of verses broken only by the verses of the psalm, and she speaks not only with the voice of a mother grieving for her only son but also almost as the voice of the cosmos:

> Tears of lamentation the pure Virgin shed over Thee, Jesus, and with a mother's grief she cried: 'How shall I bury Thee, my Son?'[41]

> 'Woe is me, Light of the world! Woe is me, my Light! Jesus my heart's desire!' cried the Virgin in bitter grief.[42]

> 'Who will give me water and springs of tears,' cried the Virgin Bride of God, 'that I may weep for my sweet Jesus?
> 'O hills and valleys, the multitude of men, and all creation, weep and lament with me, the Mother of our God.
> 'When shall I see Thee, Saviour, Light eternal, the joy and gladness of my heart?' cried the Virgin in her bitter grief.[43]

Yet in between, the Praises are couched in paradoxes which suggest that not withstanding the dereliction of the moment in the visible world, the absent Giver of Life has, all unseen, shifted the centre of his activity to the darkness of death itself:

> O Life, how canst thou die? How canst Thou dwell in a tomb? Yet dost Thou destroy death's kingdom and raise the dead from hell.
> Thou who art the Life wast laid in a tomb, O Christ: by Thy death Thou hast destroyed death and become a fountain of life for the world.[44]

The Praises are thus a turning point at which a changed perception of death begins to be emphasized, and though they again resemble in form the *moirológia,* their contrast with them is also sharp.

[41] *Lenten Triodion*, p. 626.
[42] Ibid. p. 630.
[43] Ibid. p. 631.
[44] Ibid. p. 623.

The *moirológia,* driven by unrelieved grief at the ending of a life and the devastation of a house, despite a consolatory aspect which derives from the archetypal quality of their poetic symbols, reveal chiefly the tragedy of death; but the Lament at the Tomb combines the depth of grief due to the dead God with the intimation that this is a death that destroys death as we know it, that it is not only an end but a beginning.

In this way the perception of death is changed through the entry of God into the world of the dead, and it becomes possible for death no longer to be experienced as violence, but as a way to be set free from the sins of Adam, so that the mourners can sing:

> I venerate Thy Passion, I sing the praises of Thy burial,
> and I magnify Thy power, O loving Lord:
> through them I am set free from corrupting passions.[45]

This service marks a definitive turning point from the old understanding of death to the new: the Christ who suffers for and with his people turns his death into man's freedom from the passions, and the *moirológi*a, the lay laments, into the 'Praises'.

At the close of the service the bier is lifted up[46] and, headed by a man or boy carrying the large cross from the centre of the nave and by a deacon or member of the laity with the incense, and followed by the priest with the book of the Gospels, it is taken out into the village with the entire congregation following, carrying lighted candles. Throughout this procession the priest continuously chants the verse 'Holy God, Holy and Strong, Holy and Immortal, have mercy on us', as at every funeral when the body is being carried from the church to the graveyard. Small tins of burning incense will have been placed in the roads by those old women who have not been able to stand through the service, and over these the bier is taken as it is carried through the village in a right-handed circle until it returns to the church, and again, as with any ordinary village funeral, the

[45] *Lenten Triodion*, p. 628.

[46] In the rubrics this is the *Epitáphios* alone, held by the clergy over the head of the celebrant, and carried in procession right-handed round the outside of the church (*Lenten Triodion*, p. 653), but in the villages the procession is carried out with the flower-decked bier in which the *Epitáphios* lies, and winds right-handed through the village paths.

mourners walking behind the bier must not look back 'because Charos comes from there'. On arrival back at the church the bearers of the bier hold it up inside the doorway so that everyone stoops to pass under it as they come back in—a symbolic action not in the church rubrics but which has grown up spontaneously, unexplained, and is undertaken simply with a sense that it is propitious. When all the congregation have come back into the church and the bier is placed again in the centre of the nave, the icon of the *Epitáphios* is lifted from the bier by the priest, carried through the Royal Doors into the sanctuary, and after being taken in procession once round the Holy Table, is then laid on the Table itself.

The right-handed circle, already associated with an auspicious journey in marriage and death, thus reappears on Holy Friday as Christ goes from his crucifixion to his laying out and from his laying out to his burial. Into this movement the faithful also are drawn as they follow the bier around the village, and their re-entry into the church by stooping under the bier is a further rite of passage by which the people symbolically share in the death of Christ.[47] Further, the funeral incense which accompanies the procession of the bier around the village points to the myrrh which, being 'fitting for the dead',[48] was brought by the women who laid out Christ's body—myrrh which has in the Church ever after typified these women as the 'myrrh-bearing women'. The congregation, following the bier as it is carried round the village and over the tins of incense, and bowing beneath the bier on their entry back into the church, are thus collectively identified with the role of the myrrh-bearers and the mourners who sang the lament at Christ's burial and became the first witnesses to the transformation of death which followed.

At the conclusion of the Lamentations, the customary fast of Holy Friday is ended and the people go to their homes to eat their sombre meal of bracken fronds and vinegar. Holy Saturday is a day of quiet expectation which begins with the celebration of the vesperal Liturgy of St Basil, after which the men slaughter the lambs for the Easter meal and the women wash out the entrails for the

[47] For the spiritual concept of sharing in Christ's death and its link with the right-handed dance movement see pp. 411–5.

[48] Third *troparion* of the Myrrh-Bearing Women, cf. *Pentecostarion*, p. 109 (but alternative translation used here).

mageirítsa (*μαγειρίτσα*), the spicy soup that ends the fast in the small hours of Sunday morning. An hour before midnight the night office is sung quietly, and just before midnight the church is darkened, except for a single oil lamp on the altar.

The Easter Vigil begins with the priest, now robed in white vestments, lighting a candle at this oil lamp, and emerging from the sanctuary with the lighted candle, proclaiming:

> Come and receive the light from the light without evening,
> And glorify Christ, who is risen from the dead.[49]

Everyone now comes up to light their paschal candles from the flame of the priest's candle and pass it on to each other, after which a great candle-lit procession moves out of the church to the singing of words which again describe this service as an echo of the liturgy of the angelic hosts in heaven:[50]

> Thy resurrection, Christ our Saviour,
> The angels sing in heaven;
> Grant also now that we on earth
> With pure hearts may glorify Thee.

The resurrection Gospel is then intoned to the whole village in the open air, followed by the Easter proclamation, three times repeated:

> Christ is risen from the dead,
> Trampling down death by death,
> And to those in the tombs He has given life.[51]

Easter verses, punctuated by this ubiquitous refrain, then follow, while time after time the priest shouts: 'Christ is risen!', and to each proclamation the people raise their candles and shout their answer: 'He is risen indeed!' All the while the church bells are ringing, and finally the priest turns to lead the people back into the

[49] Translated from Orthros, Kyriaki tou Pascha in *Μεγάλη Ἑβδομάς* [*Holy Week*] (Athens: Ἀστήρ - Παπαδημητρίου, n.d.), p. 419.

[50] Cf. pp. 129–30 above, where a text from the Liturgy sees what is happening as an extension of the liturgy of the angels.

[51] From this point the service can be followed in English in *The Pentecostarion*, but unpublished Church translations which are less ornate are used. Here cf. *The Pentecostarion*, p. 27.

church, now bright with lights. At this point another spontaneous village interruption may play out the harrowing of hell in a graphic enactment: the priest's entry into the church is resisted by a villager waiting behind the door as the guardian of the gates of hell, holding it shut and challenging his right to come in. A voice from behind the door, somewhat tremulous with suppressed laughter, three times asks, 'Who are you? I don't know you!', to be answered the third time by the priest giving the door a great kick, 'Na! This is who I am!' Then is sung the rest of Easter Matins followed by the Liturgy of the Resurrection, which finishes at three or four in the morning.

Just as the service of the Twelve Gospels and the vespers of Holy Friday are marked by the paradox that in some sense God can die and the visible cosmos be bereft, and just as the Praises are marked by the other half of the paradox, that the Giver of Life cannot cease to pour out life, and therefore even while hidden in the other world brings life to the dead, so in the same way the Resurrection Vigil gains its extraordinary tension by reuniting the world of death with the world of life, so that the creator's life-giving energy bursts through the whole cosmos. This image is re-presented again and again in the liturgical offices of Easter—in the *kontákion* of Easter, for example:

> Though Thou didst descend into the grave, O Immortal One,
> Yet didst Thou destroy the power of Hades,
> And didst arise as victor, O Christ, God,
> Calling to the myrrh-bearing women 'Rejoice!',
> And giving peace to Thine apostles,
> O Thou who dost grant resurrection to the fallen.[52]

Again the same theme recurs in the *tropárion* of Holy Saturday Matins:

> Going down to death, O Life immortal,
> Thou hast slain hell with the dazzling light of Thy divinity,
> And when Thou hadst raised up the dead from their dwelling place beneath the earth,
> All the powers of heaven cried aloud:
> 'Giver of Life, O Christ our God, glory to thee.'[53]

[52] Cf. *The Pentecostarion*, p. 31.

[53] *Lenten Triodion*, p. 622.

The Homily of St John Chrysostom, read by the priest at the conclusion of Easter Matins, expresses this movement of God entering the other world of death, and then reuniting both worlds in a new synthesis of life, as God's most unexpected and masterly coup. Hades, like humankind, recognizes Christ's mortal body, and assumes that it cannot be linked with an immortal nature, picking up a theme which has already been expressed in the vesperal Liturgy of St Basil in the morning of this day:

> My power has been destroyed. I accepted a mortal man as one of the dead; yet I cannot keep him prisoner, and with Him I shall lose all those over whom I ruled. I held in my power the dead from all the ages; but see, He is raising them all.[54]

In the crucifixion and the resurrection then, Christ provides the archetype for snatching victory from the jaws of defeat, turning his crucifixion into a Trojan horse by which he breaches the ramparts of the kingdom of death and frees all its prisoners. The Christ of the folk imagination, ever able to make a fool of the devil, exactly images this reality, and thus the folk tales, however colloquial or comic they may be, are deeply theological, with an irony which has its initial impulse in the theology of the resurrection.

In this theology hell is portrayed as for an instant gloating over getting another dead body into its realm, only to find, as the icon of the resurrection portrays, this body radiant with life, the locks bursting off the gates, and imprisoned souls being hauled out to freedom. And just as in the folk tales the triumph of good comes at the moment at which evil seems most powerful and the devil's hand outstretched, so the homily depicts the central theme in the same terms and death turns out to be its own worst enemy. The words 'He has despoiled Hades, who descended into Hades' are the cue for a well-known passage declaring the chagrin of Hades in the words, 'Hell was embittered', many times repeated, and each time this is read out by the priest, an answering shout of 'It was embittered!' goes up from the congregation, while at the same time, in a gesture antithetical to the raising of the candles as they shout 'Christ is risen!', everyone lowers the hand holding their candle, gesturing as it were towards Hades:

[54] *Lenten Triodion*, Stichera, p. 656.

Hell was embittered ('It was embittered!') when it met Thee below face to face. It was embittered ('It was embittered!') because it was set at nought. It was embittered ('It was embittered!') for it was mocked. It was embittered ('It was embittered!') for it was slain. It was embittered ('It was embittered!') for it was cast down. It was embittered ('It was embittered!') for it was fettered. It received a body and it encountered God. It received earth, and came face to face with Heaven. It received what is seen, and fell because of what is unseen. O death, where is thy sting? O Hell, where is thy victory? Christ is risen and thou art cast down. Christ has risen and the demons have fallen. Christ is risen and the angels rejoice. Christ is risen and life is made free. Christ is risen and there is none dead in the tomb. For Christ is raised from the dead and is become the first fruits of them that slept. To Him be glory and dominion from all ages to all ages.[55]

Here too, then, priest and people take part in an energetic dialogue which punctuates with shouts of triumph the services of Easter night.

With the reunion of the worlds of the living and the dead in Christ therefore, the liturgy has re-entered the dimension which is 'from all ages to all ages'—the world beyond time. These last words from the homily near the end of Easter Matins echo the opening call to receive the 'light without evening'. And in this world not only is death overcome, but also the distorted and fallen world ruled by sin and fate.

The meaning of the resurrection for the sinful and the fated is sketched in the first part of the Homily of St John Chrysostom, and is based on the parable of Jesus about the workers hired for a vineyard at the first, third, sixth, ninth, and eleventh hour of the day, who all received the same reward.[56] The homily applies the parable to the Easter feast, which also represents the feast beyond time in the restored cosmos of the resurrection, and is presented as being offered by Christ to all without distinction, disregarding merit, and having regard to the intention as well as the act. To disregard merit is also to disregard sin, and to regard the intention is to take account of hard circumstances which prevent its enactment; thus both the sinful and the fated are included in the scope of this first part of the homily:

If any be devout and a lover of God, let him partake of this fair and radiant festival. If any be a faithful servant, let him come in rejoicing in the joy

[55] Cf. *The Pentecostarion*, p. 37. [56] Matthew 20 :1–16.

of his Lord. If any have wearied himself with fasting, let him now enjoy his reward. If any laboured from the first hour, let him today receive his rightful due. If any have come at the third hour, let him feast with thankfulness. If any have arrived at the sixth, let him in no wise be in doubt, for in nothing shall he suffer loss. If any be as late as the ninth, let him draw near, let him in no way hesitate. If any arrive only at the eleventh hour, let him not be fearful on account of his slowness. For the Master is bountiful and receives the last even as the first. He gives rest to him of the eleventh hour even as to him who has laboured from the first. He is merciful to the last and provides for the first. To one he gives, and to another he shows kindness. He receives the works and welcomes the intention. He honours the act and commends the purpose. Enter ye all therefore into the joy of our Lord, and let both the first and those who came after partake of the reward.[57]

This emphatic statement of generosity to the undeserving and recompense to the unfortunate is accompanied by the concrete image of the food which has been prepared in all the houses as a pouring out of the gift of life by the risen Christ: 'The table is fully laden: do ye all fare sumptuously. The feast is ample: let none go forth hungry.' This feast is thus the feast of life in the eternal world: a gift beyond reward and punishment and beyond good and bad fortune, superseding the rigours of the law, the writings of fate, and the reign of death. Just as the fast expresses in every house the penitential nature of the sacred time, so the Easter feast with the tables laden with bowls of thick sheep's yogurt, red dyed hard-boiled eggs, hunks of bread, slabs of salty cheese, and bowls of spicy *mageirítsa*, is a natural language within the house for the kingdom of Christ inaugurated in the Church. The room, filled with lamp-lit faces in the unaccustomed pre-dawn hour, continues the spreading of the light from the sanctuary, and the shouts in the church of 'Christ is risen!' resonate into the following days when the greeting 'Christ is risen!' replaces the customary 'Good day'.[58] In this way the risen Christ becomes for a period part of the currency of daily greetings, and re-

[57] Cf. *The Pentecostarion*, pp. 36–7.

[58] In monastic rubrics (*Pentecostarion*, p. 40) this greeting continues until the forty days culminates in the Ascension, but in village practice it is thought to lapse on the third day after Easter.

mains at all times the basis not only for the familiar phrase 'Christ conquers' but also for the ever-present sign of the cross in village life, and for all the various folk tales in which Christ's superiority to the devil is invoked, for it is Christ's victory over death that establishes his definitive supremacy over the powers of evil.

The celebration of life over death in Holy Week is thus an event which occurs on all levels of the human person, as release from sin and punishment, as recompense for unmerited suffering, and as participation with Christ in his eternal life. In this view of things, the struggle for life in this world is not resolved, but it is filled with an undying hope.

At any one moment, then, the world of the fall and the redeemed world of Christ are locked in struggle in village consciousness, and the frontier between these two ways of looking at the world shifts backward and forward according to the character of the thinker and the context. The logic of just but merciless punishment, the unappealable fate of random sufferings, and death in this 'deluding world', can seem ineluctable at times; yet the hand of Christ continues to be stretched out in folk tale and liturgy, paying the cost of sin and giving the hope of mercy, accepting and overcoming innocent suffering, and trampling down death by death. In the village culture the liturgical tradition finds an authentic voice, and it is this that keeps alive in the people an understanding of their faith so vital that they can absorb the essence of the liturgical offices even while they are not able to understand word for word what is being said. It is the interplay between these two forces, ecclesiastical teaching and village culture, which is the great strength of village life, for the teaching kept intact by the Church and released into anecdote, folk tale, legend, and village custom and practice is transmitted into every area of life and work, feeding into talk and jokes, dreams and visions, prohibitions and prescriptions, and allowing the people to keep company with Christ, the saints, and the Mother of God, and to see in rock and stream and mountain the powers of the unseen world. The incarnate God of the Gospels becomes a figure so known to them that at times they are not only 'servants of God', but also his friends, mourners, and parents, and they know him not only as the Great Almighty who reigns over all and disposes as he wills, but also as the Giver of Life who, as mortal, died and entered hell, and, as

God, broke its power and set them free. So although on the one side the people face with unflinching realism the awful power of the violence of death, they live also in the light of the resurrection and of the God who turned death against itself and emptied its halls. It is a personal encounter with this aspect of their tradition which is being lived at Easter, and it can find expression in the simplest of village words: 'Christ rose from the dead and that is our joy.'

12
THE DANCE OF LIFE

TWO questions were posed in the introduction to this book: first, what symbols are central to the life of the Greek village described here—mainly a subsistence village—and second, how far do these symbols have links with the Orthodox liturgy?

The first question is of interest to anyone who wants to know about the experience of living in a face-to-face society in direct encounter with the natural world. It is a question which captured my imagination from the beginning of my experience of the Greek villages in the 1960s, before I knew anything about the Orthodox liturgy; and my initial answers to it, published in the 1980s, emerged from my fieldwork alone.

The second question, though, is one which thrust itself on my mind increasingly when in the 1990s I became familiar with the Orthodox liturgy in English. This question is of interest to the whole story of the cultures formed by Christian peoples—in this case the peoples of the Eastern Roman Empire, centred on its capital in Constantinople which, for over eleven hundred years until its fall in 1453 to the Ottomans, was the principal Christian influence east of a variable line from the Adriatic to the Baltic. In these cultures, in the centuries following, one of the most constant and unchanging elements has been the Orthodox liturgy, and though my knowledge of it has not substantially changed my initial conclusions from Ambeli, it has revealed much about the historical depth and complexity of what I experienced there.

This question about the role of Orthodox Christianity in forming the cultures of eastern Europe is one on which the literature about Greece in general has cast only a variable and tangential light. The interest of many writers was at first on the ancient world of classical Greece, and what might still be thought to remain of it in daily life. Then an effort was made to move on from this to understand the situation of the modern Greek state and the difficulties it inherited from its struggle with the Ottoman Empire. As a result of these two concerns, a good deal of previous writing about twentieth-century Greece has implied, perhaps unintentionally, that the influence of Orthodoxy has been quite marginal, even in subsistence villages. It has been argued that, even apart from the secularizing influence of western thought (now increasingly important), the culture of pre-Christian classical Greece lived on, especially in the villages before the 1970s; or again that the Ottoman period has left behind a general cynicism about public institutions, including the Church, which is expressed in sceptical attitudes that have become habitual. Certainly areas of cynicism about the Church have been pointed out in the preceding chapters, as well as some pre-Christian cultural elements. In addition, there are practices which are opposed by the Church as superstitious or magical, even if they are not often securely attributable to any specific pre-Christian or post-Ottoman origin; and these practices are discussed a few pages further on.

However, in looking afresh at the question of pre-Christian survivals and post-Ottoman cynicism, one of the strongest features which has emerged from this portrayal of village life is that what may strike a western reader as antique or sceptical aspects of its religious imagination are things which are often present in the Orthodox liturgy itself, as well as in the contradictions of a village symbolism which is lived out rather than being forced into a logical framework. For the liturgy, and the local symbolism with which it has been in dialogue, often express a reiterated movement from ancient imagery or disillusioned realism to the Christian world view. This is not syncretism, for syncretism is the indiscriminate fusion of logically incoherent elements from different religious sources. Here, on the contrary, images which come spontaneously to the people's minds from tragic or sceptical sources are expressed and located as part of the fallen view of the world, and set beside related images of ways back into the unfallen condition. In this way the meaning of the image changes because the context has been transformed—despair is set in the context of hope, guilt in the context of forgiveness, tragedy in the context of re-birth.

For example, the ancient view of earth as indifferently both nourisher and destroyer is expressed and then re-ordered to portray the earth as a partial reflection in the material world of the Mother of God. As she gives birth to the body of Christ, so the earth gives birth to its counterpart, the bread of the household and of the eucharist; and as she intercedes at death for the forgiveness of the dead person's sins, so the earth purges away the flesh which produced them.[1] Again, the ancient image of water, typified in the nereids who combine qualities 'sometimes good, sometimes bad', is given new and coherent meanings as Christ enters it and returns it to its primal goodness at his baptism.[2] Fear of desecration of the dead, and of a vengeance for it which now is clothed in more recent Slavic vampire imagery, is laid to rest by the accumulated symbols of a Christian death.[3] The ancient view of death as a half life under the earth is met and moved on by the juxtaposition with it of Christian images at the wake, by funeral imagery of the life of the soul, and by bringing the bones up into the light and air as a first sign of the resurrection.[4] And the ancient view of a God who punishes sin, hands out random sufferings fated from birth, and ends every illusion with death, is expressed, transformed, and resolved in the liturgy of Holy Week and Easter.[5]

In this way the Orthodox liturgy, and village symbolism with it, have over time absorbed dissonant experiences of doubt, despair, and loss, not least because both have taken and reshaped much of the symbolic language of the ancient world, both Jewish and Greek, in which these experiences were already embedded; and in identifying many of them with the world of the fall they have contrasted them with a corresponding divine world, charting paths from the one to the other. Some of these paths are systematic: they are part of a steady, transforming, integrating movement which informs the ritual patterns of the yearly cycle. In other cases however, where a shock throws those concerned back into the world of the fall, and liturgy and village symbolism mark a pattern of recovery and reinstatement in the divine world, the movement is typically back and forth between these poles of experience. Such cases are connected especially with death or bereavement, or sufferings of a similar order, and are dictated to a considerable extent by where people are in this cycle of shock and reconciliation.

It is in fact death that provides one of the clearest examples of how village symbolism and the Orthodox liturgy can express the view from the world of the fall and the view from the divine world

[1] pp. 66–9, 73–6.
[2] pp. 93–8.
[3] pp. 258–64.
[4] pp. 266–8, 299–301.
[5] pp. 338–82.

at the same time, or in close juxtaposition. Village laments at the wake about the black earth which covers the face of the dead are followed by verses chanted before and during the last kiss in the church which make the same uncompromising statement. The singers at the funeral speak on behalf of the dead and of all those present with the voice of Adam returned to the earth from which he was taken. But at the same time, Church and people continually reaffirm forgiveness for the dead, and the *sávano* with which the dead is clothed betokens the start of his journey to become, in the words of the service, 'once more a citizen of Paradise'.[6] And while village symbolism draws seamlessly on tragic, sceptical pre-Christian Greek imagery as well as on Christian expressions of faith and hope, the Church's language draws on equally tragic and sceptical pre-Christian Jewish imagery alongside its Christian poetry. These parallel juxtapositions are indeed inevitable throughout Orthodox liturgy, because the Orthodox daily offices are founded on the weekly recital of the whole cycle of the ancient Jewish psalms, in which psalms of desolation are juxtaposed in dialogue with psalms of hope and with the poetry of the Christian era. A succinct example relevant to the theme of death is the recital of a series of six psalms in the early part of daily matins, in which Psalm 88 (LXX 87), expressing the ancient image of death as the pit into which all go down into silence, is among three similar psalms which are answered by others, like Psalm 103 (LXX 102), which express confidence in the eternal mercy of God. The parallel with ancient Greek imagery of death is thus apparent, though often with the difference that these psalms of desolation, in their complaint against mortal predicaments, are tinged more deeply with repentance; and in both Jewish and Christian tradition it is repentance that is the chief pathway from the world of the fall to the divine world.

In all these areas, then, the Orthodox liturgy and village symbolism make very similar statements, both of them reflecting the imagery of the fallen world and of the divine world, and, in the case of death, moving between one and the other until a resolution is found. There are, however, a few areas where the relations between ecclesiastical and village thinking are not so harmonious, and where friction between Church and village is reflected in unrepentant village

[6] pp. 237–45, 250–5.

practice of things regarded by the Church as superstitious or magical.

The instances of these practices described here have arisen because they are part of village ideas about the cosmic element of water (used amongst other things in spells and divination), or about the critical balance of water and fire in ripening the harvest, or about the role of fate. Spells, healing, and divination, and attitudes to the elements which might in the past have been given labels like 'animism' or 'sympathetic magic', are topics too obscure and complex for more than a passing comment in this book, and there is much still to learn about them. So the brief summary given here does no more than suggest that in these instances attention to the practical context of what is done may help more in understanding it than the notion that it is part of some unitary body of ideas called 'animism' or 'paganism'.

These frictions between Church and villagers occur in matters great and small, but many certainly arise out of concerns vital in a subsistence economy: health, the success of the harvest, things affecting the marriage or survival of children. In dealing with these anxieties villagers seldom have knowledge or means adequate for influencing events, and turn to a stock of ideas inherited not only from the Church, but also from ancient scientific conjecture, from ancient images of chance and fate, and from the perennial human tendency to use symbolic language and actions to express intuitions or enact hopes. But use of these varied materials in extreme need differs from less serious or even contradictory uses at other times. Symbolic actions, for instance, especially where children are conscripted as actors, as in the *Piperiá*, may do no more than dramatize. Points where villagers actively try to manipulate are not always easy to discern, but even in their repertoire of self-help in health matters, where results are vital to them, they still accept that the outcome is uncertain; they will say for example of a healing spell, 'It will work if the illness is its own thing' (*ἂν εἶναι δικό του*). Again, while they actively hope and believe in the possibility of a cure through such means, the wish of a fellow villager to help someone who is suffering, and to provide company and compassion in distress, may bring part of the relief in itself. Divination, similarly, can be a serious attempt to imagine possible marriages, or possible risks to family members, or to find animals or valuables which are lost, and it is difficult to see how people under the constraints of subsistence living could avoid from time to time trying everything available to improve on such guesses as they have already made; but it can also be undertaken as a sociable activity, for fun and with frank scepticism. Again, while fate is regarded as an irresistible and intimidating force, people are not 'fatalistic', and the notion has a particular value as, in the last resort, freeing them from anxiety and self-recrimination, and providing consolation when things have gone wrong. Correspondingly, the Church objects to the notion that a person's fate is from birth inevitable, and is critical of spells and divinatory practices which it sees as undermining the reliance on prayer and patience before the will of God; however its acceptance as 'tradition' of such things as the ban on boiling cauldrons of water for washing on holy days, which villagers relate not only to the day but to the success of the harvest, witnesses to its tolerance of ideas which may be put into cruder words than liturgical prayer for the harvest, but are accepted as broadly continuous with it.

If frictions arise between the Church and the villagers, therefore, over such perennial bones of contention as divination, cures for illness, and ideas of fate, this perhaps reflects contradictions which can be expected of any cross-section of humanity who have little control over their lives, in this case under the harsh pressures of subsistence living. Such practices mix symbolic actions with rational considerations and conscious trial and error, and there is little basis for regarding them as the product of a pre-Christian magical repertoire, or of general cynicism about Orthodox Christianity. Certainly, cynicism about the institutional failures of the Church, as was noted earlier, is commonplace, but in a village like Ambeli there is little tendency to dismiss Orthodox tradition as a whole, and village defiance in these instances testifies chiefly to a pragmatic, unreflective confidence in the value of self-help, to intractable difficulties which provoke a search for any chance of self-help, or at the other extreme, to a sociable wish to console or entertain.[7]

There are, then, specific areas where Church and villagers disagree, but they are limited, and may reflect the constraints of isolated subsistence living more than any coherent or unitary body of ideas. More generally, the Orthodox inheritance in Greece does not

[7] These last three paragraphs refer chiefly to material discussed on pp. 50–2, 85–9, and 348–51. On cynicism about institutional failures, see p. 309 and n. 7 appended there.

exclude images from pre-Christian cultures or profound expressions of doubt and loss, but rather seeks to articulate them, to distinguish what in all this belongs to the fallen consciousness, and to show how to find the way back from it to the divine world. As a result, the commonalities between Orthodox liturgy and village symbolism on such matters as death have emerged as considerable. The question to be asked, therefore, is how far these commonalities hold good in all the chief aspects of village life. And this question can be answered, first by identifying which symbols are central to the life of the village described here, and then by comparing the liturgical parallels which have been found.

In exploring first the symbolism which serves to order the main course of life in Ambeli, this book has taken as its starting point a village cosmos which at first sight could be taken for a static three-dimensional map of the world—something whose relevance to village life might seem far from clear. But the map has turned out, as pre-Copernican cosmologies often do, to be something more—a plan for a journey towards the good. The nature of the journey becomes evident when the story of the fall from paradise is told: paradise, in village thought, is our origin and (in a different form) our destiny, but the fallen world in which we find ourselves has intervened, and our task is to redeem the consequences of the fall and to keep re-making this world as the garden which it still, in glimpses, is. Thus time is also part of this cosmology, and liturgical time in particular, which, as a 'moving image of eternity', is intended to link the present moment with our origin and destiny in the eternal world.[8] These ideas about the cosmos, paradise and fall, and time, are therefore preconceptions which set the context for the villagers' collective enactment of symbols which tell them where they are and what at each point they must do—symbols which guide the meaning given to work, marriage, hospitality, kinship, community, death, mourning, and their relationship with the natural

[8] The phrase quoted is from Plato's Timaeus (*Timaeus*, p. 50 in Plato, *Timaeus and Critias*, tr. Desmond Lee (London: Penguin, 1971)), but is used here merely as a convenient means to encapsulate the village experience of time, deeply influenced by the liturgical year, as described in Ch. 4. For a later version of this Platonic idea which seems to have influenced the Christian notion of time worked out in the liturgical year see p. 397–8 and n. 9 below.

and the divine worlds. So in order to see the force of these central symbols it is necessary now to retrace, in brief, the nature of the cosmic preconceptions which form their context.

The most important function of the village cosmos is to define the dual world of good and evil where man is placed, and at the same time to identify those aspects of the cosmos which give hope that these all-pervading opposites can be reconciled. This dualism exists within a cosmos which is perceived on three levels: the divine powers in the heavens above the earth, the demons in the caverns below, and the world of nature between the two which is the dwelling-place of man and the meeting ground of God and the devil. In this sacred cosmos, holiness is increasingly present towards the further reaches of the sky, and evil increasingly towards the depths of the earth: God has his habitation at the outer limits of the universe among the sun, moon and stars, whereas Satan, the author of evil, lies down in the centre of the earth. While God is One, however, the Almighty and Creator of All, 'everywhere and at all times' (*παντοῦ καὶ πάντα*) as the people say, his power is also diffused in an infinity of spiritual presences—saints and angels, seraphim and cherubim. Satan also is not confined to a single unique presence but has under his command legions of demons who speed about the world doing his bidding after which, as it is said, they report back to him and are awarded medals for good work.

There is in this way a hierarchy according to which spiritual good and spiritual evil inhabit the highest and the lowest levels of the universe, and these areas again consist of a number of subordinate levels inhabited by ranks of angelic or infernal powers, and also, both above and below, by what is termed 'the other world', that is to say the world of the hallowed or unhallowed dead. The darkness of the earth is the first destination of the newly-dead, where the body, now symbolically dissociated from the blood which is the defining substance of fleshly life, is given over to corruption. By contrast however, the bones of the long dead, cleaned and purified by the earth, are brought up 'into the air' and their souls by the same action freed to go 'elsewhere'.

Nevertheless, while 'under the earth' is a place of darkness associated with the demons and with corruption, it is also associated with the world tree from which springs all life, and the middle ground of the earth itself reflects this composite nature, for it is a place both of beneficence and danger, giving life but also destroying life, nourishing creatures for a while and then devouring them. The earth, in this way receiving material corruption and giving nourishment to all physical life, is both destroyer and creator, and this dual nature allows it to be open to a range of spiritual influences to do with both the divine and the diabolical, open to both life and death.

This dual nature pervades the universe, penetrating not only the earth but also fire, air and water, as well as the attributes of the sun and the moon. The sun as 'lord' of the physical cosmos is giver of both life and death, bringing on the young growth but able also to shrivel it up entirely, and the fire of the sun is the subject of a persistent symbolism which balances the necessity for heat and light with the necessity for tenderness and rain. In addition, the sun holds transitional moments of disequilibrium as the day and the year turn: midday and midnight contain a moment of danger when demonic influence can irrupt into the world, and at the winter and summer solstices the equivocal position of the sun allows the *skalikandzoúria*—the Christmas demons—to invade, and promotes the lighting of the fires of St John to ward off evil. The moon, the feminine power which brings on the sprouting seed and the embryo in the egg, also has its times of strength tempered by periodic moments of change and uncertainty, pivotal moments when evil gains force; and its cycle holds an inauspicious phase as it 'turns back' from the full, and a moment of acute danger when the old moon turns into the new, and uncertainty and loss of equilibrium presents a serious, though split-second, threat. Water has a fluid and transient character which makes it a home either for spiritual evil or for blessing, receptive both to demons and to Christ, potentially a source of destruction but also of renewal. And finally air, characteristically a pure element in so far as it is associated with the heavens, also shares in a similar polarity, for while the heights of the heavens are God's alone, the lower reaches of the air can carry evil influences—demonic 'spirits of the air' which bring sudden malady—and can become sinister in rushing winds that betoken that 'something evil is happening somewhere today'.

This ambiguity in-built in the cosmos lessens as the ascent is made into the further reaches of the sky, for these regions are indisputably the abode of God alone, and here the sun and the moon reign, high in the heavens, sacred and untouchable. Both, however, even in their transcendent aspect, have a range of symbolic attributes which relate them to earthly life. The sun as lord, set in the element of fire and air, finds a primary association with the spirit and with masculine qualities of power, stability, permanence and finality, while the moon presides over the nurturing feminine forces of process, growth, and change, whose seed bed is the earth and water which form the humus sustaining all plant and animal life. These two cosmic forces thus epitomize the essence of masculine and feminine, and these attributes of the sun and the moon are closely related to the symbolism of gender in the human world where the nature of men involves permanence and strength and the nature of women involves change and fertility. The structure of the world and the structure of human relations are part of the same cosmos and both are informed by the same principles and ideas.

The sun and the moon of this universe rise and set on a world which lies at its centre—the place where man is not only the focus of the blessings that flow from the cosmos in which he is placed, but also the focus of the battle waged between God and the devil over possession of the world and of the human souls within it. This middle level between the heights and the depths is thus the place where the ultimate and original battle between God and the devil is fought out, where saints or demons can invest and inhabit any aspect of society and of the natural world, and where the presence of good and evil at every turn is an image of the critical choices permanently confronting every man.

The middle world of man and society thus has a complex spiritual nature, for at the same time as being man's home in the universe it is a place of physical and spiritual danger, highly charged with divine or diabolical influences, a place morally and spiritually ambiguous where the outcome of the battle between the various forces is from moment to moment uncertain. Even though the devil is not autonomous but exists only by permission of God, his existence is real enough as part of the freedom God gives to man to decide whether he will follow the good or the evil path. At either end God or the devil, heaven or hell, are the final outcomes of the battle for each individual soul.

However, this uncertainty built into the cosmos is, ultimately, relative only, for an essential part of its ordering is the absolute dominion of God over all things including the power of evil. And this reality, too, enters the structure of the cosmos in that while the devil cannot enter the heavens, the voice of God is able to penetrate the underworld and summon the *skalikandzoúria* from their work of destruction, and even in his dominion in the centre of the earth the devil is said to lie 'bound'. Again, in the world of men the devil's power is always defeated if Christ is summoned. Thus for all the tension that exists between good and evil, both in the ordering of the cosmos itself and in the battle between God and the devil within it, there is an in-built presumption in favour of the supremacy of the good and the triumph of life over death. The universe, although harbouring demons and devils and containing awesome powers of destruction, is a place also where man can at all times receive blessings, and can find rest.

With man's cooperation, too, the reign of God, already supreme in the upper level, can also be extended over the middle level of the cosmos, presaging the final defeat of the demonic hosts beneath the earth; and this consummation can be realized through the communication which exists between these cosmic levels. Not only do incorporeal beings such as the saints, the angels, and the dead, find passage between them, but also the spirit of man, in prayer and in visionary or prophetic experience. Means of access allowing vision into the other worlds through wells and from mountain tops figure in the symbolism of communication between the worlds, and at certain random moments, and at midnight in particular, the veil separating the middle world from the divine world is especially thin. These channels are built into the cosmos, even if such communication between the visible and the invisible worlds remains for the living incomplete, a question of partial vision, an orientation towards the good, but one which always confronts the uncertainties of living and the mystery of the other world.

This orientation towards the spiritual world is one which pervades daily life, in a number of oppositions which comprise a symbolic language for openness to good or evil—describing things which are up or down, straight or squint, right or left, oriented towards order or chaos. The demons issuing from holes in the ground present man with a realm of seductions, dangers, and temptations; the angelic powers entering the world from on high help to repel of these evils both by direct assistance and by calling man's attention to the divine world in which alone his good is to be found. Man, desperately weak but placed nevertheless in charge of his world as the 'the superior intelligent creature', stands at the centre of the battleground, capable of orienting himself either towards the higher or the lower worlds, providing the link between the natural world and God, or the link between the natural world and the devil. In this way man, a feeble but free being at the centre of the cosmos, caught up in the moral and spiritual drama being played out within it, and with the power to choose between good and evil, is the pivot on whom all things turn.

Man's freedom is, however, compromised by the fall. Central to the cosmos is its original nature as paradise in which Adam and Eve, representing the human race, lived in a communion with God which held all things in harmony. Snakes walked upright, trees bore fruit in abundance, the world gave food without work, stones were bread and there was abundant water. But with the eating of the fruit, that is to say with the wilful separation of human will from the will of God—in village terms the seduction of Eve by the serpent and of Adam by Eve—paradise was lost, and man became an outcast in the creation of which he had been intended to be the head. The natural processes of the earth were set against men, the process of birth against women, relations of power and authority of the stronger over the weaker became part of the natural order. Human rebellion against God thus precipitated the rebellion of the rest of the created world against man, and instead of an easeful and blessed life in a paradise in harmony with itself, toil and sweat in a divided world, pain and suffering, became the hallmark of man's struggle for existence.

This view of things underpins the villagers' life, especially in their work in fields and forest, and, because of the theme of gender in the story of the fall, in sexual relations. It is a view which above all claims realism. For the origin of man's present plight people look no further than God's judgement, 'With toil and with sweat shall you till the fields', for the comment this evokes is unanswerable: 'Do we have things otherwise now?' In relations between the sexes the association with the fall is expressed with still greater disillusion. Women are referred to—and refer to themselves—as 'Eves', imaging their prototype who betrayed her man and initiated the loss of paradise. Thus women are thought by nature to lack responsibility and self-control, showing a tendency to gossip and quarrel, and revealing the consequences of the fall directly in the 'disgrace' of their menstrual periods. The exercise of self-discipline and obedience within a life-long marriage is (with the rare exception of entry into the monastic life) the only answer to this innate weakness in woman's character, and in this marriage she must be in all things subordinate to her husband. Man as 'Adam' is also associated with the fall and his toil in fields and forest that resist him is an image of this. But in contrast to Eve's opportunism and weakness he is felt to retain an element of intelligence and moral strength, and to regain his due place in the order of creation he must exercise the authority which he abandoned in the fall, tilling his fields, providing for his family and children, and keeping control of his wife. It is a scheme of things in which relations between the sexes are unequal, dominated by men's use of physical and economic power; and while this can be for the protection of women it is also easily misused, leading to a society in which young brides can be systematically overworked and neglected, and wives must accept without question their husbands' sexual demands, and may have to absorb as a matter of course the irritation and blows of a husband who happens to be drunk, anxious, or displeased.

These power relations between men and women do not occur in isolation, for they are part of an entire world view of which sin against God is the basis, so alongside the struggle between man and nature and that between the sexes runs also the struggle against neighbours for limited resources, the battle against death, and a view of sacred relations in which the Almighty Power rules by a dictate whose logic, known only to himself, is inspired not only by justice but also by whim.

Within the house, aside from the possibility of initial tensions between in-laws, mutual trust and support is expected and in the main achieved, and it is the house which defines the sacred centre around which all revolves. Thereafter, however, relations with people outside the house become subject increasingly to some degree of competition, either over tangibles like land or intangibles like reputation and honour, and though this can be fiercest between siblings and over inheritance, it becomes more prevalent as 'kinship decreases'. Thus with 'strangers'—those who have passed beyond blood relationship at second or third cousin—competition becomes the norm, so much so that the many quarrels and disturbances of village life are described by the people as due to the 'enmity' which they feel to be endemic to their society. In this scheme of things, marginal theft—of sheep, of land by shifting a boundary stone, of firewood or random articles left lying around—is all part of the way life goes on, and scandalous accusation, speculative gossip, or laughter at others' expense, is part of the spice of everyday conversation. All this is the product of a view of life as continual struggle, of one man's harm being another man's good and vice versa, of survival as involving the conquest of the weaker by the stronger, and of the pursuit of 'self-interest' as a morally justified activity even if it involves damage to others.

Yet self-interest itself is ultimately pointless in the face of the arch enemy, death, who comes with drawn sword on his black horse, deaf to cries for mercy, slaughtering old and young and consigning their bloodless shades to the underworld. In the face of this ultimate reality, the world in all its colour, violence, passion, and beauty is shown to be 'deluding' or 'false', a world that tricks people with an appearance of permanence, and then snatches all away. This reality, which is the reality of the fallen world, must in this view be faced unflinchingly. Survival is a prize gained in the teeth of competition from others, and the answer to death is a life lived with panache in glorious defiance of its inevitable end. The earth that will eat the dancers must be trodden down under their feet while they still have strength to do so, for in the end there is no avoiding the embrace of the earth's 'black mantle' and the dancer's own reduction to 'a handful of little bones', and even the soul is in peril from desecration of the body by animals or by a careless action between death and burial. Life is a struggle, intense but ultimately doomed, and it reaches its tragic culmination in the great image from Greek folk poetry—the 'struggle' with Charos on the marble threshing floor.

Just as in this fallen view of the world death is victorious, so in the same view relations between man and God tend to be seen in terms of power play in which man is invariably the loser. God Almighty who made a world innately predisposed for the survival of man and beast, nevertheless permits the devil to operate within it, and gives man free will to make his own choices. While mercy is built into this economy in the idea that 'God doesn't lose you', so too is justice in the idea of punishment for the wrong choice: 'Is that what you're like? Take that!' And since there is in the fallen world such a strong predisposition in man to sin, what might from one perspective be seen as justice, in another is seen as the exercise of tyranny, so that a common reaction to the hardships of life comes in the form of the reflection, 'That's how God has made us—to suffer'. This is the God who himself appears to be the author of man's calamities, who exacts retribution from those who are too fortunate, and acts through motives so inscrutable as to turn men simply into objects of his play.

This idea of an unpredictable and all-powerful God is given its most complete articulation in the idea of fate, where every detail of a person's life is 'written' at birth and 'cannot be unwritten'. All characteristics and events, however random and unconnected, are in the last resort explained by this force acting in the lives of men, a force inseparable from God himself. Thus ordained, a person's fate—his or her share of fortune and misfortune—carries with it a kind of acceptance simply because it is to do with that element in God which is beyond argument or resistance.

This, then, is the fallen world, and it is in this world and with the attitudes consistent with it that people live for much of the time. This view is dominated by the idea of the hostility of nature to man; the dominance of men over women; the competition of neighbours; subjection to an inscrutable and tyrannical God or fate; and the triumph of death. Yet this world is perpetually countered, challenged, and penetrated by another world, and another view of things, in which all these elements are configured differently. The presence of this other world within the fallen world reveals the fallen world not as the final reality but as something waiting to be transformed; and in this way it exposes the realism of the fallen world as transitory and ultimately insubstantial—as itself a fallen consciousness which produces the reality that it describes. A greater reality transcends this fallen world and its characteristic view of things, and it is made present by liturgy—that is to say, the creation of a way of life as a symbolic whole, a 'work of the people', made manifest in all those areas of life where village symbolism echoes the liturgy of the Church.

The first vital shift which liturgy makes between these two views of the world is in the understanding of time. The fall as a once-and-for-all event trapping succeeding generations into a causal sequence of sin and punishment gains its power in part because in this mode it is seen as an event in the past, inevitably conditioning all events which follow it. The power of the liturgical understanding, however, lies in the way it apprehends a many-dimensional reality through its freedom from sequential, or linear, time. It does not negate the reality of the fall, but it presents against it the reality of the kingdom of God, and it places both the fall and the kingdom of God in the present, as opposite poles in a continuing drama in the life of each person.

The key to this understanding of the presence of the kingdom of God, not in some unthinkably mysterious future but pervading this present world, is the practice, both in village life and in the liturgy, of returning through a circle of time to a familiar moment, and of doing so in cycles which nest one inside the other, so that the day, the week, the year, and cycles within the year, each come back to the same sacred event and to the same company of sacred persons who enact that event. These are the circles of eternity in time, through which a remembrance takes place which is not a memory of the past, but a recovery of an encounter with the divine which is ever-present, continually unearthed from the forgetfulness engendered by the fall—the recovery which is intimated in the Greek and English Church term *anamnesis*.[9]

The entry into linear time of the sacred persons of the eternal world thus occurs through the interpenetration of the two orders of time, first in the story of Christ, and then in the nested cycles of the liturgical year by which his life, death, and resurrection and the lives of the Mother of God and the saints are celebrated and seen to be re-

[9] The Christian philosopher Boethius, elaborating on neo-Platonic sources in 523–4 AD (*The Consolation of Philosophy*, tr. Patrick Gerard Walsh (Oxford: Oxford University Press, 1999), 4.6.14–17), formulated the notion of time as 'a series of concentric circles revolving around the same axis' of which 'the innermost one lies closest to the single nature of the central point [the Godhead], and itself acts as a sort of axis round which the other circles lying outside it can turn.' This notion had a profound influence on medieval Christian thought (see, on the influence of Boethius, Lewis, *Discarded Image*, pp. 75–90, and on the part played by the circles of time in particular, p. 87). In the Latin West, for example, it continued to be recalled as late as T. S. Eliot's reference (*Four Quartets* (London: Faber and Faber, 1944), Burnt Norton II) to 'the still point of the turning world.' The development of a similar notion in the Greek East is referred to later in this chapter (p. 417 and nn. 30–1). It seems to be this concept of nested circles of time, converging on God who at the still point is outside time, which is worked out in the structure of the Orthodox (and more generally the Christian) liturgical year.

flected in the material world. The concurrence of these two time schemes opens up for those involved in them two worlds of experience—fallen and unfallen, which are themselves two ways of looking at the world.

Both world views are simultaneously available, so that from moment to moment each person can slip into the one or the other, and it is this that allows deeply contrasting philosophies of the destiny of man to co-exist in a vital symbiosis, and this that is amongst the factors that provide the extraordinary vitality and complexity of conversation and discussion and argument in the village. In a café, for instance, the edict of fate counterposed with the idea of personal responsibility can occasion a roar of the most lively debate about unforeseen results from apparently chance circumstances, or mention of life after death can provoke a prolonged discussion in which a natural scepticism about the destiny of the soul after death—'No one's come back to tell us'—will find in another habitual sceptic an unexpected rebuttal: 'There are all these teachings and writings in the Church, they wouldn't be there for nothing. Something exists.' At a memorial service a bystander will rebuke a mourner who bursts into a *moirológi* for her young son, arguing that it 'doesn't do' to sing a lament 'in front of Christ', but arouse a scornful rejection of such reticence from the mourner, *sotto voce*, later on, 'A lot she knows.' In a house, a woman, weighing the speculative enjoyments of divination by throwing beans against an uneasy sense that this is forbidden, ponders: 'Is it a sin? Isn't it? I don't know. I haven't an idea.' And then, in decision: 'Shall we?' Again, people will ponder the value of spells, which they carry out themselves and which they feel certain are effective, against the value of the 'reading' from the priest which is enjoined by confessors, at the same time weighing the presentiment that they should desist from incantations if they are getting old and nearing death, or wish to take communion, which 'takes precedence'. Or in discussion they may follow out with ruthless honesty the implications for salvation of sins in which they know they are complicit: 'Will Christ save us?' 'Only if we are good and follow Christ's road.' 'Do we follow Christ's road?' 'We don't.' This rich awareness of opposing choices arises in part from the complexity of a culture which has long roots back into the pre-Christian past, though its insights have to a great extent been incorporated and baptized by Christian tradition;

but it also arises from knowledge of the fundamental choices posed by human life in any circumstances, which are especially clear in the circumstances of subsistence living face to face with the natural world. The fallen world, then, is a living presence alongside the unfallen one; but it is felt to be possible at any time to make a reconnection with the timeless world beyond this middle ground of the cosmos and of time, and this in turn brings about a series of radical transformations.

The action which is felt to reconnect with this timeless world, and to transform the doomed cycle of the fallen world, has been described again and again in the typical sayings of the villagers. It is the movement away from the evil choice towards the good, away from the devil and towards Christ, from the fallen consciousness and towards the paradisal one. This movement the Church's liturgy further defines as being from the remorseless sequence of cause and effect, sin and punishment, power and subjection, fate and suffering, which are locked together in the linear stream of this world's time, and towards the potentialities of the present moment, 'Today'. For in the eternal 'Today', the liberating energies of the risen Christ, and the intercession of the holy figures of the Church who have already been sanctified by him, can draw the powerless, the sinner, and the fated back into the divine world.

In village life it is in the house and family, the heart of society, that many of these transformations are embodied, for it is in the house that all that is most sacred in the community can best flourish. Here, over time and with dedicated labour, the man who supports the house can become within it the shadowed, half-hinted image of Christ, while the woman, over time, and with a deep chastity which applies to control over every detail of her behaviour, can take on herself explicitly the likeness to the *Panaghía*. In furtherance of the parallel drawn between the Holy Family and the earthly family, the child also, the product of the union of the blood on marriage and the bringer of a 'future' to the family, can take on within the family the relation of the Christ child to the Holy Family. It is in such a house that the meal becomes a communion in a second sense, a sacrament presided over by Christ invoked in the sign of the cross and by the *Panaghía* invited to 'eat with us', and enabled by the work of the man on the land and the woman in the house. This is the transfigured house, redeemed from the conse-

29. Holy Friday: 'There may be a special place where white peonies bloom in the mountains, [and] the younger women and children go out…looking for them to adorn the bier on which the Epitaphios is laid' (p. 361).

30. Holy Saturday: 'Christ... the one who suffered every indignity and then broke down the doors of death' (p. 370). (Cover of 17th c. Gospel book, Monastery of Simonopetra, Mount Athos.)

quences of the fall, and it is from such moments in a house that the great giving of food at marriage and death, the reverence for bread as holy, and the response to the stranger as a sacred being, can arise.

The hospitality of the house is called forth at marriages, funerals, and memorial services, and to a lesser extent on name days also. The flow of hospitality out of the house is irreversible and free, linking the members of the community in good feeling, and giving opportunity for the mending of quarrels and the forgiveness of the dead. And while these notable occasions necessarily occur only from time to time in the life of any house, the wish to give is expressed on a different level from day to day simply by the giving and receiving of good wishes, and by the offerings of help or of food that are passed between the houses. The enmity and competition that bedevils the houses is still a fact, but these gifts springing from a spontaneous impulse are critical in providing a touchstone for a different order of things and re-establishing the reality of a world free from jealousy and competition.

Although on these great occasions hospitality is given without thought of return, it is natural within the village economy that the giver will over time receive something themselves, since marriages, festivals, and deaths happen to everyone. Again, on a different level, although the impulse to give to relatives and neighbours is uncalculated, in fact it is known that reciprocity is a part of human relations and that help must be mutual if people are to live. However, there are occasions when even at some hypothetical time in the future no return will ever be possible, and this is hospitality in its purest form.

This pure and indeed sacred hospitality is associated with giving to the poor and to those in need, to beggars, gypsies, and above all to the visitor—the 'stranger' not as the unrelated fellow villager but as the traveller passing through. It is here that the open-ended irreversible flow of hospitality from the house finds its most exalted expression, for this stranger, characteristically offered the very best the house can give and from whom no return will ever be asked, is the one who reveals within the wider community the sacred nature of the house. The stranger is a witness to this transfigured reality, and in this capacity, as so often indicated in the folk tales about hospitality, a stranger becomes a mysterious visitant who may (and often does) turn out to be the unrecognized Christ.

In the house, then, a series of transformations can take place which, never complete but touched and lost and touched again, are gained in despite of the fallen world and by means of the self-sacrificial but redeeming labour of man in the fields and woman in the house. The redemption becomes possible if the labour is experienced as part of the sanctifying cycle of the liturgical year and shaped by fast and feast, by days of self-denial and days of rejoicing, and by the penetration into the time of the fallen world of the sacred presences of the eternal world.

The liturgical action reaches further than the house however, for through work undertaken as liturgy not only are transformations enacted in the house, but also in the natural world. By means of the man the fields are tilled, the wheat sown and harvested; by means of the woman the 'house becomes a garden' and the harvest becomes the liturgical bread, so that the action of the housewife's hands in preparing the household bread echoes at a lower level the action of the priest at the preparation of the Holy Gifts. It is through the work of the married couple that the marriage itself becomes 'paradise' and the earth bears the bread of communion between God and man. Thus the transformations within the house enable the transformations within the natural world whereby the earth becomes reintegrated with the garden of paradise, taking on associations of the one who gives birth to God and through whom 'the Fields of Eden flower again'.

While earth nourishes man, however, villagers also know from first hand experience that it devours him when he dies; yet here too the deeper village insight from the story of Eden is that man was taken from the earth, and as he returns in his fallen state, the earth's action over time frees the soul from the sinful flesh, and completes his forgiveness. This forgiveness is also the gift of the mourner who offers the boiled wheat of the *kóllyva*, the significance of which is expressed in the words of Christ before his own death: 'Except a grain of wheat fall into the ground and die, it abideth alone: but if it die, it bringeth forth much fruit.'[10] The words, 'may God forgive him', 'may God forgive her', invariably accompany the receiving of the *kóllyva*, so that forgiveness of the dead person's sins is one of the first fruits of a body which has fallen to the ground and died—an exchange echoed in the disso-

[10] John 12 : 24.

lution of the body and its accompanying symbolism of the dissolution of its sins in the 'black earth'. And once this exchange is completed, the bones must come up into the air, because, as some say, Christ is risen.

As earth is redeemed by the action of the house from its hostile and fallen state, and correspondingly frees the dead from their fleshly sins, so water also is freed from its associations with spiritual danger by the action of the Church. Its innate capacity for good is brought progressively to a higher level as it becomes water for the 'first blessing' at birth, then the water of baptism, and finally the water of the Theophany, the baptism of Christ, which defeats all the hidden powers of evil in water, releasing mankind from 'our ancient lamentation', causing 'earth and sea' to 'share the joy of the world....'[11] Thus the same transformation that occurs in the earth at the harvest, whereby it takes on associations with the Mother of God, is wrought in water at the Theophany through Christ's baptism: water is redeemed from the curse and reintegrated with its unfallen nature, becoming a cause of cosmic rejoicing and the medium of 'the baptism of salvation'.

Finally, one of the greatest of these transformations lies in the change between the fallen and the redeemed modes in which God himself is understood. In the fallen perspective God, though creating a beneficent world full of living things, is nevertheless Lord of an order in which man, though free to choose, cannot avoid sin and is rewarded justly by punishment. Also in this perspective, man's freedom is enclosed within an immutable fate which allocates to each person their meed of suffering, which it is their task simply to endure. It is a world in which power relations are uppermost, and stoicism is the only appropriate response from those lower in the hierarchy. Into this fallen world, however, Christ enters together with his Mother and the familiar saints, prepared to bend the rules to an almost infinite extent to save a soul. The Mother of God as a suffering and merciful mother prays constantly to her son for her people, the saints are always at hand to help, and Christ, through remaining sinless through the worst of temptations in the fallen world, triumphs even over death. It is a perspective which does not rule out apparently random suffering, justice, and judgement, but it transfigures these things with blessings, hope, and forgiveness.

[11] *Festal Menaion*, pp. 354–5.

When this deep liturgical understanding is touched in village life, it brings into being another order of reality from that presented by the fallen consciousness. Woman who is so often trapped in the image of Eve can suddenly be glimpsed as the *Panaghía*; the village family living in bare subsistence as the Holy Family; bread as the body of Christ; the house as the church; the hostile world of nature as a garden; the winter days of late November as the time of the Mother of God Half-Way-Through-the-Sowing; the ambivalent water of the wild as the source of blessing for man and beast; burial in the 'black earth' as the eating up of sins by forgiveness; the bringing up of the bones from the earth as a journey into the light of the sun; the writing of fate and the tyranny of God transmuted into a world of undeserved mercy. In this way, the dangers and constraints of village experience can be transformed by a sense of obedience to the irreversible onward giving of life.

There remains a recurrent symbol of this onward movement, this fortunate journey out of the fallen world—the ring dance of rural Greece, never 'turning back' but continuing right-handed or anti-clockwise 'towards the sun', and circling and re-circling the dancing floor though without ever closing up on itself. Individuals join into groups of kin already in the dance, and groups of kin enter where they can, but where there are new groups wishing to lead the dance they stand at the point 'where the dance crosses' or 'at the crossing of the dance'. Always open-ended, if more dancers enter the line than the floor can hold, an inner spiral forms from the centre leading into the outer ring where the single leader keeps the movement going forward. The dance is thus an enactment not simply of a circle but of an open ended circle with an inner impulse forwards and onwards, that is to say a right-handed spiral or (when imagined in three dimensions) a helix, and it involves three elements—right-handed orientation, continuous recapitulation, and irreversible movement forwards. It is to the dance so conceived that the spiralling right-handed movement used in action and in image throughout village life is constantly referred. Right-handedness as the auspicious orientation runs not only through society but through the cosmos—in humans the right hand is the 'good hand'; in the cosmos to face the sun, that is to say the east, is to face the auspicious quarter, because the sun itself is 'right-handed'; and in the third dimension the path upward is auspicious also. The innate orientation of the cosmos is towards its creator, towards God, and in the face of this in-built yearning, man's intentional reversal of the auspicious movement indicates an option for evil which is particularly perverse. To 'turn back' or 'reverse' this movement and send it 'towards the devil' is to reverse the dance of life in which all things conspire, and to invoke terrifying consequences. The dance is in fact a reflection of the circling and healing patterns of the natural and liturgical worlds moving forward under the impulse of time.[12]

This circling yet forward-moving impulse has lent its overtones to some well-used proverbial phrases in village speech. To keep a livelihood going is to 'keep things going round' (*τὰ φέρουμε βόλτα*); a new phase of history is explained as 'the years have come full circle' (*γύρισαν τὰ χρόνια*). And this sense of continuity by which similar patterns are recreated in a new time, is the universal explanation of why things are done in one way and not in another: 'That's how we found it and that's how we leave it', 'That's how we found it and that's how we pass it on' (*ἔτσι τὰ μάθαμε καὶ ἔτσι τὰ ἀφίνουμε/βγάλουμε πέρα*). This act of 'passing on' involves a deep fidelity to time-honoured practice and inherited wisdom, yet it is far from static, since such continuity does not arise from an obedience to a stereotypical or externalized rule but from an intuitive response to an archetypal understanding; and this presupposes a constant creative work to bring into renewed life the central elements of the tradition in changing historical and demographic contexts. The act of remembrance articulated in the phrase 'That's how we found it and

[12] From a much more secular perspective Jane Cowan (*Dance and the Body Politic*, pp. 132–3) has also described something akin to what this village symbol conveys. She records her experience of how the dance can make tangible at a deeper level the unity of people divided by their social positions, and points to a like pattern of two simultaneous opposed experiences: on the one hand 'the iniquitous elements of social inequality', and on the other 'that sense of recognition—which though not inevitable is by no means rare—that one is morally part of, just as one is corporeally merged with, a larger collectivity, a recognition that, as a profoundly visceral knowledge, carries the force of absolute conviction.'

Note that a dance movement 'towards the sun' is in Greece a movement which, viewed from above, is anticlockwise, although in many places in north-west Europe it is clockwise motion which is seen as 'sunwise'. This ambiguity in practical interpretation does not affect the symbolic status of the movement since locally each interpretation is a convention agreed by all.

that's how we leave it' is thus on its own level a kind of *anamnesis* involving a constant recalling of sacred understandings enshrined within the culture, and as *anamnesis* it is in its own way an enactment of the circling of the dance, recalling each generation to a renewed understanding of itself and of the cosmos, and taking the dance on for one more turn.

The necessity for both moral choices and ritual movements to be 'like the dance', that is to say in a symbolically right-handed and irreversible sequence, becomes highly noticeable in certain precise and specific contexts. Baptism, marriage, kinship, and the rituals of death, all explicitly or implicitly share in this fundamentally similar pattern, echoing the way in which hospitality is seen to be governed by a similar dynamic in which gifts flow on and no return is sought.

After the harvest is carried in, the threshing is conducted as a great celebration. Festive food of batter-puffs and honey, served with *rakí*, is offered freely; it is the circling movement which governs the movement of the workers at the end of the day as they turn over the trampled stalks and grain for the fifth and last time; and it is the dancing in the houses of all those associated with the day's work which ends the day on the threshing floor whose outcome is the bread of the eucharist and food for the living and for the dead.

At baptism the gift of life to the child through the blood of its parents is echoed on a higher level by the gift to it of spiritual life through the anointing by the godparent with the oil. The gift must flow one way however, *katameriá*, with no return baptisms being permitted from the godchild or the godchild's close relatives to the godparent's close kin, lest the 'oil turn back' and misfortune follow. The *zinári*—the long belt whose winding on is illustrated by a spiralling anticlockwise movement of the hand—which is bound at death round the waist of a man with godchildren, illustrates the spiralling progression of the gift of spiritual life; and more is involved here than baptism alone, for in baptism the godparent initiates a chain in which he or she is also sponsor at the child's marriage and then baptizes its first born. The sacrament of baptism thus involves an auspicious one-way movement of oil and crowns, in which the godparent is always the giver: the first sacrament in which he 'makes the child a Christian' is followed by a second in which he crowns godchild and spouse as a source of new life, and then by a third in which, if he is still alive, he recapitulates his gift of spiritual life through anointing their child in baptism.

In the act of marriage the dance is especially emphasized, for to marry is to 'take one's place in the line of dance'. Marriage is itself the dance, and it follows that at all the wedding celebrations the dance is the main motif. At a wedding, as at every formal event, all the processional movements down the village paths are right-handed; and there is dancing at the dowry celebrations and before and after the marriage service. The theme of the dance also recurs, though cryptically, in the rule of *katameriá* in marriage which prescribes that the kindred which 'takes' a bride may not 'give' a bride in return. The symbolism of gender, dowry, and patterns of residence, all indicate men as the stable elements to whom the women move in marriage, and *katameriá* reveals that the movement of the women as brides to their new homes must not be 'turned back' through the return gift of another woman.

It is as bearers of the blood that the women are most vital to their families of marriage, and the right-handed, auspicious, and irreversible movement of the blood, revealed in the rule of *katameriá*, is again elaborated in the image of the *zinári* to represent the growth of the kindred, to measure the inflow of new blood into the 'one blood' of the original sibling group, and to direct the blood so that it flows right-handed and irreversibly into each marriage and to all its descendants. Thus while the various dance movements at marriage reveal marriage itself as the enactment of the dance of life, the bride is also revealed as the most complete embodiment of the dancer, for she represents in herself the blood which links 'strange' houses together. It is in acknowledgement of this that a girl will be given by her groom the red *tsibér* to wear for the first time on her wedding day, and on that day will wind around her waist under her clothes a thin red cord woven with goat's yarn, and put on for the first time the highly-prized spiralling red silk belt, the *kadém*.

A further reference of the dance lies behind the concept of *katameriá* taken together with the prohibition on marriages up to and including second cousins—a development brought about by successive early Church councils and extended in popular belief to include third cousins. When marriage must be outside these wide limits of blood relationship, and when *katameriá* prohibits the return of women between groups of affines, the effect is profound, for it ever more widely makes kin out of strangers. This effect was fully understood already in the fourth century, for St Augustine in the *City of God*, endorsing the Church's movement away from endogamy with close kin, specified its merit as being that 'charity' and 'concord' should be increased by the spread of kinship and affinal links, with 'social amity' being 'scattered, and not gathered together all into two or three'. The dance of life in the union of marriage is therefore not only the dance of the blood and of the women from house to house, not only the promise of house and children, it is the dance of hospitality between previously opposed households by which daughters with their honour, their dowries, their skills, and the fertility of their new blood, are given totally and permanently to their new home, in the knowledge that no return in kind can be made. So it is that the deep necessity to give away, which inspires the giving of daughters in marriage, finds on a different level a natural reflection in the majestic scale of the hospitality at a wedding, for which even poor households impoverish themselves further by baking oven-loads of bread and stewing cauldrons of meat to feed the numerous guests.

Just as in hospitality at a marriage the inner pattern of the dance lies behind any free flow of gifts, so at death the symbolism of the dance expresses on a series of levels the importance of freely giving up the soul. The spiralling *ísou* stands on the spiralling navel of the dead person, and the image is continued in the right-handed circling of community activity at the wake around the body, and in the passing of the laments from left to right round the body, all of which represent and ensure the auspicious and irreversible outpouring of the blood from the dead person by which alone the bloodless soul may begin its journey to the other world. In all the contexts mentioned, the 'turning back' of the free-flowing auspicious movement onwards brings misfortune or death; but it is in death itself that the irreversibility of the dance pattern finds its most dramatic expression, for if the circle is broken or reversed by passing something across the body rather than right-handed round it, it brings about an irreversible demonic possession, the life-in-death of the vampire—the only corollary of the dance which is incompatible with Orthodox Christianity, and seems to have been drawn in from another source.

In mourning however the auspicious movement is unchallenged, for here the giving of the mourner is completely without self-interest, and this sacrificial giving releases in the recipients the impulse to forgive. And the sign which presages this act of forgiveness—an essential act of these memorial services—is the irreversible right-handed movement of three 'grown girls' round the village with gifts of wheat, wine, and bread.

The right-handed dance pattern therefore stands universally for the undeviating forward movement of blessed and auspicious giving which must at all costs not be turned back—in baptism it is the auspicious chain of giving of oil and crowns; in marriage it is the life-giving movement of new blood to revitalize the house of the stranger; in hospitality at a marriage it is the impulse towards free and unconditional giving of food and drink; in kinship and in *katameriá* it is the *zinári* of the blood and the oil moving outwards in the creation of amity and concord in kinship links with strangers; at death it is the free giving up of the soul to move onward into the spiritual world; at the memorial services it is the impetus given to the soul's spiritual journey by the mourner whose sacrificial gift wins forgiveness of its earthly sins. In every context the pattern of the dance takes on a precise application, but the basic meaning, common to all, links disparate situations in a shared symbolism which makes them extraordinarily rich and many-layered. Thus the vampire returning to destroy its own kin resonates with the image of death-bringing marriages within the kindred; the auspicious movement of the bloodless soul into the other world parallels the dance of the living community in the *zinári* of the blood passed on by marriage to the stranger; the announcement of a memorial by three 'grown girls', moving right-handed with their gifts of wheat, wine, and bread, encapsulates not only the idea of forgiveness, but also of hospitality and marriage. And it is because of these overtones linking together common meanings in different situations that the round dance itself encompasses the movement between both kin and strangers, this world and the next, death and life, in a single compact symbol of giving onward freely and not looking back.

These, then, are the symbols of inner values which seem to be central to the life of the village described here: first the house, and the hospitality which expresses the house's essential nature (Chapter 6), the relationship of the house with the land, and the eucharistic bread and wine which is the gift of the land, or rather of work on the land (Chapters 2 and 5); second, the relationship of the village with its sources of water, which in their consecrated form bless land, flocks and people (Chapter 3); third, the release from the finality of death, and from consciousness of sins and a hard fate, which can be achieved in the villagers' relationship with Christ and the Mother of God and the saints of the Church (Chapters 8–11); and fourth, the round dance, recurrent image of the yearning of the whole cosmos towards its maker in many overlapping contexts of village life.

Here the second question posed at the beginning of this chapter becomes relevant—how far these symbols have links with the Orthodox liturgy. Enough has perhaps been said already about the obvious liturgical or other Christian connections of the first three, and the relevant chapters can provide any reminders which are necessary (see also the index entry on liturgy and village symbolism). At the same time, naturally, these connections are not only liturgical but also local and practical, and have a specific appropriateness to the life of a village which mostly grows its own food on its own land. Both links, the liturgical and the local, are necessary for a faith to form a culture, and it has already become apparent from the literature that connections which, though similar, are also different may be made in shepherding communities, in the islands, or in urban communities in the Orthodox world.[13]

However, the fourth symbol which is central in Ambeli, the round dance, is probably better known in the West as a feature of the ancient world, connected with the Athenian drama, though more is generally known about the choral poetry of that drama than about the dance itself and what it might have meant. It might indeed be tempting to read back into ancient times some of the detailed meanings of the dance which have been described here; but among the hazards of such an attempt would be the early adoption, and probably transformation, of the language of the dance by eastern Christian

[13] Shepherding communities—see du Boulay, 'Bread and Sheep'; islands—see Stewart, *Demons and the Devil,* especially Chs. 3 (saints), 3 and 5 (cosmology), 7 (baptism); urban communities—see Hirschon, *Heirs of the Greek Catastrophe,* especially Chs. 7 (house and marriage), 9 (time), 10 (religion, death, fall and resurrection). See also references in the Introduction to this book, nn. 14–28.

writers. This last section of the book looks briefly at this question.

Thus far all the meanings of the dance have been found in the life of the community outside the doors of the Church; but in fact the dance lies also within the Church, embedded in its liturgy, and it is with the meanings expressed within this microcosm that the dance permeates the social world in all its varied contexts. In fact it is the history of the dance in the Church which has reshaped the meaning of the dance in the villages, and this final section discusses this reshaping in terms of the history of some key symbols in the Orthodox liturgy.

At baptism the godparents and the child are, in the villagers' words, 'danced'—that is to say, led by the priest three times, right-handed, round the font. After the 'crowning' of marriage, too, the couple are in the same way 'danced' around the table on which stands the common cup, a symbol of marriage. More than this though, the dance at marriage is repeated also at the ordination of a priest, and both at marriage and at ordination this dance is accompanied by the singing of what is called the Dance of Isaiah,[14] and so accepted is the term 'dance' or *khorós* (*χορός*) for these rites of passage, that a married priest can say of his marriage and ordination, 'I have had two dances' (*εἶχα δύο χορούς*).

These three rites at which the 'dance' occurs might be thought to have little in common, coming as they typically do at very different stages in life; but all three share the most fundamental of all Christian themes. In baptism, the person baptized has undertaken the path of death to self. This is clearly stated in the Epistle[15] always read at baptism: 'Therefore we are buried with him by baptism into death, that like as Christ was raised from the dead by the glory of the Father, even so we also should walk in newness of life', and these words are also paraphrased in the prayer with which the baptismal water is blessed: 'That being buried, after the pattern of thy death, he may, in like manner, be partaker of thy Resurrection.'[16] In marriage, the placing of the crowns on the heads of the couple is immediately followed by the wedding Epistle,[17] in which the wife gives herself to

[14] In the dance of Isaiah, the words run: 'Dance, O Isaiah, the Virgin is with child and shall bear a son, and shall call his name Emmanuel, both God and Man; him do we magnify, and we call the Virgin blessed.' Cf. Hapgood, *Service Book*, p. 300.

[15] Romans 6 : 3–11, quotation from v. 4.

[16] Hapgood, *Service Book*, pp. 278–9.

[17] Ephesians 5 : 20–33.

her husband as to Christ, and he gives himself to her as Christ gave himself for the Church; and this interpretation of the crowns is confirmed, while the liturgical dance is still continuing, by an invocation of the martyrs who likewise have received their crowns through self-sacrifice.[18] Finally, this invocation of the martyrs' self-giving actually begins the liturgical dance at the ordination of a priest.[19] Thus one explicit meaning of the liturgical dance is centred in self-giving: and self-giving, as we have seen, is also the impulse of the one-way onward movement of the dance in village imagery.

The relation of this imagery of self-giving to the story of Christ is already apparent from the words of the baptismal reading just quoted; but the parallel is underlined in the words sung as each of these liturgical dances is accomplished. In the dance at baptism the baptized person, after emerging stripped of his old self from the font, is conceived as being clothed with Christ.[20] In the Dance of Isaiah at marriage and ordination Isaiah is called to rejoice at the fulfilment of his prophecy of the birth of Christ,[21] imaged by the self-giving of those who are married or ordained, just as the death to self of the person baptized is the 'putting on' of Christ over the nakedness of the human person.

This, then, is the meaning given to the one-way, onward-moving aspect of the liturgical dance; but the circling, recapitulatory aspect of the dance is also given a liturgical meaning as an image of eternity, and in these and other liturgical uses the circle is repeated three times in reference to the Christian Trinity, the Father, Son, and Holy Spirit, one God who is the eternal source of all things.[22] Baptism, marriage, and ordination, being intended as once for all and to eternity, are thus apt occasions for this symbol. Similarly, the third defining attribute of the dance, its auspicious right-handed direction, echoes the blessing hand of the priest which is always the right hand and stands for the blessing hand of Christ, a meaning revealed when

[18] 'O holy martyrs, who have fought the good fight and have received your crowns, pray you unto the Lord that he will have mercy on our souls.' Hapgood, *Service Book*, p. 300.

[19] Hapgood, *Service Book*, p. 316.

[20] Here the words of St Paul (Galatians 3 : 27) are sung: 'As many as have been baptized into Christ have put on Christ, alleluia.'

[21] See n. 14 above.

[22] Hapgood, Service Book, pp. 603 n. 7, 604 n. 6, 606 n. 5.

the request for a blessing is made to an Orthodox priest, to which the answer is made, 'It is the Lord's [blessing]' (*τοῦ Κυρίου*). In this way the round dance in all its defining dimensions—of right-handedness, open-ended circling, and irreversibility—has evolved into a many-layered liturgical symbol of the central concepts of the Orthodox Christian faith.

Further instances of the right-handed movement, though not explicitly called a 'dance', also occur in the liturgy of the Church, and confirm that it is associated with the self-sacrifice of Christ in entering into this world. In the Divine Liturgy, the main processional movements by the priest are right-handed: at the Little Entrance he carries the Gospel right-handed round the altar through the north door of the icon screen to the people in the nave of the church, then back to the sanctuary through the Royal Doors in the centre of the screen to the altar; and similarly at the Great Entrance he carries the Holy Gifts, the bread and wine, from the table of preparation on the north side of the sanctuary, down the north side of the church, back up through the nave, and through the Royal Doors to the altar for the consecration. The common content of this dance symbolism, discernible in both of these processional movements, is self-sacrifice, and draws on the Christian story of God's son, who came from heaven to earth and who 'being in the form of God... made himself of no reputation and took upon himself the form of a servant', becoming 'obedient unto death, even the death of the cross', and returned from death and from the visible world to receive 'a name which is above every name'.[23] Thus by the seventh century, in the *Mystagogy* of Maximus the Confessor (an early liturgical commentary), the sanctuary had become identified with heaven and the nave with the world, and the entrance of the bishop with the Gospel 'is a figure and image of the first appearance in the flesh of Jesus Christ the Son of God and our Saviour in this world'.[24] By the eighth century the liturgical commentary of Germanus takes this for granted: 'The entrance of the Gospel shows the appearance of the Son of God into this world',[25] and adds an interpretation of the Great

[23] Philippians 2 : 6–11.

[24] Maximus the Confessor, The Church's Mystagogy, in *Maximus Confessor: Selected Writings*, tr. George C. Berthold (New York: Paulist Press, 1985), pp. 189, 198.

[25] Robert F. Taft, *The Byzantine Rite: A Short History* (Collegeville, Minn.: The Liturgical Press, 1992) p. 46.

Entrance with the Holy Gifts, as 'Christ the Great King proceeding to the Mystical Sacrifice'.[26] Thereafter these interpretations are constant, and a right-handed on-going movement evolved in the entry with the Gospel and in the Great Entrance which acquired these meanings: the outgoing movement representing Christ's self-giving to the world, and the circling return to the sanctuary indicating his re-assumption of his unceasing place beside his Father. Thus the movement of self-giving in the liturgical dance is, at baptism, marriage, and ordination, and in the Little and Great Entrances in the Liturgy, explicitly associated with the birth or entrance of Christ into this world, while at the Great Entrance it is also associated with Christ's willing death, and his communion with his people through his body and blood.[27]

In these liturgical examples of the dance, therefore, it is Christ the

[26] Taft, *The Byzantine Rite*, p. 47.

[27] Similarly, the last great Byzantine commentary on the liturgy, the 14th c. commentary of Nicholas Cabasilas, *A Commentary on the Divine Liturgy*, tr. J. M. Hussey and P. A. McNulty (London: SPCK, 1966; first published 1960) describes the entrance with the Gospel as 'symbolizing the manifestation of the Lord when he began to appear to the multitudes' (p. 59), and the Great Entrance as 'the last manifestation of Christ...when he embarked on the journey from his native country to Jerusalem' (p. 65)—this being where he would die. Note that the connection of these meanings with the right-handed circling movement developed only gradually in the case of the entry with the Gospel and the Great Entrance, which at first were simple movements from west to east. They became right-handed circling movements when the book of the Gospel was no longer carried in procession into the church at the start of the liturgy, but was already placed on the altar, and when the place of preparation of the Holy Gifts became the chapel close to the north side of the sanctuary—positions which were normative in the middle Byzantine rite—see Taft, *Byzantine Rite*, Ch. 6. The link of these meanings with the circling movement echoed and harmonized with the 6th c. Greek interpretation of the processional censing, found in *The Ecclesiastical Hierarchy* of Dionysius 3.3 (Migne 3, 428D–429B). That the censing begins in the sanctuary and returns to the sanctuary indicates to Dionysius the eternal constancy of the divine; while at the same time the movement of the censing outwards to the furthest reaches of the church is an image of the creator's mercy and self-giving to his creation in all its diversity. Like the processional movements in the Divine Liturgy, the person censing goes out by the north door and returns through the Royal Doors in the centre, or if they are closed, by the south door. (The censing of the people occurs at the midpoint of this circle, in the centre of the nave, but has a different rationale, going from the people's right, where the bishop's throne is, to the people's left. See eg *Ieratikon*, pp. 8 and 58–9.)

son of God whose archetypal dance this is, the dance in which he is born, gives himself to the world to save it, dies, and rises again; and he continues to enter the world and to clothe, or be 'put on' by, those who are baptized into the Church and into the dance of the community. This liturgical dance in village symbolism first entails the mutual sacrifice of marriage through which Christ is born, children are raised, and the wheat of the field becomes the bread of the eucharist. Then, following on from this, the dance embodies the sacrificial and free passing on of the gifts of blood kinship, spiritual kinship, and hospitality to strangers, and at the last, prepares people for the handing on of life and acceptance of death as a journey of forgiveness to a place elsewhere, awaiting a dispensation known to Christ and the saints but beyond our mortal sight.

How many of these meanings were associated with the dance before the advent of Christianity is a question which cannot be answered here; but whatever its meanings when Christianity encountered it, it is plain that the Church recognized in this symbol something which was akin to its own vision of things, and added to it and enriched it in every way it could. Just as the round dance created the ancient context for the stories of the Greek gods, and for the Athenian drama, so early Christian writers were soon adapting it to the story of God's son, his death for his people and rising again. For example, Clement of Alexandria (second century AD), both an early critic of paganism and a lover of Greek philosophy, contrasted the round dance of the Dionysia (the occasion of the Athenian drama) with that in the 'holy rites of the Word' where 'the daughters of God keep festival... assembling a sober dance (*χορὸν ἀγείρουσαι σώφρονα*). The dancers are those who act justly; the music a hymn of the King of All'.[28] Elsewhere, he uses the same image of Christ, calling the Church 'the body of the Lord, a spiritual and holy dance' (*πνευματικὸς καὶ ἅγιος χορός*).[29] From this imagery arose the numerous early descriptions of saints, prophets, angels, and Christians generally as forming a *khorós*, the round dance accompanied by singing, which has passed into western usage too, but frozen into the static image of a 'choir'. By these steps Greek Christian thinking

[28] Clement of Alexandria, *Protrepticus*, Ch. 12 (Migne 8, 240C)

[29] Ibid. *Stromateis*, 7.14 (Migne 9, 521B).

incorporated the dance, and made it an image of self-giving, death, and renewal in a multiplicity of contexts.

In this way the dance, a quintessential liturgical action of village life, takes place on two levels. Central is the microcosm of the Divine Liturgy in which the symbols of a rich and complex reshaping of Greek thought and life by its Christian inheritance are re-presented week by week and feast by feast in the village church. But alongside this runs a movement penetrating the life of the whole village community as its households struggle to win a living from the earth. This is the liturgy which is the work of man and woman in marriage, the liturgy of the work of the houses linked with one another in a dance of giving onward which overcomes the harshness of nature and the cruelty of death.

But while patterns of reconciliation in the village accompany the microcosmic liturgy in church, early liturgical and contemplative thought also developed a view of the Divine Liturgy as itself two liturgies, one of which reflects the other; for, as has been said, the service refers again and again to the fact that it is the reflection of the liturgy in heaven, where, as the Orthodox eucharistic prayer puts it, there attend on God 'thousands of archangels and tens of thousands of angels, cherubim and seraphim six-winged, many-eyed, soaring aloft upon their wings, singing, crying, shouting the triumphal hymn and saying: Holy, Holy, Holy, Lord of Sabaoth, heaven and earth are full of thy glory. Hosannah in the highest.' This heavenly liturgy, first described in the vision of the Jewish prophet Isaiah in the eighth century BC, is thus the paradigm which is reflected by the liturgy on earth, and into this heavenly liturgy, too, later Greek contemplative writing introduced the circling movement, formed in an onward or upward spiral, identical with the round dance both in village life and the village church. This circling movement is described by Dionysius, the author of the sixth century whose writings were to become a fountainhead of both eastern and western mystical tradition. In *The Divine Names* Dionysius describes the heavenly liturgy as follows:

> The divine intelligences are said to move, when at one with the glories of the Good and the Beautiful which has no beginning and no ending, in a circle; and when they go out to care for those below them, in a straight

31. The dance (1): 'The work of man and woman in marriage... the work of the houses linked with one another in a dance of giving onward' (p. 416).

32. The dance (2): 'The microcosm of the Divine Liturgy... a rich and complex reshaping of Greek thought and life by its Christian inheritance' (p. 416).

Fresco from the narthex of the Catholicon, Monastery of Koutloumousiou on Mount Athos (also on the front cover), which quotes phrases from the Lauds psalms (the last part of Orthodox daily matins). The upper fresco of forests and wild life refers to Ps. 148 vv. 9-10: '[Praise the Lord] mountains, and all hills; fruitful trees and all cedars: beasts and all cattle; creeping things and flying fowl.' The lower fresco, seen here in more detail, refers to Ps. 50 v. 4: 'Praise him with the timbrel and dance: praise him upon the strings and pipe.' The Lauds psalms are also prominent in Easter Matins, where they are interwoven with references to the Resurrection.

line, passing directly through all that intervenes; but when caring for those more needy while remaining undisturbed in constancy around the Beautiful and the Good, which is the cause of all constancy, they move in a spiral, unceasing in the round dance (*περιχορεύοντες*).[30]

And again, in *The Celestial Hierarchy*:

This then, according to my understanding, is the first order of the heavenly beings, which stands in a circle immediately round God, revolving the eternal knowledge of Him in a simple and unceasing round dance, in accordance with the highest station which is, as among the angels, ever-moving...[31]

These passages, echoed later in the Byzantine tradition by Maximus the Confessor and Gregory Palamas,[32] affirm the image of the dance in the heavenly liturgy, whose pattern is repeated in the liturgy of the Eastern Church, and in the round dance of the village celebrations.

Thus in early eastern Christian contemplative thought, the liturgy in eternity, the liturgy in the Church, and the liturgy in the community, have to resonate together if the cosmos is to become one. In this thinking the world we know is divided, the paradisal world separated by a flaming sword from the world of the fall. Yet the two worlds are also seen to be in reality one, and the division is in fact a division in man himself at a deep level of consciousness. It is man's fallen consciousness with its constricted realism which chokes itself off from paradise, and sets difficulties in the way of the repentance or 'changed perception' (*metánoia*) which would reintegrate him with it. Yet the gateway to this changed perception, the gateway to paradise, is also identified: it is Christ, who re-enters time in the liturgy of the Church and in his self-giving calls forth an answering self-giving from the people.

In the little tradition of villages given mainly to subsistence farming, it is easy to see how these ideas could resonate. There, dedicated toil in

[30] Dionysius, *The Divine Names*, 4.8 (Migne 3, 704D–705A). For a similar notion of Boethius, see n. 9 above.

[31] Dionysius, *The Celestial Hierarchies*, 7.4 (Migne 3, 209D–212A).

[32] Maximus the Confessor, Ambiguum 7, in *On the Cosmic Mystery of Jesus Christ*, tr. Paul M. Blowers and Robert Louis Wilken (Crestwood, N.Y.: St Vladimir's Seminary Press, 2003), pp. 47–8; Gregory Palamas, *The Triads*, tr. Nicholas Gendle (New York: Paulist Press, 1983) pp. 44, 99, 101.

the natural world is inevitable, but to this necessary self-sacrifice a liturgical dimension is given by the sense that the cosmos is sacred and that times of labour are enfolded in the timeless. Likewise in countless other details of the communal life, which this book has tried to illustrate, the call to self-giving awakens a flow of responses which, recurring again and again, touch meanings which are always the same. At the deepest level of this way of thought lies an engagement with giving on and giving away, of which the dance was, in the early centuries of the Christian era, reshaped as an icon. And in this way the three levels of the dance—that of the divine intelligences around God, that of the faithful before the sanctuary, and that of the whole village gathered in the round dance—have together come to form in this Orthodox culture a single cosmic liturgy.

APPENDIX · BIBLIOGRAPHY · GLOSSARY · INDEX

APPENDIX

PRACTICES NO LONGER EXTANT IN AMBELI AT THE TIME OF FIELDWORK

The entries here concern practices no longer extant in Ambeli by 1966–73 (the time of fieldwork), but reported as occurring within recent memory. All other practices referred to were current among many or all of the villagers in 1966–68, although there was a steady falling off after the early 1970s, so uniformity cannot be claimed for the whole of the period.

Page

Chapter 1: WORLD

28 *The middle parting of women's hair.* This was specified for traditional dress. When this dress began to be left off (see reference to p. 281 below) the older women continued to wear their hair this way though the younger women began to have their hair short and with a side parting.

36–7 *Childbirth in the villages together with associated customs.* In 1961 a young wife died giving birth in the village, and after this all the women decided to have their babies in the clinic in the local market town. The services of local midwives were no longer needed and traditional birth practices lapsed.

37 *Old women overhearing the Fates.* The belief in the ability of the old women to overhear the Fates was commonly held, but referred to as in the past. No one living in the village claimed to have such powers at the time of fieldwork.

38–9 *Traditional building of a house.* No new houses were being built in the village during my time there, but the custom of slaughtering a cock on the day of laying the foundations of a new house has continued to the present day in those villages which have livestock. The slaughtering is now done in the yard, but nevertheless in some cases the blood is still poured into the foundations.

Chapter 2: EARTH

67 *Boiling wheat for saints' days.* This custom lapsed shortly before 1966. Th last saint to be commemorated in this way was St Modestas, the patron saint of animals.

70, 72 *Childbirth customs.* See reference above to Ch. 1, p. 36–7.

Chapter 3: WATER

79 *Use of oxen for ploughing.* Oxen were still being used up to about 1950, but after that they were replaced by mules and horses.

81–3 *Dhrystélla.* The mill in Ambeli, and the *dhrystélla* (*nerotriví*) with it, was abandoned in 1961 or 1962, but these contrivances are still used in some places in northern Evia.

86 *Klídhonas.* The last *klídhonas* in Ambeli took place in the early 1950s.

88 *Piperiá.* The last *Piperiá* in Ambeli took place in 1961 or 1962.

91–2 *Childbirth customs.* See reference above to Ch.1, p. 36–7.

Chapter 4: TIME

106 *Sowing large acreages of wheat with oxen, and continuing up to Christmas and beyond.* The advent of fertilizer in the mid-fifties quadrupled the crops, and this, coupled with the emigration of many of the young men from the village, meant that the great acreage once needed for the wheat was very much diminished. Again, the adoption of horses and mules as plough animals, instead of the slow-plodding oxen, speeded up the rate of ploughing.

111 *Open air festivals.* During my time in the village there were no open air festivals celebrated at the four nearby country churches although a liturgy was celebrated in all of them on the feast day, and elsewhere in Evia communal meals and dancing were still following these liturgies as late as 1964. Recently, however, in a deliberate effort to maintain old traditions, the celebration of these annual festivals and the eating of a communal meal outside have been revived at all of Ambeli's country churches. Nowadays, though, meat, instead of being bought by the church, is bought by members of the association recently formed to regenerate village life, but it is still cooked outside in large cauldrons, and paid for by those who eat it.

115 *The greeting, 'Christ is Risen!'.* By 1966 this was no longer exchanged on days other than the Sunday of the Resurrection.

123 *Klídhonas*. See reference above to Ch. 3, p. 86.

Chapter 5: WORK AND BREAD

135 *The making of shepherd's capes and traditional costume.* Neither the heavy shepherd's cloaks nor the traditional costume were any longer being made in the village by 1966, though the costume was still being worn in the area by some older women (see reference below to Ch. 9, p. 281).

156–9 *Open air festivals*. See reference above to Ch. 4, p. 111.

Chapter 6: THE HOUSE AND THE STRANGER

162–3 *Engagements in which the bridegroom did not see the bride until the wedding day.* Marriages were still being arranged at the time of fieldwork but increasingly it was expected that the bride would visit the bridegroom before marriage and that during that time sexual relations would have taken place.

164 *Incoming brides*. By the time of fieldwork all girls were marrying out of the village.

167 *The communal round dance.* The great unified village dances on the threshing floor lapsed in the 1950s partly as a result of competition from the cafés. By 1966 the patronal festival was celebrated separately by patrons of three cafés, with round dancing to recorded music or music from hired urban musicians using amplifiers. Small groups of kin would take a turn dancing and then leave the floor for others to have their turn.

168 *Stuffing the trousseau.* Mattresses were no longer being stuffed with straw by 1966, but the phrase 'stuffing the trousseau' had survived to indicate the celebration of the laying out of the trousseau in an ornamental pile.

168 *Weddings lasting for three days.* These great weddings had lapsed by 1966, to be replaced by one day of festivities before the departure of the bride to her new home. In the seventies this could be replaced by a wedding in the town, after which the guests repaired to a coffee shop for cakes or ice-creams before dispersing.

172 *Gifts of garments and jewellery to adorn the traditional costume.* With the abandonment of the traditional dress by most women (see reference above to Ch. 5, p. 135), the gifts of the groom to the bride had been replaced by modern equivalents (see du Boulay, 'The Meaning of Dowry').

175–6 *Incorporation rituals.* After 1966 all the girls married out of Ambeli and no new brides came in.

182–3 *Visiting on name days involving the entire community.* By 1966 only those with positive 'relations' (friendship or kinship) would go to each other's name days, so only relatively small quantities of batter puffs were prepared. People without such 'relations', or those not on good terms with any house celebrating a name day, would not go.

Chapter 7: THE LIFE IN THE BLOOD

203 *The wearing of the zinári by men.* Men in Ambeli had abandoned traditional dress well before 1960.

210–11 *Avoidance by parents of the baptism in church.* This custom was still being observed in the early 1960s, but was abandoned after that.

213 *Wearing of the zinári at death.* This lapsed with the abandonment of traditional dress.

Chapter 8: THE VIOLENCE OF DEATH

257–8 *Unidirectional right-handed movement around the body.* The injunction not to pass anything over the body was scrupulously obeyed, but during the time of fieldwork things were passed impartially either way round the head or round the feet. The insistence that the movement should be right-handed came from an old woman respected for her knowledge of how things should be done, and often referred to by the villagers themselves in cases of doubt.

257–8 *The antiphonal singing of laments.* Laments were sung in Ambeli during the time of fieldwork, but not by antiphonal groups. The description of the antiphonal lament comes from Alexiou, *The Ritual Lament.*

Chapter 9: THE PROGRESS OF MOURNING

280–1 *The general wearing of traditional dress.* The last woman to wear traditional dress in the village died in 1966, but the dress was still being worn in neighbouring villages at that time by some women, even those in their forties. The dress then adopted was said by some to be 'like the gypsies'—headscarf, long dress or skirt with a long apron, shirt or jersey covered with a cardigan or jacket. With this was worn thick stockings and shoes often of thick plastic. (For the wearing by men of traditional dress see reference above to Ch. 7, p. 203). In Ambeli when the traditional dress was being worn it was customary for the change to mourning dress to be deferred until the third day after the death 'so that Charos should distance himself'. After traditional dress was put off, the change to deep mourning became immediate after a death, and the women's dress became entirely black. Men observed mourning only to the extent of wearing a black armband.

285 *Prostrations made on the grave of a woman who has died in childbirth.* During my fieldwork the most recent death in childbirth had been in 1961, but I was not told that prostrations had been made then and the custom had probably lapsed. But it had been practised within my elderly informant's lifetime.

287–90 *Gifts of food at funerals and memorials for the dead.* The last funeral to be celebrated with the full giving of food was in 1947. By the early seventies the great giving of food for all at the *makáries* was carried out by some, but in some cases was replaced simply by the giving of *kóllyva* and 'pieces' after the liturgy. By late 1966 the custom of the three 'grown' girls taking the bread, wheat, and wine round the village, as preparation for the memorial to come, was no longer being observed.

Chapter 10: THE GODBEARERS

None.

Chapter 11: THE INCARNATE GOD

380 *The Easter greeting.* See Ch. 4, p. 115.

Chapter 12: THE DANCE OF LIFE

407 *The general wearing of traditional dress.* See reference above to Ch. 9, p. 280–1.

Wearing of the kadém. See reference above to Ch. 9, p. 280–1.

408 *Antiphonal singing of laments.* See reference above to Ch. 8, pp. 257–8.

BIBLIOGRAPHY

ALEXAKIS, ELEUTHERIOS, VRAKHIONIDHOU, MARIA, and OIKONOMOU, ANDROMAKHI, (eds.), *Ἀνθρωπολογία καί Συμβολισμός στήν Ελλάδα* [*Anthropology and Symbolism in Greece*] (Athens: Ἑλληνική Ἑταιρεία Ἐθνολογίας, 2008).

ALEXIOU, MARGARET, *The Ritual Lament in Greek Tradition* (Cambridge: Cambridge University Press, 1974).

—, *After Antiquity* (Ithaca: Cornell University Press, 2002).

AUGUSTINE OF HIPPO, *The City of God*, tr. John Healey (London: Dent, 1945).

BAILEY, K. E., 'Burial Customs', in *The Oxford Companion to the Bible*, pp. 95–96.

BARBER, PAUL, 'Forensic Pathology and the European Vampire', in Dundes (ed.), *The Vampire*, pp. 109–42.

BASIL THE GREAT, *The Hexaemeron*, tr. B. Jackson, first published 1894, in Philip Schaff and Henry Wace (eds.), *Nicene and post-Nicene Fathers of the Christian Church*, vol. 8 (Grand Rapids, Michigan: Eerdmans, 1983).

BOETHIUS, *The Consolation of Philosophy*, tr. Patrick Gerard Walsh (Oxford: Oxford University Press, 1999).

BOULAY, JULIET DU, see DU BOULAY.

BULGAKOV, SERGIUS, *The Orthodox Church*, tr. L. Kesich (Crestwood, N.Y.: St Vladimir's Seminary Press, 1988).

Burial of the Dead, Office for a Lay Person, tr. by the Liturgical Translations Committee, Diocese of Sourozh, Russian Orthodox Church in Britain and Ireland (Oxford: St Stephen's Press, 2004).

BUXTON, JEAN C., *Religion and Healing in Mandari* (Oxford: Clarendon Press, 1973).

CABASILAS, NICHOLAS, *A Commentary on the Divine Liturgy*, tr. J. M. Hussey and P. A. McNulty (London: SPCK, 1966; first published 1960).

CAMPBELL, JOHN K., *Honour, Family and Patronage: A Study of Institutions and Moral Values in a Greek Mountain Community* (Oxford: Clarendon Press, 1964).

—, and SHERRARD, PHILIP, *Modern Greece* (London: Benn, 1968).

CLEMENT OF ALEXANDRIA, *Protrepticus*, in Migne, *Patrologiae cursus completus, Series Graeca*, vol. 8 (1891).

—, *Stromateis*, in Migne, *Patrologiae cursus completus, Series Graeca*, vol. 9 (1890).

COWAN, JANE K., *Dance and the Body Politic in Northern Greece* (Princeton: Princeton University Press, 1990).

DAMIANAKOS, S. (ed.), *Brothers and Others: Essays in Honour of John Peristiany* (Athens: Centre National de Recherches Sociales (E.K.K.E.), 1995).

DANFORTH, LORING M., *The Death Rituals of Rural Greece* (Princeton: Princeton University Press, 1982).

DAWKINS, RICHARD, *The God Delusion* (London: Bantam Press, 2006).

DE PINA-CABRAL, JOAO, *Sons of Adam, Daughters of Eve: The Peasant Worldview of the Alto Minho* (Oxford: Clarendon Press, 1986).

DIMEN, MURIEL, and FRIEDL, ERNESTINE (eds.), 'Regional Variation in Modern Greece and Cyprus: Toward a Perspective on the Ethnography of Greece', *Annals of the New York Academy of Sciences*, 268 (1976), pp. 1–465.

DIONYSIUS, see PSEUDO-DIONYSIUS.

Divine Liturgy of St John Chrysostom, tr. by the Liturgical Translations Committee, Diocese of Sourozh, Russian Orthodox Church in Britain and Ireland (Oxford: St Stephen's Press, 1999).

DUBISCH, JILL (ed.), *Gender and Power in Rural Greece* (Princeton: Princeton University Press, 1986).

—, *In a Different Place: Pilgrimage, Gender and Politics at a Greek Island Shrine* (Princeton: Princeton University Press, 1995).

DU BOULAY, JULIET, *Portrait of a Greek Mountain Village* (Oxford: Clarendon Press, 1974, reprinted as paperback, 1979; reprinted Limni, Greece: D. Harvey, 1994, 2001).

—, 'The Greek Vampire: A Study of Cyclic Symbolism in Marriage and Death', *Man* (N.S.) 17 (1982) pp. 219–38.

—, 'The Meaning of Dowry: Changing Values in Rural Greece', *Journal of Modern Greek Studies* 1 (1983), pp. 243–70.

—, 'The Blood: Symbolic Relationships between Descent, Marriage, Incest Prohibitions and Spiritual Kinship in Greece', Man (N.S.) 19 (1984), pp. 533–56.

—, 'Women: Images of their Nature and Destiny in Rural Greece', in Dubisch (ed.) *Gender and Power*, pp. 139–68.

—, 'La mariée et sa belle-mère. Aspects du rituel du marriage dans un

village de Grèce', in Peristiany and Handman (eds), *Le prix de l'alliance*, pp. 379–95.
—, 'Strangers and Gifts: Hostility and Hospitality in Rural Greece', *Journal of Mediterranean Studies* 1 (1991), pp. 37–53.
—, 'Cosmos and Gender in Village Greece', in Loizos and Papataxiarchis (eds.), *Contested Identities*, pp. 47–78.
—, 'Time and Society in Rural Greece', in Damianakos (ed.), *Brothers and Others*, pp. 147–62.
—, 'Bread and Sheep: A Comparative Study of Sacred Meanings among the Ambeliots and the Sarakatsani', in Mazower (ed.), *Networks of Power*, pp. 209–30.
—, '*Ο συμβολισμός της γης σ' ένα χωριό της Ορθόδοξης Ελλάδας*' ['The symbolism of the earth in a Greek Orthodox village'], in Alexakis, Vrakhionidhou and Oikonomou (eds.), *Ἀνθρωπολογία καί Συμβολισμός στήν Ελλάδα*, pp.145–73.
— and WILLIAMS, RORY, 'Amoral Familism and the Image of Limited Good: A Critique from a European Perspective', *Anthropological Quarterly* 60 (1987), pp. 12–24.
DUFFY, EAMON, *The Stripping of the Altars: Traditional Religion in England c.1400–c.1580* (New Haven and London: Yale University Press, 1992).
DUNDES, ALAN (ed.), *The Vampire: A Casebook* (Madison: University of Wisconsin Press, 1998).
ELIOT, T. S., *Four Quartets* (London: Faber, 1944).
EVANS-PRITCHARD, E. E., *Witchcraft, Oracles and Magic among the Azande* (Oxford: Clarendon Press, 1937).
EVDOKIMOV, PAUL, *L'Orthodoxie* (Neuchatel and Paris: Presses de Taizé, 1959).
Festal Menaion, The, The Service Books of the Orthodox Church, tr. Mother Mary and Archimadrite Kallistos Ware (London: Faber,1969; reprinted in Faber Paperbacks, 1977).
FINE, J. V. A., 'In Defense of Vampires', in Dundes (ed.), *The Vampire*, pp. 57–66.
GAUNTLETT, STATHIS, 'Between Orientalism and Occidentalism: The Contribution of Asia Minor Refugees to Greek Popular Song and its Reception', in Hirschon (ed.), *Crossing the Aegean*, pp. 247–60.
GLEICK, JAMES, *Chaos: Making a New Science* (London: Heinemann, 1988).
GOODY, JACK, *The Development of the Family and Marriage in Europe* (Cambridge: Cambridge University Press, 1983).
HAPGOOD, ISABELLA F. (ed.), *Service Book of the Holy Orthodox-Catholic*

Apostolic Church, compiled, translated and arranged from the Old Church Slavonic Service Books of the Russian Church and Collated with the Service Books of the Greek Church, 5th edition (Englewood: Antiochian Orthodox Christian Archdiocese of New York and all North America, 1975).

HART, LAURIE KAIN, *Time, Religion and Social Experience in Rural Greece* (Lanham: Rowman and Littlefield, 1992).

HERZFELD, MICHAEL, *Ours Once More: Folklore, Ideology and the Making of Modern Greece* (Austin: University of Texas Press, 1982).

—, 'The Significance of the Insignificant: Blasphemy as Ideology' (Man (N.S.) 19 (1984), pp. 653–64.

—, *The Poetics of Manhood: Contest and Identity in a Cretan Mountain Village* (Princeton: Princeton University Press, 1985).

—, *Anthropology through the Looking-glass: Critical Ethnography in the Margins of Europe* (Cambridge: Cambridge University Press, 1987).

—, 'The Ethnographer as Theorist: John Campbell and the Power of Detail', in Mazower (ed.), *Networks of Power*, pp. 147–68.

HIRSCHON, RENÉE, *Heirs of the Greek Catastrophe: The Social Life of Asia Minor Refugees in Piraeus* (Oxford: Clarendon Press, 1989; reprinted by Berghahn Books, New York, 1998).

— (ed.), *Crossing the Aegean: An Appraisal of the 1923 Compulsory Population Exchange between Greece and Turkey* (New York and Oxford: Berghahn Books, 2003).

HUNTINGTON, SAMUEL P., *The Clash of Civilisations and the Remaking of World Order* (London: Simon and Schuster, 1996).

—, *The Clash of Civilisations? The Debate* (New York: Foreign Affairs, 1996).

HUTTON, RONALD, *The Rise and Fall of Merry England: the Ritual Year, 1400–1700* (Oxford: Oxford University Press, 1994).

IERA MONI OSIOU DAVID TOU GERONTOS, *Ἕνας ἅγιος Γέροντας, Ὁ μακαριστὸς π. Ἰάκωβος* [*A holy Elder, the blessed Fr Iákovos*] (Rovies, Evia, Greece: Ἱ. Μ. Ὁσίου Δαβὶδ τοῦ Γέροντος, 1993).

Ἱερατικόν [Service Book] (Athens: Ἀποστολικὴ Διακονία τῆς Ἐκκλησίας τῆς Ἑλλάδος, 1998).

IOANNIDES, K., *Ὁ Γερὼν Πορφύριος: μαρτυρίες καὶ ἐμπειρίες* [*Elder Porphyrios: testimonies and insights*] (Athens: Ἱερὸν Γυναικεῖον Ἡσυχαστήριον ἡ Μεταμόρφωσις τοῦ Σωτῆρος, 1995).

IOSSIFIDES (OR JOSSIFIDES), A. M., 'Sisters in Christ: Metaphors of Kinship among Greek Nuns', in Loizos and Papataxiarchis (eds.), *Contested Identities*, pp. 135–55.

—, 'Earthly Lives and Life Everlasting; Secular and Religious Values in two Convents and a Village in Western Greece', Ph.D thesis (University of London: London School of Economics, 1990).

JUST, ROGER, *A Greek Island Cosmos: Kinship and Community on Meganisi* (Oxford: John Curry, 2000).

KENNA, MARGARET, 'Houses, Fields and Graves: Property and Ritual Obligations on a Greek Island', *Ethnology* 15 (1976), pp. 21–34.

—, 'Icons in Theory and Practice: An Orthodox Christian Example', *History of Religions*, 24 (1985), pp. 345–68.

—, 'Why does Incense smell Religious? Greek Orthodoxy and the Anthropology of Smell', *Journal of Mediterranean Studies* 15 (2005), pp. 51–70.

KLEIN, CHARLOTTE, 'The Oriental Liturgies and the Jews', *Sobornost,* series 6, number 7 (1973) pp. 503–8.

KYRIAKIDHOU-NESTOROS, A., *Οἱ δώδεκα μήνες: τά λαογραφικά* [*The twelve months: folk traditions*, 2nd edn. (Athens: Μαλλιάρης Παιδεία, 1986).

LADURIE, EMMANUEL LE ROY, *Montaillou: Cathars and Catholics in a French Village, 1294–1324*, tr. Barbara Bray (London: Scholar Press, 1978; reprinted by Penguin Books, 1980).

LANTSCHOOT, ARNOLD VAN, see VAN LANTSCHOOT.

LAWSON, JOHN CUTHBERT, *Modern Greek Folklore and Ancient Greek Religion* (Cambridge: Cambridge University Press, 1910).

LEIGH FERMOR, PATRICK, *Roumeli: Travels in Northern Greece* (London: John Murray, 1966).

Lenten Triodion, The, The service books of the Orthodox Church, tr. Mother Mary and Archimandrite Kallistos Ware (London: Faber, 1978).

LEWIS, C. S., *The Discarded Image: An Introduction to Medieval and Renaissance Literature* (Cambridge: Cambridge University Press, 1964).

LIENHARDT, R. G., *Divinity and Experience: The Religion of the Dinka* (Oxford: Clarendon Press, 1961).

LLEWELLYN SMITH, MICHAEL, *Ionian Vision: Greece in Asia Minor 1919–1922* (London: Allen Lane, 1973; reprinted with new introduction, London: C. Hurst, 1998).

LOIZOS, PETER, and PAPATAXIARCHIS, EVTHYMIOS (eds.), *Contested Identities: Gender and Kinship in Modern Greece* (Princeton: Princeton University Press, 1991).

LORENZATOS, ZISSIMOS, *The Drama of Quality: Selected Essays*, tr. Liadain Sherrard (Limni, Greece: D. Harvey, 2000).

LOUTH, ANDREW, 'Eastern Orthodox Eschatology', in *The Oxford Handbook of Eschatology*, pp. 233–47.

MARKIDES, KYRIAKOS C., *The Mountain of Silence: A Search for Orthodox Spirituality* (New York: Doubleday, 2001).

—, *Gifts of the Desert: The Forgotten Path of Christian Spirituality* (New York: Doubleday, 2005).

MAXIMUS THE CONFESSOR, 'The Church's Mystagogy' in *Maximus Confessor, Selected Writings*, tr. George C. Berthold, Classics of Western Spirituality (New York: Paulist Press, 1985).

—, *On the Cosmic Mystery of Jesus Christ*, tr. Paul M. Blowers and Robert Louis Wilken (Crestwood, N.Y.: St Vladimir's Seminary Press, 2003).

MAZOWER, MARK (ed.), *Networks of Power in Modern Greece* (London: Hurst & Co., 2008).

Μεγάλη Ἑβδομάς [*Holy Week*] (Athens: Ἀστήρ - Παπαδημητρίου, n.d.).

Memorial for the Departed, tr. by the Liturgical Translations Committee, Diocese of Sourozh, Russian Orthodox Church in Britain and Ireland (Oxford: St Stephen's Press, 2002).

MERTON, THOMAS, *The Seven-Storey Mountain* (New York: Harcourt, Brace Jovanovich, 1948).

MIGNE, J. P., *Patrologiae cursus completus, Series Graeca* (Paris: Migne, 1857–1866).

Μικρὸν Εὐχολόγιον [Small Prayer Book], Ἐπιμέλεια Ἐπισκόπου Ταλαντίου Παντελεήμονος (Athens: Βασιλείου Σαλιβέρου, n.d. (1960s)).

OINAS, FELIX, 'East European Vampires', in Dundes (ed.), *The Vampire*, pp. 47–56.

OTT, SANDRA, *The Circle of Mountains: A Basque Shepherding Community* (Oxford: Clarendon Press, 1981).

Oxford Companion to the Bible, Bruce M. Metzger and Michael D. Coogan (eds.), (Oxford: Oxford University Press, 1993).

Oxford Dictionary of the Christian Church, 2nd edn., F. L. Cross and E. A. Livingstone (eds.) (Oxford: Oxford University Press, 1974).

Oxford Handbook of Eschatology, ed. Jerry L. Walls (New York: Oxford University Press, 2007).

PALAMAS, GREGORY, *The Triads*, tr. Nicholas Gendle, Classics of Western Spirituality (New York: Paulist Press, 1983).

PAPADOPOULOS, STYLIANOS G., *Ὁ μακαριστὸς Ἰάκωβος Τσαλίκης* [*The blessed Iákovos Tsalíkis*] (Athens: Ἱ. Μ. Ὁσίου Δαβίδ τοῦ Γέροντος, 1992).

PAXSON, MARGARET, *Solovyovo: The Story of Memory in a Russian Village*

(Washington, D.C.: Woodrow Wilson Center Press, and Bloomington: Indiana University, 2005).

Pentecostarion, The, tr. by the Holy Transfiguration Monastery (Boston: Holy Transfiguration Monastery, 1990).

PERISTIANY, JOHN (ed.), *Strategies et prestations matrimoniales en Mediterranée* (Marseilles: Editions Jeanne Laffitte, 1987), and *Dote y matrimonio, en los países mediterráneos* (Madrid: Centro de Investigaciones Sociológicas, 1987).

—, and HANDMAN, MARIE-ELISABETH (eds.), *Le prix de l'alliance en Mediterranée* (Paris: Editions du Centre National de la Recherche Scientifique, 1989),

PERKOWSKI, JAN LOUIS, 'The Romanian Folkloric Vampire', in Dundes (ed.), *The Vampire*, pp. 35–46.

PHOUNDOULES, IOANNES M., *Ἀπαντήσεις εἰς λειτουργικάς ἀπορίας* [*Answers to liturgical questions*] (Thessaloniki: Πουρνάρος, 1982), vol. 4, pp. 234–5.

PINA-CABRAL, J. DE, see DE PINA-CABRAL.

PITARD, W. T., and WHITE, S. A., 'Afterlife and Immortality', in *Oxford Companion to the Bible*, pp. 15–17.

PSEUDO-DIONYSIUS, *The Ecclesiastical Hierarchy*, in Migne, *Patrologiae cursus completus, Series Graeca*, vol. 3 (1866).

—, *The Divine Names*, in Migne, *Patrologiae cursus completus, Series Graeca*, vol. 3 (1866).

—, *The Celestial Hierarchy*, in Migne, *Patrologiae cursus completus, Series Graeca*, vol. 3 (1866).

RUNCIMAN, STEVEN, *Byzantine Civilisation* (London: E. Arnold, 1933).

RUSHTON, LUCY, 'Religion and Identity in a Rural Greek Community', D.Phil. thesis (University of Sussex, 1983).

SCHMEMANN, ALEXANDER, *Introduction to Liturgical Theology*, tr. Asheleigh Moorhouse, 2nd edn. (Crestwood, N.Y.: St Vladimir's Seminary Press, 1975).

SHERRARD, PHILIP, *The Marble Threshing Floor: Studies in Modern Greek Poetry* (London: Vallentine, Mitchell, 1956; reprinted Limni, Greece: D. Harvey, 1981, 1992).

—, *The Greek East and the Latin West: A Study in the Christian Tradition* (London: Oxford University Press, 1959; reprinted Limni, Greece: D. Harvey, 1992, 1995, 2002).

—, *Constantinople: Iconography of a Sacred City* (London: Oxford University Press, 1965).

—, *The Sacred in Life and Art* (Ipswich: Golgonooza Press, 1990; reprinted Limni, Greece: D. Harvey, 2004).

SHEVZOV, VERA, *Russian Orthodoxy on the Eve of the Revolution* (Oxford: Oxford University Press, 2004).

SOPHOCLES, *Antigone*, tr. H. D. F. Kitto,World's Classics (Oxford: Oxford University Press, 1994).

STEWART, CHARLES, *Demons and the Devil: Moral Imagination in Modern Greek Culture* (Princeton: Princeton University Press, 1991).

—, 'Dreaming of Buried Icons in Rural Greece', in Mazower (ed.), *Networks of Power*, pp. 89–108.

TAFT, ROBERT F., *The Liturgy of the Hours in East and West* (Collegeville, Minn.: The Liturgical Press, 1986).

—, *The Byzantine Rite: A Short History* (Collegeville, Minn.: The Liturgical Press, 1992).

THEODOSSOPOULOS, D., 'What use is the Turtle? Cultural Perceptions of Land, Work, Animals and "Ecologists" in a Greek Farming Community', Ph.D. thesis (University of London, 1997).

THOMAS, K., *Religion and the Decline of Magic* (London: Weidenfeld and Nicolson, 1971).

TISCHENDORF, CONSTANTINE VON, *Apocalypses apocryphae Mosis, Esdrae, Pauli, Johannis, item Mariae dormitio: additis evangeliorum et actuum apocryphorum supplementis. Maximam partem nunc primum edidit* (Leipzig: H. Mendelssohn, 1866).

VAN LANTSCHOOT, ARNOLD (ed.), 'Révélations de Macaire et de Marc de Tarmaqa sur le sort de l'âme après la mort', *Le Muséon*, 63 (1950), pp. 159–89.

WARE, TIMOTHY, (Bishop Kallistos of Diokleia), *The Orthodox Church*, 3rd edn. (London: Penguin, 1997).

—, Bishop Kallistos, *The Orthodox Way*, revised edn. (Crestwood: N.Y., St Vladimir's Seminary Press, 1995).

WILSON, KATHARINA M., 'The History of the Word *Vampire*', in Dundes (ed.), *The Vampire*, pp. 3–11.

GLOSSARY OF GREEK TERMS USED IN THE ANALYSIS IN ROMANIZED SCRIPT

Ádhis: Hades.

Akáthistos Hýmnos: The Unsitting Hymn, or hymn through which everyone stands.

Anámnesis: The recovery of an encounter with the divine which is ever-present, but needs to be continually unearthed from the forgetfulness engendered by the fall.

Andaínei: This word signifies 'meeting' or 'connecting' as in 'if the time connects', 'if the moment takes effect'.

Andídhoro: Bread which is blessed at the service of preparation before the celebration of the Divine Liturgy.

Ártos: Breads baked with sugar, cinnamon, and aniseed, made for the church in fives, commemorating the five loaves and the fishes.

Cháos: The ancestor of our own word 'chaos', sometimes used to indicate disorder, but in contexts concerning the cosmos it indicates an unbelievable infinity, void even of God.

Christoutzikós mou: An endearment for Christ, 'My little Christ'.

Dhouleiá: Work.

Dhrystélla: Pit lined with planks in which rugs are worked in water from the mill lade.

Dhrýmes: Spirits of the wood.

Dhiávolos: Devil.

Epitáphios: Specifically, a rectangular cloth on which is embroidered or painted an icon of the dead Christ laid out for burial, which is brought out into the nave on Holy Friday, and on Holy Saturday is laid on the altar until Ascension. It also means, by extension, the bier of Christ—the table-like structure surmounted with arched wooden struts like a crown in which this icon is laid.

Epitrachílion: The stole worn by a priest in the performance of any sacred function.

Exaptériga: Long poles topped with gilt images of the seraphim used in some ecclesiastical processions.

Féta: A soft cheese which is stored in brine.

Griés: Old women.

Ísou: A unique kind of candle whose name is derived from *ísos* meaning 'equal' or 'equivalent' (to the person's height), which is placed on the navel of a dead body during the wake.

Kadém: A long red silk belt given by the bridegroom to the bride at the engagement ceremony.

Kalamatianós: A popular pan-Hellenic round dance named after the town of Kalamata, danced to a 7/8 rhythm.

Katameriá: A movement in marriage or spiritual kinship which goes one way only. For example, in the case of marriage, if a man A marries a woman B, more kinsmen of A may marry more kinswomen of B, but no kinsman of B may 'turn back' to take a woman from the kin of A—successive marriages between affines are only countenanced so long as they preserve the original movement of the sexes in marriage.

Khorós: Dance.

Klídhonas: A ritual carried out on the feast day of John the Baptist in which girls' 'fate' in marriage is foretold.

Kóllyva: A generic term covering all the various types of food for the dead, and thus properly includes the two types of bread *leitourgiés /prósphora*, and the 'soul breads' and 'pieces' which are baked especially for the great memorials, as well as the wine and the boiled wheat which is also offered to the community at such a time. However, since the most commonly made memorial food is the boiled wheat which is a prerequisite not only of the great memorials but also of the lesser memorials as well, the word *kóllyva* is commonly used to represent just the boiled wheat, whether plain or mixed with walnuts, pomegranate seeds, sultanas, parsley, and a little sugar.

Kommátia: 'Pieces', that is to say bread baked for a funeral, either incised into diamond shapes before baking or shaped separately into tiny loaves. Both are stamped with a seal bearing the initials for Jesus Christ Conquers.

Kontákion: A hymn in strophes, especially the 'Kontakion of the day', sung after the 6th ode of the canon at matins and repeated at the Divine Liturgy after the Little Entrance.

Kossónes: Decorated breads baked principally for children.

Kouloúria: Circular bread rings.

Koumbáros (fem. *-a*): A spiritual kinsman or woman who, together with his or her spouse, is sponsor at a wedding or godparent at a baptism.

Kourambiédhes: Sweet pastries.

Lápatha: Long leafy stems used for the adornment of the *Piperiá* (see below).

Lechóna: A woman within forty days of having given birth.

Leitourgeiá: Bread especially baked and given by various households to be consecrated for the Divine Liturgy.

Leitourgeía: Communal service, hence liturgy.

Loukoumádhes: Fried batter puffs eaten with honey on festive occasions.

Mageirítsa: A spicy soup, eaten after the Easter Vigil, which is made of the entrails of the lamb killed for the midday Easter meal.

Makaríes: A term used for the great memorials for the dead, of which there are five in Ambeli.

Mandilónei: 'To give a kerchief to'.

Metánoia: A change of perception involving repentance.

Midzíthra: A cheese made mainly from whey, hard when mature.

Moíra: Fate.

Moirológi: A formal lament.

Morphoménos: Educated or 'shaped'.

Panaghía: The 'All-holy One', the name by which the Virgin Mary is most commonly referred to in Greece.

Pandodhýnamos: Almighty.

Paráklisis: A service of prayer to a saint or to the Mother of God.

Patrídha: A person's family village of origin.

Phelónion: Over garment worn by the priest in the liturgy.

Piánetai, or *piánei*: 'Being effective', or to 'take', in the sense in which a graft is said to 'take'.

Piperiá: A ritual carried out by young girls on 1 May to ensure rain during the growing season.

Pítta: Festive decorated bread baked with a little oil and sometimes anointed with honey.

Prósphoro: Bread that is 'offered' to Christ, another name for the *leitourgeiá* (see above).

Prozými: A piece of naturally-leavened dough kept aside from the previous baking.

Psychónia: 'Soul loaves', similar to '*kommátia*' (see above).

Psýchisma: A form of diagnosis, carried out with certain words and said over water and hot embers.

Rakí: A spirit distilled from the grape skins which have been pressed for wine.

Sávano: This garment is an unsewn length of white material which is approximately one foot wide and measured to be twice the height of the dead person, with a hole cut in the middle so that it fits over the head and stretches the full length of the body both front and back.

Sighanós: A round dance with slow walking steps.

Skalikandzoúria: Local dialect for *kalikándzaroi*. The demons who work all year to cut down the world tree, emerging into the upper world for the Twelve Days of Christmas.

Syrtós: One of the basic Greek round dances, *syrtós* derives from the word *sérno* meaning 'to drag' and refers to the way in which the dancers' feet brush against the ground; there are many regional versions of the dance.

Táma: Vow (verb *tázo*), to make a promise to a saint. '*Táma*' is also the word used for the votive offerings which, in the form of miniature replicas of parts of the body for which the saint's help is sought, or precious pieces of jewellery, are hung around the icons of particular shrines in prayer for a favour sought or in thanksgiving for one granted.

Téknon: Offspring or child.

Theophánia: Feast of the Baptism of Christ, literally the Manifestation of God.

Theophóroi, sing. *-os*: Those who carry God within them.

Theós: God.

Theotókos: The 'One who gives birth to God'.

Tíkto: To bear, or give birth to.

Toú Christoú: The time 'of Christ' or the Christmas season.

Trachanás: A dried porridge of coarse ground wheat boiled with milk, which is then dried and crumbled for storage.

Trachomándilo: Dialect for *epitrachílion* (see above).

Trisághio: 'Thrice Holy': a short service sung at encounters with the body of a dead person, as well as at the graveside and at memorial services.

Tropárion: A sung stanza of religious poetry, especially the '*tropárion* of the day' which is sung at the end of vespers and repeated in the Divine Liturgy after the Little Entrance.

Tsibér: A woman's kerchief which, tied tightly around the hair but with a raised roll in front, causes the light decorated headscarf arranged over it to make an attractive frame round the face.

Tsournás: Balkan double reeded shawm, used in dances and sometimes in laments.

Tycheró: Fated, or lucky.

Týchi: Fate, or luck.

Vasilévo: 'To reign', a word which can carry a reference to St Basil.

Vasilópitta: *Pítta* (see above) made on 1 January in honour of St Basil.

Velédzes: Heavy rugs softened and felted in the *dhrystélla* (q.v.)

Yítio: Spell.

Vrikólakas: Vampire.

Yérondes (fem. *yeróndisses*): Elders of the Church.

Ypapandí: The feast of the Meeting of the Lord with the aged Symeon in the Temple when his mother comes to be purified 'according to the law'.

Yposchethó: I promise.

Zinári: Dialect from *zóni* or *zonári*; the long belt which is worn wound right-handed or anticlockwise round the waist of the men's traditional dress.

INDEX